Anthropocene Alerts

Anthropocene Alerts

Critical Theory of the Contemporary as Ecocritique

Timothy W. Luke

Telos Press Publishing
Candor, NY

Printed in the United States of America

23   22   21   20   19   1   2   3   4

ISBN 978-0-914386-75-9 (paperback)
ISBN 978-0-914386-76-6 (ebook)

Library of Congress Cataloging-in-Publication Data

Names: Luke, Timothy W., author.
Title: Anthropocene alerts : critical theory of the contemporary as ecocritique / Timothy W. Luke.
Description: Candor, NY : Telos Press Publishing, [2020] | Includes bibliographical references.
Identifiers: LCCN 2019046980 (print) | LCCN 2019046981 (ebook) | ISBN 9780914386759 (paperback) | ISBN 9780914386766 (ebook)
Subjects: LCSH: Human ecology—Political aspects. | Environmental sociology. | Ecocriticism.
Classification: LCC GF21 .L85 2020 (print) | LCC GF21 (ebook) | DDC 304.2—dc23
LC record available at https://lccn.loc.gov/2019046980
LC ebook record available at https://lccn.loc.gov/2019046981

Cover design by Amanda Trager and Erik Moskowitz
Cover image courtesy of NASA Visible Earth, Jacques Descloitres, MODIS Rapid Response Team, NASA/GSFC

Telos Press Publishing
PO Box 811
Candor, NY 13743
www.telospress.com

Contents

Preface

THE GENESIS OF this book rises directly for me from two closely connected events that gave contemporary human beings the power to cause extreme environmental change on a planetary scale capable of registering in deep geological time: the atomic bomb tests on July 16, 1945, at the Trinity Test Site near Alamogordo, New Mexico, and August 29, 1949, at the Semipalatinsk Test Site near Kurchatov City, Kazakhstan. Having organized a secret "weapons of mass destruction" (WMD) program during World War II, the United States held a nuclear monopoly from 1945 to 1949 that accelerated the Soviet Union's secret, but much more slowly developing, nuclear weapons program, which culminated in the Semipalatinsk bomb test. There were few alerts for either secret test, but both events were signs of more destructive tests to come. Indeed, they became national priorities as these two superpowers exploded scores of nuclear weapons in their own countries to sustain the devestating dramas of nuclear deterrence.

During the next fourteen years, the United States exploded another 119 nuclear devices in atmospheric or ground tests at its more isolated Nevada Test Site, while the Soviet Union tested 116 comparable devices at Semipalatinsk until the Partial Test Ban Treaty was signed on August 5, 1963, by the United States, the Soviet Union, and the United Kingdom to outlaw all atmospheric, outer space, and underwater nuclear tests after October 10, 1963. Even though there is quite plausible evidence, as I have argued elsewhere, that many signs of the Anthropocene were evident long before 1945,[1] these eighteen years of environmentally destructive weapons testing left the indisputable mark of artificial nuclear isotopes in the earth's geological record, which has been identified as one of several possible definitive "golden spikes" to alert humanity about the radical shift to the Anthropocene emerging from the Holocene epoch.

This endangerment is personal for me because my family and I lived two counties away from the Nevada Test Site in Kingman, Arizona, which is the county seat of Mohave County, during the 1950s and 1960s. Alerts about some tests occasionally were made for "public information," and residents of the region could not wait to witness them. Not knowing much about their peril, many tourists poolside at resorts in Las Vegas, Nevada, would also often watch these atomic and thermonuclear tests, regarding them as another dazzling technological spectacle afforded to them in "The Entertainment Capital of the World." All of us, however, in this region during the years of atmospheric tests could be regarded, which Rob Nixon suggests about other ecological crimes, as essentially human "uninhabitants" caught within "a national sacrifice zone" by the nuclear testing regime inasmuch as this landscape was treated "as if it were uninhabited by the living, the unborn, and the animate deceased,"[2] or as if the Anthropocene had already attained its catastrophic climax. Those showered by bursts of radioactive isotopes or irradiated dust clouds became "Downwinders," who carried with them forever the "known unknowns" of radiological toxic burdens, particularly if they remained in the region drinking the water, eating plants from the soil, and coexisting with the settled dust.[3]

Coincidentally in 1963, biologist Barry Commoner published the first edition of his book *Science and Survival*. In the opening pages, he noted disturbing news (from the contiguous Washington County, Utah, north of Mohave County) about the growing incidence of "abnormal

1. See, for example, Timothy W. Luke, "The Anthropocene and Freedom," *Platypus Review* 60, October 2013, https://platypus1917.org/2013/10/01/anthropocene-and-freedom/.

2. Rob Nixon, *Slow Violence and the Environmentalism of the Poor* (Cambridge, MA: Harvard Univ. Press, 2013), p. 17.

3. See Jessica Boehm, "Kingman 'Downwinders' Seek Recognition Long after U.S. Atomic Tests," *Cronkite News*, December 12, 2014, http://cronkitenewsonline.com/2014/12/kingmans-downwinders-seek-recognition-restitution-decades-after-atomic-tests/.

thyroid nodules" that can be "an indication of possible thyroid disease," including "nontoxic goiter, inflammation, [and] benign or malignant tumors,"[4] in the glands of children and young adults. These initial detections were only the tip of the iceberg, and the residents in these "Downwinder" counties continue to be plagued by serious cancers and leukemias today.[5] The deleterious effects of these nuclear tests already have devastated the environment of this region, and their long-lived toxic consequences have degraded the health of many friends, family, and me for decades.

Like fossil fuel burning, overuse of plastics, bioengineered seeds, and oil-based chemicals in agriculture, radioactive contaminants have been desolating biodiversity and taking lives for decades in the de-Holocenating decades before the official debates about recognizing the Anthropocene were convened. Hence, my approaches to ecocritique express life-long trepidations about the uneasy balance between "science and survival" in how I articulate the critical theory of the contemporary. Arguing that humanity is creating innumerable poorly understood dangers with its new complex scientific technologies, Commoner asserts that such technical achievements "suffer from a common and catastrophic fault," namely, "they threaten our very survival."[6] Even though they create the material means for economic abundance, rapid transportation, good housing, more food, and weapons of immense power, the inventors and users of high technologies blunder into perpetuating old dangerous styles of production. Those exploitative patterns developed only "by plundering the earth's natural resources," whose destruction and depletion inevitably must "be paid by later generations."[7]

Commoner in 1963 felt these trends would soon cause severe ill effects in the earth's environment despite bringing material benefits to many people since the 1940s. He was right. And now, over seventy-five years later, the "long-range effects" of such environmental plunder are

4. Barry Commoner, *Science and Survival* (New York: Ballantine Books, 1979), p. 7.

5. See Hubble Ray Smith, "Downwinders: Survivors Losing Hope of Compensation," *Kingman Daily Miner*, January 17, 2018; Brandon Messick, "Decades after Nuclear Testing in the Nevada Desert, Mohave County's 'Downwinders' Still Seeking Help," *Kingman Daily Miner*, January 28, 2019; and Keith Ridler, "Western Governors Want Nuclear Testing Compensation Expanded," *Kingman Daily Miner*, October 15, 2019.

6. Commoner, *Science and Survival*, p. 151.

7. Ibid.

tragically apparent, and their catastrophic faults are more manifest everyday. Humanity, however, continues to avoid solving the "very grave economic, social, and political problems" behind such embedded extractive patterns of relentless technological innovation, which steal "from future generations not just their lumber or their coal, but the basic necessities of life: air, water, and soil."[8]

The coming condition of "uninhabitancy" for all life in the Anthropocene actually has been under intensive critical discussion in political, intellectual, and cultural circles tied to Marxian, neo-Marxist, or Frankfurt School–inspired critical theory for many decades. This reality generally is ignored by experts in the geological, life, and physical sciences, who have been working hard to manufacture definitive meanings and manage the practical applications of the Anthropocene concepts in a nearly monopolistic manner. But many environmental humanities, social science, and policy studies groups are pushing back. In resisting those narrow efforts to construct, circulate, and curate this destabilizing notion in debates in biology and geoscience, my ecocritique-focused "Anthropocene alerts" also aim to crack apart the monopoly and seek further understandings drawn from more critical perspectives.[9] Indeed, this selection from my *Telos* essays published since 1980 sharply criticizes the destructive disruption that the Anthropocene concept describes—both before and after it was branded as "The Anthropocene Epoch."

However, I have not done this work alone. Over the years of my activities with the St. Louis *Telos* Group, and later on the journal's editorial board, I also have served as a faculty member at different universities. At these jobs, numerous colleagues, friends, and other readers shared their reactions at academic meetings, on coffee breaks, in hallway conversations, and in email exchanges to the evolving approach I have developed in these ecocritique-driven essays. Their criticism and comments gave me important encouragement and guidance for advancing this piece of my research program. In particular, I appreciate the invaluable insights provided by Frank Adler, Ben Agger, David Arditi,

8. Ibid.

9. See, for example, Timothy W. Luke, *Ecocritique: Contesting the Politics of Nature, Economy and Culture* (Minneapolis: Univ. of Minnesota Press, 1997); and Timothy W. Luke, *Capitalism, Democracy, and Ecology: Departing from Marx* (Urbana: Univ. of Illinois Press, 1999). Edited sections or expanded versions of chapters 1 through 7 here are found in one or both of these earlier volumes.

Joseph W. Bendersky, Russell A. Berman, Terrell Carver, Bill Chaloupka, Simon Dalby, François Debrix, Frank Fischer, Ellsworth R. Fuhrman, Mary Hawkesworth, Robert D. Holsworth, Doug Kellner, Roger Keil, Nancy Love, Warren Magnusson, Bryan McDonald, Michael A. Peters, Wolfgang Natter, Brian Opie, Gearóid Ó Tuathail, David Pan, Adrian Pabst, Paul Piccone, Mark Poster, Adolph Reed, Jr., Alan Rudy, James Rowe, Ariel Salleh, Catriona Sandilands, Andrew J. Scerri, Karena Shaw, Antonio Y. Vázquez-Arroyo, Florindo Volpacchio, Edward Weisband, Damian White, and Stephen K. White.

More recently, I have been fortunate in having the opportunity to help develop and work closely with another circle of close colleagues in an intellectual affinity group that we have named "Environmental Political Theory." Also known by its acronym, "EPT," this growing association of green thinkers has held its own interesting pre-conferences the day before the Western Political Science Association's (WPSA) annual conference, while it also has managed a robust series of panels at the WPSA's professional meetings for nearly two decades. Several chapters of this book were first field-tested as conference papers, pre-conference presentations, or roundtable comments in this scholarly network. I am pleased to participate in all of these interactions and have enjoyed greatly my ongoing discussions with John Barry, Nir Barak, Andrew Biro, Phil Brick, Peter Cannavò, Chris Crews, Teena J. Gabrielson, George Gonzalez, Cheryl Hall, Breena Holland, Christian Hunold, Kyle Haines, Yogi Hale Hendlin, Anatoli Ignatov, Joel Kassiola, Robert Kirsch, Joseph Lane, Jennifer Lawrence, Michael Lipscomb, Manuel Arias Maldonado, John M. Meyer, Sean Parson, Emily Ray, David Schlosberg, Sarah Surak, Sarah Wiebe, Rafi Youatt, Steve Vanderheiden, Steve Vogel, Harlan Wilson, Zev Trachtenberg, and many others.

At Telos Press Publishing, Maria Piccone and Robert Richardson first encouraged me to draw together these unedited original contributions from *Telos*, Telos-Paul Piccone Institute conferences, and *Fast Capitalism* into a book-length manuscript. Rob's dedicated and professional editing work greatly assisted me, and Mary's publishing savvy truly accelerated pulling this book together. Amanda Trager and Erik Moskowitz also worked closely with me to design the book's cover.

At Virginia Polytechnic Institute and State University, I would like to acknowledge the support of the College of Liberal Arts and Human

Sciences as well as the Department of Political Science. My time spent with colleagues and graduate students at the university in the Alliance for Social, Political, Ethical, and Cultural Thought doctoral program as well as the Government and International Affairs program in the School of Public and International Affairs also has been very rewarding. Finally, I continue to enjoy never-ending assistance and solid support in the Department of Political Science from Kim Hedge and Karen Nicholson, whose professionalism, expertise, dedication, and acumen are exemplary models for me and my colleagues.

Tim Luke
Blacksburg, Virginia
November 16, 2019

Introduction

THIS SELECTION OF critical essays maps out my approach to "eco-critique," or the relentless contestation of the politics of nature, economy, and culture as the core of a critical theory of the contemporary. For nearly a decade, the rhetorical mobilization in the popular press and scholarly literature of an obscure geological date-setting concept drawn from the nomenclature and taxonomy of stratigraphy, namely, "the Anthropocene," rapidly has reframed contemporary economic, historical, and political debates about human civilization. The claim is stark: the earth and all its inhabitants are deeply endangered by the sudden advent of this unpredictable new era. As it eclipses the most recent geological time period, known as "the Holocene," which spans the last 11,000 to 12,000 years BCE (Before Current Era) cradling the emergence and development of all human civilizations, the Anthropocene marks a new epoch of great loss, growing instability, and grand catastrophe.

The prevailing Anthropocenic narrative identifies the explosive proliferation of fossil fuel extraction and combustion during the last 250 years, in turn, as the key cause of the rapid climate change, extensive biodiversity loss, and deep ecospheric disruption triggering today's unanticipated and unwanted worldwide state of emergency. This account reduces the great variety of human histories to one basic material foundation—the increasing use of fossil fuels since the 1770s—to define and document how the accelerating output of benign *industrial products* behind economic progress during the Age of Industrialization brings with it tremendous floods of toxic *industrial by-products* that despoil the biosphere to the point of registering now in deep geological time the worldwide ecological disasters linked to accelerating climate changes. Yet this essentially climatological conception of history obscures many decades of alert radical materialist critiques of everyday capitalist life in Marxist discourses that foresaw the alienation of humanity from nature becoming permanent and destructive for both. Tremendously urgent alerts were sounded about the rapidly degrading ethical, economic, and ecological conditions of "the earth" as the processed world of global capitalism took hold worldwide with steam power in the nineteenth and twentieth centuries. In this respect, Marx and Engels anticipate in *The Communist Manifesto*, for example, today's outlines for global articulations of informationalism, the emergence of the Anthropocene turn, and the waning of the Holocene, given how contemporary capitalism "must nestle everywhere, settle everywhere, establish connexions everywhere," since it always "creates a world after its own image."[1]

During its five decades of publication, intellectual debates in *Telos* have worked out important new theoretical frameworks to elaborate a "critical theory of the contemporary" to respond and react systematically to these cultural, political, and social changes, which are coming at even more unstable conjunctures in the early twenty-first century. Many of the journal's writers and readers participated in the political struggles of the 1960s, but they also brought into broader circulation and greater discussion the green edges in Western Marxist theoretical discourses.[2] Drawn from the short-lived urban "red republics" all across Central and Southern Europe in 1918–1919, the Frankfurt School in Germany and its exile during the 1930s and 1940s in the British Empire and the United States, and the humanist Marxian thought that sparked back to

---

1. Karl Marx and Friedrich Engels, *Manifesto of the Communist Party*, in *The Marx-Engels Reader*, ed. Robert C. Tucker (New York: W. W. Norton, 1978), pp. 476, 477.

2. See, for example, Robert D'Amico "The Domination of Nature" *Telos* 15 (Spring 1973): 142–47; Murray Bookchin, "Beyond Neo-Marxism," *Telos* 36 (Summer 1978): 5–28; Joel Whitebook, "The Problem of Nature in Habermas," *Telos* 40 (Summer 1979): 41–69; The Carbondale Telos Group, "Ecology and the Welfare State: A Conference Report," *Telos* 52 (Summer 1982): 129–40; and Isaac D. Balbus, "A Neo-Hegelian, Feminist, Psychoanalytic Perspective on Ecology," *Telos* 52 (Summer 1982): 140–55.

life during in the 1950s, aspects of this critical theory of the contemporary have provided many "Anthropocene alerts," flashing their warnings in various articulations of ecocritique.[3]

Ranging from intra-party debates within the Second or Third Internationals to more radical popular resistance movements against, or outside of, the pre-1914 Social Democratic parties or post-1918 Marxist-Leninist communist parties, many Western Marxist thinkers were cautious about the emergence of an "actually developing socialist regime" under Bolshevik rule as it struggled to win a civil war and then revive the country's economy in the 1920s. With the turn to forced industrialization and the politics of intra-party purges, some became critical of Moscow's Stalinist turn during the 1930s. Many leftist intellectuals tied to the Frankfurt School sought refuge from fascism in France, Great Britain, or the United States and then developed new critical approaches in critiques of liberal democracy, fascist totalitarianism, and communist autarky. To avoid the red-baiting that came in the 1940s and 1950s from supporting the Soviet Union, some worked with Western governments, others started more conventional social science research or became popular public intellectuals, addressing more general concerns in the fields of aesthetic, economics, psychology, or sociology without losing their critical neo-Marxist viewpoints. It was these thinkers that *Telos* brought into broader discussion since 1968, revitalizing many neglected, if not nearly lost, cultural and intellectual insights gained by the Frankfurt School and other neo-Marxist analysts from these earlier

---

3. See William Leiss, "Husserl and the Mastery of Nature," *Telos* 5 (Spring 1970): 82–97; Ray Morrow, "The Dialectic of Ideology and Technology: The Origins, Grammar, and Future of Ideology," *Telos* 32 (Summer 1977): 193–214; Fred Alford, "Autonomous Technology," *Telos* 33 (Fall 1977): 249–52; Stuart Ewen and Elizabeth Ewen, "Americanization and Consumption," *Telos* 37 (Fall 1978): 42–51; Andrew McLaughlin, "The Destruction of Nature in the Soviet Union," *Telos* 47 (Spring 1981): 235–37; Robert John, "The Sun Betrayed: A Report on the Corporate Seizure of U.S. Solar Energy Development," *Telos* 48 (Summer 1981): 236–39; André Gorz, "The Reconquest of Time," *Telos* 55 (Spring 1983): 212–17; Claus Leggewie and Brice Lalonde, "Ecoliberalism Lives," *Telos* 61 (Fall 1984): 129–34; Ferenc Feher and Ágnes Heller, "From Red to Green," *Telos* 59 (Spring 1984): 35–44; John Bokina, "The Domination of Nature Revisited: A Critique of Edward O. Wilson," *Telos* 80 (Summer 1989): 138–48; Louise Fortmann and Emery Roe, "On Really Existing Communities—Organic or Otherwise," *Telos* 95 (Spring 1993): 139–46; John Zerzan, "Why Primitivism?," *Telos* 124 (Summer 2002): 166–72; and Eileen Crist, "Beyond the Climate Crisis: A Critique of Climate Change Discourse," *Telos* 141 (Winter 2007): 29–55.

struggles abroad. To fuel new approaches to critical theory in the West during the Nixon-Ford era, the journal also published important translations of underground anti-Soviet dissident writings from across the Eastern Bloc, new works by Frankfurt School authors getting back to work in West Germany, in addition to other nearly forgotten writings by Antonio Gramsci, Georg Lukács, Anton Pannekoek, and Karl Korsch. Along with fresh voices from Europe and North America, which were heard during and after the events of May 1968, this eclectic scholarship focused on the flaws of so-called "actually existing socialism" and "liberal democratic capitalism" everywhere in the world. Moreover, as policies of détente between the Eastern and Western Blocs led to the gradual deradicalization of mass political struggle after 1968 despite the recourse to armed direct action by small groups in Germany, Italy, and North and South America, *Telos* served as reliable forum for continuing crucial debates as well as a reliable source for translating significant radical dissident texts into English that rarely were available elsewhere.

From these commitments, Marxism as "a philosophy of praxis" gained another chance to be heard in the Cold War years. On the one hand, without the extraordinary intervention of the Bolsheviks in 1917, as Paul Piccone notes, "Marxism would have gone the way of other 19th-century philosophies of progress, like those of Comte, Spencer, and various Social Darwinists."[4] On the other hand, the Soviet Union's deepening deformation under the pressures of bureaucratic collectivism, industrialization from above, Communist Party infighting, and Stalinist militarism by 1928 pushed many Western radical intellectuals to rediscover Hegelianized readings of Marxism and propose anti-Stalinist forms of communism from the 1920s through 1950s, which *Telos* more widely publicized after 1968.

This prickly engagement with Western Marxism during the 1960s and 1970s, then, was significant. The journal took serious interest in these largely overlooked currents of anti-capitalist critique, which were frozen over during the anti-fascist struggles of the 1930s and 1940s as well as the early decades of the Cold War. Yet *Telos* did not flinch from calling out the dictatorial acts and exploitative policies of "actually existing socialism," which stumbled from atrocity to atrocity after 1928 all

---

4. Paul Piccone, "From the New Left to the New Populism," *Telos* 101 (Fall 1994): 176.

around the world as its devotees became more nationalistic, colonialist, and authoritarian. Some New Left movements during the 1960s decried Moscow's policies locally and globally as the self-serving nationalistic expressions of an "obsolete communism," but others in these movements were distracted into supporting the anti-imperialism of ill-focused Third World socialist and communist groups during the darkest days of the Cold War. Nonetheless, the New Left in the years leading up to 1968 took hold of Western Marxism's ambivalent and amorphous critical discourses, which were about "as sophisticated as any available in Europe at the time," in order gain "a political vision and a better self-understanding" of itself in a vast capitalist world system with complexities and contradictions far beyond the coal-fired Victorian lifeworlds of 1848, 1871, or 1905 underpinning classical Marxism.[5]

In the 1970s, *Telos* began carving out its own theoretical spaces for articulating nonconformist modes of intellectual and materialist criticism to ground fresh critical theories of the contemporary. Along with Herbert Marcuse and Jürgen Habermas, the thought of different thinkers (such as Jean Baudrillard, Murray Bookchin, Michel Foucault, Cornelius Castoriadis, Ágnes Heller, Christopher Lasch, and Antonio Negri) as well as dissident voices from Eastern Europe (ranging from Polish labor radicals, Charter 77 figures, the Budapest School, East German dissidents, Praxis 48 writers, and Soviet émigrés after 1956) frequently peppered the ebb-and-flow of *Telos* debates. Not surprisingly, the political ossification of the Soviet Union after Khrushchev's ouster by Brezhnev and Kosygin, along with the rise of neoliberal regimes in London and Washington, also preoccupied many *Telos* debates in the 1970s and 1980s. Due to these developments, as Piccone observed, it was increasingly true by 1989 that "analyses of specifically American themes from perspectives rooted neither in the old Critical Theory nor in the Theory of Communicative Action, nor, for that matter, in standard objectivistic social science are increasingly finding their way in the pages of *Telos*."[6] As disruptive political discourses were stirred up by new middle-class populism, or subnational regional anti-statism, or even full-blown paleoconservatism in many advanced industrial cultures and

---

5. Ibid., p. 180.

6. Paul Piccone, "20 Years of *Telos*," *Telos* 75 (Spring 1988): 25; and Piccone, "The Changing Function of Critical Theory," *New German Critique* 12 (Autumn 1977): 28–37.

societies, leaders in both the capitalist West and the Communist East were forced to reappraise the rapid rise of globalized neoliberalism as it disrupted their economies and states. During the Carter, Reagan, and Bush years, *Telos* in turn also opened up debates around another mix of theoretical perspectives from Ernesto Laclau and Alain de Benoist to Christopher Lasch and Carl Schmitt. In different ways, their ideas refocused critical attention on the tumultuous effects of rapid neoliberal transformations, including devastating economic crises, the collapse of traditional legitimation discourses, and new popular political movements in the East and West.

The prevailing political order during the post-1945 boom years in the West was organized upon, as David Harvey suggests, an "embedded liberalism" designed "to construct the right blend of state, market, and democratic institutions to guarantee peace, inclusion, well-being, and stability."[7] As a result, whether one looks at the United States, Japan, or Western Europe, this ideological agenda guided a strong Fordist-Keynesian institutional apparatus to abide by a collective social contract sustained by fossil-fueled urban-industrial growth. As Harvey asserts, there was a general consensus

> that the state should focus on full employment, economic growth, and the welfare of its citizens, and that state power should be freely deployed, alongside of or, if necessary, intervening in or substituting for market processes to achieve these ends. Fiscal and monetary policies usually dubbed "Keynesian" were widely deployed to dampen business cycles and to ensure reasonably full employment. A "class compromise" between capital and labor was generally advocated as the key guarantor of domestic peace and tranquility. States actively intervened in industrial policy and moved to set standards for the social wage by constructing a variety of welfare systems (health care, education, and the like).[8]

Such national policies delivered fairly predictable high rates of growth in both fossil fuel consumption and industrial production into the mid-1970s, especially given Washington's willingness to rack up major trade

---

7. David Harvey, *A Brief History of Neoliberalism* (Oxford: Oxford Univ. Press, 2005), p. 10.

8. Ibid., pp. 10–11.

imbalances with the rest of the world to defend Cold War–era liberal democratic capitalism. However, after 1979, a new agenda formed around making aggressive alterations to this social contract. After the oil crises of the 1970s, nuclear détente between the United States and the Soviet Union, and the launch of the "four modernizations" by Deng Xiaoping in China, it was clear that this neoliberal project would soon free capital from embedded liberalism's constraints.[9]

Telos authors clearly took the "embedded liberalism" of the postwar era to task for not going far or fast enough to fulfill its own collective promise. Hobbled by New Class technocratic practices, state bureaucrats' insufficient ability to use state power to realize greater social democracy, and excessive regulatory administration, so-called "big government" pushed beyond the point of diminishing returns, as the conventions of liberal democratic capitalist governance proved to be less and less democratic, liberal, and capitalist. Consequently, during the Carter and Reagan administrations, fluid coalitions of academics, citizens, entrepreneurs, managers, and taxpayers agitated to reconfigure Keynesian social welfare practices from the New Deal to the Great Society era around "neoliberal reforms."[10]

Harvey's succinct appraisals of neoliberalism capture many of these shifts in the larger world economy and society that *Telos* began addressing quite critically during the last thirty years. With the dismantling of embedded liberalism, neoliberalism emerged as a complex new regimen that, insofar as it

> values market exchange as "an ethic in itself, capable of acting as a guide to all human action, and substituting for all previously held ethical beliefs," it emphasizes the significance of contractual relations in the marketplace. It holds that the social good will be maximized by maximizing the reach and frequency of market transactions, and it seeks to bring all human action into the domain of the market. This requires technologies of information creation and capacities to accumulate, store, transfer, analyze, and use massive databases to guide decisions in the global marketplace. Hence neoliberalism's intense

9. Ibid., p. 11.

10. For more on this conjuncture in neoliberalism's development, see Paul Piccone, "The Crisis of One-Dimensionality," *Telos* 35 (Spring 1978): 43–54; and Timothy W. Luke, "Culture and Politics in the Age of Artificial Negativity," *Telos* 35 (1978): 56–72.

interest in and pursuit of information technologies (leading some to proclaim the emergence of a new kind of "information society"). These technologies have compressed the rising density of market transactions in both space and time.[11]

As this neoliberal project unfolded in Europe, China, and the United States during the 1980s and 1990s, "the critical theory of contemporary" responded rapidly in *Telos*.[12]

These collected essays, for example, looked at the new environmental politics and radical ecological thinkers gaining attention during these social changes. My studies explore both alternative contemporary movements and unusual past moments of unorthodox resistance to the institutional and ideological developments of "embedded liberalism" as well as the new emergent neoliberalism, but I also focus on the role of various visions of the "information society" unfolding along with these changing forms of capitalism. While the criticism of the early Frankfurt School still holds up, the new analyses made by the contemporary Frankfurt School after 1973–1974, as advanced by Habermas and his followers in "the communicative turn," or by other avowedly liberal thinkers who were struggling to maintain the illusion that the embedded liberalism of the Fordist-Keynesian welfare states of 1933 to 1973 years might somehow survive intact, soon proved to be less instructive. The energy-intensive growth policies to sustain continuous economic development globally after 1980 at the same levels that had been so costly since the 1950s locally were guaranteed to explode into permanent environmental disasters.

In the American context, these critical essays from *Telos*, *Fast Capitalism*, and Telos-Paul Piccone Institute conferences articulate different aspects of my approach to developing a critical theory of the contemporary expressed through the registers of ecocritique, which continuously question the interwoven politics of nature, economy, and culture. Since the 1970s, the discourses and practices of both neoliberal institutions and professional-technical classes working on behalf of these social for-

11. Harvey, *A Brief History of Neoliberalism*, pp. 3–4.
12. See Timothy W. Luke and Ben Agger, eds., *A Journal of No Illusions: Telos, Paul Piccone, and the Americanization of Critical Theory* (New York: Telos Press Publishing, 2011); and Patricia Mooney Nickel, *North American Critical Theory after Postmodernism: Contemporary Dialogues* (New York: Palgrave Macmillan, 2012).

mations have operated above the heads of the average citizen, while also working against the concrete interests of the working classes, the underclass, and the environment. As Pierre Bourdieu and Loïc Wacquant argue, the information-intensive practices underpinning the symbolic analytical mindsets of mobile global elites are among the main drivers of ongoing modernization campaigns, which ironically are "borne not just by the champions of the neoliberal revolution, who under cover of modernization are seeking to remake the world by making a clean slate of the social and economic gains resulting from a hundred years of social struggle, depicted today as so many archaisms and obstacles to the nascent new order, but also by cultural producers (scholars, writers, artists) and even political figures of the left, the majority of whom still see themselves as progressive."[13] It is precisely such contradictory zones of allegedly progressive cultural practices and actually regressive economic policies that I target in these selected works of ecocritique since the 1980s.

Informationalization on a global scale is just one moment of capitalist industrial materiality that draws individuals and groups into the virtual collectives of social media, Internet commerce, and political polarization. The hyperreal simulation of society, acceleration of exchange, and reduction of civility since 1980, in turn, are accelerating the neoliberal fetishization of markets, deregulation, and corporations as the practice of "globalization," or a planetary collective tethered to what Jean Baudrillard describes as "the generation by models of a real without origin or a reality: a hyperreal...it is the map that engenders the territory."[14] With its aggressive globalizing networks, worn-down domestic governments, and overtaxed local communities, neoliberal governance exalts "the individual" interacting with millions of others in "the market." Neoliberalism's most bitter truth, as its own continuous

13. Pierre Bourdieu and Loïc Wacquant, "The New Planetary Vulgate," in Pierre Bourdieu, *Political Interventions: Social Science and Political Action*, ed. Franck Poupeau and Thierry Discepolo (London: Verso, 2008), p. 364. See also Robert Reich, *The Work of Nations: Preparing Ourselves for 21st-Century Capitalism* (New York: Knopf, 1991); Christopher Lasch, *The Revolt of the Elites and the Betrayal of Democracy* (New York: W. W. Norton, 1996); and Timothy W. Luke, *Capitalism, Democracy, and Ecology: Departing from Marx* (Urbana: Univ. of Illinois Press, 1999).

14. Jean Baudrillard, *Simulations*, trans. Paul Foss, Paul Patton, and Philip Beitchman (New York: Semiotext(e), 1983), p. 2.

commercial chaos and periodic power outages have illustrated, "no longer has to be rational, since it is no longer measured against some ideal or negative instance. It is nothing more than operational."[15]

The world created after informationalism connects everywhere, commodification settles everywhere, and pollution nestles everywhere is packaged today as "the Anthropocene." While this term is still open to debate, each of these essays serves as either an alert about its advent before it was branded or an alarm after anthropogenic ecological changes added more destruction to an already damaged planet. Even before the Anthropocene concept gained such currency, the critical theory of the contemporary searched the earth's ecologies to highlight how "all that is solid melts into air, all that is holy is profaned, and man is at last compelled to face with sober senses, his real conditions of life, and relations with his kind"[16] turn on the growing domination of nature and worsening domination of humanity.

The new global Anthropocene culture industry's mapping of both twentieth-century history and current events in the twenty-first century is still imprecise. Many of its conceptual cartographers still treat "humanity" as a collective subject with the singular drive always to seek greater energy and more material progress. This Anthropocene's new narrative frame must be recognized as yet another Western, or largely westernized, technoscience project and governance assemblage meant to control the earth and other human beings from afar.[17] And it is striving to maintain, or reassert, technological, political, economic, and cultural dominance by pushing this climatological conception of geopolitical trends. The strategic goals, whether they relate to the opening of the Arctic Ocean to greater ocean-borne commerce with climate change or keeping rapid decarbonization policies running slowly, still

---

15. Ibid., p. 3.

16. Marx and Engels, *Manifesto of the Communist Party*, p. 476. See Timothy W. Luke, "Lives as Half-Life: The Nuclear Condition and Biopolitical Disaster," in *Biopolitical Disaster*, ed. Jennifer L. Lawrence and Sarah Marie Wiebe (New York: Routledge, 2018), pp. 47–61.

17. See, for example, J. R. McNeill and Peter Engelke, *The Great Acceleration: An Environmental History of the Anthropocene* (Cambridge, MA: Harvard Univ. Press, 2016); and Timothy W. Luke, "Sustainability and the City," in *Handbook of Cities and the Environment*, ed. Kevin Archer and Kris Bezdecny (Cheltenham: Edward Elgar, 2016), pp. 433–53.

keep the command-control-communication of climate change adaptation over the near term and long run in the hands of the G-7 (or maybe the G-20 economic coalitions of wealthy nation-states) to justify the policy conditions their ruling expert elites set for the earth's planetary stewardship.

Even though *Telos* is rarely in the spotlight, many wide-ranging studies of environmental politics that channel environmental political theory into North American critical thought have been developed in *Telos*. Although I share Adorno's worries about the possible effectiveness of any critique, I do not despair about what must be done. Indeed, these instances for the ecocritique of mass consumerism, mainstream environmentalism, blind informationalism, biopolitical localism, green managerialism, and ecological urbanism do not concede the alleged inability of thought to face the totality of what must be confronted. In turn, some of these essays address radical activists and thinkers who always have refused the postmodern reluctance to come forth as active engaged subjects. Their engagements may have been extreme, violent, misconceived, or maladroit, but they all have sparked significant political responses well worth consideration in the critical theory of the contemporary.

The following chapters unfold, more or less, in chronological order and appear mostly in their original unedited form. Chapter 1, "Radical Ecology and the Crisis of Political Economy" (*Telos* 46, Winter 1980–81), was written during Ronald Reagan's first victorious campaign for the White House, two years into Deng Xiaoping's call to China's toiling masses "to enrich yourselves," and seven years after the Yom Kippur War, in which President Nixon backed Israel to the point of pushing the Arab petro-states in OPEC to impose an oil embargo on "The West." Instead of accelerating technological efforts to find more diverse, renewable, and stable energy sources, both "The West" and "The East" played geopolitical cards in accepting their locked-in dependence on fossil fuels by maneuvering against OPEC, intervening forcefully and more frequently across the Middle East, and vying militarily to ensure "the security of the world's oil supply." Carbon dioxide (CO_2) concentrations during 1980 were measured at 371 ppm, but "the entropy state" criticized in this early ecocritique of how sustainably such regimes have degraded the development of global economy already had launched misbegotten new growth programs that have raised atmospheric CO_2 concentrations up to 415 ppm in 2019.[18]

Such contradictions spurred my engagement in contesting these politics of economy, nature, and society. Chapter 2, "Informationalism and Ecology" (*Telos* 56, Summer 1983), probes the contradictory tendencies in informationalizing advanced industrial economies to use data-driven production and management tools for creating more efficient ecological administrative outcomes as well as triggering bigger bursts of environmentally destructive economic growth. The emerging project of planetarian ecomanagerialism, guided by continuous informational surveillance from space, at sea, on the ground, or in the air, quickly turned into a contradictory set of opportunities to stabilize such fragile ecologies of everyday life and/or simply discipline the existing regime of unrelenting growth as fossil-fueled sustainable degradation.

Chapter 3, "The Dreams of Deep Ecology" (*Telos* 76, Summer 1988), and chapter 4, "Community and Ecology" (*Telos* 88, Summer 1991), examine divergent intellectual and political responses to the growing environmental crisis in the Reagan-Bush era. In the first case, I argue that deep ecology turns back to favor nature over society; in the second case, I examine how more communitarian politics might attain tangible ecological improvements through more local nature and society balances. Chapter 5, "The Politics of Arcological Utopia: Soleri on Ecology, Architecture, and Society" (*Telos* 101, Fall 1994), closely examines the alternative urban forms of "arcology" that Paolo Soleri developed to hybridize aesthetically and efficiently an ecological city (or "architecture") with social nature (or "ecology") to forge a better urban existence. Unfortunately, his utopian experimental city in central Arizona, Arcosanti, continues to become more depopulated and derelict, while the massive citified exurban formations he detested all around Phoenix, Arizona, blossom up bigger every year. Nonetheless, as the sprawling Phoenix metropolitan area has grown in size to become almost three times as

18. See the CO_2 Earth website, https://www.co2.earth/daily-co2. These figures are amalgamated measurements from the Mauna Loa Observatory as reported by CO_2 Earth, an independent, citizen-led public science initiative. In 1950, global fossil fuel consumption (coal, natural gas, and petroleum) was roughly 20,000 terawatt-hours (TWh); by 1980 it had tripled to just over 60,000 TWh, and then it more than doubled from 1980 to over 120,000 TWh in 2017. See Hannah Ritchie and Max Roser, "Fossil Fuels," *Our World in Data*, https://ourworldindata.org/fossil-fuels.

large as Jamaica and nearly twice as large as Israel or Slovenia, its elites cynically celebrate the high aesthetics of Soleri's architectural vision, even though it was the road they would not take to create a new ecological urbanism.[19]

Chapter 6, "Searching for Alternatives: Postmodern Populism and Ecology" (*Telos* 103, Spring 1995), and chapter 7, "Re-Reading the Unabomber Manifesto" (*Telos* 107, Spring 1996), also explore two radically different political modes of resisting advanced informational society. One pushes to reintegrate rural towns and small cities materially together in order to forge ecological ways of living within contemporary global capitalism by resurrecting individual lives resting upon real economic individual competence. The other involves going off the grid to attack the professional-technical elites that steer "industrial civilization" with the hope of cataclysmically crashing it.

Chapter 8, "A Harsh and Hostile Land: Edward Abbey's Politics and the Great American Desert" (*Telos* 141, Fall 2007), delves into yet other boisterous lifestyles for going off the grid in the American West, as celebrated in the fictional works of Edward Abbey. Chapter 9, "Hashing It Over: Green Governmentality and the Political Economy of Food" (*Fast Capitalism* 10.1, August 2011), on the other hand, looks to how re-agrarianizing the daily lives of the urban underclass, the time of overstretched suburbanites, and the skill of back-to-the-community gardeners now serves as a complex set of tactics for the neoliberal state to "care for the self and others" through a green governmentality. With minimal state support, such campaigns try to balance the slow degradation of cities and their inhabitants' existence by granting them greater measures of "food sovereignty" amid urban "food deserts" through community

19. See Claire C. Carter, *Repositioning Paolo Soleri: The City is Nature* (Scottsdale, AZ: Scottsdale Museum of Contemporary Art, 2017), https://smoca.org/exhibition/repositioning-paolo-soleri-the-city-is-nature/, which documents how Soleri explored "thousands of possibilities for the urban built environment," but these explorations of new urban megastructures largely were aesthetic, "drawings, architecture models, sketchbooks, sculpting, prints, and photographs." Instead of taking this path, global capitalism tries instead to retain a conventionalized "sustainable materialism." See Timothy W. Luke, "Caring for the Low-Carbon Self: The Government of Self and Others in the World as a Gas Greenhouse," in *Towards a Cultural Politics of Climate Change: Devices, Desires, and Dissent*, ed. Harriett Bulkeley, Matthew Patterson, and Johannes Stripple (Cambridge: Cambridge Univ. Press, 2016), pp. 66–80, as well as David Schlosberg and Luke Craven, *Sustainable Materialism: Environmental Movements and the Politics of Everyday Life* (Oxford: Oxford Univ. Press, 2019).

farming experiments. Chapter 10, "On the Politics of the Anthropocene" (*Telos* 172, Fall 2015), provides a more in-depth critique of the intellectual contours in the Anthropocene debate and the political stakes of accepting its new cultural, economic, and social agendas in a world increasingly beset by rising seas, worsening weather, and extreme temperatures: arguing about what to name a geological epoch—whether it is new or not—will not change what is already coming to the world as it burns more fossil fuels to invent its future.

Chapter 11, "On the Road to Marrakesh: A Politics of Mitigation or Mystification for Global Climate Change?" (*Telos* 177, Winter 2016), chapter 12, "Seven Days in January: The Trump Administration's New Environmental Nationalism" (*Telos* 178, Spring 2017), and chapter 13, "Science at Dusk in the Twilight of Expertise: The Worst Hundred Days," (*Telos* 179, Summer 2017), are all more direct assaults on the international arrangements for policing climate change or administering environmental policies in the United States during the Obama and Trump administrations. The toothless programs for countries capping-and-measuring their own greenhouse gas emissions with the good intentions of realizing future reductions, the mindless embrace of environmental nationalist prerogatives that worsen the ecological amenities of citizens at home and the world at large, and the entrenched know-nothing assault on environmental science when it gets in the way of economic growth campaigns simply to gain political adulation by short-sighted democratic leaders are all sharply criticized for cynically deepening the destruction already ravaging a damaged planet.[20] In a way, these topical ecocritiques also are cases in point of today's new post-truth forms of state failure, which only lend more credibility to the spread of the Dark Enlightenment.

Chapter 14, "The Dark Enlightenment and the Anthropocene: Readings from the Book of Third Nature as Political Theology" (delivered at the 2019 Telos-Paul Piccone Institute Conference on Political Theology), looks at small circles of interesting writers and tech workers emerging in the "dusk of expertise" across the world. Together, they are pushing

20. These chapters also anticipate the declaration of "a climate emergency" in November 2019 to mark the alarm raised at the First World Climate Conference in Geneva during 1979. See William J. Ripple, Christopher Wolf, Thomas M. Newsome, Phoebe Barnard, William R. Moomaw, and 11,258 scientist signatories from 153 countries, "World Scientists' Warning of a Climate Emergency," *BioScience*, biz088, November 5, 2019, https://doi.org/10.1093/biosci/biz088.

extreme responses to the Anthropocene that turn away from mainstream policy and science to advance "the Dark Enlightenment" and "accelerationism"—both projects meant to collapse existing "technological civilization" from within in order to rebuild a New World Order around radically different values, practices, and scales of action to serve those with the material means to thrive in such a collapse. In addition, some proponents of accelerationism accept the new dire conditions of the Anthropocene as a full-blown post-natural environment as a "new normal." Hence, they imaginatively dream in polemical fantasias of reengineering themselves, and a few chosen elements of humanity per se, to become new superhuman, transhuman, or posthuman organisms, who will better adapt to the extreme ecological conditions of a synthetic post-nature looming ahead for the planet at this time of uneven but rapid "de-Holocenation."

Finally, chapter 15, "Reflections from a Damaged Planet: Adorno as Accompaniment to Environmentalism in the Anthropocene" (*Telos* 183, Summer 2018), recalls Adorno's clear sense of risk and indeterminacy in any "damaged life" to better understand the conditions of living on a "damaged planet." Beset by tremendous ecological uncertainties already recognized as either the "known unknowns" or "unknown unknowns" of the deep doom soon to happen, the alert is crystal clear. The earth today is a badly damaged planet. Even though it is not yet thoroughly under 24x7x365 observation to measure fully what, how fast, why, and where exactly ecological collapse will be coming first, the dialectics of visibility and manageability pushing for such knowledge implicitly telegraph the growing barbaric fixation on the domination of nature under these post-natural conditions for life itself all the way down as well as all the way over the horizon. Remaining alert and engaged to these trends, therefore, through continuously developing more engaged ecocritique through critical theories of the contemporary is vital. With such insights, collapse need not be complete, resilience might well prevail over the ravages of ecosystemic degradation, and the pragmatics of continuous environmental resourcification for greater growth could be forsaken to embrace a more ethical way of life for human and nonhuman beings' existence in different political communities, even amid the deep daily disruptions to the earth itself now in a new epoch eagerly being branded as the Anthropocene.

1

Radical Ecology and the Crisis of Political Economy

L EFT PROGRAMS TODAY are in crisis because capitalism, on whose productive capacity leftists have anchored their hopes since the late nineteenth century, has itself entered into a series of structural crises that seem to have no obvious solutions. Indeed, the Left is presently in crisis since, like the system it opposes, it refuses to acknowledge the ecological constraints limiting further developments of advanced industrial societies. Instead, as stagflation, structural unemployment, and escalating energy costs intensify the crisis, the Left continues to debate how this creaking social and economic edifice might be propped up with yet more of the organizational buttresses that have accelerated its collapse, namely, *more* state intervention, bureaucratic planning, and public control of the technical means of production in order to exploit diminishing natural resources. Leftist political organizations such as John W. Gardner's Common Cause, Barry Commoner's Citizens Party, or Tom Hayden's Campaign for Economic Democracy, generally propose *statist* solutions—especially if the state would come under their allegedly more enlightened direction. Having never been the primary building contractors of America's industrial order and, at best, having only served as consulting engineers, most American leftists can only call for more populist state intervention to salvage advanced industrial society from the excesses of technocratic state intervention.

* Originally published in *Telos* 46 (Winter 1980–81): 63–72.

But the current crises are far deeper than conventional Left programs suggest. For nearly three generations the "emerging post-industrial order" has been winning illusory victories against nature in the war against material scarcity. Its triumph arrived in a fit of moral blindness that refused to acknowledge that unprecedented material affluence for 6 percent of the world's population has required consumption of 35 to 40 percent of the planet's annual production of material goods. As the oil shocks of 1973 and 1979 have indicated, however, the endless age of abundance and the attainment of the affluent society globally are gross mystifications of the severe imbalances between advanced industrial metropolitan nations and poor peripheral countries, technological efficiency and ecological irrationality, present consumption and future production, and organizational effectiveness and structural inequity. Rather than conquering scarcity, advanced industrial society has been creating new scarcities, both in advanced industrial states and dependent Third World countries, which, in turn, are fueling new conflicts between the OECD states and the Group of Seventy-Seven, between the United States and the Soviet Union, and between the European Economic Community (EEC), Japan, and the United States. In the final analysis, advanced industrial society, like the Holy Roman Empire, is turning out to be neither advanced, nor industrial, nor very sociable as both the EEC and the United States rearm themselves to militarily seize vital stocks of raw materials in the Third and Fourth Worlds, as whole sectors of American industrial production are either moving abroad or collapsing under foreign corporate pressures, and as the intrinsic dynamic of a consumption-based economy continues to generate false needs and narcissistic character traits. In the United States these trends are finding their most telling expression in the multimillion-dollar "survivalism" industry, whose magnates vend all of the products needed by the average consumer to prepare for the Hobbesian war of all against all looming beyond the materials shortages of the 1980s—home gasoline storage tanks, freeze-dried foods, and automatic assault rifles.

On the whole, only the radical social ecologists' work seems to fully understand the current crises. Some conventional leftist groups occasionally pay lip service to the concerns of radical ecology. Yet they continue to believe that modern science and technology will find acceptable solutions to economic problems and material scarcities. Consequently, the Left either discounts or ignores the heedless destruction of nature and nonrenewable natural resources. Just as the Soviet Union, the People's Republic of China, and East Germany are more than willing to employ almost any technique that promises to improve their over-all economic performance, the Western Left is largely blind to the real costs of retaining the present industrial system. Instead of developing *real* alternatives that do not presume the input of multiple megawatts of electrical power, environmentally minded leftist groups such as the Citizens Party openly advocate digging up half of the Rocky Mountains and using all their available water resources to extract the oil, gas, coal, and shale petroleum needed to "keep industry working" in the Atlantic and Pacific coastal states. Such environmentalist thinking may provide a needed dose of artificial negativity for the extremely unprofitable nu-clear power state-corporate combine, but it is not radical ecology.

The Left refuses to recognize what radical ecologists have for many years, i.e., that an unanticipated development, "the entropy state," has unexpectedly risen from the rational designs of advanced corporate capitalism. More concretely, "the entropy state is a society at the stage when complexity and interdependence have reached the point where the transaction costs that are generated equal or exceed the society's pro-ductive capabilities."[1] Advanced industrial capitalism has now reached this conjuncture of overpromoted irrational overproduction.

The apparently unavoidable costs of maintaining the necessary "throughput" of goods, services, and information at least matches if not surpasses the input capacity of the environment. This excessive de-mand, in turn, not only endangers monopoly capitalism's satisfaction of its clients' expectations of eternal plenty but also threatens to wreck entire natural biomes for centuries. For example, Brazil, in its rush to-ward industrial development, is looting the resources of the entire Amazon basin by using forestry, agricultural, and mining techniques that are largely ill-suited to the fragile tropical ecology of the Brazilian rain forests and savannahs. Thus, in emulating the high-energy, high-technology, high-consumption industrial regime of North America, the Brazilian "economic miracle" is eradicating the world's largest body of

---

1. Hazel Henderson, "The Entropy State," in *Creating Alternative Futures: The End of Economics* (New York: Berkley Pub. Corp., 1978), p. 83.

natural vegetation, and thus its largest exchanger of carbon dioxide and oxygen, as it creates vast eroded mudflats, dust bowls, and over-silted watercourses.[2] In turn, this "development trade-off" is significantly contributing to the buildup of carbon dioxide in the atmosphere that is leading to the warmest temperatures in over ten centuries over many parts of the globe.

The widespread assumption is that continuing advances of scientific research and technological innovation will inevitably solve these worrisome problems. Yet it is precisely this faith in a science and technology that presume an instrumental approach to nature that must be challenged. While some critical theorists have been struggling with this problem for decades,[3] nothing has changed. Indeed, this problem goes to the very essence of modern domination inasmuch as practically no one can conceive of moving beyond or outside of the present technological regime. The critique of social democrats, Marxist-Leninists, or even anarcho-socialists remains fairly simple and direct, namely, that the problem is not in *how* the technological regime functions but rather in *who* controls, manages, and benefits from its operations. Thus, if the bourgeoisie, or the corporate sector, or the New Class, or the Enlightenment schema, or the party, or the professional-technocratic intelligentsia were removed, then the intrinsic virtues of technological production would come into full play. These positions are nonsensical.

Advanced technology has built into its operational parameters a number of irrational, destructive, and inefficient assumptions that any group who uses these methods will have to confront. Yet in genuinely confronting them, the alleged efficiency of advanced technology self-destructs. By intensifying the inputs of nonrenewable energy, management, advanced technological expertise, and capital, there has been an improvement in the material culture of a small minority of humanity. But the true costs of these processes are never calculated or even taken into consideration. The invisible, intangible, and external *costs* of advanced technologies' visible, tangible, and internal *benefits* are continually charged off because they cannot be conceptually, financially, or

---

2. Richard J. Barnet, *The Lean Years: Politics in the Age of Scarcity* (New York: Simon and Schuster, 1980), pp. 75, 149.

3. See William Leiss, *The Domination of Nature* (Boston: Beacon, 1971).

fiscally accounted for under non-ecological modes of thinking. Consequently, many today would argue that the battle against scarcity in agricultural production has been won forever. The development of corporate agriculture in the United States promises to deliver increasingly larger amounts of food to increasingly larger groups of consumers with increasingly smaller contributions of human labor. Yet this agriculture is doomed to collapse precisely because it has substituted energy and organization for labor. Today, as the farm belts around American cities are covered over by suburbia with its service industry centers, and as the food production of the nation is concentrated in a few scattered areas bound together by interstate trucking, it takes six calories of nonrenewable fossil fuel energy to produce one calorie of renewable food energy, and one bushel of good topsoil is lost for every two bushels of corn produced under these energy-intensive means of production. Thus, in less than a century, nearly one-half of the topsoil in the American plains states has been lost to erosion, nearly one-sixth of all known reserves of fossil fuels have been dissipated, and these losses are accounted for as "gains" by advanced technological society because the external and invisible costs of accumulating petroleum energy and topsoil over the millennia enter into modern industrial social thinking as "free" goods ready to be exploited at a profit.

The vaunted rational efficiency of advanced technology actually hides gross irrationalities, such as Love Canal, the *Torrey Canyon* oil spill, New England's acid rain, Three Mile Island, and the Hanford nuclear site, that are an integral and not an accidental part of modern life. Presumably, these ecological disasters would be worthwhile trade-offs if the material utopia that advanced society promised were indeed a reality. But it is not. Instead, there are a few select centers of privatized commodity consumption in Europe, Japan, and North America, which have bullied their way into existence over the past century by despoiling the material resources of eons. Basically, present-day technology does not have the technical answers for using the planet's finite fund of material, intellectual, and cultural resources at levels enjoyed by the more affluent classes of the OECD countries for everyone in the world. At best, it aims in the future to provide the same level of goods and services given a small growth in population with a diminishing input of resources. Thus, the goal of IBM, Exxon, or General Foods has become the provision of the same material standard of living to a population that is perhaps 7 percent of the world's populace and uses only 30 percent of its resources rather than being 6 percent and getting 40 percent of its material resources.

The Left today is not facing these problems, much less dealing with them. On the whole, they are attributed to a crisis of political leadership, of managerial command, or of economic control that all ties back to their criticism of the advanced capitalist system on the grounds of *who* controls it and for *whom*. Having failed to consolidate its inchoate cultural revolution in the late 1960s and early 1970s, the New Left and its contemporary heirs have mainly set traditional Old Left goals for themselves—organize the workers, mobilize the people, inform the masses, raise funds for the cause, work within the system to keep it partially rational, regulate social institutions to aid the dispossessed, and seize command over the society in order to slowly fulfill the leftist program of economic equalization, personal liberation, and social emancipation. In addition to the real scarcities that existed prior to worldwide industrialization beginning in the 1880s, artificial scarcities have been created and aggravated by the new productive processes of advanced industrial society. Deforestation has caused massive desertification, irrigation has led to tremendous salination of agricultural land and freshwater supplies, fossil fuel consumption has altered weather patterns and activities, chemical fertilizers and pesticides have destroyed food chains, cheap energy has given way to expensive energy, and corporate farm mechanization has depleted once immense stocks of arable soils. Until the Left confronts these issues, its program, like that of moderate centrists and liberals, will fail to address the real crises. While posing as social and political revolutionaries, then, the Left remains allied with ecological and technological tories.

Today, the only social forces engaged in truly radical activity are those radical or social ecologists seeking a viable, alternative social, economic, and technical model that consciously stands both within and outside of the present technological and economic assumptions of advanced industrial society. Thus, radical ecology circles are presently developing on a small-scale, local, and decentralized level the technological, ecological, and social alternatives to advanced industry's totalitarian technical regime. Through the cooperative, communal, and community action movement, a number of significantly effective alternative technologies are being developed that assume a relation of stewardship and cooperation with nature rather than one of exploitation and domination. Moreover, the creation of these alternative housing, energy, agricultural, transportation, communication, and organizational technologies is aimed at generating both material hardware and cultural software that presumes individual autonomy, skill, discipline, and activity. By moving from energy-intensive to energy-saving techniques, from capital-intensive to capital-saving investments, from hierarchical complexity to nonhierarchical simplicity, and from inaccessible technology to accessible crafts, radical ecologists are stimulating the fabrication of appropriate technological and economic forms that are "the hardware and the processes that allow for the efficient production to support materially comfortable lives for all, based on machinery that is understandable and maintainable at the local level, that draws on renewable sources of energy, uses recycled materials and builds self-confident personalities and local control, while it reduces the artificially created need for 'more' goods regardless of quality or utility."[4]

Ultimately, the radical ecologists are working from within the technological traditions of advanced industrial society, but they are bending its techniques to new, more rational, more effective fulfillment of human needs by attacking directly the anomic dependency, consumeristic narcissism, and cretinization that advanced industrial society purposely creates among its client populations. Similarly, the radical ecologists' advocacy of self-reliance, voluntary simplicity, personal discipline, collective democratic decision-making, and individual reskilling all pose a revolutionary challenge to contemporary social practices, which presume dependency upon experts, conformist consumption to sustain the economy's need for unwanted aggregate demand, concentrated ownership, hierarchical control, centralized technocratic decision-making, and personal deskilling. Yet because the radical ecologists have no explicit organizational structures, no commitment to lobbying, public hearing, or electoral politics, and no institutional program, it is difficult to argue that they serve as real sources of artificial negativity

4. Neil Seldman, "Reviving Common Sense in the USA," *Ekistics* 43, no. 259 (1977): 376.

within the present order. Instead, they seem to represent a new collection of genuine "outsiders," whose opposition to technocratic regimes is fundamental, total, and inherently antagonistic. Nonetheless, these social, political, intellectual, and cultural forces are operating outside of the current political economy of advanced industrial society in a fashion that challenges the conditions, costs, and controls of advanced technology, which the conventional Left continues to regard as sacrosanct to its world-historical mission.

2

Informationalism and Ecology

THE DISRUPTION OF the ecological balance sustaining human life has become one of the major products of advanced industrial society. Nature has been despoiled at the expense of all life for the benefit of a handful of recent generations who have been "fortunate" enough to enjoy the role of consumers in the twentieth century.[1] This consumerist model thrives upon the wasteful production of private goods by destroying the collective resources of the natural habitat.

Having overloaded the ecological system of North America, American firms have shifted capital and jobs to other continents, forging a transnational industrial regime out of their untapped ecological poten-

* Originally published in *Telos* 56 (Summer 1983): 59–73.

1. For a further discussion in this vein, see Barry Commoner, *The Closing Circle: Man, Nature, and Technology* (New York: Knopf, 1971); Barry Commoner, *The Poverty of Power: Energy and the Economic Crisis* (New York: Knopf, 1976); René Dumont, *Utopia or Else*, trans. Vivienne Menkes (London: Deutsch 1974); Ivan Illich, *Toward a History of Needs* (New York: Pantheon Books, 1978); and Harry Rothman, *A Murderous Providence: A Study of Pollution in Industrial Societies* (London: R. Hart-Davis, 1972). For a critique of consumerism, see Jean Baudrillard, *For a Critique of the Political Economy of the Sign*, trans. Charles Levin (St. Louis: Telos Press, 1981); Ivan Illich, *Energy and Equity* (New York: Harper & Row, 1974); William Leiss, *The Limits of Satisfaction: An Essay on the Problem of Needs and Commodities* (Toronto: Univ. of Toronto Press, 1976); and Timothy W. Luke, "Regulating the Haven in a Heartless World: The State and Family under Advanced Capitalism," *New Political Science* 2, no. 3 (1981): 51–74.

tial. In turn, the character of American capital has shifted profoundly as its traditional *industrial* goods-producing activity has fallen behind *informational* knowledge-producing activities in economic and political importance. Ironically, however, the interests of American informational capital in this deindustrializing trend now parallel those of ecological activists, who seek to build new ecologically sound communities to coexist with nature in diverse habitats without qualitatively lowering standards of living.

By elaborating the impact of this informational revolution on America's industrial economy, one can explore the possibilities for an ecological transformation emerging out of the contradictions between informational and industrial society. Already, some observers—like the "Atari Democrats"—see a post-industrial informationalized society as an environmentally sound economic order.[2] Still, their high-tech solutions for the current industrial malaise, such as the construction of massive solar collectors in earth orbit to generate electricity or the relocation of America's polluting industries abroad, must not be mistaken for an authentic ecological revolution. The ecological crisis is a global problem. It can only be aggravated by internationalizing industrial pollution or microwaving megawatts of electricity through the planet's atmosphere. Instead, informational capital's program for cybernetically managing the earth's ecological collapse from space must be recognized as an environmental false promise that neither America's neoconservatives nor its neoliberals can really fulfill.

The Crisis of Advanced Industrialism

The deep structural crises of advanced industrial capitalism, as it has developed in the United States, extend beyond the current recession. Behind 11% unemployment and the $125 billion plus deficit of 1982, the entire American industrial complex has decayed to near collapse. In 1947, the United States produced 60% of all the world's steel. By 1975,

2. See Lester C. Thurow, *The Zero-Sum Society: Distribution and the Possibilities for Economic Change* (New York: Basic Books, 1980), for the classic example of neoliberal thought. Also see Barry Bluestone and Bennett Harrison, *The Deindustrialization of America: Plant Closings, Community Abandonment, and the Dismantling of Basic Industry* (New York: Basic Books, 1982), and Hazel Henderson, *The Politics of the Solar Age: Alternatives to Economics* (Garden City, NY: Anchor Press/Doubleday, 1981), for the neoliberal program for a cybernetic "reindustrialization with a human face."

U.S. production declined to 16% of world production and has dropped to near 12% in the early 1980s. Similarly, in 1959 American companies were the largest firms in 11 out of the 13 major industrial sectors, while U.S. interests controlled 111 out of the world's largest 156 companies in these 13 industrial sectors. By 1976, however, U.S. companies controlled only 7 of the 13 major industrial groups and 68 of the 156 biggest firms. Moreover, American technological primacy has declined significantly in all 13 groups save aerospace and electrical equipment.[3]

American industries after 1945 energized the world economy for over two decades as U.S. GNP consistently grew over 3% per year. Even in 1960, the United States dominated 25% of the world's manufacturing output, while American firms produced 95% of the consumer electronics, steel, and automobiles sold in the home market. Yet with market saturation and the energy crisis, American productivity decreased 1% per year from 1973 to 1978 and 2% in 1979. At the same time, American firms sold less than 50% of consumer electronics, 85% of steel, and 80% of all automobiles in the U.S. market. From 1960 to 1981, America's piece of the world export pie has from declined 16 to 11%.[4]

These trends can be driven home by examining the keystone of American industrial primacy since the 1900s: the automobile industry. Automobile industries employ one out of every six U.S. workers, and 26% of all retail sales are dependent upon automotive production. During the 1970s, however, American automobile firms lost control. In 1977, foreign imports comprised 18% of American auto sales. By 1982 Japanese imports alone held nearly 30% of the American market as all imports verged on gaining 40% of U.S. auto sales. Imports in 1982 were

3. Richard J. Barnet, *The Lean Years: Politics in the Age of Scarcity* (New York: Simon and Schuster, 1980), pp. 273, 241. Also see "Steelyard Blues: New Structures in Steel," *NACLA Report on the Americas* 13, no. 1 (January/February 1979).

4. John Naisbitt, *Megatrends: Ten New Directions Transforming Our Lives* (New York: Warner Books, 1982), pp. 55–56. By the mid-1980s, Third World producers will account for 13% of all exported manufactured products and 64% of all Third World exports will be manufactured goods. In the mid-1970s, Third World countries exported only 9% of all manufactured products and only 25% of their exports were manufactured goods. These newly industrialized countries have quadrupled their steel output since 1960 and will both produce and consume 25% of world steel production by 2000. In addition to steel, autos, shoes, textiles, and electronic goods, the United States also now has lost its primacy in machine tools as it imports more foreign-made assemblies than it exports American-made units. See Barnet, *The Lean Years*, pp. 265, 274–75.

70% of California auto sales, the major American market. In 1980, Japan surpassed the United States as the world's major automobile producer with 11 million vehicles—40% greater than U.S. production. Japanese productivity also has grown to be three times greater than American productivity. American factories build a car in 31 hours versus 11 hours in Japan for a comparable car. U.S. firms also largely have lost out in the new booming Third World automobile market, which will equal the American market at 15 million vehicles in 1990, to European and Japanese automobile companies.[5] With this industrial decay, unemployment rates in 1982 throughout the Midwestern industrial states hovered between 10 and 20%.

Much of America's unemployment problem can be traced to this global reorganization of world industry and the emergence of a more service-oriented economy in the United States. In the early 1950s, nearly 60% of America's workforce was employed in industrial occupations. By the early 1980s, however, only about 15% of America's workers, out of a workforce of nearly 100 million, were occupying traditional manufacturing jobs. Of the new jobs created in the 1970s—19 million in all—only 11% were in the goods-producing sector and only 5% were in traditional manufacturing industries. Nearly 90%—17 million new jobs—were generated instead in the professions, service companies, government, and informational firms.[6]

Public employment has increased tremendously with America's industrial stagnation. While one out of ten workers was a government employee in 1932, one of every six workers is employed directly in the United States at the federal, state, or local level in 1980. One of every ten works for Washington alone. With the collapse of America's basic industries and with agricultural employment falling to only 3% in the 1970s, the public sector has become the employer of the last resort either directly in public agencies or indirectly through new government subsidies and protectionist rules to support failing industrial enterprises. In addition to those directly employed by all levels of government, several

---

5. Naisbitt, *Megatrends*, p. 66; Louis Kraar, "Make Way for the New Japans," *Fortune*, August 10, 1981, pp. 176–84. Also see Emma Rothschild, *Paradise Lost: The Decline of the Auto-Industrial Age* (New York: Random House, 1973); and Barnet, *The Lean Years*, p. 244.

6. Naisbitt, *Megatrends*, p. 39; Barnet, *The Lean Years*, p. 273; David L. Birch, "Who Creates Jobs?," *Public Interest* 65 (1981): 3–14.

million more work as private contractors, defense employees, and out-side consultants. Adding these workers together, nearly one in four workers is dependent on the public sector for employment.

Informationalization as Post-Industrialism

Despite this massive growth in state employment and private service industries, it is incorrect to identify "de-industrializing" or "post-industrial" America as essentially a service society.[7] Merely because American workers no longer produce as many *goods*, it should not be assumed that only *services*, except for food services and the medical professions, therefore are necessarily growing in importance. Instead, American producers increasingly are engaged either directly in the production of *information* or indirectly in the informationalization of goods-production and services-provision.

Informationalization represents the new dominance of data-intensive techniques, cybernetic knowledge, and electronic technologies as the strategic resource in corporate production. The invention, production, management, and distribution of *information*—as words, numbers, images, or audio—now overshadows the manufacture of goods or provision of services in the truly advanced capitalist economies. This qualitative shift in production toward *informational* productivity separates the United States, Japan, and West Germany from other advancing industrial systems in the Soviet Union, Spain, Italy, Taiwan, Brazil, or South Korea, which still measure their "advances" in terms of *industrial* activity. Informational society has been defined partially as the "service economy," the "technological society," or "post-industrialism."[8]

7. See Daniel Bell, *The Coming of Post-Industrial Society: A Venture in Social Forecasting* (New York: Basic Books, 1973), pp. 121–64; Bell, "The Social Framework of the Information Society," in *The Microelectronics Revolution: The Complete Guide to the New Technology and Its Impact on Society*, ed. Tom Forester (Oxford: Blackwell, 1980), pp. 500–549.

8. Daniel Bell observes, "A postindustrial society is based on services. What counts is not raw muscle power, or energy, but information." See Bell, *The Coming of Post-Industrial Society*, pp. 126–27; Victor C. Ferkiss, *Technological Man: The Myth and the Reality* (New York: Braziller, 1970); and Alan Gartner and Frank Riessman, *The Service Society and the Consumer Vanguard* (New York: Harper & Row, 1974). For further discussion, see Christopher Evans, *The Micro Millennium* (New York: Viking, 1979); and Fritz Machlup, *The Production and Distribution of Knowledge in the United States* (Princeton, NJ: Princeton Univ. Press 1962), pp. 362–400. Also see J. Rose, *The Cybernetic Revolution*

Each of these incomplete notions, however, does not fully account for the transformations wrought by the informational revolution of American industrial society.

An entirely new social formation tied to the production, interpretation, and distribution of information has emerged from within American industrial capitalism since the mid-1950s. These trends were launched in the 1920s and 1930s as the telecommunications and electric power grids were extended throughout the entire nation. The primary centers of informational activity accounted for 18% of national income in 1929 and 17% in 1948. In the 1950s, however, informational growth rapidly accelerated with widespread computerization. The annual growth rates in knowledge production in primary informational activities from 1949 to 1958 are astounding: 16.4% in research and development, 10.9% in telephone systems, 77.2% in television station revenues, 104.2% in electronic computers, and 10.6% for total knowledge production.[9] These productivity advances were made possible by several technological and organizational breakthroughs. By 1954, for example, Texas Instruments had constructed the first silicon junction transistor for electronics applications, General Electric purchased the first UNIVAC computer used exclusively for business data processing, and IBM began to dominate computing markets with its mass-produced 701 systems.

In 1956, white-collar workers in technical, clerical, and managerial positions outnumbered blue-collar industrial workers for the first time in American history.[10] With the Sputnik challenge in 1957, an unprecedented mode of industrial production, based upon these white-collar workers generating data-intensive scientific knowledge and complex electronic technology, came together in American aerospace, defense, computer, and electronics industries to produce wholly new genres of technological information. In 1959, the semiconductor integrated cir-

---

(London: Elek, 1974); Wickham Skinner and Kishore Chakraborty, *The Impact of New Technology: People and Organizations in Manufacturing and Allied Industries* (New York: Pergamon Press, 1982); and Ronald Stamper, *Information in Business and Administrative Systems* (London: Batsford, 1973).

9. Marc Uri Porat, *The Information Economy: Definition and Measurement*, U.S. Office of Telecommunication Special Publication 77-12 (1) (Washington, DC: U.S. Government Printing Office, 1977), pp. 64-65.

10. Daniel Bell, "Notes on the Post-Industrial Society," *Public Interest* 6 and 7 (Winter and Spring 1967): 24-35, 102-18.

cuit was developed. By 1963, IBM introduced its first family of computers, the 360 line, with standardized programming, architecture, and software—over 30,000 were sold in the 1960s to government, business, and universities. AT&T, with NASA, launched the world's first communications satellite, Telstar, in 1962, which was the initial step toward a multimodal telecommunications network capable of receiving and transmitting video, audio, and digital information in the 1970s. Finally, during the 1970s, Intel introduced in 1970 the 1103 Random Access Memory (RAM) chip and in 1974 the 8080 microprocessor chip, an improved model of its first four-bit 4004 microprocessing unit (MPU). By 1975, thirty years after ENIAC, the first electronic computer, over 200,000 large computers were in operation along with 750,000 microprocessor units worldwide.[11]

With these technological innovations, American industrial capitalism has been greatly augmented if not nearly displaced by American informational capitalism. Admittedly, most information production now derives from the programming and management needs of complex government or corporate operations. Similarly, many informational jobs are undemanding, repetitive, low-paid, and essentially uncreative. Nonetheless, job definitions, skills, and duties increasingly have been defined in both the blue-collar and white-collar strata by their relation to informational activity. As the computer console has replaced the factory smokestack as the determinant sign of economic power, informationalization has reconstituted labor and management. By the late 1960s, the *primary information sector* of the economy—computer manufacturing, telecommunications, mass media, advertising, publishing, accounting, education, research and development, and risk management in finance, banking, and insurance—produced 25.1% of the national income. In turn, the *secondary information sector*—the work performed by information workers in government, goods-producing firms, and service-producing firms for internal consumption—produced 21.1% of the national income. Already by the late 1960s, prior to widespread computerization, data-intensification in manufacturing, and microprocessing technology, informational activities alone produced 46% of America's national income and earned 53% of total national wages. By the mid-1970s, the

11. Dirk Hanson, *The New Alchemists: Silicon Valley and the Microelectronics Revolution* (Boston: Little, Brown, 1982), pp. 65, 82, 84, 97, 103–4, 120–28, 246.

primary information sector's overall share of national income production alone rose from 25 to 30%, while all information workers in both sectors surpassed non-information workers in numbers.[12]

Of course, informational capital has not eliminated industrial or agricultural capital. Rather, it has begun to informationalize industrial production (using CAD/CAM, group technology, and automated assembly) and agricultural production (using biotechnology, genetic engineering, and computer-assisted farm management) just as industrial capital industrialized agriculture in the early twentieth century. America's industrial and agricultural products remain vital to its present overall economic structures. Still, with the transnationalization of manufacturing and food cultivation in Second and Third World export platforms, the informationalized production of words, images, and numbers increasingly dominates the American workplace.

The collapse of America's industrial economy, however, will be followed by additional employment losses as the informationalization of economic life becomes more pervasive. Current projections hold that 40% of all economic productivity can be improved, in one way or another, by microprocessing technology. Data-intensive production could mean that at least 50% of current shop-floor workers will be replaced by highly skilled technicians and robots by 1990. With over 130,000 workers laid off, General Motors began buying 14,000 industrial robots in March 1982. Once the robots are online, 40,000 to 50,000 jobs will be replaced, which equals the Chrysler Corporation's total hourly U.S. labor force in 1982.[13]

12. See Porat, *The Information Economy: Definition and Measurement*, pp. 65, 119–23; and Marc Uri Porat, *The Information Economy: Sources and Methods for Measuring the Primary Information Sector*, U.S. Office of Telecommunication Special Publication 77-12 (2) (Washington, DC: U.S. Government Printing Office, 1977).

13. John Siansell "The Social Impact of Microprocessors," *New Scientist* 8, no. 1124 (1978): 104–6. By 2000, nearly all industrial workers could be displaced by robotic units, while 50 to 75% of all industrial jobs could be lost in the process. By 1990, the United States, which is lagging behind Japan and some EEC nations, could be producing 17,000 to 20,000 robots a year to augment a robotic base of 80,000 to 160,000 units. U.S. auto producers today already employ 1,000 complex robots to increase their productivity. The most sophisticated units cost $50,000 each, yet they work two shifts a day for eight years in a normal work span—or $5 per hour versus $15 per hour for human workers. Along with manufacturing, informational technology is predicted to displace 30% of the human workers in banking and insurance, 40% of all office workers, and up to 50% of all mid-level corporate and industrial management. Already, the relatively low capital

Some of these displaced workers either will be retrained as informational workers to return to private sector jobs or will be absorbed into service occupations in public employment. Nevertheless, neither the private nor the public sector can entirely absorb the tremendous new displacement of labor promised by robotization and informationalization. Most of the displaced workers will not get jobs of equal status or pay as they fall into the high-turnover, low-wage niche of the labor markets. With informationalization, *hundreds* of *thousands* of stable, medium- and high-wage jobs will be lost forever, while only *thousands* of new high-wage professional jobs in the informational industries can be developed to replace them.[14]

Consequently, some corporate planners argue that the informationalizing economy and the contracting welfare state must develop a "third sector" (beyond the "private" and "public" sectors) or a "third system" (beyond the "market system" and the "planning system") to accommodate the de-industrialized workforce of the coming decades.[15] Being unable to maintain the incomes of the unemployed and underemployed through either transfer payment schemes or full-employment programs, the "technologically competent" elites now in control of the informationalizing industrial state and transnational firms are promoting a hybrid package of structural unemployment, volunteerism, soft energy paths, frugality, voluntary simplicity, decentralization, and local

---

intensitivity of office work—$2,000 to $6,000 per worker in 1980—will rise to over $10,000 per worker by 1985 as informational capital displaces labor. The labor-displacing qualities of informational capital can be seen, for example, in New York Telephone's handling of 30% more calls in 1980 than 1969 with 15,000 fewer employees. Desmond Smith, "Info City," *New York*, February 9, 1981, p. 28; Skinner and Chakraborty, *The Impact of New Technology*, p. 2; Naisbitt, *Megatrends*, p. 74; Hanson, *The New Alchemists*, p. 163; Wickham Skinner and Kishore Chakraborty, *The Impact of New Technology: People and Organization in Service Industries* (New York: Pergamon Press, 1982), p. 6; and Harry Anderson, "Jobs: Putting America Back to Work," *Newsweek*, October 18, 1982, pp. 80–81.

14. One labor analyst in New York noted in 1981, for example, as the Ford auto plant closed in Mahwah, New Jersey, with a loss of 6,000 jobs, that 6,000 new hotel rooms in New York would open in 1981. In-house projections suggest one domestic helper is needed for each room; thus 6,000 new jobs also were created in New York—at lower pay with less status for those displaced auto workers. See Smith, "Info City," p. 29.

15. For a discussion of the "Third Sector," see Richard C. Carlson, Willis W. Harman, Peter Schwartz, and Associates, *Energy Futures, Human Values, and Lifestyles: A New Look at the Energy Crisis* (Boulder, CO: Westview Press, 1982).

actionism to meliorate the deteriorating situations of the "technologically obsolescent" and "technologically superfluous" classes.[16] Within
this "third sector," Ivan Illich's notions of the "subsistent household,"
"useful unemployment," and "vernacular economics" might come to
prevail. Consumers will be encouraged to produce their own goods and
services for their own frugal consumption as the larger informational
economy discredits the ideas and infrastructure of mass consumerism
on the lines of post–World War II American suburbia.[17]

According to one corporate forecast, generated by the Values and
Lifestyles program at SRI International in 1980, American consumers
fall into three groups: *need-driven consumers* living at the poverty level
and buying bare necessities are 11 percent of the adult population, or
19 million people; *outer-directed consumers* living affluent middle-class
lifestyles and buying the complete package of consumer society are 69
percent of the adult population, or 110 million people; and *inner-directed consumers* living "consciously" or "voluntarily" simple lives, or
non-consumeristic lifestyles compared to outer-directed consumers,
make up 20 percent of the adult population, or 33 million people.[18] Although the inner-directed consumers do not see their lifestyles as forming an austerity or downward-mobility movement, its ultimate impact,
in the context of the de-industrialization and ultra-informationalization
of America's economy, is that of austerity. With scores of millions of
outer-directed consumers losing their industrial or service jobs to informational technology, and only a few million jobs being created in the
new informational sphere of production, it becomes imperative for the
system's continuous functioning to legitimate this new materially de-
prived era as a "quality of life" revolution that is morally desirable.

Most consumers will not fall in the underclass of *need-driven consumption*. Yet they cannot hope to have in material wealth or symbolic

16. For a discussion of technology as the basis of class formation and conflict, see
David E. Apter, "Ideology and Discontent," in *Ideology and Discontent*, ed. David E. Apter (New York: Free Press of Glencoe, 1964), pp. 15–43.

17. These alternative social and economic institutions are discussed more completely in Ivan Illich, *Toward a History of Needs* (New York: Pantheon Books, 1978); and
Illich, *Shadow Work* (Boston: Marion Boyars, 1981).

18. See *Leading Edge* 1, no. 1 (1980); and Duane Elgin, *Voluntary Simplicity: Toward a Way of Life That Is Outwardly Simple, Inwardly Rich* (New York: Morrow, 1981),
pp. 129–30.

fashions what *outer-directed consumption* has promised in America since industrialization in the 1890s. Corporate product demography already has targeted these trends. The high-volume, low-cost downscale marketing of mass consumption of the 1950s and 1960s, which always stressed *accessibility*, slowly is giving way to the low-volume, high-cost upscale markets of elite consumers that primarily emphasize *exclusivity*. Outer-directed consumption will continue under informational capitalism, but it increasingly will center on smaller enclaves of elite consumers.

Hence, "voluntary simplicity," "frugality," "ecological lifestyles," "conspicuous conservation," "small is beautiful," "conserver society," or "simple living" are the new master codes of mass consumption in the age of informational capitalism, which produces less *goods* at higher costs for fewer people in specialized markets. Yet image systems, value codes, knowledge bases, and information networks are readily produced under informational capitalism to ground an *inner-directed consumption* tied to innovative *information* packages of "post-affluence," such as personal fulfillment, physical fitness, self-actualization, or spiritual awakening.[19] Outer-directed consumerism provided expensive weeklong vacations at Waikiki on a mass basis for conspicuous consumption. The emerging inner-directed consumerism celebrates frugal ongoing "journeys of moral rebirth" performed at home on an individual basis for personal fulfillment. It is cheaper, saves energy, does not abuse the ecosphere, and the market is nowhere near saturation.

Transnational informationalizing capital wants to break down these consumeristic dependencies in the mass population on national industrial capital and the welfare state. Needing capital for informational development, informationalized firms do not want their backward industrial competitors to fritter away financial resources on consumer goods production—autos, housing, appliances, etc.—or the overextended welfare state to redistribute the social surplus—CETA workers, interstate highways, MX systems, etc.[20] Informational capital instead

---

19. See, for example, one pollster's efforts to chart these changes in Daniel Yankelovich, *New Rules: Searching for Self-Fulfillment in a World Turned Upside Down* (New York: Random House, 1981). Likewise, a handbook for the "new rules" might be Warren Johnson, *Muddling toward Frugality: A Blueprint for Survival in the 1980s* (Boulder, CO: Shambhala, 1979).

20. See "The Reindustrialization of America," special issue of *Business Week*, June 1980, pp. 126–34, on the central importance of finding new pools of capital in wasteful

seeks to displace industrial capital and government from financial markets. It then can invest available funds in the new producer goods of informational economies, soaking its fresh capital out of consumer production and the public sector. As a substitute for affordable, diverse consumer goods and dependable, substantive welfare payments, transnational informational firms are backing volunteerism, frugality, and spiritual reawakening to take up the slack during the informationalizing transition. Dirty, labor-mobilizing industry is moved abroad, leaving millions without jobs, incomes, or purpose. Hence, the technologically competent classes in control of informational capital now urge the technologically obsolescent and superfluous strata to muddle toward frugality and voluntarily simplify their lives.

To restratify American society along the lines of technological competence, informational capital totally contradicts many of the egalitarian-democratic myths underpinning mass electoral politics. These political conflicts, moreover, have strongly influenced recent political events and movements. The contradictions between the "sunbelt and snowbelt" economies, the western "cowboy" and eastern "yankee" elites, workers in "sunrise" and "sunset" industries, or the cultural styles of New Class "Chablis-and-brie" groups versus blue-collar "pools-and-patios" strata all embody a vicious politics of redistribution within the informationalizing society. In turn, the frustrations of the technologically obsolete working classes in America, who have lost immense purchasing power since 1967, increasingly support reactionary appeals from both Democrats and Republicans, which promise to restore America's greatness, economic prosperity, and social consensus.[21] Advanced industrial America, cast along the lines of the United States from 1890 to 1950, however, is not fading away gracefully or easily. Similarly, the new informational society, which already has promoted massive unemployment, urban decay, social dislocation, and international turmoil,

---

government and consumer spending to meet the needs of "reindustrializing" America; and Timothy W. Luke, "Rationalization Redux: From the New Deal to the New Beginning," *New Political Science* 2, no. 4 (1982): 63–72.

21. For a discussion of the "apple pie fascism" or "friendly fascism" that might emerge from these conflicts, see Paul Blumberg, *Inequality in an Age of Decline* (New York: Oxford Univ. Press, 1980); Bertram Gross, *Friendly Fascism: The New Face of Power in America* (New York: M. Evans, 1980); and Kevin Phillips, *Post-Conservative America: People, Politics, and Ideology in a Time of Crisis* (New York: Random House, 1982).

hardly appears attractive or benevolent. These complex trends are mis-understood, fragmentary, and disorganized. Yet to the extent that the strategies for easing the informational transition are unrationalized, open-ended, and disorderly, ecological activists might appropriate some of these new institutional, technological, and cultural possibilities for the cause of ecological transformation.

Outlines for an Ecological Politics

Since the Industrial Revolution, technical advances have progressively robbed individuals and communities of their rights to self-definition, self-determination, and self-direction. This process of rationalization without representation has engendered new modes of human and eco-logical domination in everyday life. The authority of technical experts and specialized knowledge exerts itself through the material artifacts and organization processes of corporate culture, benefiting its anony-mous controllers and designers in the technologically competent classes. It is this anonymous authoritarianism that needs to be attacked. Being grounded in a modern welfare state that tends toward total adminis-tration, any meaningful ecological critique must also recognize that transnational capital inescapably moderates, limits, and defines its revo-lutionary thrusts.

Informationalization, particularly when mediated through micro-processing technology, has promoted its own version of an ecologically viable society. Informational developments have advanced the growth of exurban and rural communities by downsizing and automating in-dustrial plants. New communications and cybernetics media keep these far-flung smaller factories under centralized management. The older in-dustrial cities and regions, in turn, are decaying as they lose their popula-tion, industries, tax base, and services to new informational communities and regions.

Microprocessing technology has been heralded as the true *avant garde* of a democratic decentralization of society. In 1975, a micro-processing chip cost $360; but by 1980 the same chip cost $5, making computer-processing capacity virtually free. Its coinventor, Robert Noyce, predicted in 1973 that computerization after the microprocessor implies radical *decentralization* rather than the complete *centralization* charac-teristic of early mainframe systems. Microprocessing units are diffusing rapidly. Use estimates rose from under one million in 1975 to sixty million in 1980 (compared to 100 years to reach 440 million telephones) worldwide.[22] While the decentralizing potential of computerization is evident, it is not certain that it will become a reality.

The informational revolution will not guarantee necessarily a more democratic, small-scale, ecological society. Microprocessing units can be used equally well on a handful of massive orbital solar satellites or in millions of tiny rooftop solar panels to generate power. An ecologically sound politics must guide informational economies to technological options more suited to ecologically reasonable forms of production. Otherwise, the power centers of industrial capitalism will continue to divert informational development to reinforce their centralized transnational hierarchies.

The institutional basis for a deconstructionist ecology exists *in nuce* in certain tendencies of advanced corporate capitalism. Yet it exists in fragments, unrealized possibilities, and unchosen options that need to be fully identified, correctly implemented, and openly practiced to be realized. More specifically, an objective basis for ecological action might be found in six trends: new population patterns; the growth of single-issue political action groups centered on local or regional politics; the expansion of cooperative exchange and social services; the development of alternative communal institutions; the rise of an anti-corporate/anti-state underground economy; and a growing population of people, perhaps as many as ten million, already practicing aspects of anti-consumerist ecological lifestyles.

One critical trend is the overall return of population to the small cities and rural areas. From 1820 to 1970, large cities grew faster than small cities and country regions, and by 1920 the United States was predominately urban. Yet since the early 1970s, small towns and rural areas have grown faster than large cities. For every 100 people that moved into cities from 1970 to 1975, 131 people moved out. Over 42 percent of the population, or 95 million people, now live in small towns, small cities, and the country, which provides the solid possibility for developing

22. Hanson, *The New Alchemists*, p. 159; "Microcomputers Aim at Huge New Market," *Business Week*, May 12, 1973, p. 180; and "The Microprocessor/Microcomputer Industry," Industrial Analysis Service, Creative Strategies, Inc., San Jose, CA, 1977. Quoted in Hanson, *The New Alchemists*, p. 144.

a new exurban mode of existence, as towns under 2,500 people are now the fastest growing form of settlement.[23]

These population movements reflect a developing interest in the pace, scenery, and stability of rural living. Similarly, they accord with the population decentralization implicit in informationalization and de-industrialization. Along with this rapid growth in the rural population, many new jobs have moved into exurban regions as urban industrial jobs diminish in numbers. Over 700,000 new manufacturing jobs and 3,500,000 new informational and service slots were created in non-metropolitan areas from 1970 to 1978 alone.

With this growth in exurban communities, a new movement toward localism in economic activity, political decisions, and social structures also has developed. State, county, and local governments are being pressured to be more responsive, participatory, and effective. Nearly 20 million citizens belong to single-issue or comprehensive action groups tied into local political concerns. Citizen action groups like ACORN (Arkansas Community Organizations for Reform Now), Virginia Action, CED (Campaign for Economic Democracy), Carolina Action, and the Illinois Public Action Committee have formed to put *local* economic, political, and social issues onto the public agenda.[24] Much of this change has been manipulated from above to legitimize and rationalize the existing system of administration. Nonetheless, these new localist citizens movements also are providing the structural possibilities for realizing an ecologically sensible politics.

In the economic sphere, 70 million Americans participate in some kind of producer, credit, or consumer co-op. These aboveground alternative economic institutions also are augmented by a tremendous underground economy that amounts to hundreds of billions of dollars. Nearly 15 percent of the GNP probably turns over underground off the books; 4.5 million get all their income and 15 million more obtain part of their incomes off this noncorporate shadow economy. Similarly, over

23. Naisbitt, *Megatrends*, pp. 126–27; and Kirkpatrick Sale, *Human Scale* (New York: Coward, McCann & Geoghegan, 1980), p. 44.

24. See Harry C. Boyte, *The Backyard Revolution: Understanding the New Citizen Movement* (Philadelphia: Temple Univ. Press, 1980), pp. 100–102. For a discussion of how such movements have been purposely stimulated to provide badly needed administrative rationality, also see my "Culture and Politics in the Age of Artificial Negativity," *Telos* 35 (Spring 1978): 55–72.

32 million households engage in backyard or commons home gardening—a 100 percent increase since the 1950s—and produce $13 billion in agricultural commodities.[25]

Apart from and completely outside of corporate capitalism and the welfare state, the self-production of goods and services has started in free schools, food co-ops, free clinics, women's groups, community media, credit unions, community day care, neighborhood councils, flea markets, health foods, counterculture publishing, law clinics, cooperative housing, and localist politics. Single-issue action groups and citizens movements now have more contributing members (1.4 million to 520,000) and funds ($16.6 million to $13.6 million in 1976) than the two major political parties. Many of these groups and their members have been instrumentalized by mainstream politicians and public agencies. Still, they are only a tendential indication and a possible basis for moving toward ecologically sound institution-building on a local level. Likewise, 1977 and 1980 studies argue that 4 or 5 million people in the late 1970s, and nearly 10 million in the early 1980s, have withdrawn from consumer society to pursue "voluntary simplicity."[26] In other words, 5 to 6 percent of the U.S. adult population already may be working, in one way or another, toward some of the goals of an ecologically reasonable society.

It is technically possible, particularly with present-day informational technology, to design technical instruments that are simple, durable, useful, and accessible to individual, household, or community use.[27] Such tools, once disengaged from the constraints imposed by corporate control, can provide the inorganic energy and mechanical efficiency necessary for a humane standard of living. Virtually every tool possesses a self-subversive dimension that ecological activists can tap to serve the purpose of ecological development.

The alternative technology groups, which formed concretely as a movement only in the mid-1970s, already have developed into a consid-

25. Sale, *Human Scale*, pp. 45–46, 236. Also see John Case and Rosemary C. Taylor, eds., *Co-ops, Communes and Collectives Experiments in Social Change in the 1960s and 1970s* (New York: Pantheon Books, 1979).

26. Elgin, *Voluntary Simplicity*, p. 132; and Milton Kotler, "Citizen Action: New Life for American Politics," *Nation*, October 30, 1976, pp. 429–31.

27. See Richard C. Dorf and Yvonne C. Hunter, eds., *Appropriate Visions: Technology, the Environment, and the Individual* (San Francisco: Boyd & Fraser Pub. Co., 1978).

erable technical community and are promoting several viable technologies. Many access journals, like *RAIN, Appropriate Technology, Solar Energy, Appropriate Technology Quarterly*, and others, have a circulation of nearly a million and constitute both a developing technical discourse and public sphere for articulating ecologically sound alternatives. In addition to these journals and the publication of hundreds of related pamphlets and books, over 2,000 alternative technology groups have also formed to popularize these techniques. These alternative technologies have not yet transformed economic production in the United States. Still, these advances provide a potential technological basis for living a labor-intensive, self-sufficient, and ecologically sound existence for millions of households.

An ecologically sound politics also necessitates a transition to a spatial-practical setting that ecologically fuses the rural and urban into a new mode of existence.[28] This *deconcentration* of urban resources would bring "urban" commerce, art, society, and letters into balance with "rural" crafts, culture, community, and customs. The anthropocentrism of orthodox urban leftists and the nature chauvinism of traditional romantic rebellion, in turn, could be lessened in this new exurban culture, which would redefine the human–nature relation.

Orthodox leftists have wrongly confused large industrial cities with progressive social formations. Echoing Marx's diatribes against peasant and rural life, most leftist movements and thinkers hold that the modern model of industrial urbanism, such as twentieth-century London, Paris, Berlin, or New York, promises the most hospitable milieu for a socialist economy and society. In fact, such urban agglomerations probably can never become socialist, ecological, or democratic.

Large American cities, which have developed with advanced industrialization, have expanded quantitatively with little qualitative improvement in cultural benefits, social services, public utilities, or physical infrastructure. Rather, size itself imposes a cost on these collective goods, making them less accessible, enjoyable, and useful as more people are concentrated around them. Yet it would not be necessary to entirely relocate urban rhythms in the reconstitution of corporate

---

28. For a suggestive treatment of how to rebuild rural society, see Wendell Berry, *The Unsettling of America: Culture and Agriculture* (San Francisco: Sierra Club Books, 1978); and Murray Bookchin, *The Limits of the City* (New York: Harper & Row, 1974).

society. Rather, transport, communications, and land use could be re-ordered to reconnect the rural and urban through small-scale interdependent linkages, and the benefits of rural and urban life can be unified to eliminate the personal costs imposed by rural isolation and urban giganticism.

These new institutions, in turn, would guarantee popular participation and operational accountability in the management of the localist economy and community. The *municipalization* of industry rather than the *nationalization* of industry emerges as the optimal mode for socializing the means of production in the ecological revolution to create a post-anthropocentric ethic of natural cooperation, close affinal association, and skilled craft practice of situating people in nature and by reintroducing nature's needs to society.

Combining a participatory democracy with a communitarian ethos will demand tremendous exertions to assure that the obligations and benefits of producership are not unequally distributed. This issue crops up immediately in discussions of the ecological revolution. Ecological concerns are conventionally identified with elite, white-collar, New Class groups, which are alleged to be inattentive to working-class concerns or blue-collar constituencies. An ecologically viable organization, however, must go beyond these class-specific conventions by demanding a balance of manual and mental labor from all producers and an equitable sharing of resources within the networks of an ecological society. This change implies the adoption of a lifestyle grounded in "voluntary simplicity." This strategy, however, does not imply an uncritically embraced austerity, which mystifies the falling rate of material satisfaction in informationalizing American society. Instead, it suggests the self-definition and self-realization of needs independent of corporate capital's "coercive complexity."

Preserving Ecological Possibilities

In the last analysis, the political goals of an ecological revolution and the structural directions intrinsic to the trends of the informational revolution only coincidently complement each other. One must not presume that the ecologically minded new citizens movements or the rise of localism are simply stalking horses for transnational capital. These ideas and the new institutions grounded on them can continually be reappropriated and redeployed to serve progressive ends and preserve emancipatory possibilities.

In the short run, corporate capital and the welfare state might stimulate the advent of free schools, neighborhood councils, backyard gardening, and frugality philosophies to compensate for the withering away of public goods and consumer commodities as capital flows into informationalizing firms, as jobs are exported abroad, and as consumer markets shift into specialized upscale boutiques. Yet in the long run, these alternative institutions and techniques hold the potential for developing a more rational, equal, and participatory society through self-reliance and communal interaction. Thus, in the intermediate run, ecological activists must nurture the emancipatory potential of corporate capital's "third sector," "new volunteerism," or "voluntary simplicity." Ecological political action represents an emancipatory dimension: an oppositional possibility within the informationalizing corporate order that can be organized to reorder everyday life.

Such activism delimits the class conflict of informational societies as consumer and client groups struggle locally to gain greater collective control and individual benefit from the informationalized means of production controlled by corporate producers and professional providers. By refusing to accept the corporate and professional administration of informational capital, consumers and clients can organize to reappropriate their alienated energies and skills communally from the technologically competent classes, overcoming their technological obsolescence in a more universal ecological competence.

Informational capital and ecological activists both seek to dismantle rapidly advanced industrial society in order to create a less centralized, hierarchical, and environmentally destructive economy in the United States. Still, informational capital stops at the limits imposed by capitalist exchange as it merely seeks to reconstruct industrialized manufacturing and agriculture along informational lines, making them more data-intensive, robotized, numerically controlled, and downsized. It does not, however, end the domination of man and nature. Instead, informationalized technology promises to extend and elaborate that domination. Individuals are to be reduced to word processors, number crunchers, and image consumers in their cyberneticized frugal households, while nature is bioengineered or genetically technologized to unfold along

corporate-planned lines of evolution. The politics of informationalization, now forming inchoately as neoliberalism or "Atari Democracy,"
must not be mistaken for a progressive new wave of the future.

On the contrary, the ecological revolution must push beyond these
limits to resist the ongoing domination of man and nature by challenging both industrial and informational capital. Ecological activists must
demystify, repossess, and decode the material packages and behavioral
scripts being produced by informational capital to advance the emancipatory interests of average producers and consumers in everyday life.[29]
The struggle centers on the different meanings being reassigned to acts
and artifacts in industrial life by informational capitalism. One syntax
of signification points toward an official informational pragmatics in
labor and leisure that would revitalize the reification of labor in the production and consumption of information. On the other hand, a more
subversive ecological pragmatics derived from localist vernaculars can
empower producers and consumers with their own meanings for informationalizing development, which could turn labor and leisure into
emancipatory modes of ecologically sound living.

---

29. See Jacques Donzelot, *The Policing of Families*, trans. Robert Hurley (New York:
Pantheon Books, 1979); Stuart Ewen and Elizabeth Ewen, *Channels of Mass Desire: Mass
Images and the Shaping of American Consciousness* (New York: McGraw-Hill, 1982);
Ivan Illich, *Disabling Professions* (Boston: Marion Boyars, 1978); and Christopher Lasch,
The Culture of Narcissism: American Life in an Age of Diminishing Expectations (New
York: Norton, 1979), for an introduction to this process of critically identifying eman-
cipatory possibilities.

3

The Dreams of Deep Ecology

"DEEP ECOLOGY" PRINCIPLES are more than a new philosophy of nature. Deep ecologists have provided the basic inspiration for numerous bioregional, national, and even transnational political action groups.[1] Local "place defense" organizations across America, Western Europe, and Japan, like oppositions to new hydroelectric dams, power lines, airports, highways, timbering programs, dredging and draining schemes, or power plants, draw from deep ecological ideas.[2] On a regional level, ecological resistance to new nuclear weaponry systems, nuclear power stations, military bases, or communications networks has often drawn guidance from deep ecology. Many radical activists, like the "eco-raiders" or "monkeywrenchers" of the American Southwest and Pacific Northwest, also have deep ecological sympathies. Other activist groups, including Earth First!, Greenpeace, Friends of the Earth, the Sea Shepherds, and the various Green political parties share close affinities with deep ecology.[3] In other words, deep ecology has cast itself as one of

* Originally published in *Telos* 76 (Summer 1988): 65–92.

1. George Sessions, "The Deep Ecology Movement: A Review," *Environmental Review* 11, no. 2 (1987): 105–26.

2. Bill Devall, "Ecological Consciousness and Ecological Resisting: Guidelines for Comprehension and Research," *Humboldt Journal of Social Relations* 9, no. 2 (1979): 177–96.

3. See Fritjof Capra and Charlene Spretnak, *Green Politics* (New York: Dutton, 1985); David Foreman, ed., *Ecodefense: A Field Guide to Monkey Wrenching* (Tucson, AZ: Earth

the primary theoretical forces behind many popular social movements' efforts to defend the quality of everyday life from further rationalization by the state and transnational commerce.[4] As such, it deserves careful but critical consideration.

The deep ecology movement emerged in the 1970s in reaction to the reform environmentalism of the 1960s, which had developed, in turn, as a response to the unfettered exploitation of nature during the global economic boom of the 1950s and 1960s. Yet, in seeking to improve on reform environmentalism, the deep ecologists have taken a number of problematic political positions. The most prominent exponents of deep ecology are Arne Naess, Bill Devall, George Sessions, and Gary Snyder.

One can sympathize with certain aspects of the deep ecology project. Most importantly, it could constitute *in nuce* new other-regarding norms of justice. By seeing nature as a significant form of otherness with properties of sentient subjectivity, deep ecology proposes that we adopt new codes of ethical responsibility to move away from the exploitation of nature. However, its practitioners often weaken and marginalize their appeal by adopting ancillary positions that are poorly thought out, ineffectively argued, or politically naive. As a result, the dreams of deep ecology often take on nightmarish qualities.

State, Society, and the Environment

Modern industrial production, as Joseph Schumpeter claims, presupposes "creative destruction." Vast waste is a primary product of both modern capitalism and socialism. In the United States, this wasteful destruction has sparked at least three major social conservation movements during the twentieth century. The first two took hold within the federal bureaucracy during the Progressive Era and New Deal period under Theodore and Franklin D. Roosevelt.[5] Both of these movements,

---

First! Books, 1985); and Jonathan Porritt, *Seeing Green: The Politics of Ecology Explained* (Oxford: Basil Blackwell, 1985).

4. See Bill Devall and George Sessions, *Deep Ecology* (Layton, UT: Peregrine Smith Books, 1985); Bill Devall, "The Development of Natural Resources and the Integrity of Nature," *Environmental Ethics* 6, no. 4 (1984): 293–323; Bill Devall, "The Deep Ecology Movement," *Natural Resources Journal* 20, no. 2 (1980): 295–322; Kirkpatrick Sale, *Dwellers in the Land: The Bioregional Vision* (San Francisco: Sierra Club Books, 1985); and Michael Tobias, ed., *Deep Ecology* (San Diego: Avant Books, 1985).

5. See Donald Worster, *Nature's Economy: The Roots of Ecology* (San Francisco: Sierra Club Books, 1977).

however, aimed only at conservation. Their agenda was to impose limits on the most destructive abuses of land, timber, water, and mineral resources in the private sector by charging federal agencies with their scientific management. Economic growth was not proscribed; it was simply rationalized.

Environmental conditions, however, worsened during the "long prosperity" following World War II. Commoner observes that "most pollution problems made their first appearance, or became very much worse, in the years following World War II, having made their environmental debut in the war years: smog (first noticed in Los Angeles in 1943), man-made radioactive elements (first produced in the wartime atomic bomb project), DDT (widely used for the first time in 1944), detergents (which began to displace soap in 1946), synthetic plastics (which became a contributor to the rubbish problem only after the war)."[6] In the United States, these problems sparked critical attention and then government action in the 1960s on Kennedy's "New Frontier" in a third national conservation movement, beginning with Rachel Carson's and Stewart Udall's work.[7]

Yet, as George Sessions claims, the more urgent crises of the 1960s split critical thinking about the environment as well as political strategies for its protection. "Something happened, however, in the mid-1960s which one author describes as a movement 'from conservation to ecology.' There was a rapidly emerging awareness that increased population, pollution, resource depletion, nuclear radiation, pesticide and chemical poisoning, the deterioration of the cities, the disappearance of wildlife and wilderness, decreases in the 'quality of life,' and continued economic growth and development under the rhetoric of 'progress' were biologically interrelated. There was a growing suspicion of the ability of technologists to manage natural systems successfully."[8] As a result, a

6. Barry Commoner, *The Closing Circle: Nature, Man, and Technology* (New York: Bantam Books, 1971), pp. 124–25.

7. Carson's severe criticism of modern pesticides called for greater attention to be given to "ecological" networks, or "the complex, precise, and highly integrated system of relationships between living things which cannot be safely ignored." Rachel Carson, *Silent Spring* (Boston: Houghton, Mifflin, 1962), p. 218. Also see Stewart Udall, *The Quiet Crisis* (New York: Holt, Rinehart and Winston, 1963).

8. George Sessions, "Shallow and Deep Ecology: A Review of the Philosophical Literature," in *Ecological Consciousness: Essays From the Earthday X Colloquium* (Washington, DC: University Press of America, 1981), p. 392.

state-sanctioned reform environmentalism developed out of this new conservation movement, while more radical ecological groups reacted both against its moderation and the growing severity of the environmental crisis.

Reform environmentalism movements, according to deep ecology, focus on the *unintended social costs* of economic growth, complexity, scale, and productivity. Most reform environmentalists still treat them as minor problems that can be managed from the public and not-for-profit sectors with technocratically planned changes in government regulation or market-driven incentives in the private sector.[9] Business and government always have known about these costs, but they purposely suppress efforts to fully contain or eradicate them. Deep ecologists argue that an industrial economy inherently presumes the imposition of such costs as externalities, and regulating them only postpones the final collapse or shifts the costs elsewhere. Hence, a radical change is necessary to attack the more basic problems—untrammeled economic growth, instrumental rationality, and the reification of nature implicit in capitalist and socialist industrialism. As their solution, deep ecologists want to resurrect the alternative, repressed, ignored, or forgotten visions of ecological living behind or beyond the structures of industrial society.

Deep Ecology: Origins and Outlines

Most deep ecologists argue that their principles are nothing new. They see themselves as borrowing the "ancient truths" of pre-industrial, non-urban, and pre-capitalist societies. Because such societies have been either destroyed or marginalized within the current world-system, however, deep ecologists identify these basic beliefs as "the minority tradition." Devall and Sessions claim that "the minority tradition focuses on personal growth within a small community and selects a path to cultivating ecological consciousness while protecting the ecological integrity of the place."[10] As examples of such thinking, Sessions tags a panoply of traditions from around the world as inspirations for deep ecology: Christian Franciscanism, Heideggerian philosophy, Aldo Leopold's

---

9. See Commoner, *The Closing Circle*; Bill Devall, "Reformist Environmentalism," *Humboldt Journal of Social Relations* 6, no. 2 (1979): 129–55; and John Dryzek, *Rational Ecology: Environment and Political Economy* (Oxford: Basil Blackwell, 1987).

10. Devall and Sessions, *Deep Ecology*, p. 3.

ecosystem ethics, Taoism, Buddhism, hunter-gatherer tribal religions, Western process metaphysics (Heraclitus, Whitehead, and Spinoza), American Indian culture, European romanticism (Goethe, Rousseau, Blake, Wordsworth, Coleridge, Shelley), American transcendentalism (Emerson, Thoreau, Whitman, Muir), "beat philosophy" (Ginsberg and Snyder), 1960s counterculture (Watts, Reich, Roszak), social ecology (Bookchin), and eco-resistance (Rodman, Berg, Dasmann, and Abbey).[11] In one way or another, each of these cultural pieces are placed into the deep ecology conceptual mosaic.

The idea of deep ecology was first outlined in 1972, and in 1973 Naess articulated his distinction between "shallow environmentalism" and "deep ecology."[12] Naess claims the conservation movements of the Progressive and New Deal eras, environmental pressure groups, the Club of Rome "limits to growth" school, and animal rights activists all fail to challenge the existing institutionalized worldview of advanced industrial society. Instead, such "shallow" ecologies are seen as adhering to an "anthropocentric" view of nature. This view separates humanity from nature and deadens it by seeing nature as inanimate, while empowering humans to dominate it because they are defined as the crown of creation. Working with such values, shallow environmentalism is merely a kind of "enlightened despotism." It would ease, but not end, the ravages of human domination of nature by eliminating its worst waste, regulating inefficiencies, or acting more humanely.

Naess's latter notion of a "deep ecology" accepts shallow environmentalism's intentions, but it pushes beyond this limited approach into a totalistic critique of modern industrialism. He stresses a post-anthropocentric "biospherical egalitarianism" to create "an awareness of the equal right [of all things] *to live and blossom*."[13] By calling for the return of people to nature, Naess claims a normative role for deep ecologists in working out a "New Philosophy of Nature." Accordingly, "the significant tenets of the Deep Ecology movement are dearly and forcefully *normative*. They express a value priority system only in part based on results of scientific research.... [I]n so far as ecology movements deserve our

---

11. Sessions, "Shallow and Deep Ecology."

12. Arne Naess, "The Shallow and Deep, Long-Range Ecology Movement: A Summary," *Inquiry* 16, no. 4 (1973): 95–100.

13. Ibid., p. 100.

attention, they are *ecophilosophical* rather than ecological. Ecology is a *limited* science which makes *use* of scientific methods. Philosophy is the most general forum of debate on fundamentals, descriptive as well as prescriptive, and political philosophy is one of its subsections. By an *ecosophy* I mean a philosophy of ecological harmony or equilibrium. A philosophy is a kind of *sofia* wisdom, is openly normative, it contains both norms, rules, announcements and hypotheses concerning the state of affairs in our universe. Wisdom is policy wisdom, prescription, not only scientific description and prediction."[14] Rather than accepting shallow environmentalism to preserve the dominant worldview, Naess envisions deep ecologists developing his ecosophical system as a new mediation of humanity and society with nature. Devall and Session's *Deep Ecology* elaborates the conceptual underpinnings of deep ecology in much more detail. Following Naess, they see today's basic conflict as one of consciousness: "Thus deep ecology goes beyond the so-called factual level to the level of self and earth wisdom. Deep ecology goes beyond a limited piecemeal shallow approach to environmental problems and attempts to articulate a comprehensive religious and philosophical worldview. The foundations of deep ecology are the basic intuitions and experiencing of ourselves and Nature which comprise ecological consciousness."[15]

The central problem of the dominant worldview for Devall and Sessions is the human desire to dominate nature or the anthropocentric fallacy of man's separation from and control over nature: "Ecological consciousness and deep ecology are in sharp contrast with the dominant worldview of technocratic-industrial societies with regard to humans as isolated and fundamentally separate from the rest of Nature, as superior to, and in charge of, the rest of creation. But the view of humans as separate and superior to the rest of Nature is only part of larger cultural patterns. For thousands of years, Western culture has become increasingly obsessed with the idea of dominance: with dominance of humans over nonhuman Nature, masculine over the feminine, wealthy and powerful over the poor, with the dominance of West over non-Western cultures. Deep ecological consciousness allows us to see through these

---

14. Ibid., p. 99.
15. Devall and Sessions, *Deep Ecology*, p. 65.

erroneous and dangerous illusions."[16] To acquire this non-dominating mode of ecological consciousness, Devall and Sessions adopt Naess's two ultimate norms: self-realization and biocentric equality.

First, self-realization is framed by Snyder's vision of "real work," which stresses becoming a "whole person" rather than remaining an isolated ego struggling to accumulate material possessions.[17] It is a new ethic of "being" or "doing" rather than a credo of "experiencing" or "having." Self-realization is defined as spiritual growth, or the unfolding of inner essence, which "begins when we cease to understand or see ourselves as isolated and narrow competing egos and begin to identify with other humans from our family and friends to, eventually, our species. But the deep ecology sense of self requires a further maturity and growth, an identification which goes beyond humanity to include the nonhuman world. We must see beyond our narrow contemporary cultural assumptions and values, and the conventional wisdom of our time and place, and this is best achieved by the meditative deep questioning process. Only in this way can we hope to attain full mature personhood and uniqueness."[18] Second, the norm of biocentrism maintains that "all things in the biosphere have an equal right to live and blossom and to reach their own individual forms of unfolding and self-realization within the larger Self-realization."[19] This principle does not necessarily preclude mutual predation; instead, it stresses the larger concern of living "with minimal rather than maximal impact on other species and the earth in general."[20] Consequently, they argue that "biocentric equality is intimately related to the all-inclusive Self-realization in the sense that if we harm the rest of Nature then we are harming ourselves. There are no boundaries and everything is interrelated. But insofar as we perceive things as individual organisms or entities, the insight draws us to respect all human and nonhuman individuals in their own right as parts of the whole without feeling the need to set up hierarchies of species with humans at the top."[21] This awareness could then move people

16. Ibid., pp. 65–66.
17. Gary Snyder, *Turtle Island* (New York: New Directions, 1974).
18. Devall and Sessions, *Deep Ecology*, p. 67.
19. Ibid.
20. Ibid., p. 68.
21. Ibid.

to change in accord with principles like "voluntary simplicity" or living life as "simple in means, rich in ends."

After defining "ecosophy" during the 1970s by its opposition to both advanced industrialism and the co-opted thinking of shallow environmentalism, in 1984 Naess and Sessions developed eight essential principles for deep ecology: (1) the well-being of human and nonhuman life on earth has intrinsic values, separate from human uses or purposes; (2) the diverse richness of all life-forms contributes to realizing these intrinsic values; (3) humans have no right to reduce this richness and diversity of life except to satisfy vital needs; (4) the flourishing of human life and culture is compatible with a substantial decrease in human populations—indeed, the flourishing of nonhuman life requires such a decrease; (5) human interference with the nonhuman world is excessive and worsening; (6) policies must be changed to transform economic, ideological, and technological structures into a situation much different from the present; (7) human satisfaction must shift to appreciating the quality of life (dwelling in situations of inherent value) rather than adhering to higher material standards of living; and (8) those who subscribe to these points have an obligation, directly or indirectly, to try to implement the necessary changes.[22]

Conceptual Contradictions in Deep Ecology

Where have the deep ecologists dug their intellectual foundations? In citing "the minority tradition" as their basic inspiration, deep ecologists have combed selectively through the cultural traditions of pre-capitalist, non-urban, pre-industrial primal peoples, seeking "a basis for philosophy, religion, cosmology, and conservation practices that can be applied to our own society."[23] By taking this line, deep ecology seems to stand firmly on one essential point, namely, as a systematic negation of the "Enlightenment schema."

As Max Horkheimer and Theodor W. Adorno wrote, "[t]he program of the Enlightenment was the disenchantment of the world; the dissolution of myths and the substitution of knowledge for fancy."[24] The

22. Ibid., p. 70.
23. Ibid., p. 96.
24. Max Horkheimer and Theodor W. Adorno, *Dialectic of Enlightenment*, trans. John Cumming (New York: Seabury, 1972), p. 3.

essence of this new knowledge is instrumental reason *qua* technology: "It does not work by concepts and images, by the fortunate insight, but refers to method, the exploitation of others' work and capital.... What men want to learn from nature is how to use it in order wholly to dominate it and other men. That is the only aim.... For the Enlightenment, whatever does not conform to the rule of computation and utility is suspect.... Enlightenment is totalitarian."[25] Horkheimer and Adorno detail how the Enlightenment systematically extirpated animism and mythological thinking to disenchant nature. If any mode of thought failed to attain closure with these rational assumptions and judgments, then enlightened consciousness reduced it to mere fictions. "Enlightenment has always taken the basic principle of myth to be anthropomorphism, the projection onto nature of the subjective.... It makes the dissimilar comparable by reducing it to abstract quantities. To the Enlightenment, that which does not reduce to numbers, and ultimately to the one, becomes illusion; modern positivism writes it off as literature.... The destruction of gods and qualities alike is insisted upon.... Myth turns into enlightenment, and nature into mere objectivity. Men pay for the increases of their power with alienation from that over which they exercise their power. Enlightenment behaves toward things as a dictator toward men."[26] Deep ecologists want to overthrow this dictatorship of Enlightenment, returning human consciousness back to a reenchanted world, an animate resubjectified nature, and more mythic modes of knowing to overcome man's alienation from and domination of nature.

This anti-Enlightenment stance is plain in Naess's principles of self-realization and biocentric equality. Devall and Sessions deny enlightened instrumental reasoning any jurisdiction over these basic precepts: "They are arrived at by the deep questioning process and reveal the importance of moving to the philosophical and religious level of wisdom. They cannot be validated, of course, by the methodology of modern science based on its usual mechanistic assumptions and its very narrow definition of data."[27] Deep ecology, as Michael Tobias suggests, concerns "personal moods, values, aesthetic and philosophical convictions which serve no necessarily utilitarian, nor rational end. By

25. Ibid., pp. 4–6.
26. Ibid., pp. 6–9.
27. Devall and Sessions, *Deep Ecology*, p. 66.

definition their sole justification rests upon the goodness, balance, truth and beauty of the natural world, and of a human being's biological and psychological need to be fully integrated into it."[28] Given this disposition, deep ecology also draws from the beliefs of primal traditions. "The natural and supernatural worlds are inseparable; each is intrinsically a part of the other. Humans and natural entities are in constant spiritual interchange and reciprocity" because, in Devall and Sessions's view, anthropological evidence indicates that "the primal mind holds the totality of human-centered artifacts, such as language, social organization, norms, shared meanings, and magic, within the first world of Nature. For the primal mind there is no sharp break between humans and the rest of Nature."[29]

Deep ecological self-realization is to be the antithesis of consumerism in which the isolated ego strives for hedonistic pleasures or personal salvation in consuming. Instead, it projects autonomous subjectivity onto nature and seeks a fusion of the personal self with the "organic wholeness" of nature's self.[30] Both people and nature are defined as enchanted fields of conscious being, interlocked by natural necessity and human mythic understanding. This "full unfolding of the self can also be summarized by the phrase 'no one is saved until we are all saved,' where the phrase 'one' includes not only me, an individual human, but all humans, whales, grizzly bears, whole rain forest ecosystems, mountains and rivers, the tiniest microbes in the soil, and so on."[31]

In this liberation of nature, everything is to be treated as an animate subject with intrinsic value and inherent rights for self-realization: "The intuition of biocentric equality is that all things in the biosphere have an equal right to live and blossom and to reach their individual forms of unfolding and self-realization with the larger self-realization. The basic intuition is that all entities in the ecosphere, as parts of an interrelated whole, are equal in intrinsic worth."[32] Deep ecologists embrace this principle to affirm that people are nature, and nature is, at

28. Ibid., p. v.

29. Ibid., p. 97.

30. Arne Naess, "Identification as a Source of Deep Ecology Attitudes," in Tobias, *Deep Ecology*, pp. 256–70.

31. Devall and Sessions, *Deep Ecology*, p. 67.

32. Ibid.

least in part, people. To harm nature, then, is to commit slow suicide or engage in self-mutilation. When humans technologically intervene in nature, it often means that we abuse or murder other animate selves, from river systems to animals to rain forests. Still, natural subjects are empowered under this rule in Naess's system to use each other as food, shelter, or security because "mutual predation is a biological fact of life." However, given humanity's tremendous destructive powers in Enlightenment-based technology, people must treat nature and other natural subjects as ends not means, living "with minimum rather than maximum impact on other species and on the earth in general." As modes of mythic construction for a reenchanted world, these animistic appercep-tions of subjectivity in nature, Devall and Sessions conclude, "cannot be grasped intellectually but are ultimately experiential."

Some aspects of these arguments are attractive. Like many others, deep ecologists want to treat other forms of natural life and nonlife with a good conscience and an ethic of moral responsibility. In this sense, it potentially offers the beginnings for a new system of morality, stress-ing an ethic of minimal impact, rather than maximum exploitation, for living within nature. Deep ecology also presents some initial rules for enacting and legitimating this nature consciousness as a mode of human good conscience. Nonetheless, beyond these promising ideas, one must ask what kind of "new morality" would arise from mythic knowledge, an animate conception of nature, and an anti-Enlightenment mode of reasoning. When looking at these issues, deep ecology's challenge to the Enlightenment schema seems deeply flawed.

A Myth of Humanity's Fall: The "Retro" Rationality of Primalism

The quest for self-realization and biocentric equality as the foundation of this new ecosophy implicitly assumes its own myth of man's fall. Once upon a time, or elsewhere in more primitive regions of the world, humanity lived in a state of innocence. But now, due to technological domination, humanity lives in a state of corruption or alienation. For deep ecology, however, redemption is possible, in accord with the ex-amples set by primal societies, by attaining correct moral consciousness. Consequently, the idea of "primal peoples," which is as questionable as "world communism" or "the Third World," serves as a reified symbol of virtuous praxis and a "retro" rationality for social organization.

Deep ecologists lump the many primitive cultures into one "primal" cultural pile and then privilege these values and practices unquestioningly in their ecosophical thought. To stave off ecological crisis in post-industrial society, deep ecologists recommend that individuals appropriate the selectively perceived norms of preliterate/pre-industrial peoples into their everyday activity. Supposedly, "primal peoples are characterized by individuation, personalism, nominalism, and existentialism," whereas the pathology of advanced industrialism "consists in our dedication to abstractions, to our collectivism, pseudo-individualism, and lack of institutional means for the expression and transcendence of human ambivalence."[33] Such retro generalizations are totally suspect. The warring, slavery, tribalism, sexism, or racism practiced in primitive societies is simply denied by virtuous definition. Devall and Sessions, for example, continually stress the wisdom of American Indians, but this approval reduces a wide range of different cultures to a privileged, reified symbol that virtually denies contradiction. Their vision of "primal virtue" keys off images of the silent brave who sheds a tear over the white man's garbage in anti-littering ad spots. It is nothing but a romanticized mystification, as Vine Deloria suggests, "reciting a past that is basically mythological, thrilling, and comforting,"[34] because it casts a pre-Columbian America as peopled by noble savages. Unlike us, they "give a hoot and don't pollute." Moreover, the myths are tremendously unclear about which "Indians" are the most virtuous. Are we to emulate "the old ways" of tribes like the Aztecs, Incas, and Mayans or the Mohaves, Supai, and Cocopahs? Have any Native American societies systematically practiced slavery, war-making, or ecological destruction? Thus, Native American groups today, for example, hunt "endangered species" of animals merely to procure religious totems vital to their religious practices. Likewise, modern Navajos and Apaches are very active promoters of strip-mining, power station construction, aggressive timbering, and industrial tourism on their lands in the Southwest. Did any agricultural groups in the pre-Columbian American Southwest or Mesoamerica promote ecological disasters by destroying their lands through overcultivation or overirrigation, somewhat like corporate agriculturalists today? In other words, why define all Indian

33. Ibid., pp. 20–21.
34. Vine Deloria, Jr., *God Is Red* (New York: Dell, 1973), p. 56.

societies as truly "primal" or equally peaceful, nature-regarding, and respectful of the individual?[35]

By the same token, in the larger picture of all primitive societies, do all primal cultures share these nature-regarding norms as ethical universals? Could primal peoples develop anti-ecological values? Have primal peoples created ecological crises or abused the environment with their technologies? Does this moral alternative really exist, or is it a psychosocial projection discovered in post-industrial social scientists' dissatisfaction with advanced industrialism as they systematize their one-sided understanding of primal people?

When deep ecologists claim that primal peoples unfailingly used nature reverently so that a "richness of ends was achieved with material technology that was elegant, sophisticated, appropriate, and controlled within the contest of a traditional society,"[36] red flags must be raised. Such values may have been true of small nomadic bands of hunters and gatherers or slash-and-burn agriculturalists. Can the same rules, however, be followed today by ecologizing post-industrial peoples re-inhabiting nature? Devall and Sessions deny that they are resurrecting the myth of noble savages; still, their search for inspiration from primal traditions verges upon becoming such a covering myth. Deep ecology stresses its anti-modern disposition by calling for a reinhabitation of varying bioregions in the future along the primitive lines of primal societies. The myth of man's fall from primitive grace is false, but it justifies mythologically deep ecology's anti-modern, future-primitive vision of social change.

The Dialectic of Reenchantment

In advocating a reenchantment of the world, deep ecology's privileging of primal traditions ignores the extent to which primal society's myth, magic, and ritual are partially the functional equivalents (and perhaps the conceptual antecedents) of Enlightenment science and technology. Ritual and myth may be the "nondominating science" that Naess,

---

35. See William Cronon, *Changes in the Land: Indians, Colonists, and the Ecology of New England* (New York: Hill and Wang, 1983); and Peter Farb, *Man's Rise to Civilization as Shown by the Indians of North America from Primeval Times to the Coming of the Industrial State* (New York: E. P. Dutton, 1968).

36. Devall and Sessions, *Deep Ecology*, p. 97.

Devall, and Sessions support; yet, as Horkheimer and Adorno argue, these modes of knowing can anticipate scientific domination. In mythic reasoning, "[e]verything unknown and alien is primary and undifferentiated: that which transcends the confines of experience; whatever in things is more than their previously known reality.... The dualization of nature as appearance and sequence, effort and power, which first makes possible both myth and science, originates in human fear, the expression of which becomes explanation.... The separation of the animate and the inanimate, the occupation of certain places by demons and deities, first arises from this pre-animism, which contains the first lines of the separation of the subject and object."[37] In some respects, then, primal myths and rituals actually are an operationalist mode of thinking, mediating primal people's efforts to control or influence nature.[38]

"Myth intended report, naming, the narration of the beginning," as Horkheimer and Adorno admit, "but also presentation, confirmation, explanation.... Every ritual includes the idea of activity as a determined process which magic can nevertheless influence.... The myths...are already characterized by the discipline and power that Bacon celebrated as the 'right mark.'"[39] Magic is based on the specific not the universal, concrete representation not substitutional abstractions, and impersonations of demonic or divine spirits not methodical operational manipulations of matter. It can contain its own dialectic of enlightenment. Mythological ritual sets off the process of enlightenment until enlightenment itself becomes an animistic magic. "Just as myths already realize enlightenment, so enlightenment with every step becomes more deeply engulfed in mythology."[40]

Devall and Sessions endorsement of the "new physics" of holistic interrelation reflects this confusion.[41] Enlightenment science cannot be disinvented or destroyed. It is fully embedded in many of our existing acts and artifacts. Sensuous, participative, metaphysical views of reality—when fused into technical potentials of modern science for

37. Horkheimer and Adorno, *Dialectic of Enlightenment*, p. 15.

38. See Bronislaw Malinowski, *Magic, Science and Religion* (Garden City, NY: Anchor Books, 1955), pp. 79–87.

39. Horkheimer and Adorno, *Dialectic of Enlightenment*, p. 8.

40. Ibid., pp. 11–12.

41. See Morris Berman, *The Reenchantment of the World* (Ithaca, NY: Cornell Univ. Press, 1981); and Fritjof Capra, *The Tao of Physics* (Boulder, CO: Shambhala Press, 1975).

destructive misapplication—could promote a more domineering rather than less destructive science. There are no guarantees. New Age thinkers already treat ecological reasoning as a model of automatic cybernetic management intrinsic to nature (the "Spaceship Earth" metaphor) that scientists can modify to realize greater micro/macro efficiencies in global production, like weather modification, ocean farming, or genetic engineering.[42] Like Stewart Brand, deep ecology can too easily slip into "Whole Earth Catalogism," fusing the quest for more woodstoves, tepees, and windmills with lobbying for interplanetary colonization, space stations, and hypercomputerization.

Deep ecologists forget how much of modern Newtonian-Cartesian-Galilean-Baconian science was itself wrapped up in morally enchanted mystical visions of nature.[43] Newtonian mechanics was created not only to make possible new technical engineering feats of nature's subjugation but also to attain some new moral understanding from the universe and its celestial spheres. The unintended consequences of reenchantment and myth may express the operational wish for new instrumental control as much as primal man's co-participation in the natural and supernatural worlds. In modern times, this confusing conflation of enchanted mythic ritual and instrumentally rational science best reveals its stark contradictions in Nazi Germany.[44] A reenchantment of nature in Nordic myth and new Aryan ritual produced V-2s, Auschwitz, Me-262s, and nuclear fission, while covering itself in fables of Teutonic warriors true to tribal *Blut und Boden*. Ideologists of industrial fascism openly proclaimed it to be *anti-modern* and *future primitive*. Nazism also condemned industrialism and the overpopulation of most other societies as it propounded a very peculiar vision of reinhabiting its self-proclaimed and historically denied *Lebensraum*. One should not assume that deep ecology will lead necessarily to a fascist outcome, yet the deep ecologists must demonstrate why their philosophy would not conclude in a similarly deformed fusion of modernity with premodernity.

42. See Marilyn Ferguson, *The Aquarian Conspiracy* (New York: St. Martin's, 1980); and R. Buckminster Fuller, *Operating Manual for Spaceship Earth* (New York: Dutton, 1971).

43. See Timothy J. Reiss, *The Discourse of Modernism* (Ithaca, NY: Cornell Univ. Press, 1982); and William Leiss, *The Domination of Nature* (Boston: Beacon Press, 1974).

44. See Robert A. Pois, *National Socialism and the Religion of Nature* (New York: St. Martin's 1986).

In addition, deep ecology's evocation of "Eastern spiritual process traditions," namely, Taoism and Buddhism, is lifted out of its cultural context with little consideration of any sociocultural grounding. On one level, these religions may enable one "to relate to the process of becoming more mature, of awakening from illusion and delusion," and to help "groups of people engaged in the 'real work' of cultivating their own ecological consciousness."[45] Yet, on another level, these traditions embrace myths of "organic unity" and, as the Tao bids, quest for "production without possession, action without self-assertion, development without domination,"[46] which gives away their origins in traditional bureaucratic empires prior to or outside of the modern world-system.

In peasant villages bound by kinship-driven collectivism, limited agricultural productivity, and imperial bureaucratic oversight, as Max Weber notes, these religions served as a salvation ethic based on attaining perfect changelessness. For such an "Eastern spiritual process tradition," "when such salvation is gained, the deep joy and tender, undifferentiated love characterizing such illumination provides the highest blessing possible in this existence, short of absorption into the eternal dreamless sleep of *Nirvana*, the only state in which no change occurs," which comes, in turn, by freeing oneself "from all personal ties to family and world, pursuing the goal of mystical illumination by fulfilling the injunctions relating to the correct path (*dharma*)."[47] In Weber's view, these ethics led down a path of world rejection by directing their followers to avoid individual self-realization. On the wheel of karma causality, each new incarnation of an individual creates or denies new chances to attain nirvana in the future. Any attempt at rational purposive activity in the methodical control of life leads away from salvation. Similarly, full individual self-realization in existential individuation would seem to make nirvana more remote by ensnaring the individual in the illusory (even if they are ecologically grounded) concerns of this changing, suffering world.

Such ethical codes, if closely adhered to, are essentially ill-suited to a purposive cultural revival of ecological consciousness to revolutionize advanced industrialism. They have been credos of world rejection and

---

45. Devall and Sessions, *Deep Ecology*, p. 100.
46. Sessions, "Shallow and Deep Ecology," p. 412.
47. See Max Weber, *The Sociology of Religion* (Boston: Beacon Press, 1975), p. 26.

individual effacement (as might suit the spiritual needs of overburdened agricultural producers under oriental despotism) rather than a continuation of the individuation, personalism, nominalism, and existentialism that Devall and Sessions endorse in primal cultures. To evoke such religious outlooks in post-industrial America, on one level, may promote maturity and forsaking consumerist illusions, while, on another level, providing an ineffectual opiate for the masses as their current material standard of living disappears in deep ecological reforms.

The Myth of Nature's Subjectivity

In addition to reducing a broad range of primal cultures into one complex univocal tradition, deep ecologists also construct nature as an active subject that can teach people, if they cultivate their intuition or introspective consciousness, a special redemptive "Earth Wisdom."[48] Devall and Sessions maintain that "we may not need something new, but need to reawaken something very old, to reawaken our understanding of Earth Wisdom. In the broadest sense, we need to accept the invitation to the dance—the dance of unity of humans, plants, animals, the Earth. We need to cultivate an ecological consciousness."[49] Nature is seen as speaking, knowing, having needs, suffering, sharing selfhood, expressing, and growing. Primal traditions, in the last analysis, are vital because they have remained open to nature's subjectivity, following its wisdom and sharing in its being.

Deep ecology's ultimate value of self-realization claims to go "beyond the modern Western *self* which is defined as an isolated ego striving primarily for hedonistic gratification or for a narrow sense of individual salvation in this life or the next."[50] Real selfhood, it is claimed, derives from human unity with nature, realizing our mature personhood and uniqueness with all other human and nonhuman forms of being. Humanity must be "naturalized." The "human self" is not an atomistic ego, but a species-being and a nature-being, a "'self-in-Self' where 'Self' stands for organic wholeness."[51] Here, the essence of nature appears to be a projection of an idealized humanity onto the natural world. Nature

48. See Doris LaChapelle, *Earth Wisdom* (San Diego: Guild of Tudors Press, 1978).
49. Devall and Sessions, *Deep Ecology*, p. ix.
50. Ibid., pp. 66–67.
51. Ibid., p. 67.

is "humanized" in a myth of subjectivity to change human behavior. The reanimation of nature in deep ecology extends this selfhood to all natural entities—rocks, bacteria, trees, clouds, river systems, animals—and allegedly permits the realization of their inner essence.

As deep ecology depicts it, and as Georg Lukács would observe, this mythical vision of nature actually "refers to authentic humanity, the true essence of man liberated from the false, mechanizing forms of society: man as a perfected whole who inwardly has overcome, or is in the process of overcoming, the dichotomies of theory and practice, reason and the senses, form and content; man whose tendency to create his own forms does not imply an abstract rationalism which ignores concrete content; man for whom freedom and necessity are identical."[52] Deep ecologists, however, cannot really enter into an intersubjective discourse with or know concretely the being of rocks, rivers, or rhinos, despite Muir's injunction "to think like glaciers" when confronting nature. "The meditative deep questioning process" might allow humanity "an identification which goes beyond humanity to include the nonhuman world."[53] Still, a hypostatization of human species-being with whales, grizzlies, rain forests, mountains, rivers, and bacteria is no more than the individual ecosphere's identification of his/her self with those particular aspects of nature that idiosyncratically express their peculiarly personal human liberation. This ideological appropriation can only be (human) self-serving. One must ask if humanity is naturalized in such self-realization or is nature merely humanized to the degree that its components promote this peculiar human agenda for "maturity and growth."

This vision of self-realization appears to go beyond a modern Western notion of self tied to hedonistic gratification, but it does not transcend a narrow sense of individual salvation in this life or the next. Nature in deep ecology simply becomes a new transcendent identical subject-object to redeem humanity. By projecting selfhood into nature, humans are to be saved by finding their self-maturation and spiritual growth in it. These goals are found in one's life by indwelling psychically and physically in organic wholeness as well as in the next life by recognizing that one may survive (physically in fact) within other humans,

52. Georg Lukács, *History and Class Consciousness: Studies in Marxist Dialectics*, trans. Rodney Livingstone (Cambridge, MA: MIT Press, 1971), p. 136.

53. Devall and Sessions, *Deep Ecology*, p. 67.

whales, grizzlies, rain forests, mountains, rivers, and bacteria or (psychically in faith) as an essential part of an organic whole. Nature, then, becomes ecosophical humanity's alienated self-understanding, partly reflected back to itself and selectively perceived as self-realization, rediscovered in biospheric processes.

Biocentrism as "Soft Anthropocentrism"

Given deep ecology's vision of nature, biocentrism might simply be a spiritually refreshing or psychically rewarding form of anthropocentrism. Under certain conditions, Naess's claim that all organisms and entities in the ecosphere are equal in intrinsic worth and share an equal right to self-realization makes sense. If we deforest tropical Brazil or vent fluorocarbons into the atmosphere, we deny rain forests and the ozone layer the right to their own existence. By fooling with nature in this way, we are foolishly harming it and ourselves. As Devall and Sessions claim, "There are no boundaries and everything is interrelated. But insofar as we perceive things as individual organisms or entities, the insight draws us to respect all human and nonhuman individuals in their own right as parts of the whole without feeling the need to set up hierarchies of species with humans at the top."[54]

Still, Naess's "mutual predation" proviso largely belies this principle because "in the process of living, all species use each other as food, shelter, etc.," which is "a biological fact of life." In turn, he observes, "a culture of hunters, where identification with hunted animals reaches a remarkably high level, does not prohibit killing for food. But a great variety of ceremonies and rituals have the function to express the gravity of the alienating incident and restore the identification."[55] This vision of biocentrism, then, mystifies the workings of a "soft anthropocentrism." Even if people reduce their needs, and live with minimum rather than maximum impact on other species and the earth in general, humans' interrelations with nature still will remain anthropocentric given human technological powers and biological facts of life. Rocks and trees do not use humans—except for perhaps recycling the stray molecules from decayed human bodies—for their survival or self-realization. Humans, however, do move, crush, and chip rocks as well as chop, carve,

54. Ibid., p. 68.
55. Naess, "Identification as a Source of Deep Ecology Attitudes," p. 262.

and burn trees to create shelter, tools, food, or medicines. Individual nonhuman entities or organisms are treated with less respect, equality, and rights by humans. Even if people abdicate as lords and masters of nature, the latter still will feel the pressure of human hunters and gatherers. Although humans could change many of their ways, such predation still would be far from mutual. We might let great white sharks, like "Jaws," eat as many swimmers as he can find without fear of reprisal or allow grizzlies to chow down on campers and livestock as their mode of self-realization. But will we allow anthrax or cholera microbes to attain self-realization in wiping out sheep herds or human kindergartens? Will we continue to deny salmonella or botulism microorganisms their equal rights when we process the dead carcasses of animals and plants that we eat? In the end, people inevitably put themselves above other species and natural entities, as deep ecology accepts, "simply to live." Rituals of atonement or identification clearly may limit the extent of destruction by changing the overall perception of nature, but these mystifications of humans "not coming first" do not necessarily drive a stake through the heart of anthropocentrism. Human predators, who say their nature prayers or do their atonement rituals, are still predatory anthropocentrists as far as their prey is concerned.

The norms of biocentrism, then, would reenchant nature to make new, more limited anthropocentric claims against the ecosphere. Polluted or abused natural settings cannot satisfy these spiritual demands; thus, deep ecology extends subjectivity to nature as a means of limiting environmental abuse. As Devall and Sessions basically admit, the norm of biocentric equality would guarantee "an overriding vital human need for a healthy and high-quality natural environment for humans, if not for all life, with minimum intrusion of toxic waste, nuclear radiation from human enterprises, minimum acid rain and smog, and enough free flowing wilderness so humans can get in touch with their sources, the natural rhythms and flow of time and place."[56] The emphasis still falls on people and their needs. Dressing up such human-centered appropriation of nature in rituals or myths would make it more psychically rewarding or spiritually refreshing, but biocentric equality comes across as the "soft anthropocentrism" befitting a minimal pressure on the earth. Yet it seems doubtful that even a primal hunting-and-gathering society

56. Devall and Sessions, *Deep Ecology*, p. 68.

could consistently meet the strictures of a "hard biocentrism," much less an ecologizing post-industrial society.

The "Modern" Core of Deep Ecological Subjectivity?

Deep ecology's critique of the Enlightenment schema is neither as thorough nor as a radical as its advocates claim. By citing new norms to constrain humanity's destruction of the ecosphere, deep ecologists aspire to overturn the Enlightenment schema underpinning advanced industrialism's instrumental rationality. In adopting examples they see in primal cultures, deep ecologists believe they can effectuate nature's reenchantment, the development of non-dominating sciences, and an emergence of a new ecological society by creating new forms of human selfhood. Although deep ecology presents these goals as tantamount to the abolition of man's domineering power over nature, it would appear instead that human power would not be replaced by biocentric equality as much as it would be displaced by a silent anthropocentrism in this new human subjectivity.

The new philosophy of nature might seal "the death of man" in ecological functioning by supplanting a coercive set of human power relations with a new discipline of ethical surveillance (self-administered by the subject in Taoist meditation, Buddhist self-in-Self introspection, and mythic Native American purification rituals) to reconstitute human subjectivity within natural subjectivity. The sites of power plainly would shift because the disciplines of self and social understanding would be forced into new polarities of value and practice.[57] In constituting ecospheric or biospheric entities as subjects, humanity would become, following Leopold's paradoxical idealization, just "plain citizens" in an egalitarian biotic/geological/atmospheric community.[58] The strategies of ecosophy might shift human power over nature (and man by implication) from external sovereign control in a Hobbesian sense to internal participative normalization with nature in a new Foucauldian sense.

Much of the modern Enlightenment schema could survive these transformations. Enforcing harmony with nature might be as destructive and domineering as attaining dominance over nature. Deep ecology's

57. See Michel Foucault, *Discipline and Punish: The Birth of the Prison*, trans. Alan Sheridan (New York: Vintage, 1979).
58. Aldo Leopold, *Sand County Almanac* (New York: Oxford Univ. Press, 1968).

construction of reenchantment, mature selfhood, and nature bear the birthmarks of modernity in its conception of the postmodern as primal premodernity. In this regard, deep ecology's confrontation with technocratic industrialism mirrors Rousseau's confrontation with the Enlightenment.[59] The good person, or ecosophical people, should follow "the voice of nature" (biocentrism) not "the voice of reason" (anthropocentrism), which simply expresses instrumental strategies for satisfying corrupt social desires. As subjects of the dominant worldview, people disenchant the world and seek instrumental control in the false voice of reason. Yet these corrupting social forces interfere with people's following their true natural sentiments. If we develop, as Naess, Devall, Sessions, and Snyder claim, our alleged intuition of Earth Wisdom or attune our sentiments to nature, then we can tap into new realms of true freedom. Even so, this pure voice of nature, speaking through individual conscience in the language of virtue, still expresses a very modern concern for individual self-realization of every subject's being.

While deep ecology casts this shift in subjectivity as a revival of primalism, it also might be a Rousseauian revitalization of self-expressive modernism.[60] Nature here speaks of virtues and freedoms that are those of sovereign individuals, creating themselves by rescuing themselves from the corruptions of modernity in finding their personal freedom in its "natural rhythms" or "flows of time and place." Once recovered in the "real work" of self-realization, nature as a healing force or foundation of virtue empowers people to attain full self-expression. Like Rousseau's modern ethic of individual expression, each of us—humans, rocks, or rivers—has a nature to be revealed, expressed, and realized in complete and equal self-fulfillment for deep ecologists. Modern subjectivity, then, is not so much overcome as it is made into an equal entitlement and guaranteed to everything in the ecosphere, knowing all along that humans still have the best crack at enjoying these benefits.

Deep ecology actually may not go far enough and essentially can go no further. It tends to "green" or "soften" the Enlightenment schema,

59. See Timothy W. Luke, "On Nature and Society: Rousseau versus the Enlightenment," *History of Political Thought* 5, no. 2 (1984): 211–43.

60. See Marshall Berman, *The Politics of Authenticity: Radical Individualism and the Emergence of Modern Society* (New York: Atheneum, 1970); and Robert Nisbet, *The Quest for Community* (New York: Oxford Univ. Press, 1953).

but it does not actually overturn its workings. Primal pre-Enlightenment traditions are pared down to suit the particular needs of some postmodern intellectuals, who take from them only what they need to assail advanced industrialism's ecological abuse. Diverse types of reenchantment, myth, and ritual also are embraced categorically without much thought to their potential operational interests nor their probable legitimation of a new hyper-instrumental science. An ethic of self-realization is espoused that projects modern individual self-expression as an ontological quality of nature. By the same token, the precept of biocentrism seems to occlude a soft anthropocentrism in issuing a license of "mutual predation" to nature's most successful and destructive predator—people. Finally, deep ecology could function as a new strategy of power for normalizing new ecological subjects—human and nonhuman—in disciplines of self-effacing moral consciousness. In endorsing self-expression as the inherent value of all ecospheric entities, deep ecology also could advance the modern logic of domination by retraining humans to surveil and steer themselves as well as other beings in accord with "nature's" dictates. As a new philosophy of nature, then, deep ecology provides the essential discursive grid for a few enthusiastic ecosophical mandarins to interpret nature and impose its deep ecological dictates on the unwilling many.

The "Politics" of Deep Ecology

Given these conceptual problems in the deep ecological program, how can deep ecology be situated politically within the existing system of power? In the last analysis, Naess, Devall, and Sessions respond to the environmental crisis with "an examination of the dominant worldview in our society, which has led directly to the continuing crisis of culture."[61] Their practical political answers essentially present "an ecological, philosophical, spiritual approach for dealing with the crisis." Still, as Marx suggests, if "it is not the consciousness of men that determines their being, but, on the contrary, their social being that determines their consciousness," then what sort of social existence or class position has determined the shape of deep ecological consciousness? Basically, as Chim Blea states, "deep ecology has been developed by

---

61. Devall and Sessions, *Deep Ecology*, p. ix.

outdoors persons—mountain climbers, backpackers, field biologists—with experience in observing natural phenomena and comes from the conservation/preservation movement." It "seeks to develop a new paradigm, questions the essence of human civilization, fundamentally condemns human overpopulation and industrialism, is *anti-modern* and *future primitive,* bio-regional, reinhabitory, and resacralizational."[62] Not surprisingly, then, deep ecologists now look to these people and their practice for the discipline, rituals, and teaching of ecological consciousness. Taking care of a place, bringing an attitude of watchful attention to the environment, focusing on self in nature, finding maturity and joy in natural being, and simply doing outdoors activities are basic values shared by many outdoors persons. If they are done "with the proper attitude," many personal leisure pursuits, "like fishing, hunting, surfing, sunbathing, kayaking, canoeing, sailing, mountain climbing, hang gliding, skiing, running, bicycling, and birdwatching,"[63] are endorsed by deep ecologists as a clear path to ecological awareness.

These modes of social existence do determine the consciousness and practical programs of the deep ecology movement, but they also expose a mystification. Many of these outdoor activities for finding the right ecological dharma also are highly industrialized, overstylized modes of corporate consumerist leisure. Admittedly, free-form mountain climbing, fishing, running, and sunbathing do not necessarily demand high-tech equipment, but bicycling, surfing, hang gliding, skiing, hunting, and kayaking are among the most deeply entrenched bastions, as Edward Abbey decries, of "industrial tourism." A self-contained industrial tourist, who brings all of his/her food, clothing, shelter, and equipment from the leisure industry or supermarket, can pretend to relate to nature as a biospherical equal by finding self-realization on a sunny weekend. A great many ordinary workers, shopkeepers, and farmers also might know and enjoy the outdoors on ecological terms, but deep ecology, as a philosophy for properly outfitted mountain climbers, backpackers, and field biologists, could also be mistaken here for the ideology of white-collar intellectuals or professional-technical workers defending

62. Chim Blea, "Animal Rights and Deep Ecology Movements," *Synthesis* 23 (1986): 13–14; excerpted from *Earth First!* 6, no. 6 (June 21, 1986).

63. Devall and Sessions, *Deep Ecology,* p. 70.

their environmental "positional goods."[64] Rock cliffs, backcountry powder, trout pools, forest trails, monster breakers, elk herds, class three river rapids, or bird preserves clearly can be enjoyed more thoroughly by a few individuals to the extent that most others cannot enjoy them. It makes sense for deep ecologists to condemn human overpopulation or resacralize the bioregion they wish to enjoy; it would revalorize these environmental benefits as their positional goods. Unfortunately, nomadic grub eaters cannot produce high-tech composite surfboards, eighteen-speed trail bikes, or sophisticated hang gliders. Who will make such goods or produce food while others seek self-realization and biocentric equality? The anti-modern, future primitive condemnation of industrial civilization by many deep ecologists is not really total, but its contradictory partialities are mystified in the social forms of life that generate this consciousness.

Beyond these basic mystifications of its class origins, the eight essential principles of deep ecology elaborated by Naess and Sessions are lacking as practical dicta or as a political program.[65] First, the notions that (1) the well-being of human and nonhuman life has intrinsic value apart from human uses, that (2) the diversity of life-forms contributes to these intrinsic values, and, finally, that (3) humans have no right to reduce this rich diversity except to satisfy vital needs are all important goals. Blea, for example, argues that all things are equally valuable, from plants to people to clouds, but animals are no more crucial than plants or mammals than insects. However, rare species and endangered individuals in rare species as they become endangered are more valuable than more abundant species and individuals of such species. Thus, if one were caught in a spring brushfire, a deep ecologist would be bound ethically to save a California condor hatchling over a human child because the former—given its rarity—is much more valuable. Likewise, how should a deep ecologist react to a Native American killing eagles, which are an endangered species, merely for its totemically valued feathers? Nature is believed to know best; hence, humanity should not assign good or evil labels to the cycles of suffering, pain, and death in nature—people should just let it be. Such attitudes, in turn, clearly ful-

---

64. See Fred Hirsch, *Social Limits to Growth* (London: Routledge & Kegan Paul, 1977).

65. Devall and Sessions, *Deep Ecology*, p. 70.

fill the fourth principle of deep ecology, namely, that the flourishing of nonhuman life necessarily requires a decrease in human life.

Yet deep ecologists offer few criteria or no standards for practicing these precepts. If humans have no right to reduce the diversity of life, except to satisfy vital needs, then what are the standards for identifying vital needs? Suffering, pain, and death are defined as natural or inevitable. Can humans destroy viruses and bacteria to cure disease? Can humans eat all plants if game is meager or turn to any game animals if crops or natural grazing foods fail? Can humans reduce the diversity of a river basin with dams to control floods that let rivers or rain become what they are, and allow crops to displace natural vegetation and alter nitrogen fixation cycles in the existing topsoil? Nature has let California condors, the tiger, African elephants, and blue whales suffer and die in their ecological niches as humans or draft animals supplant them. Should humanity act otherwise or let it be?

Deep ecologists should not necessarily have all the answers now, but they do need substantive criteria for arriving at such answers in the future. Right now, however, all that deep ecology seems to offer are new symbolic rituals of sacralization instead of substantive rational criteria for choosing between alternatives. As Blea suggests, "I thank pieces of wood I gather for my fire, I treat as sacred whatever I eat or use to fulfill vital needs whether it be animal, plant or mineral.... We, as Deep Ecologists recognize the transcendence of the community over any individual, we should deal with all individuals—animal, plant, mineral, etc.—with whom we come into contact with compassion and *bonhomie*. Some we will use to fulfill vital needs, some will use us to fulfill their own vital needs, some (like burros in the Grand Canyon) we may need to kill to protect the integrity of the community, but all should be treated with respect and love."[66] Here, again, one sees a soft anthropocentrism at work in nature sacralization. People will continue to cut and burn trees, kill and eat plants and animals, or isolate and kill germs to fulfill vital human needs or protect the integrity of humanly defined ecocommunities. As Alan Watts noted, when people want food, "cows do scream louder than carrots,"[67] but deep ecologists do not seem troubled by such distinctions

66. Blea, "Animal Rights and Deep Ecology Movements," p. 14.
67. See Warwick Fox, "Deep Ecology: A New Philosophy for Our Time?," *Ecologist* 14, nos. 5–6 (1984): 194–200.

or provide criteria for judging between cows and carrots, rocks and rivers, or people and ptomaine. After deep ecological training, it appears that a ritual prayer, the right attitude of respect, or compassionate loving gratitude will rationalize and legitimate softer anthropocentric actions. In other words, deep ecologists ultimately are "outdoors persons" who are brave, clean, thrifty, reverent, and obedient to the laws of the pack. Serious abuses of nature will probably lessen, but the human being still is "more equal" than other beings in deep ecology's Animal Farm.

Second, the idea that (4) human life must reduce its population to flourish itself as well as to promote nonhuman life, because (5) human interference in the nonhuman world is excessive and worsening, presents many practical difficulties. These principles might be true, but who decides how to decrease human populations where, when, and why? In the developed world, many people see the underdeveloped world overpopulating itself, forcing nature into collapse. While in the underdeveloped world, more human life in new children promotes the continuation of their parents' individual human lives. And excessive consumerism in the developed world is seen by the underdeveloped world as excessive and worsening, causing nature to collapse. Most people will not voluntarily stop reproducing to protect the survival of nature. Even so, if people did come into Earth Wisdom, it also would seem that reproduction is "natural." It is "letting nature be" by finding one form of self-realization in new life. To make these principles actually work, vital human needs, like those of food, shelter, clothing, health, or life itself, probably cannot be satisfied. A "hard biocentrism" versus a "soft anthropocentrism" would reduce the population. Yet existing technologies of comfort and security would have to be suspended or outlawed as famine, disease, the elements, or reinhabitory predators reduced populations.

Third, principle (6) is the least developed and the most problematic: policies must change to transform economic, ideological, and technological structures into something not like today's, which implicitly will fulfill the dictates of principles one through six. Beyond (7) shifting human satisfaction to appreciate the quality of life over higher quantitative standards of living, deep ecology has no program. At best, in ridiculing the strategies of reform environmentalism, it only offers the traditional solutions of moral anarchism, namely, changing the self to change society with individual acts of will guided by "correct" conscience/

consciousness in a pressing situation of necessity to save humanity. Devall and Sessions claim that "if we seek only personal redemption we could become solitary ecological saints among the masses of those we might classify as 'sinners' who continue to pollute. Change in people requires a change in culture and vice versa. We cannot ignore the personal area nor the social, for our project is to enhance harmony with each other, the planet and ourselves."[68] This outlook leads to the last principle (8), namely, those who subscribe to these points have an obligation to directly or indirectly implement them.

Unfortunately, these feeble injunctions will not empower the minority tradition in new ecological communities. There is not a secure theory of the state, ideology, technology, or the economy here. Deep ecology fails to admit how many people willingly and enthusiastically will volunteer in the rape of nature to enjoy corporate consumerism. Today's Michelob philosophy of "you can have it all" while "living on the edge" often is seen as spiritually much more satisfying than Earth Wisdom. As revolutionaries, deep ecologists fail to ask or answer Lenin's question of advanced industrialism: "Who, Whom?"

Deep ecology in the last analysis is "utopian ecologism." As a utopia, it presents alluring moral visions of what might be; at the same time, it fails to outline practicable means for realizing these ecologically moral visions. Deep ecologists are caught in the trap of endorsing new visions for new "ecotopias," but they do not even have a practical program for future primitive reinhabitation or bioregional community building. Political action is displaced into the realm of ethical ideals, making it every individual's moral duty to change himself or herself in advancing cultural change. Yet, without the opportunity to change collective activity—in the economy, ideology, technology, or polity—these personal moral regenerations might become only a quietistic, postmodern Taoism of finding the right path in an evil society.[69] On the one hand, Naess suggests his vision of deep ecology is virtually idiosyncratic; he strongly enjoins others to concoct their own ecological omelettes.[70] On

68. Devall and Sessions, *Deep Ecology*, p. 14.

69. Timothy W. Luke, "Informationalism and Ecology," *Telos* 56 (Summer 1983): 59–73, reprinted in this volume.

70. See Arne Naess, "Intuition, Intrinsic Value and Deep Ecology," *Ecologist* 14, nos. 5–6 (1984): 201–4.

the other hand, Devall and Sessions conclude that deep ecology stands for these ultimate values: "Inward and outward direction, two aspects of the same process. We are not alone. We are part and parcel of the larger community, the land community. Each life in its own sense is heroic and connected. In the Bodhisativa's words, 'No one is saved until we are all saved.'... The process of developing maturity is simpler than many think. Like water flowing through the canyons, always yielding, always finding its way back, simple in means, rich in ends."[71] Deep ecologists can claim these values as their final goals. However, such principles for "interpreting the world" have little political promise for "changing it."

If the economy, ideology, and technology of corporate consumerism are to change, then one must ask: Who dominates whom? How? Why? Where? What is to be done? Deep ecology does not address these basic questions or provide convincing answers. Deep ecologists also prematurely dismiss the contributions, which initially may be needed in their new society, being made by reform environmentalism in the areas of alternative agriculture, alternative technology, and appropriate architecture.[72] More importantly, they also ignore the promise of social ecology in the areas of ecological politics, urban reconstruction, and practical strategies of transformation.[73] Beyond engaging in nonviolent resistance while acting from deep principles "to touch the earth," there are no effective strategies for advancing real change in deep ecological thought, save those of continuing the symbolic politics or pressure tactics of reform environmentalism at the local level with a new, deep, long-range attitude "to better public policy" through frugality, modesty, and restraint.

Conclusions: Justice and Deep Ecology

As political philosophy, deep ecology has failed to show how and why it should be implemented. Like many revolutionary programs, deep ecology lacks a "theory of transition." There are no practical means for changing people's everyday consumerist habits into those of an

71. Devall and Sessions, *Deep Ecology*, p. 205.

72. See Lester R. Brown et al., *The State of the World 1988* (New York: W. W. Norton, 1988); and Lester Brown, *Toward a Sustainable Society* (New York: W. W. Norton, 1981).

73. See Murray Bookchin, *The Ecology of Freedom* (Palo Alto, CA: Cheshire Books, 1982); and Bookchin, *Toward an Ecological Society* (Montreal: Black Rose Books, 1980).

ecotopian community without tremendous costs. One can agree with Snyder that "we must change the very foundations of our society and our minds. Nothing short of total transformation will do much good."[74] But how does any highly developed society, like the United States in the 1980s with 235 million people, living because of the global imports and exports of transnational corporate capitalism in and out of huge metroplexes, reinhabit its bioregions such that "the human population lives harmoniously and dynamically by employing a sophisticated and unobtrusive technology in a world environment which is 'left natural'"?[75] Current world urbanism is nothing but an obtrusive technology that renders the organic into the inorganic. What happens to Los Angeles, Chicago, New York? If their corporate agricultural or municipal service supports are cut simply to return the Los Angeles Basin, Lake Michigan's South Shores, and Manhattan Island to nature, then nature does know best how to cope—these people will suffer and/or die. The philosophical dreams of deep ecology ultimately entail a moral and political nightmare.

Deep ecological justice ultimately is post-distributional. It defines away distribution systems or codes with human norms of fairness and equality as the sustaining apparatus of corrupt techno-industrial society. By calling for biospherical egalitarianism, deep ecology subjectifies nature. Only by extending the right of life, liberty, and the pursuit of happiness (as the freedom of self-realization) to nonhuman life and inanimate entities can humans, in the vision of deep ecologists, for the first time allegedly enjoy their rights to life, liberty, and the pursuit of happiness in emancipated nature. Justice is made into an attribute of all-selves-in-Self working toward their peculiar self-realization.[76] Therefore, humans must transform their hitherto anthropocentric modes of existence, out of the new sense of "fairness" to all otherness growing from an ecosophical consciousness, to promote this new biocentric justice.

This quest for "natural unity in process" or "biospherical egalitarianism" bears the marks of deep ecology's inner contradictions. The soft

74. Snyder, *Turtle Island*, p. 99.

75. Ibid. For example, see the sympathetic but also realistic appraisal of some deep ecological political strategies employed by the Earth First! group in Charles Bowden, *Blue Desert* (Tucson: Univ. of Arizona Press, 1986), pp. 87–98.

76. Naess, "Identification as a Source of Deep Ecology Attitudes," pp. 256–70.

anthropocentrism of deep ecology, which favors the nature-regarding interests of humans, spreads intrinsic value evenly across the ecosphere in principle as it continues to overvalue certain humans over other humans, animals, plants, and inanimate entities. Yet, as Warwick Fox argues, "the only universe where value is spread evenly across the field is a dead universe."[77] Deep ecologists, in stressing first principles and new macrological forms of consciousness, really do not develop an adequate theory of justice or a workable system of ethics beyond the retro-reasoning of a mythic primalism. While acknowledging that killing, pain, and suffering are natural and necessary, they advance no consistent criteria for deciding between alternatives when such acts are necessary. We ought to treat all of nature better by not polluting or abusing the earth, but this is a clear choice between an obvious good and certain evil. How do we decide between two "goods" or two "bads" in conflict? Deep ecology provides few guideposts on this rougher ground. Until it comes to grips with its conceptual flaws and political contradictions, the answers that deep ecology provides as political philosophy must be held suspect. Otherwise, deep ecologists simply could reproduce at different levels of destruction the many tragedies they decry happening under the dominant worldview of advanced industrialism.

---

77. Fox, "Deep Ecology," p. 199.

4

Community and Ecology

Community, Class, and Modernity

T HE POPULIST CRITIQUE of the New Class and its liberal agenda
usually takes one of two lines of attack. The first, like Alasdair Mac-
Intyre's, "holds that liberal political theory accurately represents liberal
social practice."[1] For populists to criticize liberal society, it is sufficient to
take liberal theory on its own terms and accept the vision of subjectivity
advocated by Locke, Smith, or Bentham as true. That is, contemporary
society is an aggregation of rational economic agents, existentially fragmented in an endless game of complex instrumental calculations. But,
as Christopher Lasch points out, ordinary people do not want to live
this way—a lifestyle they associate with New Class behavior.[2] Within
that framework, there are no moral criteria to guide individual choice
except personal utility or the unstable interests of loosely aggregated
voluntary associations. The inevitable result is a series of crises.

The second response, such as Robert Bellah's, "holds that liberal
theory radically misrepresents real life."[3] In this view, most people live in

* Originally published in *Telos* 88 (Summer 1991): 69–79.

1. See Michael Walzer, "The Communitarian Critique of Liberalism," *Political Theory* 18, no. 1 (1990): 7. See also Alasdair MacIntyre, *After Virtue: A Study in Moral
Theory* (Notre Dame, IN: Univ. of Notre Dame Press, 1981).

2. See Christopher Lasch, *The True and Only Heaven: Progress and Its Critics* (New
York: Norton, 1991), pp. 476–508.

3. Walzer, "The Communitarian Critique of Liberalism," p. 9. Also see Robert Bellah
et al., *Habits of the Heart: Individualism and Commitment in American Life* (Berkeley:
Univ. of California Press, 1985).

a world of complex social ties lying beyond the scope of liberal theory. Atomized economic agents, set free to act instrumentally, will follow New Class ideals of upward social mobility and leave local communities.[4] Therefore, to criticize modern society, all one has to do is reject liberal theory on its own false terms, while attending to its surviving pre-liberal, non-liberal, or post-liberal attributes that make it work, since they are the only possible basis for building a viable social order.[5] Both of these critiques contain an element of truth, but they do not go far enough. Any political discussion of community today must confront the fundamental question of ecology.[6]

Today, however, any evocation of "community" and "ecology" immediately comes under attack as a reactionary response to modernity and is associated with conservative images of "going back to nature"— a rejection of modernity's unilinear and irreversible character. Despite what sociological theory assumes, however, modernity is neither unilinear nor irreversible, going from primitive community to complex society. It is the result of critical choices made within particular historical conditions.[7] Earlier projects seeking alternative social arrangements providing for broader community autonomy can be reactivated to challenge increasing New Class domination. By interposing between production and consumption technical expertise and complex hierarchical organization centered in massive state bureaucracies and transnational corporations, the New Class systematically disempowers all

---

4. Lasch, *The True and Only Heaven*, pp. 509–32.

5. Cf. Gérard Raulet, "The New Utopia: Communication Technologies," *Telos* 87 (Spring 1991): 39–58.

6. Lasch vindicates populism as an alternative, but he ignores the American political traditions that have best approximated his ideal, i.e., those of ecological activism.

7. For a critique of this modernization model of progress, see Timothy W. Luke, *Social Theory and Modernity: Critique, Dissent, and Revolution* (Newbury Park, CA: Sage, 1990), pp. 211–68. The most recent sociological analysis predicated on such modernization dynamics is to be found in Jürgen Habermas. However, his framework of "system" and "lifeworld," which casts the system as an integrative force colonizing the lifeworld, represents system as society and lifeworld as community in essentially the same old unidirectional, irreversible, and inexorable roles of modernization theory, even though the epicyclical construct of "civil society" can be interposed between the two to make communication theory look like it mediates a serious struggle between system and lifeworld forces. See Jürgen Habermas, *The Theory of Communicative Action*, vol. 2, *Lifeworld and System: A Critique of Functionalist Reason*, trans. Thomas McCarthy (Boston: Beacon Press, 1987).

other social agents. In substituting nonrenewable, energy-intensive production techniques for organic labor-intensive ones, it has severed what were once close ties of communities to their particular ecological settings. The ecological destruction wrought around the globe indicates how costly these economic and political trade-offs have become.

The New Class

New Class ideological agitprop constantly celebrates the unlimited abundance that high-tech industry and scientific research will make possible. These promises of universal abundance and a more egalitarian distribution of its many benefits have not been and cannot be kept.[8] It is physically impossible to produce enough wealth to bring everyone up to New Class "throwaway" standards of living, because the earth's already severely strained ecosystems simply cannot carry this load.

Generally speaking, the New Class designates the professional-technical intelligentsia or the knowledge-manipulating social strata that articulate and apply their expertise in both state bureaucracies and corporate enterprises.[9] Internally divided, the ranks of this New Class encompass both the adversary culture and the technical elites, liberal reformers and conservative technocrats, bureaucratic *apparatchiki* and cybernetic entrepreneurs. Nonetheless, their collective commitment to

8. This public relations blitz is the utopian literature of the present. For example, Rockwell International shows the technical breakthroughs that can be realized "Where Science Gets Down to Business." DuPont's timeless call to achieve "Better Living through Chemistry" is matched by today's General Electric pledging to "Bring Good Things to Light." AT&T empowers one "To Reach Out and Touch Someone" because "The System is the Solution" if you only make "The Right Choice." Toyota/Lexus promises "The Relentless Pursuit of Perfection," but Chevron unifies expert scientific producer and everyday energy consumer in its Zen-like "People Do." However, the tao of Dow Chemical perhaps surpasses them all as its corporate imagery shows soon-to-graduate, professional-technical students instructing their families, who are diversely shown as black ghetto-dwellers, comfortable white suburbanites, and hard-working farm folks, on how a New Class–based higher education will pay off technologically for them and humanity, while an unseen chorus of happy consumers jubilantly sings the musical score, "You Can Make a Difference in What Tomorrow Brings, Dow Lets You Do Great Things!"

9. In the United States, inequality has grown since 1967 and has been increasing at a faster pace. See Kevin Phillips, *The Politics of Rich and Poor: Wealth and the American Electorate in the Reagan Aftermath* (New York: Random House, 1990), pp. 3–32; and Robert Reich, *The Work of Nations: Preparing Ourselves for 21st-Century Capitalism* (New York: Times Books, 1991).

knowledge-driven projects of technological development and economic growth embroils them in elaborate schemes that disempower ordinary people and reduce nature to an alien entity that needs to be dominated. These attitudes lead to the destruction of nature and mystify the actual brutality and irresponsibility of New Class power by associating it with the plethora of material goods, cultural benefits, and social services that the presently unsustainable rate of exploiting nature now provides only for the few. These self-destructive dynamics need to be reexamined against a backdrop of concrete alternatives.

Community and Populism

Within this New Class framework, community tends to decay into the most "minimal" features with very little popular content. Composed of clients and consumers, communities today are not much more than an aggregation of atomized individuals organized into discrete geo-graphic-legal units. Community becomes so thin because workplace and residence, production and consumption, identity and interests, administration and allocation are so divided in the New Class project of an advanced industrial society predicated primarily on geographic and social mobility. The division of interests, loss of common historical consciousness, weakening of shared beliefs, and lessening of ecological responsibility are what necessitates alternative approaches to under-standing community.

Social theory, New Class ideology *par excellence*, interprets com-munities entirely in terms of modernization. Allegedly, with the spread of national and international networks of capitalist exchange, the close ties of organic local community (*Gemeinschaft*) crumbled into rubble as formalized social relations (*Gesellschaft*) buried it under the bet-ter-organized and rational practices of modernity.[10] According to this logic, "community" is depicted as the warm, close, past-and-present social condition within an oversimplified conceptual dichotomy that opposes it to the cold, distant, present-and-future social condition of "society."[11] Thus sociological analyses have interpreted community and

10. The original and problematic source in modern sociological theory for these notions is Ferdinand Tönnies, *Gemeinschaft und Gesellschaft* (Leipzig: Reisland, 1987).

11. Although Rousseau, Smith, and Marx make similar arguments about modern-ization, these ideas gain their fullest professional-technical articulation only in modern

its "premodern" institutions as a primitivism to be eliminated by the rational progress made possible by modernity's state bureaucracies and global markets. The alleged stasis of premodern communities provides a legitimating writ for imposing more fluid, mobile, and variable forms of everyday life, such as those manufactured by New Class experts.

Once community is framed in these categories, its meaning becomes even more problematic because New Class assumptions guard against "thicker" populist understandings. Social theory deals with alternative visions of community in three equally distorted ways. First, it interprets any emphasis on community as *conservatism*, or an effort by privileged interests to defend traditional practices. This approach, however, undermines New Class accounts of the irreversibility of the evolution from community to society embedded in modern social theory. It implicitly acknowledges that some community-tradition-folk practices do survive and coexist with society-modernity-secular practices. It stigmatizes concerns for surviving traditions as "conservative" because accepting traditional continuities implies an endorsement of organic hierarchies rooted in age-old prejudices, inequality, and oppression. As the architect and guardian of modern thin communities, the New Class takes great pains to argue that attempts to reconstitute traditional thick communities necessarily lead to perpetuating premodern evils.

The second New Class criticism of community casts concerns with its "thick" reconstitution as *romanticism*, or a wish to return to long-lost but not forgotten sets of primitive relations. This reaction also undercuts the vision of community inexorably evolving into society by acknowledging the moral emptiness of modern society and admitting that the closeness of traditional community returns as an unfulfilled utopian image. The New Class sanctions any engagement with notions such as "voluntary simplicity" or "small is beautiful" as nostalgia. Rather than embracing the unsettling uncertainty of market exchange, this romanticism would turn back the clock to recapture communal solidarity.

---

social theory. See Henry Maine, *Ancient Law* (London: Murray, 1861); Émile Durkheim, *The Division of Labor in Society* (New York: Macmillan, 1933); Max Weber, *The Theory of Social and Economic Organization*, ed. Talcott Parsons (New York: Free Press, 1947); Charles Horton Cooley, *Social Organization* (New York: Scribner, 1909); Ralph Linton, *The Study of Man* (New York: Appleton-Century, 1936); and Talcott Parsons, *The Social System* (Glencoe, IL: Free Press, 1952).

Yet the New Class also argues that such forms of communal life never really existed and, even if they did, that it would be impossible and undesirable to revitalize them. The teleological role of an idealized past to help shape new projects of social reconstruction thus flattens out within the New Class dogma of "the end of history," reducing all future developments to the mere extension of instrumental rationality and ever-growing consumption.

The third approach sees longing for "thick" communities as *collectivism*, or an impatience with the divisions, instability, and mobility of capitalist society. The New Class has closely policed these aspirations for maximal community because collectivist alternatives are but another form of New Class domination—as can be seen from recent East European experiences, within which the very concept of the New Class originally arose. Radical visions of a future condition of rational collectivist control threaten more modest advances in the present. Instead of dealing with present problems of minimal community on their own terms, such radical collectivism would rush the clock forward into some technologically defined maximal communitarianism constituting a perfect rational utopia. The New Class may eventually gain these powers, but prematurely calling for their realization only exposes the fragility of power and sparks fears of the despotic collectivist nightmares of "really existing socialism."

Talking about communal life, then, is hazardous. None of these dangers in maximal populist community are necessarily guaranteed to occur, but New Class ideology continues to issue its ironclad warranties. Unless one accepts the thinnest, most minimal constructions of society, New Class interests feel threatened. Any program to reconstruct today's thin/minimal communities as new forms of thicker/maximal community draws stern disciplinary indictments. Because of their allegedly *conservative*, *romantic*, or *collectivist* aspirations, populist projects continue to be hassled by New Class "concept cops" eager to defend against ordinary people seeking to shape their lives and determine their destinies.

"Environmentalism" as New Class Ideology

In the United States today, calling for greater ecological responsibility has become politically imperative. While environmental concerns are still associated with an all but vanished counterculture, many New Class insiders have "gone green" by integrating ecological concerns within bureaucratic corporate agendas. Thus, the World Bank endorses "environmentalist" economic growth, transnational corporations claim that everyday is "Earth Day," and large government bureaucracies manage their office waste by buying "100% recycled paper" file folders. Behind such mediagenic window-dressing, however, lurk new projects of "environmental defense," "waste containment," or "worldwatching" to legitimate expanding New Class interventionist power and knowledge.

Ecological problems are global, borderless, and transnational. As the Cold War has faded, so has the concrete threat of communist subversion that once justified state as well as corporate projects of modernization. Yet the global economy and the interventionist state constructed as anti-communist bulwarks remain, grow, and continue to ravage the environment. These New Class "worldwatchers" today "think globally" but "act locally" to shore up their power by defending the environment, containing waste, and watching the world in ways that ensure their clients will remain passive, dependent, and powerless.

"Global thinking" has become the ideology of growth-minded nation-states and transnational corporations. It demands uncritical acceptance of formal codes of instrumental rationality able to deal with elaborate statistical models assumed to be identical to and exhaustive of the forms of life captured within their disciplinary grids. It is reductionist, instrumental, and destructive. Everything not disclosed by its professional rules of statistical standard deviation or mathematical multiple regression is crushed, ignored, or distorted to fit standardized uniform results on the projected slopes of statistical extrapolations.

The New Class empowers itself and disempowers local communities all over the globe through a simple bargain. In exchange for accepting their systems of knowledge and power, the New Class promises that the short-term flow of goods and services on a global scale will continue and grow for a few more decades—even if only for the benefit of various elites. To resist this project, the flow of goods and services may slow or stop, which could lead to major social and economic crises. The New Class is clearly transnational and highly homogenized. The elite professional spaces delimited within telecommunication links, jetports, high-tech office complexes, upper-income neighborhoods, new science centers, and powerful bureaucratic agencies all tend to reproduce the same sets of expectations. "Acting locally" while "thinking globally" means surfing in Maui and thinking about the next business deal in Manila, working at home but commuting cybernetically to the bond business pits in Tokyo, or contributing to the local PBS television station to pay its share of producing a documentary in London about saving elephants in Africa.

Beyond the New Class's environmentalist rhetoric, these increasingly borderless minimal "communities" remain ensnared in global exchange networks, living off millennia of slowly accumulated fossil fuels. Their major concern is with maximizing mobility rather than ensuring sustainability. Often none of their vital ecological support mechanisms are in the immediate environmental vicinity. Environmental inputs are not used on a sustainable scale appropriate to each bioregional setting. Instead, these supporting flows are sourced from around the larger nation-state or even the world, bound together by the wasteful expenditure of scarce nonrenewable energy. Due to their location in the global network, some neighborhoods, cities, regions, and nation-states either enjoy exceptionally high rates of excess consumption or suffer from outrageously inadequate levels of basic goods and services.

The New Class is, first and foremost, grounded in transnational exchange and not embedded in a particular ecoregional setting. Being constantly on the move, it treats most places frivolously or disrespectfully. Any place is usually no better than any other. Indeed, every place is equally subject to potential destruction as a development site, a source of economic raw material, or a fresh market to sustain the flow. Building a community in a particular location, accepting it on its own ecological terms, working to adapt a sustainable way of life, and cherishing it for its unique differences are foreign notions to the New Class's operational logic. By "outsourcing" the material basis of everyday life or organizing production around importing incomplete segments or partial components of the total array of goods and services needed to survive, New Class state and corporate planners have broken many communal and organic ties to immediate ecoregional settings. By channeling communities toward "specializing" or exporting their small, limited stream of goods and services in sufficient volume to maintain a balance of trade with other communities in a global exchange network, New Class experts make them hostage to state and corporate bureaucracies. Profitable in an exchange-based accounting system drawn up for quarterly reports to New Class management, these cycles of global trade are ultimately unsustainable.

Resisting these New Class practices must take the form of acting and thinking ecologically. Unless and until most communities reconnect their economies with their immediate supporting ecoregions, they will be subject to both New Class domination and environmental collapse. Living in balance with the local bioregional surroundings while still tied to larger networks of information and expertise, communities can turn into sustainable commonwealths instead of predatory profiteers. More importantly, new kinds of knowledge, tied to the specificities of place and the particularities of local communities, would develop in creating a sustainable society. Such knowledge is not likely to suit the expectations of today's typical New Class expert. But it could develop openly once people and communities embed themselves ecologically in the immediate region. Knowledge of place should attend to the particularities of that ecoregion by suspending universal standards in favor of what is suitable to each community. Otherwise, inappropriate cultural codes, housing forms, dietary patterns, apparel styles, technical implements, or energy systems unsuited to particular environments will give way to foreign disciplines of technological domination. These changes require demystification of New Class power and the reconstitution of communal concerns with local and regional commonwealths because the limits of environmental sustainability have already been reached and in some settings are being exceeded.

Possibilities for Populist Resistance

The New Class myth of economic progress is becoming increasingly indefensible: the high standards of living it promises are not standard, have never been very high for most people, and do not guarantee a meaningful life. Communities may do better by determining their own ecologically appropriate ethos, redefining their own standards of life, and setting their own moral criteria. New Class ideology calls for communities and individuals to "think globally, act locally" to prop up the tottering political economy of advanced industrial society. An ecological populism needs communities and individuals that can "think locally" and "act globally."

For an ecological populism, nature must be brought back directly into everyday life in more subjective aesthetic or ethical forms. Rather than being only an alien entity from which to extract resources and into which to dump waste, nature must be treated as an equal vital presence. It should not remain the object of administration by New Class experts, but the most basic subjective site defining essential ends and basic values, such as responsibility, frugality, autonomy, sustainability, and freedom. These ecological and populist notions of community must not be mistaken for utopian socialism or other long-discredited models promising organic reconciliation with nature. Returning to some idyllic past is neither likely nor necessary. An ecological populism would develop an alternative modernity by making different choices about community or forcing new popular relations of production.[12] An ecological populism must go well beyond bankrupt ecosocialist millenarianism.[13]

"Thinking locally" and "acting globally" means making several radical shifts toward some social forms conventionally regarded as "dead and gone." First would be the creation of more complex, diverse, and

12. An ecological society should be an alternative modernity, not an anti-modernity or postmodernity. See Murray Bookchin, *Toward an Ecological Society* (Montreal: Black Rose Books, 1980); and Timothy W. Luke, "Notes for a Deconstructionist Ecology," *New Political Science* 4, no. 1 (1983): 21–32.

13. For outlines of these ecosocialist programs, see Martin Ryle, *Ecology and Socialism* (London: Radius, 1988); and Stuart Hall and Martin Jacques, eds., *New Times: The Changing Face of Politics in the 1990s* (London: Lawrence and Wishart, 1989). An effective ecological populism must ask different questions to create an economy, society, and polity beyond the romantic collectivism of such ecosocialist rhetorics. Today's ecosocialist programs read like agendas of re-empowerment for some kind of centralized statist collectivism, which looks to Maoist peasant work brigades or Cuban state farms for models of "a kinder, gender socialism" serving green goals. Yet the collective mode of landholding, work organization, and technological control of these models threatens a disappointing rerun of bureaucratic *nomenklatura* and *apparat* authoritarianism. The allure of appropriate technologies in ecosocialism also evokes new ill-considered infatuations. When viewed through the soft focus and warm glow of *Mother Earth News* or the *Whole Earth Catalog*, ecosocialism bizarrely parodies Lenin's declaration that "socialism equals electrification plus soviet power" with claims that "ecosocialism equals windmills, geodesic domes, and solar panels plus nonhierarchical decision-making." The technological enthusiasms of such "back to the land, here comes the sun" manifestos promise to exhaust their force in economic fragmentation, cultural frustration, and political failure.

skilled societies of small producers, who own real property and control a significant body of skills. Owning and controlling such assets at the local level tends to reunify production and consumption in the same population centers. This means changing who owns and controls as well as who uses and profits from land, capital, and technology. Not only the benefits of consumption but also the costs of production would then be immediately evident at the local level rather than only in distant environmental "sacrifice zones." A complex society of small-scale proprietors and regional producers, in turn, could nest their economies more ecologically in the particular sustainable ecoregion.[14]

Second, such a society would cultivate a new subjectivity grounded in new kinds of empowerment—technological, economic, political, and cultural. Since "the good life" would no longer be the endless consumption obsession of contemporary permissive individualism, it could be redefined in more demanding moral codes of hard work, frugality, ecological responsibility, humility, and skill perfection.[15] This, in turn, will generate new community institutions suited to the new context.[16] Here the real advances of secular rational civilization might counterbalance potential regressions to a reactionary irrational culture. Racism, provincialism, xenophobia, sexism, and class hatreds need not be part of any populist society. Indeed, loyalty to community, ecoregion, or place need not become lines of cultural conflict or group warfare.

Third, within such a context, centralized bureaucratic state control and standardized corporate penetration of local communities would be considerably curtailed, while individual responsibility would be greatly increased. Yet self-rule, self-ownership, and self-management are de-

---

14. As Wendell Berry notes, some cities will never be sustainable, but many others can and should be. See "Out of Your Car, Off Your Horse," *Atlantic Monthly*, February 1991, pp. 60–63. Also see David Morris, *Self-Reliant Cities: Energy and the Transformation of Urban America* (San Francisco: Sierra Club Books, 1982); Richard Register, *Ecocity Berkeley: Building Cities for a Healthy Future* (Berkeley, CA: North Atlantic Books, 1987); Wendell Berry, *Meeting the Expectations of the Land: Essays in Sustainable Agriculture and Stewardship* (San Francisco: North Point Press, 1984); and Wendell Berry, *The Unsettling of America: Culture and Agriculture* (San Francisco: Sierra Club Books, 1977).

15. See an initial consideration of these goals in Ken Anderson et al., "Roundtable on Communitarianism," *Telos* 76 (Summer 1988): 2–32.

16. For more discussion, see Paul and Percival Goodman, *Communities: Means of Livelihood and Ways of Life* (New York: Random House, 1960).

manding social practices. Freedom entails the prospect of failures, reversals, and just having less at times without being automatically able to turn to centralized state powers for relief. While they are very likely to succeed at making a popular ecological community work, these communities may also collapse. This threat of failure makes their autonomy meaningful: if New Class big brothers are always standing in the background ready to pick them up, dust them off, and push them along their way, then there is little meaningful autonomy or real freedom for such populist commonwealths. The transnational character of the diminished but still very much functioning global economy with its time-and-space compressing communication and transportation systems will prevent most communities from withdrawing into isolationist self-sufficiency or collapsing after unforeseen natural disaster.

Finally, these shifts would involve reconstituting the fundamental writs of authority now underpinning public order. Propounding larger aggregates of these autonomous communities in the United States would require real federal structures to protect and preserve such ecological commonwealths from outside interference and internal insecurity. A new debate about federalism must center on local autonomy without revitalizing traditional practices of racism or sexism, preservation of national and transnational ties without aggravating liberal practices of unrepresented rationalization, arbitrary decision-making, and bureaucratic collective organization overriding popular consent.[17] By elaborating such unrealized possibilities, an ecological populism could shake many communities' traditional resistance to change as well as mount a political offensive against New Class domination.

17. For some preliminary considerations, see Murray Bookchin, *The Rise of Urbanization and the Decline of Citizenship* (San Francisco: Sierra Club Books, 1987).

5

The Politics of Arcological Utopia:
Soleri on Ecology, Architecture, and Society

ATOP A LOW MESA above the Aqua Fria River in central Arizona, a unique laboratory devoted to testing a new ecological model has been slowly developing for twenty-five years. A project of Paolo Soleri's Cosanti Foundation, Arcosanti is a working prototype for a new kind of city—one being designed, built, and inhabited as a three-dimensional, highly concentrated megastructure.[1] To house a city of 5,000 to 6,000 people, Arcosanti will occupy only fourteen acres of land in the midst of an 860-acre greenbelt/park area/agricultural zone. The closely articulated structures of Arcosanti will be not much more than one-quarter of a mile on any one side, but they will rise to as much as twenty-five stories tall. Within them, Soleri and his coworkers hope to locate all of the economic and social infrastructure of any modern city, while providing residents with up to 2,000 square feet of living space per family to use more or less as they please. Outside, everyone will be able to enjoy the expansive views of another 3,000 acres to be kept as undeveloped open space.

To respond to the mounting environmental crises, Soleri has used Arcosanti to rethink modern urban design and planning. Instead of accepting the logic of today's two-dimensional cities, such as Phoenix or

* Originally published in *Telos* 101 (Fall 1994): 55–78.

1. See Paolo Soleri, *Arcosanti: An Urban Laboratory?* (Santa Monica, CA: VTI Press, 1987); and Ralph Blumenthal, "Futuristic Visions in the Desert," *New York Times*, February 1, 1987.

Los Angeles, which follow an automobile-driven "scatterization" pattern by pushing outward as their inner cores atrophy and die, Arcosanti is a laboratory for urban implosion.[2] Soleri's unusual fusion of architecture with ecology in what he calls "arcology" bans the automobile from the city in favor of pedestrian walkways aided by fixed mechanical people-movers (elevators, escalators, and moving sidewalks).[3] In a city of such complex compactness, most journeys by foot would require no more than fifteen or twenty minutes—about the same amount of time it takes to walk from inside a major mall to the outer ring of the parking lot in Phoenix or Los Angeles. In staging this controlled implosion, Soleri seeks to stabilize his community at about 350 people per acre (ten times the population density of New York City). Its ecological superiority derives from the elimination of the automobile and all the associated space costs charged off to streets, highways, parking, dealerships, fueling, repairs, and junkyards necessary to support an automotive transportation system.[4]

By rethinking the twentieth-century industrial city from the ground up, Soleri's fusion of high technology and ecological responsibility provides one of the most realistic responses to the environmental crisis—although Arcosanti is frequently derided as the misbegotten folly of a utopian dreamer. This is not merely a paper proposal. His arcological alternative is already being built and inhabited. Despite all its promise, however, much of Arcosanti's potential remains unfulfilled. There are many unresolved problems in Soleri's ecological project, casting doubt over how successfully it has been implemented in Arizona since 1970.

Soleri's Background

Paolo Soleri was born in Turin, Italy, in 1919. Educated at the Turin Polytechnical Institute, he joined Frank Lloyd Wright at Taliesin West

2. For more discussion, see Paolo Soleri, "Flight from Flatness," in *The Bridge between Matter and Spirit Is Matter Becoming Spirit: The Arcology of Paolo Soleri* (Garden City, NJ: Anchor Books, 1973), pp. 198–201.

3. Soleri uses "arcology" in many ways: to describe a method of thinking, the practice of design, an approach to environmental organization, and some actual physical structure embodying its principles. See Luca Zevi, "Paolo Soleri: A Message to Be Dug Out," *L'Architettura: Cronache e Storia* 422 (December 1990): 849–50.

4. See Paolo Soleri, *Arcology: Architecture in the Image of Man* (Cambridge, MA: MIT Press, 1973).

outside Phoenix in 1948, and along with his wife Corolyn and Mark Mills, he built Dome House near Cave Creek, Arizona—a structure closely integrated into its environment in accord with Wright's organic architecture theories. In 1950, Soleri returned to Italy, where he built a house and a studio. Soon he was commissioned by the Solimene family to design a new ceramics factory. As the factory was being constructed, Soleri became interested in the ceramic manufacturing process. Once the plant was completed in 1955, Soleri and his wife moved back to Arizona, buying five isolated acres of land in Paradise Valley outside Phoenix (about fifteen miles southwest of Wright's Taliesin West), where they began to produce ceramic and bronze objects, including the now world-renowned windbells and wind chimes that have provided most of the funds for Arcosanti's modest yearly construction budget. In 1956, Soleri also established the Cosanti Foundation as a studio, shop, and residence to produce his ceramics and, later, to articulate his architectural ideas.[5] In the 1950s and 1960s, Soleri began developing his maverick approach to reengineering the structural interfaces of the environment and society while watching Phoenix encroach on his desert homesite. After gaining notoriety in the 1960s as an ethical philosopher, social critic, and architectural visionary, he began building the Arcosanti megastructure at Cordes Junction, Arizona, in 1970. This project occupied him until his death in 2013.

The ceramics connection is not insignificant. Casting ceramic and bronze items provided the Soleris with much of their income during these early years, while the techniques used in casting ceramic artifacts also moved Soleri to experiment with them as architectural construction techniques. Soleri notes, "I began working with earth and silt in the early 1950s. Originally I became interested in using desert soil and the silt abundant in the dry Arizona riverbeds because of their inherent properties and availability. Experimentation proved the usefulness of earth and silt as molding mediums for many types of crafts projects. Clay and plaster were the first materials that we cast in earth or silt molds. We produced ceramic windbells from earth molds, and plaster architectural models from originals which had been carved in silt. The

---

5. See Francesco Ranocchi, "From a House to a Piece of City: Paolo Soleri's Ideas and Experiments," *L'Architettura: Cronache e Storia* 422 (December 1990): 856–57.

use of earth and silt for making forms on which to cast concrete was the logical next step."[6]

From 1962 to 1974, six of the structures at Cosanti were "earth cast" using river silt forms, with the help of architecture students interested in learning these unusual building techniques. According to Soleri, "Today these structures comprise the Cosanti complex, and are used as craft studios, work areas, offices, and residences. The Cosanti complex is the result of a combination of ancient craft techniques, new variations on these techniques, scrounged and donated materials, aesthetic perceptions, unorthodox architectural concepts, and the sweat of many workers."[7] The workshops moved out to the Arcosanti site during the 1970s, and much of that structure also has been built with casting techniques extrapolated from the Cosanti ceramic production process.

Most of Soleri's writings date back to the 1960s and 1970s, when he chose to engage many of the leading pop icons—Marshall McLuhan, R. Buckminster Fuller, Pierre Teilhard de Chardin, the Woodstock Nation, transcendental meditation, hippie communes—in his discussion of arcology. Today, many of these writings seem fairly anachronistic. The Teilhardian tone can be completely baffling, even though the insights derived from this bizarre philosophy are central to the project of arcology. Yet, ironically, much of what he wrote twenty or thirty years ago is only more pertinent today. Seen as a road not taken, Soleri's vision unfolds as a concise and cogent warning about how gigantic areas of scatterized urban sprawl were leading to the ecological catastrophes of today's plundered and polluted planet.

Soleri is not a philosopher for cynical postmodernists. His thinking unfolds through rigid oppositions and hard contradictions: matter and spirit, process and growth, scatterization and complexification, Alpha God and Omega God, giganticism and miniaturization. Architecture, as a mediation of "theotechnology" to realize "the urban effect" out of chaotic nature, is the means chosen by Soleri to transform humanity and realize its inner cosmic mission.[8] This approach will rankle postmodern

6. Paolo Soleri and Scott M. Davis, *Paolo Soleri's Earthcasting for Sculpture: Models and Construction* (Salt Lake City: Peregrine Smith Books, 1984).

7. Ibid., p. 4.

8. See Paolo Soleri, *The Omega Seed: An Eschatological Hypothesis* (Garden City, NJ: Anchor Books, 1981).

sensibilities because Soleri is unabashedly anthropocentric and provocative. Yet his ideas make a significant contribution to radical ecology. Few thinkers have contributed as much to understanding how the built environment, nature, social ecologies, or modern cities actually operate.

Soleri's Project

Architecture for Soleri is a vital social calling. It can lead to an ecological revolution because it is essentially an informational process rather than a material activity. Anticipating various "new materialist" streams of thought in the 2000s, he asserts that every edifice ultimately operates as an actor: "it is actually information in and of itself instead of being a remote presence."[9] This pertains to all architecture. Thus, architecture can be apprehended as much more than mere construction. According to Soleri, "Architecture is the alterations made upon nature by the organic, the psychological, the mental, the components of man's consciousness where the social-cultural stresses operate within and emanate out of the human kind. Architecture…is not only a shelter for communication and information institutions, a medium, but it is also…mass information itself."[10] Architecture materially expresses what society does. Since architecture-as-information helps constitute personality and community, "it is then only logical that the pauperization of our soul and the soul of society coincide with the pauperization of the environment. One is the cause and reflection of the other."[11] Any radical social transformation also demands a reordering not only of ideas and institutions but also of society's most basic informational technology: its architecture. According to Soleri, ecological development must be rethought as part of theological and technological evolution. Organizing spaces and designing places are an enterprise invested in "the business of sacredness." While today's urban metroplexes fall short of this task, "the discrepancy is to be seen as a gap between what ought to be and what is." Thus, correct ecological design can be directed to attain "the *Civitas Dei*. It is that complex machine for information which by the non-expedient ways of design also becomes knowledge in itself, where the media has finally, if

---

9. Ibid., p. 217. For further discussion, see Diana Coole and Samantha Frost, eds., *New Materialisms: Ontology, Agency, and Politics* (Durham, NC: Duke Univ. Press, 2010).

10. Soleri, *The Omega Seed*, p. 223.

11. Ibid., p. 225.

only within limits, sublimated itself into the message, a large interiority reverentially turned to the handling of *particulae sacrae*, the polis dwellers."[12] These are valid insights, but to reach the end of this trail Soleri rides through the strange badlands of Teilhardian eschatology.

Soleri freely and unabashedly mingles elements of theological speculation, moral outrage, construction theory, and eschatological design to advance his "metaschematics for cosmogenesis." Along with Arcosanti, arcologies represent much more than mere experimentations with alternative urban technology or subversive communitarian resistance. Arcosanti is both, but these are secondary aspects of what Soleri sees primarily as an ethical struggle for spiritual enlightenment. His architectural ideas constitute a technology for the realization of an emergent divinity from a volatile universe: "we can say that the true God is *not yet*, but the true God *will be*, because the creational process is."[13]

These claims violate many modern assumptions: matter is not dead, spirit is not merely transcendent, the universe is not a finished process, man is not a machine, god is not an abstraction. These unusual claims, in turn, are derived from Teilhard's pantheistic musings.[14] Unfortunately, Soleri's arcological turn cannot be understood independently of Teilhard's unique fusion of faith and reason in the nexus of technology and cosmogenesis. These pronouncements, like those of many "prophets," are not particularly systematic or lucid.[15] Moreover, the Teilhardian conceptual register that Soleri adopts often leaves him way out on the

12. Ibid., pp. 231–32.

13. Paolo Soleri, *Technology and Cosmogenesis* (New York: Paragon House, 1985), p. viii.

14. For more elaboration of the philosophies advanced by Teilhard, see Pierre Teilhard de Chardin, *The Phenomenon of Man* (New York: Harper and Row, 1961); Teilhard, *Building the Earth* (Wilkes-Barre, PA: Dimension Books, 1965); Teilhard, *The Appearance of Man* (New York: Harper and Row, 1965); Teilhard, *Hymn of the Universe* (New York: Harper and Row, 1965); and Teilhard, *Man's Place in Nature: The Human Zoological Group* (New York: Harper and Row, 1965).

15. A sense of what he believes about "the true God that will be" can be garnered from passages such as these: "It is a creature, a reality, that generates within itself its own transcendence. Because of its youth, most of this creature is still in 'darkness.' What generates within and issues without begins to assume the responsibility for the creation of Omega, now roughly incarnate in fragments. This Infant God, or Gods (perhaps as many as there are solar systems) are autonomously generating organisms. They are organisms generating consciousness, consciousness generating anticipations (hypotheses and simulations), anticipations instigating action, action expressing and acting out the

margins of modern political discourse, sounding very much like a crackpot. Organism, for Soleri, is the mediation of matter and spirit, where becoming slips into being and being advances becoming. Accordingly, "Organism is the mineral complacence forced into the turmoil of the organic. Organism is the relative simplicity of the early organic becoming more and more fragile, yet more and more expectant of the unpredictable. Organism is the relatively tranquil instinctual superseded by the anguish of the mental. The Infant God is restless, demanding, harsh, violent, and prodigious."[16] The "Infant God," as autonomous conscious organism, is the promotion of "mineral reality's," or matter's, evolution into "mental reality," or mind. These primal dynamics, in turn, adhere to a normative imperative and structural regularity in the universe.

Soleri's unembarrassed representation of the transcendent social *telos* in divine terms derives from Teilhard's vision of the Omega Point: a teleological target that can and will draw humanity toward its positive effects in spite of the intervening misadventures in irrationality, inequity, and irresponsibility. For Soleri, it is important to remember: "(1) God is not because God 'will be' and (2) God 'is' the urban effect. These assertions form an eschatological argument. It is absurd and/or blasphemous unless one distinguishes between that which is potential and that which is actual. Because God is not (as yet), the urban effect is not (as yet). There is an immanent urban effect that incarnates a limited divinity, the immanent God."[17] The urban effect is "the eschatological denouement of consciousness," and its origin is to be found in "the ability that appears in matter, when matter attains certain morphological properties, to become responsive to stimuli and stresses in ways that are not the norm but the exception."[18] Matter becomes spirit as it integrates complexity, miniaturization, and duration in mass-energy, leaping beyond the physical/material into the psychological/spiritual. The urban effect is to be found in every living thing, and when organized rightly, "God, the Omega Seed, is the entelechy or the urban effect."[19] The

---

manipulative and transformational power of organism. The Infant God is operational." See Soleri, *Technology and Cosmogenesis*, pp. viii–ix.

16. Ibid.

17. Paolo Soleri, *Fragments: A Selection from the Sketch Books of Paolo Soleri* (New York: Harper and Row, 1981), p. 23.

18. Ibid., p. 25.

19. Ibid., p. 86.

superpersons of the future will not be extraordinary men or women. Instead, they will be "the totalized condition of which humans are a part. A premonition of this condition is contained in the urbis. This *Civitate Dei* is not where the divine dwells; it is the divine itself. It is not the city of God; it is the God city."[20] The invention of God is vital because by inventing God humans either invent perfection or advance the perfecting process. The fine points of Soleri's engagement with Teilhard's philosophy need not be discussed here. While Soleri clearly disagrees with Teilhard at several places, he also sees his arcologies as expressions of eschatological thinking.[21]

Ecology becomes humanity's most essential science inasmuch as the earth's ecosystems are mind-generating, spirit-attaining processes in which matter becomes spirit. Aesthetic practices, or "esthetogenesis," are a key mediation of this dialectic.[22] Aesthetic imagination and artistic discipline become the vital sparks, wholly dependent upon individual labor and communal energy, animating matter with spiritual significance. Soleri's ecological thinking is grounded on what he calls the "complexity-miniaturization-duration imperative." He sees all nature "from bacteria to God" conforming to three fundamental principles: "COMPLEXITY: Many events and processes cluster wherever a living process is going on. The make-up of the process is immensely complex and ever intensifying. MINIATURIZATION: The nature of complexity demands the rigorous utilization of all resources—mass-energy and space-time, for example. Therefore, whenever complexity is at work, miniaturization is mandated and a part of the process. DURATION: Process implies extension of time. Temporal extension is warped by living stuff into acts of duration. A possible resolution of 'living time' is the metamorphosis of time into pure duration, i.e., the eventual 'living

20. Ibid.

21. More concretely, "Arcosanti tries to 'radicalize' the proposition by attempting to reinstate the working presence of complexity-miniaturization, quite probably in the best 'Teilhardian tradition.' Therefore, the 'how-ness' of Arcosanti is the quest of a more fitting instrument for the human animal to go on in the transcendental quest for grace, also, I think, a Teilhardian aim." Soleri, *Technology and Cosmogenesis*, pp. 120–21.

22. Art is the center of an ecology-environment-theology triad: "(1) The environment: immanent manifestation of an eschatological drive. (2) Religion: simulation model of anticipated perfection, space, and the fully aware divinity of a concluded reality. (3) The esthetic: emergence of the spirit from matter in specific particles of grace (a novel, a dance and so on)." Soleri, *Fragments*, p. 190.

outside of time."[23] This idiosyncratic reading of the cosmos provides a nomological code that Soleri regards as "a clear, forceful normative light for any living process to follow."[24] There is an immanent order in nature that human reason and imagination can discover. Through arcological design, Arcosanti's construction is being organized with an awareness of these norms, because all of "nature and the living are dependent on such coherence."[25]

Contrasting the sprawl of lower life-forms (coral, bacteria, mold) to the concentration of higher ones (bees, wasps, ants) in nature, Soleri regards the most successful and sophisticated forms of life, like the human city, as those allowing complexity/miniaturization/duration to coalesce. Cities are, in fact, expressions of genuine ecological balance between city and country, even though these relations have become attenuated and/or broken in the post–World War II era as non-city/non-country exurban and suburban spaces proliferate as simpler, more hypertrophic, and more transitory sprawls. Sprawl unfolds on an inhuman scale because it is fabricated for and by the automobile. This abuse of space is the sociopathic condition Soleri seeks to cure.

Point Omega, the Omega God, and the Omega Seed are presented as the *telos* of these evolutionary struggles for the divinization of the universe. Humanity, or "wo-man" in Soleri's terms, is the outcome of three billion years of life's evolution on earth. Life's creational activities are continuously generating new life-forms, struggling to realize new existences for conscious, sensitive, creative beings like human beings.[26] As with other idealist philosophies of history, humanity is the critical

23. Soleri, *Arcosanti: An Urban Laboratory?*, p. 11.
24. Ibid.
25. Ibid.
26. The thinking and doing of such conscious beings are instances of spiritual genesis: "The premise that *homo faber* is also a symbol of *cosmos faber*, the 'fabricating' the cosmos is engaged in, the cosmo-genesis that providentially is a soul genesis. The genesis of spirit is not of spirit (God) generating matter with all the ultimately inconsequential history of a dispensable process of being; it is instead matter generating spirit within the excruciatingly noble and suffering process of metamorphosis. Therefore the urgency of *doing as thinking*. Because the thinking per se—and I include in it contemplating-mediating—is the beautiful flower of a *doing* that has generated brain-mind, that 'thinking machine-performance' of immense nobility and resourcefulness at the apex of the pyramid (hierarchy) of the food chain. Without such a monumental pyramid, thinking-mediating-transcending is impossible, in fact, inconceivable." See Soleri, *Technology and Cosmogenesis*, p. 133.

mediation of the being/becoming dialectic. Soleri gives it primacy because humans are the top of the food chain, making them the crown of creation.

Here technology jibes with cosmogenesis, and Soleri's own arcological enterprise assumes its eschatological assignment. To develop humankind, there are innumerable post-biological technologies needed to accelerate these evolutionary trends. An arcology or "ecological city" is one of these vital post-biological technologies.[27] The contemporary environmental crisis arises from the corrupt values of contemporary industrial civilization or from mindless tendencies toward simplification, giganticism, and ephemerality, disrupting and dissipating the spirit and matter needed to advance these projects.

Attacking the sprawl of contemporary metroplexes with all of their self-destructive tendencies, then, becomes a spiritual crusade to be waged by divinely charged design theory, engineering innovations, and communal revitalization. Sprawl violates the complexity/miniaturization/duration commandments of cosmogenesis; arcology can fulfill them "in such a way as to cause matter to transcend itself."[28] It registers this power because arcologies are engines of "the urban effect" or mediations of "the transformation of mineral matter into mind via the potentially unlimited power of complexification and miniaturization."[29] To invent "the idea-city" of arcology is to reinvent the ordered housing of mass-energy "capable of *serving* and *ex-pressing* what might be called the transpersonal consciousness of the society, the cultural-theological-creating genesis."[30] From the esthetogenesis implied by the urban effect, Soleri holds that the ideals of the good life will be produced: synergy, beauty, frugality, knowledge, compassion, interdependence, sensitivity, transcendence, cooperation. So along with the urban effect, cosmogenesis becomes being.[31]

---

27. Ibid., p. 19.
28. Ibid., p. 20.
29. Soleri, *Arcosanti: An Urban Laboratory?*, p. 92.
30. Soleri, *Technology and Cosmogenesis*, p. 20.
31. Ibid., p. 139. Human society, when rightly housed and morally aware, will be intent upon "the extrusion of meaning, lasting meaning, out of a mineral (mass-energy) reality, powerfully but not fatally swaying the conscience generating within it.... [T]he fruition would be the seed of the Cosmos, the Omega Seed, and within it the

The Arcological Effect

The theological twist in Soleri's thought is tied, by virtue of his reflections on the nature of life and consciousness, to ecology and technology. The genetic patterns of the Omega Seed show that *"in any given system, the most complex quantum is also the liveliest; in any given system the liveliest quantum is also the most miniaturized."*[32] To the extent that human beings make and are made by their environments, Soleri proposes to rationalize the processes of their evolution. The ends of complexity, vitality, and miniaturization must be kept in mind as societies design their habitats, because it puts them in a much better position to solve many of the most pressing environmental problems. Arcology follows these principles and captures all of the beneficial payoffs of six major architectural "effects." While they are simple, they also provide a remarkable solution for many environmental problems:

> The *greenhouse effect* is a membrane that seals off an area of ground that can be cultivated, extending the growing season to practically twelve months, and also saves a great amount of water.... With the "greenhouse," one has intensive agriculture, limited use of water and extension of seasonal cycles. This is the *horticultural effect.* Then there is the *apse effect.* Some structures can take in the benign radiation of the sun in the winter months, and tend to cut off the harsh radiation of the sun in the summer. By the *chimney effect,* which is connected with the greenhouse effect, one can convey, passively, energy through the movement of air; the heat from one area to another. So we have these four effects: there is also the capacity of masonry to accumulate and store energy—the *heat sink effect.* With relatively large masonry, one can store energy during the warm hours of the day, and give it out during cool or cold hours of the night. The intent is to see if these five effects can be organized around what I call the urban effect. The *urban effect* is the capacity of mineral matter, to become lively, sensitive, responsive, memorizing.... If we were to coordinate those six effects together, then we definitely could save on resources like land, water, time, energy, materials, and have a better ecological sanity.[33]

---

resurrection/manifestation of all and everything. *That is the end of time and the full dominion of duration."*

32. Ibid., p. 136 (italics in original).

33. Ibid., pp. 137–38.

Arcological structures can harness all these effects by suspending the two-dimensional explosion of urban areas in a new three-dimensional implosion of urban structures. Radically reconceptualizing individual houses, towns, and cities as social aggregates with immanent rational potentials, instead of seeing them as personal real estate attached to social irrationalities, is extremely difficult. But it is possible: "Arcosanti is an ongoing process pursuing the urban effect within the context of the other five effects."[34]

The arcology is pure ecological transformation in that it seeks to harmonize cities as "a biomental organism contained in a mineral structure" with their biophysical environments.[35] The scatterization of automobile/railway/streetcar urbanization is attacked by miniaturizing the logistics of energy and matter into superdense structures. Soleri believes these systems will check the degenerative decline of cities by reducing the waste of energy, material, time, and labor used to maintain their irrational and anti-ecological forms. Moreover, the concentration of inhabitants should also promote the integration of different ethnic, racial, age, and religious groups. Health care would be easier to deliver, housing would be accessible to all, and cultural development would characterize the public life of the arcological city. Similarly, good land would be freed for agricultural, forestry, and recreational uses in the areas surrounding the arcological megastructures with their now much higher residential densities.

Arcologies are not improbable utopias. As Soleri observes, the naval architecture of today's passenger ships is very closely related: "the common characteristics are compactness and definite boundary; the functional fullness of an organism designed for the care of many, if not most, of man's needs; a definite and unmistakable three dimensionality.... [T]he liner, the concept of it, can open up and, retaining its organizational suppleness, become truly a 'machine for living,' that is to say, a physical configuration that makes man physically free."[36] This analogy is exploited in several proposed arcologies, including Novanoah I (a city for 400,000 to float in coastal waters or on the open sea), Novanoah II (a city for 2,400,000 also to ply some ocean expanse), Noahbabel (a

---

34. Ibid., p. 139.
35. Soleri, *Arcology: Architecture in the Image of Man*, p. 122.
36. Ibid., p. 14.

city of 90,000 to be fixed in the sea off of some coastal setting), and Babelnoah (a city of 6,000,000 for a flat coastal region).[37] Of course, all these imaginary cities, which are little more than sketches published twenty-five years ago, have never been drawn in detail or planned on a full scale, although they substantiate Soleri's analogy between large passenger ships and arcological cities.[38] Only one of his smallest designs, Arcosanti, has gone from the drafting table to the construction site, but all of its masses are arranged to express the six effects that arcologies must exploit.

Soleri's Problems

In one way or another, like many teleological theories of history before it, Soleri's project almost presumes the preexistence of God cities and God citizens in order to make them come into being. Living amid a culture that obviously accepts, if not openly chooses to produce, urbanization on the order of the obscene metropolitan sprawl found in Atlanta, Dallas, Los Angeles, Houston, or Phoenix, Soleri slogs forward at Arcosanti with a handful of true believers sharing a vision of the ecological sense of his project. Content with casting windbells and evangelizing the few tourists who show up everyday for tours of Cosanti and Arcosanti, these faithful few perhaps already live Soleri's esthetogenetic life, transforming brass into bells and concrete into a city. By and large, however, they are young, transient, and enthusiastic residents of a place that lacks any economic or social function beyond demonstrating the possible truth of Soleri's imagination to a civilization that denies them daily in everything it does. Although its chambers of commerce are more than willing to promote visits to Arcosanti in hotel lobby flyers and travel magazine write-ups if it brings more visitors to experience

37. Ibid., pp. 36–61.
38. Ibid. pp. 62–118. Once these urban images are made plausible as extrapolations of ocean liners to ocean cities, Soleri articulates other designs for many different land-based sites: Arcoforte (a city of 20,000 on a sea cliff), Babel II A (a city of 800,000 on marsh land), Arcvillage I (a farming community of 9,000 near good farm land), Logology (a city of 900,000 for hilly flood plains), Arckibuz (a desert village for 2,500), Arcollective (a cold region village of 2,000), Veladiga (a city in or as a river dam for 15,000), Stonebow (a bridge city of 200,000 to be built over or in a large canyon), and, for the ultimate architectural challenge, Asteromo (a city of 70,000 to be build in outer space).

the region's many anti-ecological lifestyles, the state of Arizona also has done very little to advance Soleri's ideas.

The almost unreal ephemerality and wastefulness of everyday life in cities such as Phoenix act as a strong boundary condition, constraining efforts to make something like Arcosanti from becoming real. With the informational revolution, many might even argue convincingly that Soleri's arcologies are obsolete technologies for advancing the urban effect. Given the new media, such as cable television, mobile personal telephony, global satellite-based communication, and personal computers, two-dimensional scatterized sprawl can emulate three-dimensional complexity—now even on a global level.[39] "Cybertectures" are displacing "architectures," dooming Soleri's arcological dreams to sink into the telematic rifts of transnational infostructures. If complexification can advance informatically, then why bother with material manifestations in architectural megastructures? Miniaturization is better measured in bytes and gigaflops, not in square meters or population densities. Soleri, of course, objects. In his mind, informationalization makes arcologies even more necessary and desirable. If informational technology is misapplied to the partial rationalization of scatterization, it will only postpone the collapse as it aggravates their consequences. Nonetheless, in some respects, informationalization does begin to sublate the arcological effect, enabling one to treat the entire planet—when it has many mature infostructures up and running at some point in the future—as one gigantic arcological megastructure on the informational plane.

For a totalitarian civilization that mystifies its totalitarianism in the ideologies of choice, liberation, and convenience, Soleri's urban experiment can be explained away as a communitarian nightmare: an environmentalist's anthill where no one can have a car, plant a lawn, or build their "own" house because the Master Builder as Founding Legislator has deemed them all to be evil. He is probably right, but this sort of right guy has been finishing last in modern industrial cultures for three hundred years.[40] At best, as a real estate enterprise, Arcosanti

39. See Timothy W. Luke, "Informationalism and Ecology," *Telos* 56 (Summer 1983): 59–73, reprinted in this volume.

40. For a mix of these kinds of readings, see M. Basil Pennington, "Arcosanti Monastery No. 1," *America* 144, no. 10 (March 14, 1981): 207–9; "A Dream City, or a Ghost Town?," *Newsweek*, March 23, 1981, p. 14; Naomi M. Bloom, "Human Beehives: Paolo Soleri's Arcosanti," *Science Digest*, March 1981, pp. 42–47; Susan Hazen-Hammond,

may only occupy another small niche in the immense food chain of Arizona's other consumer-segmented lifestyle villages, such as Sun City and Green Valley for oldsters, Scottsdale and Oro Valley for transient yuppies, or Ahwatukee and Chandler for young families. For New Age ecological dreamers at the tail end of the psychodemographic distribution, who might otherwise settle for a New Age 1960s aura in Bisbee or Jerome, Arizona also has Arcosanti. But as real estate, Arcosanti is also utterly illogical in the capitalist space economy of place valorization and devalorization. As a devotion to permanence, no current business categories can deal with it. Its projected horizon for economic life is off of the ten- to fifty-year scale of amortization used in America to mortgage real estate. Compared to a city like Phoenix, where blocks and blocks of 1970s-era dream houses already are turning into slums, while other blocks and blocks of 1950s-era postwar "mid-century modern" ranch houses are being gutted and then rehabbed to sell the razzle-dazzle of Space Race America to those upmarket millennials not overburdened by student debt and eager for shorter commutes, Arcosanti is irrational. Arizona's entire political economy is based on rapid cycles of growth and decay, while Arcosanti is predicated on ripening slowly as a no-growth society.

In some ways, a Phoenix or a Los Angeles—in their full-blown 1945–90 Cold War forms—typifies the urban form in an era of thermonuclear confrontation. Spreading out from the ground zero of downtown government centers or central business districts, which lack any authentic "downtown" or "uptown" urban vitality, these urbanized conglomerations are thin accretions of impermanent structures operating under the menacing shadows of intense thermonuclear explosion. Lacking any civic center holding them together, such places have gained

"Mecca or Mirage?," *Discovery*, Summer 1985; Arthur Frommer, "A Pilgrimage to Arcosanti," in *The New World of Travel* (New York: Prentice Hall, 1988), pp. 272–75; Paul Weingarten, "Futuristic City: A Radical Vision Still Out of Focus," *Chicago Tribune*, July 10, 1988; Leonard David, "Paolo Soleri: Man for All Seasons," *Ad Astra* 1 (November 1989): 31; Jane Dodds, "Paolo Soleri," *Art in America* 78 (November 1990): 201; John Poppy, "Home, Sweet Home, 2001-Style," *Longevity*, May 1991, pp. 50–60; "Paolo Soleri's Arcology: Updating the Prognosis," interview by Philip Arcidi, *Progressive Architecture*, March 1991, pp. 76–78; Mark Pastin, "For Selfish Reasons, Arizonans Should Look Again to Arcosanti," *Business Journal*, May 20, 1991; David W. Dunlap, "Future Metropolis," *Omni*, October 1984, pp. 116–24.

their social identity mainly in and from televisual images. Nightly news broadcasts, detailing the murders, ballgames, and rainfall occurring within their borders, create a sense of "the Valley of the Sun" or "L.A.," but, for the most part, there still is "no there, there." Built around the high-technology industries used to construct the thermonuclear delivery systems of the federal state, their communities have been continuously deconstructed by Cold War anomie and superpower angst, reducing them to settled assemblies of megadeaths awaiting Soviet megatonnage, which in the meantime provide the televisual settings for police-state morality plays, such as *Dragnet*, *CHiPs*, *Baywatch*, or *Cops*. In a sense, they are cities where the bomb already has dropped, leaving a uniformly drab collection of rubble where communities of isolated atomized people scurry from flimsy shelters to clogged streets to dilapidated commercial strips to abusive workplaces stretching for hundreds and hundreds of square miles. Only an H-bomb could destroy them, but perhaps only an H-bomb-centered political economy likewise could create such "urbanized" places without leaving any semblance of a city within their "city limits."

At the same time, Arcosanti now is languishing because it does need a political economy to operate: an entire industry to sustain it, a real community to build it, a living society to maintain it by putting all its energies into its realization. Although Soleri argues that a city is essentially an informational construct, Arcosanti proves how limiting an informational economy can be, particularly if it has only two product lines: windbells and tourism. Now, at best, it is a prophet's manor or a monastic order's abbey, but not a city.[41] Lacking more complex ties to

---

41. The grip of a monastic allure in Soleri's thinking is quite strong. In *Technology and Cosmogenesis*, he writes: "One of the paradoxes of spirituality is that it is bound to (generated by) materiality and there, at the critical hinge of matter converting into spirit is Monakos.... Monakos, at least the Monakos, goes about the business of reality with a firm grip, at times a self-destructive vise, on body-and-soul. It is a quickening of the body in direct touch with the raw physical-physiological make-do; a quickening of the soul that is none other than the quickened body transcending the physiological splendor it embodies, the uninterrupted miracle of the self-transcending food chain. In this context of a spirituality locked in the sweat of the flesh, the techno-logy of evolution, I am going to elaborate on the environmental-architectural (arc-ology) work leading to Arcosanti and beyond" (Soleri, *Technology and Cosmogenesis*, pp. 133–34). The practice of building Arcosanti, therefore, becomes for Soleri a "neomonastic proposition" to counterbalance material consumerism with mental transcendence. "To keep things in

many industries, most markets, or more information, it cannot really become a city. It is only a house of ideas, and it may well become a ruin once the idea man is gone. Something rising on the scale of Arcosanti really requires a corporate or state agency to raise the capital, labor, and materials to make it operate, but under current conditions neither Arizona nor Soleri will allow this to happen. So in his own cosmogenetic terms, Soleri's city is simply a mineral structure lacking the biomental organism to sustain it. An intentional community of fifty or sixty has been created over the years to occupy it, but its spaces were planned to hold 5,000 or 6,000 people. To the extent that it has attracted only one percent of its ideal population, Arcosanti is a failure even as a monastic community.

The scale of a Soleri arcology reveals much about its inner contradictions. Cities are communities of people cohabiting in the same space and time. They typically start small and grow larger, although some have been planned to begin large and remain relatively stable (Reston, Virginia, or Columbia, Maryland) or begin larger and become quite grand (Washington, DC, Canberra, Brasilia, or New Delhi). Corporate capital and municipal law would be more than able to adapt to arcological criteria if the popular desire for building such spaces could be created. However, the pictures of suburban domesticity vended to modern families for over a century militate against the images of arcological living proffered by Soleri. In fact, the rhetoric of its presentation is very monastic. Unfortunately, even for those few willing to listen, it is excessively monastic. The stale auras of an architectural student practicum, grad student poverty, and holier-than-thou frugality as the moral basis of life at Arcosanti are extremely alienating for the average consumer. It flashes back to 1960s counterculture communes left behind during "the revolution" rather than moving forward to the practical necessities of 1990s ecological reality.

---

balance," he concludes, one can find in monastic models some important values, such as "tradition, learning, intellectual rigor, humility, frugality, altruism, self-discipline and transcendence," which are things "not to dismiss nonchalantly" (Soleri, *Arcosanti: An Urban Laboratory?*, p. 77). Almost fifty years later, the Arcosanti website notes, "There are about 60 adults and children who currently call Arcosanti home year around and this population greatly increases during our workshop season." See "Who Are the Arcosanti Builders," Arcosanti website, https://arcosanti.org/about/arcosanti-builders/.

Soleri's arcological speculations are an ecological manifesto, but would they work as planned? In them, Soleri is recoiling from the destruction of habitat caused by the growth of contemporary cities. His anthill cities have been maligned for their anthill qualities, but he really has changed only a couple of assumptions in urban design, moving, first, from automobile to pedestrian transport and, second, from building many ministructures to constructing a few megastructures. These changes, however, might not radically alter the city's ecological imprint on the countryside. A million people in an arcology may not be more ecologically viable, because a modern city is merely the material manifestation of many different global flows intersecting at one particular site. Soleri prematurely attributes many environmental problems to the shape of the city's architectural nexus with nature—the city as material structure/real estate/geographical site. Much could change, and undoubtedly even be improved, in arcologies of his design, but he is naive in believing that what exists now is not also an arcology—only of a highly deviant type. Destructive global flows of capital, labor, energy, material, and ideas might just as well, or even more easily, circulate through his arcological structures, altering only a few local ecologies and not significantly improving global environmental imbalances.[42]

Soleri's arcological designs also fly directly in the face of many contemporary environmentalists' notions of living in harmony with nature. He openly admits that nine or ten billion people, or double the planet's current population, could inhabit the earth if only its urban infrastructure could be arcologized to fit his specifications.[43] This is not the picture of "sustainable ecological development" envisioned by most of today's greens. He also remains very eclectic about his proposed sites of construction. Building tremendous megastructures over undeveloped canyons, in river courses, or along cliff regions is not the aesthetic of frugality and appropriateness followed by deep ecology, ecofeminism, or even social ecology. The public benefits of following Soleri's path to ecological frugality ultimately might prove to be very satisfying even to

42. For more discussion of these flows, see Robert Reich, *The Work of Nations: Preparing Ourselves for 21st-Century Capitalism* (New York: Knopf, 1989); and David Harvey, *The Condition of Postmodernity: An Enquiry into the Origins of Cultural Change* (Oxford: Blackwell, 1989).

43. See Soleri, *Arcology: Architecture in the Image of Man.*

some radical ecologists, but his methods have inappropriate technology written all over them inasmuch as he calmly plans for a doubling in the earth's population.

Arcosanti is not a complete arcology; it is at best a fragment of a future yet to come. In fact, many Arcosantis as greenplexes for ecologically inclined consumers could even be built within the current frameworks without even rippling most of its anti-ecological qualities. Only if scores of arcologies on the scale of Novanoah II (2,400,000 inhabitants), Babelnoah (population 6,000,000), or Logology (900,000 citizens) were being built all over the planet would the arcology be considered a working idea. By remaining trapped in the spiritualistic echo chambers of 1960s consciousness-raising, Arcosanti has failed to anticipate many of the most significant global changes in the 1990s. Its New Age auras have eclipsed its inhabitants' abilities to adapt Arcosanti's ecological lessons to the new times of post-Fordist informationalism.

The political economy of Arcosanti today, then, is neither tremendously political nor remarkably economic. Instead of building a city with many of its citizens already in place, this "urban laboratory" has become more of a rural retreat from the Sun Belt frenzy of Phoenix for Soleri and his coworkers. Sitting so close to I-17, a major north-south route from Phoenix to the Grand Canyon, Arcosanti has become just another roadside attraction, starring Soleri and his followers as the funky inhabitants of a bizarre living history village from the 1960s. Whereas Williamsburg features fragments of the past dressed up by the present as American history, Arcosanti presents fragments of a future that get dressed down by curious tourists from the present as a fascinating but failed expression of the Age of Aquarius. For fifty years, twenty-something dropouts have been casting windbells, baking organic muffins, leading instructional tours, or raising concrete walls at Arcosanti. Instead of creating his city, Soleri has established a neomonastic habitat. Like Williamsburg's tasteful simulation of English colonial life under the Hanoverian kings, Arcosanti too is an artful simulation, only it remains stuck upon memorializing what might have been had some of the Woodstock Nation taken power. It is a nice place to do workshops, as the frequent customers in its Elderhostel, silt-casting seminar, and New Age concert businesses prove. But most people would not want to live there. Thus it serves unwittingly as a vivid affirmation of everything that modern consumerism associates with the "small is beautiful" and "voluntary simplicity" philosophies of the 1960s—living at the dead-end of a dirt road in the desert amid the ruins of a commune to handicraft windbells and print manifestos to sell to carloads of Japanese tourists.

Not surprisingly, the capital accumulation dynamics of this quasi-manorial economy are almost nil. Arcosanti's annual construction budget is about $200,000, much less than what Phoenix suburbanites will shell out for a single-family house down the road from Cosanti in Paradise Valley. Arizona's population almost doubled from 1970 to 1995, but Arcosanti's 50 or 60 permanent residents are barely one percent of the 5,000 to 6,000 citizens Arcosanti had planned to house by now. The ecological credo of Arcosanti is the cause of this steady state in its economy. Seventy miles south, Phoenix is a growth machine that has mushroomed from 150,000 people in 1945 to 3.5 million in 1995 by treating both architecture and environment as disposable personal commodities. Housing is the engine of its growth machine because it is something tossed together in sixty days out of chipboard, two-by-fours, and spray-on stucco on tiny lots jammed together near a golf course, playground, or shopping mall. People live in it for five or six years, then resell it to move up and further out. Sold and resold for fifty or sixty years, it ends its economic life as a freeway teardown, in a barrio, or simply abandoned in the urban core. Huge amounts of water, electricity, and material resources are needed to keep this home habitable in Phoenix, all of which come from outside the Valley of the Sun at unsustainable rates. Still, there has been constant growth for five decades by reproducing the same cycles over and over. This new "sixth C," or construction, is what keeps the Arizona lifestyle rolling. Without it, the state would become the backwater that it was before this political economy was invented in the 1940s—underpopulated, economically stagnant, and politically insignificant as it pursued the traditional "five Cs" of citrus, cotton, cattle, climate, and copper in a semi–Third World extractive economy.

If this growth machine is both Arizona and America, then Arcosanti is un-Arizonan and anti-American through and through. Something that lasts for generations, some place that is ecologically sustainable, some community that is rooted in the environment is not part of the contemporary lifestyle in Arizona or America. Soleri cannot succeed, because everything he regards as ecological failure in the particular society he inhabits is also the *sine qua non* of its irrational but real economic prosperity. Still, this stark juxtaposition of Phoenix and Arcosanti must be studied in great detail. It is one of today's quintessential confrontations of anti-ecology with ecology. From the opposition and antagonism of these competing urban forms, much can be learned.

Conclusions

At the end of the day, Soleri and Arcosanti are a contradictory proposition. There is much to be discovered here among his theoretical insights as well as from his city's practical setbacks. Various ideologies and utopias freely intermingle in everything he has achieved. At first glance, Soleri's utopian arcologies often seem the wish dreams of a civilization yet to be realized. However, they can also be seen as ideological fictions for stabilizing many myths in the present social order. These ideological qualities are the most vexing product of his work.

First and foremost, Arcosanti might be regarded as just another techno-fix for the problems plaguing contemporary industrial civilization. Even though it is dressed up in the garb of theological celebration, a Soleri arcology is a tremendous megamachine dedicated to rationalizing the metabolism of urban economies and societies by building bigger to last longer. Each arcology rests on a design for concentrating the production/consumption/circulation/administration of commodities in the bowels of an immense megastructure, while arraying the spaces for residences, schools, entertainments, and the arts on its top or along the exteriors, like some super luxury steamer permanently run aground on earth. Thus, once again, rational design and logical construction on a gigantic scale by a world-historical genius are represented as the only path for the ecological salvation of society. Actually, this project has been stunted by being so closely held. It really needs to be opened up to popular feedback and community input to succeed.

Second, Arcosanti comes off as an architectural concretization of the vanguard schema of enlightened rule. Left to their own devices, the citizens of Arizona, America, or the world apparently will accept a Phoenix, Los Angeles, Lagos, or Mexico City as their habitat. Regrettably, such urban forms are an ugly urban sprawl, polluted, disorderly, overpopulated, inefficient. To survive this chaos, Soleri intones, this civilization needs new leadership: rational enlightened visionary guidance from above. Missing a sacred element in its secular hustle for progress and fun, this civilization could also use a higher purpose, like enacting the cosmogenetic realization of some God-force in human history. In other words, Soleri's arcology occasionally smacks of some desert despotism, albeit virtuous and enlightened, but not terribly unlike those that have already crashed and burned elsewhere during the twentieth century. The arcological project is not tremendously detailed, but what appears on paper already is highly overdetermined. The architect, as master builder, will dictate the shape and function of space down to the 1,000 to 2,000 square feet each family will receive.[44] There, and only there, like passengers on a ship or slaves on a plantation, might personal desires be accommodated and expressed. The thorny questions of real property law, private ownership of wealth, and public corporate organization, which are the material forces actually driving the contemporary city, are essentially ignored in this totalizing vision of ecological order. Inasmuch as legal and economic issues are neglected in Soleri's grand architectural design, one sees a major reason for its pathetic record as a working human settlement.

Third, Arcosanti could be dismissed as a true utopia—it is a "non-place" because it is no place. Plunked down in the middle of nowhere, with no industries, little arable land, few transportation links, minimal scenic attractions, and hardly any people, why would anyone want to live there? Everything about it, even if it were completed, signals that it is the negative antithesis of all that is, rightly or wrongly, regarded as life-affirming in the scatterized metroplex. You can lead millions of horses to this water, but very few of them will drink. Cosmogenesis in the Arizona desert will lose out every time when put up against plain old technogenesis in Houston, plutogenesis in New York City, or esthetogenesis in San Francisco. If Arcosanti did not exist, it might almost be necessary to invent it to reaffirm the virtues of the vices that Soleri decries in cities like Phoenix and Los Angeles. The multiple myths of mobility, fun, pleasure, power, and convenience that contemporary consumerism

---

44. For echoes of this vision of aesthetic dictatorship, see the writings of Soleri's American teacher, Frank Lloyd Wright, including his *An Organic Architecture: The Architecture of Democracy* (London: Lund, Humphries, 1939); *When Democracy Builds* (Chicago: Univ. of Chicago Press, 1945); and *The Natural House* (New York: Horizon Press, 1954).

thrives on are assuredly false promises, especially when viewed from an ecological perspective. Yet they are believed, so they become true. Arcosanti's misfortune, ironically, is to serve as tangible proof of the utopian alternative's undesirability by showing itself as an ideology based on immobility, labor, pain, powerlessness, and inconvenience.

The complexity and energy of the urban effect are real. Glimpses of it can be gained from midtown Manhattan, Chicago's Michigan Avenue, downtown Boston, or San Francisco's Market Street. However, most of these complex energies are generated by major corporations, large banks, and big governments. The arcological challenge is how to capture and concentrate these effects in more popular forms of municipal commonwealth or urban communitarianism without succumbing to Soleri's utopian ecologism. Soleri professes to have no preconceived plans about how to organize the civic administration of his arcologies. Instead, he believes they are like pianos upon which almost any kind of music could be played by the societies that acquire them. This metaphor is alluring, but it overlooks how directly any arcology, like a piano, must express the collective values and personal tastes of those who invent and build it. It takes a complex society to build a piano, and only particular types of social individuals can, in turn, play highly complicated and varied kinds of music on this instrument. Thus far, Arcosanti has failed as a city by not accounting for this essential civil element in its designs; not only must the piano be built, so too must players be trained, listeners educated, concertos composed, concert halls designed, and piano factories constructed for "piano playing" to succeed.

Fourth, in casting arcological invention as an anti-urban return to nature, Soleri picks the fight (out of some sense of purity) that cannot be won and passes on the battles that must be won (on the basis of practicality) in the existing city. By presenting the arcological alternative as one more futurology for tomorrow, by setting his new megastructures into fantastic unspoiled bioregions, he ignores the possibilities for materially improving all of today's existing arcologies already failing their inhabitants now on site in large cities. Instead of reimagining urban infrastructures from the ground up on new unspoiled sites, why not push people toward thinking about arcologically retrofitting existing cities? Phoenix easily could become a series of smaller, interconnected arcological structures, allowing the return of the desert, the river bottoms, or even the citrus groves it has annihilated with unchecked suburbia over the past five decades. Rather than avoiding real battles over contemporary styles of land use, shelter construction, property creation, habitat destruction, and urban culture by retreating to a utopia in the desert, why not join in the political struggle to redefine everyday life by pushing all existing scatterized arcologies to shed much of their irrationality in becoming more like Soleri's idealized concentrated arcologies? Over the past twenty-five years, huge malls and commercial projects occupying much more land than many of Soleri's designs have been built very rapidly in Phoenix. Indeed, large tracts of land from federal reassignments of property, failed commercial developments, or dead-and-gone 1950s shopping malls have become available for arcological experimentation in Phoenix. But these opportunities for real transformative experimentation with the structures of a thoroughly anti-ecological city have been lost for the lack of a Solerian arcological will, imagination, or desire.

Fifth, Soleri's fairly impoverished categories of critique chalk up the two-dimensional sprawl of a Phoenix, Los Angeles, or Houston to the effects of one technology—the automobile. On one level, this analysis is correct, but remarkably incomplete. In fact, one might argue more effectively that these sorts of cities grew hand-in-hand with the development of the interventionist federal state during the Cold War era. The economies of these Sun Belt urban sprawls were deeply embedded in the high-technology astronautical, aircraft, and electronics industries that rested at the heart of the Fordist American defense economy. Such cities also were made possible by federal subsidies to interstate highway construction for their transportation grids, to hydroelectric dam construction for their electricity and water supplies, to cheap residential construction for their housing stock, and to corporate agribusiness construction for their food and fiber needs. The automobile, air-conditioning, and the mass media provided the requisite technologies to move people and goods, maintain climate-controlled habitats, and organize the thoughts and desires of millions of people moving into such cities from all over the nation almost overnight to live and work in an entirely new form of urbanized space. Yet, like the national regime that made these urbanisms possible, these urbanized concentrations of population largely lack any real organic community, localistic particularity, or democratic grounding. Such sprawls are simply temporary housings or transitory habitats for thousands of families moving from place to place by corporate directive or governmental design to sustain the federally funded growth machines of the Cold War economy. Now, as the military goods once produced in helicopter plants, aircraft factories, and missile installations in Phoenix, Los Angeles, and Houston are no longer in demand, and the federal largesse that built the dams, highways, and suburbs making such places possible is drying up, these two-dimensional cities face severe new challenges simply to survive.

The concentration of population and production in compact mega-structures, as Soleri proposes, might well be a highly rational response to the post–Cold War political economy of flexible accumulation. Cities no longer can count on major subsidies from higher national authorities to pay for inefficient transportation systems, inhospitable housing tracts, and expensive water supply systems. To respond to the demands of global rather than national modes of high-technology production, cities will need compact, flexible, inexpensive spaces for offices and factories close to their population centers. Reducing everyday frictions caused by the urban sprawl, traffic gridlock, and social decay embedded in the automobile-based Cold War city's civil engineering systems and architecture will require radical innovations. Building variants of Soleri's arcological settlements might be a step toward adapting to the realities of the transnational economies of post-Fordism.

The isolated personalities and atomized families of Cold War–era suburbia, however, do not foster the sort of social individuality needed to commit any individual's life or every family's fortunes to the permanent civic commitment of constructing an arcology. Yet a real communitarian alliance or an authentic popular commonwealth tied to similar communities through a genuinely federal form of self-government could launch the reconstruction of existing urban areas as ecologically sound and architecturally enduring arcologies. Arcologies require a new form of state, rooted in the practices of popular communal governance. Populist commonwealths might generate more rational relations of production and consumption better suited to constructing such arcological cities. In turn, the urban effects of these arcologies could charge new populist commonwealths with tremendous vitality and creativity.[45]

45. See Timothy W. Luke, "Community and Ecology," *Telos* 88 (Summer 1991): 69–79, reprinted in this volume.

In spite of all these reservations, however, the positive utopian energies of Soleri's work should be acknowledged. Soleri must be praised for the innovative hints he provides to those now rethinking the dynamics of human ecology. Apart from the odd Teilhardian foundations of his reasoning, he calls for a reconceptualization of how extensive the human impact on the environment already has been. Arcologies already exist, but they work in scatterized, megalopolistic, inefficient forms, wasting energy, material, and lives in an ongoing degradation of all human and nonhuman life on the planet.

Despite the fantastic qualities of many of Soleri's arcological proposals, there are workable ideas for communities of 2,000, 20,000, or even 200,000 inhabitants in his visionary designs. The first reaction of many to Soleri's ideas is disbelief: "it can't happen here," "too big, it won't work," "nothing like this can exist." But, some stand-alone megastructures, such as the Pentagon, the World Trade Center, the Omni in Atlanta, and many other mixed-use "live, work, play" galleria-type mega-malls rising all across North America, have been built—each one on many more acres than Arcosanti—by this society, even if the existing corporate relations of production often pervert them to fulfill essentially anti-ecological uses. Moreover, every existing urbanization in the world today is a failed three-dimensional arcology consumed by the crises of two-dimensional urban systems. Popular movements and/or existing communities could choose to follow arcological ideas, as Soleri has been testing them at Arcosanti, in new attempts to build a more ecological society. In the post–Cold War world, which apparently needs some new transcendent purpose for maintaining any focused collective action, building arcological cities could provide larger goals for successive generations of people. Getting the other 5,900 people that Soleri has needed for twenty-five years to set up house at Arcosanti might be a measure of progress for this one neomonastic complex. But mobilizing these thousands of arcological activists to build one, two, three, many Arcosantis elsewhere around the country would be immensely more important as the first steps toward developing an urban civilization for a new communitarian populism.

6

Searching for Alternatives:
Postmodern Populism and Ecology

Informationalism, Populism, and Ecology

RECENT SHIFTS IN the world economy are undercutting today's existing macroenvironments still populated by suburban consumers, which raises prospects for new populists to rethink the institutions of American federalism and corporate capitalism. As corporate downsizing and government cutbacks renege on the social contracts hammered out over the past century as industrial democracy, the new entrepreneurial economy of independent subcontracting, temp workers, and structural underemployment, emerging now as post-Fordist informationalism, is forcing many to rethink old communitarian ideas, which were last seriously entertained by the populists. In the transformations being wrought by post-Fordist informationalization, radical changes "can be translated or transcoded into a narrative account in which agents of all sizes and dimensions are at work."[1] New political spaces are now coming into being, inhabited by new agents that are neither statist nor corporate.

This postmodern condition may signal the rise of "a new social system beyond classical capitalism"[2] on both local and global levels. As

---

* Originally published in *Telos* 103 (Spring 1995): 87–110.
1. Fredric Jameson, *Postmodernism, or the Cultural Logic of Late Capitalism* (Durham, NC: Duke Univ. Press, 1991), p. 408.
2. Ibid., pp. 54, 59.

David Harvey argues, this new social system is developing on the ruins of Fordist regimes of industrial production, capital accumulation, and state intervention formed during the 1930s through the 1970s in national welfare states. Since the 1970s, a new regime of flexible accumulation has emerged in loosely coupled transnational alliances of local market centers, factory concentrations, technology innovators, capital pools, and public administrators.

Out of this mix, transnational firms produce world cars, global hamburgers, planetary pants, or earth shoes from nowhere and anywhere to sell everywhere, making a travesty of either nationalist campaigns to "Buy American" or xenophobic reactions to resist "Americanization." Like Chernobyl, "America" as an economic formation, mass culture, or ecological system is everywhere. It is no longer simply the substance of a nation-state or an ethno-national population. It has become the harbinger of a new consciousness as well as a mode of production at the nucleus of a global chain reaction. As it melts down to its most critical mass, the fallout is changing life everywhere. Spatial barriers and time zones collapse in the compression of multinational capital's acceleration of global production. As Harvey observes, "flexible accumulation typically exploits a wide range of seemingly contingent geographical circumstances and reconstitutes them as structured internal elements of its own encompassing logic.... The result has been the production of fragmentation, insecurity, and ephemeral uneven development within a highly unified global space economy of capital flows."[3]

Within such a context, Jean-François Lyotard's vision of performativity may be what anchors the disorganized regime following classical economic liberalism. Today, "the State and/or company must abandon the idealist and humanist narratives of legitimation in order to justify the new goal: in the discourse of today's financial backers of research, the only credible goal is power. Scientists, technicians, and instruments are purchased not to find truth, but to augment power."[4] The New Class elites hiding behind these codes of performativity are

---

3. David Harvey, *The Condition of Postmodernity: An Enquiry into the Origins of Cultural Change* (Oxford: Blackwell, 1989), pp. 294, 296.

4. Jean-François Lyotard, *The Postmodern Condition: A Report on Knowledge*, trans. Geoff Bennington and Brian Massumi (Minneapolis: Univ. of Minnesota Press, 1984), p. 46.

global, not regional, local, or even national.[5] On the other hand, new agencies from beneath the nation-state and outside big business now stress the viability of local communities, immediate environments, and regional commerce against the designs of large national bureaucracies. The cultural dominance of post-Fordist informationalism marks one of the most basic forces at work in the current world system, which is also marked by "the moment of the multinational network...a moment in which not merely the older city but even the nation-state itself has ceased to play a central functional and formal role in the process that has in a quantum leap of capital prodigiously expanded beyond them, leaving them behind as ruined and archaic remains of earlier stages in the development of this mode of production."[6] Scanning these ruins for clues of life is essential. What are now the "traditional structures" of industrial cities and nation-states from times of high modernity no longer play as central a role in either the economy or society.[7] Arguably, they are very tangible Anthropocene alerts.

After the consolidation of the Second Industrial Revolution, the necessities of everyday life were no longer the products of individual artisans.[8] Instead, new forms of finance capital, professional organizations, interventionist bureaucracies, and applied sciences crystallized in an elaborate organization of production that linked together many complex machines, consolidating all those new devices, routines, and institutions to form larger entities to perform many different kinds of work and to provide for the needs of consumers.[9] Small holding agriculture gave way to corporate farming, little shops were displaced by big factories, local economies imploded under global commerce, and skilled trades were restructured as professional science or unskilled labor. The ecology of communities was transformed as these megamachines infiltrated everyday life in the name of efficiency, progress, or development to fabricate industrialized macroenvironments. What once

5. Christopher Lasch, "The Revolt of the Elites: Have They Cancelled Their Allegiance to America?," *Harper's Magazine*, November 1994, pp. 46–48.

6. Jameson, *Postmodernism*, p. 412.

7. Lasch, "The Revolt of the Elites," pp. 48–49.

8. David Noble, *America by Design: Science, Technology, and the Rise of Corporate Capitalism* (New York: Knopf, 1977).

9. Lewis Mumford, *The Lewis Mumford Reader*, ed. Donald Miller (New York: Pantheon, 1986), p. 345.

was homemade now could be store-bought. That which had come from local fields, streams, forests, and soils arrived from far away. Corporate marketing needs, professional scientific opinions, and uniform government requirements all set the measure of ordinary existence from elsewhere, rather than local communities based among neighbors and friends.

American populism in the 1890s was a widespread popular revolt against the new systems of ecology fabricated by these megamachines. To serve the new agendas, the more sustainable communities of small local producers, who already were adopting appropriate technologies, frugal lifestyles, and democratic philosophies as common sense solutions to many everyday problems, had to be crushed. The remaining fragments were integrated, on terms not of their own choosing, into new networks of social reproduction suited to the new megamachines.[10] If ecologies are the totality of all relations between organisms and their environments, then the relation between human organisms and their environments shifted when people allowed major corporations, pretending to be science and technology, to bring good things to life or permitted better living to come through chemistry, physics, and biology instead of hard work, self-reliance, and individual effort. For all their faults, populists sensed these dangers a century ago and resisted them.

The Populist Movement of the 1890s

Populism has been regarded negatively in the United States largely because of the meanings it acquired in the now outmoded Cold War political lexicon as defined by New Class social sciences. Anxious to contain right-wing mass resistance, 1950s political opinion research brought Seymour Martin Lipset's caricature of populism as a rancid strain of working-class authoritarianism into vogue.[11] Ignoring enlightened elites, such populists allegedly would give sway to their authoritarian tendencies by throwing in with either fascist or communist movements to

10. David A. Hounshell, *From the American System to Mass Production, 1800–1932: The Development of Manufacturing Technology in the United States* (Baltimore: Johns Hopkins Univ. Press, 1984).

11. Seymour Martin Lipset, *Political Man: The Social Bases of Politics* (Garden City, NJ: Doubleday, 1960).

upend the status quo. Thus, various populistic initiatives in the 1960s and 1970s often were dismissed as mobs of dangerous deviants threatening the basically progressive harmony of liberal welfare states. President Reagan's anti-statist and anti-elitist rhetoric in the 1980s, however, freed populism of any of its negative associations, allowing many new initiatives to lay claim to "populism" after 1980. New Leftish versions from Jesse Jackson, George McGovern, or Bill Clinton clash with New Rightish visions from Jack Kemp, Newt Gingrich, and Dan Quayle as all post-Reagan-era politicos try to outmatch each other in their attacks on the welfare state. So far, this talk has been only talk. Meanwhile, for many middle-class groups, the economic, political, and social unrest of the past decade remains, as Harry Boyte argues, "emblematic or deep and traumatic disruptions in values and ways of living themselves.... In such an environment, the call for a return of power to ordinary people—the defining project of populism—gains tremendous force. If experts, distant problem-solvers, and the rich and powerful seem perplexed, impotent, and avaricious, the appropriate solution is to devolve authority to those closer to home and to institutions grounded in the life of actual, textured communities."[12] But how, where, when, and why?

Populism in the 1890s, as well as in the 1990s, prefigures a struggle concerning how economy and society ought to be organized. It challenges the prevailing corporate or statist rules, arguing in favor of small freeholding against corporate collectivism, local economies over global diseconomy, face-to-face community against in-your-face commercial culture, and self-rule over bureaucratic clientism. American populism, as it rose and fell in the Midwest, West, and South after the 1890s, was many things for many people. In some respects, however, it was a resistance against a new industrial ecology that emerged in the 1880s as the Second Industrial Revolution remade much of America into a nation rooted in macroenvironments constructed by corporate capitalism, national statism, and technocratic professionalism.

In the generation leading up to the 1890s, the United States was radically transformed. In 1860, the United States trailed England, France, and Germany in the total value of manufactured output. By 1894, it

---

12. Harry C. Boyte, *Community Is Possible: Repairing America's Roots* (New York: Harper, 1984), p. 213.

almost equaled all of them combined.[13] Before the Civil War, the working class was outnumbered by slaves. By the mid-1890s, the American working class was the largest in the world. At the end of the 1860s, half the nation's manufacturing establishments were still powered by water. By the mid-1890s, electricity and steam drove much of America's manufacturing enterprise.[14] Before Taylorism and Fordism colonized American workplaces, a four-day work week and a three-day weekend characterized many communities, as artisan skills still gave many workers tremendous control over both "work rules" and "company time." Families and friends, good drink and good discussion, frequent breaks and fine naps all were common features of the everyday life of independent producers. Instead of corporate capital enforcing its monopolies over access to capital, technology, and markets, independent producers manufactured goods and accumulated property in local networks keyed to notions of commonwealth rather than national concentrations of wealth. The artisan economy was not perfect, but in many ways it was more humane, democratic, and accessible than the corporate order for maximizing choice and productivity. While post-Fordist informationalism brings many new uncertainties, it could also eliminate much of the standardized mechanization and centralization that undercut artisans a century ago. Within the fading old Fordist industrial system, new artisan-based forms of labor, independent entrepreneurialism, and communal production might be viable once again. With such autonomous economic activities, individuals and communities may begin to oppose big firms and bureaucracies that have hitherto clientized them.

As Christopher Lasch has pointed out, the loose alliance of corporate capital and state bureaucracy forged in the 1870s and 1880s sought to replace independent producership and classical citizenship with a narrow array of feeble surrogates tossed out of a mix of consumerism and clientism: "Attempts to achieve a redistribution of income, to equalize opportunity in various ways, to incorporate the working classes into a society of consumers, or to foster economic growth and overseas expansion as a substitute for social reform can all be considered as twentieth-century substitutes for property ownership; but none of these

---

13. Herbert G. Gutman, *Work, Culture and Society in Industrializing America: Essays in American Working-Class and Social History* (New York: Vintage, 1977), p. 33.

14. Ibid.

policies created the kind of active, enterprising citizenry envisioned by nineteenth-century democrats."[15] The freedom and equality believed necessary for a democratic commonwealth early in the 1800s were never realized because Fordism, Taylorism, Keynesianism, and Sloanism became the vendors of a new "industrial democracy" with its own peculiar forms of economic freedom and legal equality.

Populism can be associated with a productivist ideology shared by small farmers, skilled artisans, and small-town tradespeople, all working to resist the innovations of a new industrial economy from the 1880s through the 1930s. While independent agrarianism was a bedrock foundation of the movement, its ranks were much broader and deeper than those of smallholding farmers. As Lasch notes, "Artisans and even many shopkeepers shared with farmers the fear that the new order threatened their working conditions, their communities and their ability to pass on both their technical skills and their moral economy to their offspring. In the nineteenth century, 'agrarianism' served as a generic term for popular radicalism, and this usage reminds us that opposition to monopolists, middlemen, public creditors, mechanization, and the erosion of craftsmanship by the division of labor was by no means confined to those who worked the soil."[16] Populism at that time represented a wide range of people still directly tied to their land and their craft. Individual producership tied families and communities to the environment in ways unlike those in today's welfare state economies.

Because of deep shifts in the organization of labor as well as changes in the property relations most suited to flexible modes of production, new possibilities are now emerging that recycle much of what was once attacked as "populism." As Lasch suggests, these attributes would include such attitudes as "producerism; a defense of endangered crafts (including the craft of farming); opposition to the new class of public creditors and to the whole machinery of modern finance; [and] opposition to wage labor. Populists inherited from earlier political traditions, liberal as well as republican, the principle that property ownership and the personal independence it confers are absolutely essential preconditions of citizenship."[17]

15. Christopher Lasch, *The True and Only Heaven: Progress and Its Critics* (New York: Norton, 1991), pp. 224–25.

16. Ibid., p. 211.

17. Ibid., p. 224.

In light of environmental constraints, the dream of abundance on which the New Class bases its legitimacy as a form of industrial democracy is proving to be nothing more than a myth. If everyone in China, or even in the United States, lived at the consumption levels of middle-class Los Angeles suburbanites, the world would soon choke on smog, CFCs, Styrofoam, and carbon dioxide. Luxury for all will never happen. Its ideological promises only survive to legitimate luxuries for the few today. The populists' awareness of limits pushed them to value competence, shared governance, and ownership—ideas that progressive New Class managers checkmated with their utopias of consumption and clientism. As Lasch notes, "Populists...regarded a competence, as they would have called it—a piece of earth, a small shop, a useful calling—as a more reasonable as well as a more worthy ambition. 'Competence' had rich moral overtones; it referred to the livelihood conferred by property but also the skills required to maintain it. The ideal of universal proprietorship embodied a humbler set of expectations than the ideal of universal consumption, universal access to a proliferating supply of goods. At the same time, it embodied a more strenuous and morally demanding definition of the good life."[18]

The living standards of the affluent cannot be extended to the poor on either a global or a national scale. Endless economic expansion will collapse the planet's biotic sustainability long before suburban consumption is universalized. Not surprisingly, corporate ecological authoritarianism, which has forced many forms of New Class rationalization on society without popular consultation, is under fire today for the anti-ecological arrogance it displays in impoverishing culture and abusing technology. Even more ironically, what worked imperfectly in the United States from the 1880s through the 1960s has worked even more imperfectly on a global scale since the 1970s.

Moreover, the spread of consumer capitalism on a national scale has also proven to be highly destructive. State regulation of everyday life has created dependencies and insecurities. Ever greater state intervention into the routines of families, individuals, cities, and firms has made them less viable while creating major problems.[19] Just as state communism

18. Ibid., p. 531.
19. Paul Piccone, "Beyond Pseudo-Culture: Reconstituting Fundamental Political Concepts," *Telos* 95 (Spring 1993): 3–14.

collapsed of its own weight, so too is corporate consumerism proving to be an impossible dream. *Perestroika* in the United States may first appear as Reaganism or Gingrichism, but what has followed since 9/11 are darker developments whose worst outcomes are still unfolding. As Lasch observes, populism provides some possible answers: "The need for a more equitable distribution of wealth ought to be obvious, both on moral and on economic grounds, and it ought to be equally obvious that economic equality cannot be achieved under an advanced system of capitalist production. What is not so obvious is that equality now implies a more modest standard of living for all, not an extension of the lavish standards enjoyed by the favored classes in the industrial nations to the rest of the world. In the twenty-first century, equality implies a recognition of limits, both moral and material, that finds little support in the progressive tradition."[20] When populism declined, new ideologies and institutions redefined individual values, organized urban society, and unleashed a cultural revolution in the name of "industrial democracy."

As William Leach suggests, "From the 1890s on, American corporate business, in league with key institutions, began the transformation of American society into a society preoccupied with consumption, with comfort and bodily well-being, with luxury, spending, and acquisition, with more goods this year than last, more next year than this. American consumer capitalism produced a culture almost violently hostile to the past and to tradition, a future-oriented culture of desire that confused the good life with goods."[21] In the 1990s, new populists also are asking if "[c]ommodity production and consumerism alter perceptions not just of the self but of the world outside of the self. They create a world of mirrors, insubstantial images, illusions increasingly indistinguishable from reality.... The consumer lives surrounded not so much by things as by fantasies."[22] Such fantasies can be and have been normalizing. These corporate goods acquired tremendous force, allowing anyone to see themselves in them and everyone to see them as self-constituting agents of industrial democracy.

20. Lasch, *The True and Only Heaven*, p. 532.

21. William Leach, *Land of Desire: Merchants, Power, and the Rise of the New American Culture* (New York: Pantheon, 1993), p. xiii.

22. Christopher Lasch, *The Minimal Self: Psychic Survival in Troubled Times* (New York: Norton, 1984), p. 30.

Macroenvironments in Industrial Democracy

Once such macroenvironmental webs are woven, pristine nature or un-contaminated ecologies become problematic concepts. After the Second Industrial Revolution, one might ask if there is any "nature" left. Is nature gone for good now that the corporate model of modernization has expanded everywhere as a macroenvironment? All organisms are products of their environments. They may, of course, shape their environments by their actions. But they too are always shaped by their environmental settings. People are no exception, even though the rule no longer applies unconditionally. Why? Because the environment is no longer "nature," despite the frantic railings of deep ecologists about humanity's domination of nature. Bill McKibben and Carolyn Merchant are absolutely right, even though often they are not taken seriously.[23] We now live *after* "the end of nature." Nature *is* "dead." To take these insights to heart, we should admit that our real ecosystem is largely composed of commercialized artifacts, mediating the metabolism of immense megamachines thriving in their habitats of elaborate, artificial environments.

Lewis Mumford called these apparatuses "megamachines," or "mass organizations able to perform tasks that lie outside the range of small work collectives and loose tribal or territorial groups," which have, at the same time, "progressively multiplied the use of the more reliable mechanical components while not merely reducing the labor force needed for a colossal operation but, through electronics, facilitating instantaneous remote control."[24] Through bureaucratic surveillance and commercial normalization, the agendas of these machines are to control "the entire community at every point of human existence," because the global human ecology generated by such machines "escapes spatial and temporal limitations; it can operate as a single, largely invisible unit over a wide area, its functioning parts operating as a unit through instant communication."[25] The daily existence of millions of people and

23. Bill McKibben, *The End of Nature* (New York: Doubleday, 1989); and Carolyn Merchant, *The Death of Nature: Women, Ecology, and the Scientific Revolution* (San Francisco: Harper & Row, 1990).
24. Mumford, *The Lewis Mumford Reader*, p. 345.
25. Ibid.

thousands of urban settlements depends on hundreds of these machines, which interlock labor and capital, matter and energy, producers and consumers in exchanges of directed work that sustain the life of these people in their artificial environments. In other words, people are mainly products of the products that constitute the environment: supermarkets, malls, suburbs, automobiles, telecommunications, and corporate entertainment. We only exist there, and increasingly more "virtually there" in online shopping, social media communities, telecommuting labor, and digital governance.

Nature has been integrated into the megamachines of transnational corporate capitalism. Maybe this is the by-product of natural fission, creating a green "first nature" outside and a manufactured "second nature" inside. Either way, the key ecosystems of the human environment are centered in second nature and its megamachineries. Everyone who lives in a money economy depends on the artifacts produced by these megamachines—as commodified forms of shelter, food supplies, dress, climate control, work, entertainment. When easy access to this environment is interrupted by war, weather, or crime, survival itself is imperiled. Without the megamachines, life turns into the solitary, nasty, brutish, and short existence endured in Sarajevo, Haiti, Rwanda, or Grozny.

This is the ideology of commodities under industrial democracy: the primacy of the totality. Everything must work this way because everything does work this way. In an ironic concordance with Barry Commoner's first law of ecology, "everything is connected to everything else" and the whole depends on each part.[26] Megamechanic artifacts shape their inhabitants even as they, in turn, shape these artifacts. Without linking into its transnational commodity chains, few people can live any kind of satisfying life. The independent producership of dignified labor within autonomous communities that American populists dreamed of during the 1890s is almost impossible unless, of course, one sees Somali peasants combing the hills for firewood and food in these terms. Nature is becoming a utopia, existing at best in the glossy imagery of Sierra Club photos or the slick packaging of ecotourism trips, because many of its old secrets are now commodified products. In keeping with Commoner's second law of ecology, "everything has to go somewhere," both city and country are architecturally integrated, technologically linked,

26. Barry Commoner, *Making Peace with the Planet* (New York: Pantheon, 1990), p. 8.

and institutionally managed to function in corporately administered megamachines.[27] These business-based apparatuses source their inputs globally and deliver their outputs locally—albeit in extremely unequal levels—to promote the daily survival of six billion people. Most of these habitats are found in cities, which are not nature's metropolis but rather nature's necropolis.[28] High-performance machineries of speed, power, and comfort realize their ideological ends in each individual's use of their commodities. Without access to their ordinary habitats in the mall or familiar ranges in the supermarket, modern hunter-gatherer cultures created by the suburban consumerism of industrial democracy will wither and die.

Maybe the abolition of nature can be seen as a by-product of shifting collective megamachines in which individuals get caught along or inside the boundaries of two technologies. These technologies rarely operate autonomously or discretely, but the circuits commodity-production-consumption may allow an examination of the constant interaction of "technologies of production, which permit us to produce, transform, or manipulate things," and "technologies of the self, which permit individuals to effect by their own means or with the help of others a certain number of operations on their own bodies and souls, thought, conduct, and ways of being, so as to transform themselves in order to attain a certain state of happiness, purity, wisdom, perfection, or immortality."[29] Do these technologies of production and the self generate new amalgams of objective systemic productivity and subjective idiosyncratic consumption? The end users of commodities are reassigned through commodities to the role of capital asset, causing "the ultimate realization of the private individual as a productive force. The system of needs must wring liberty and pleasure from him as so many functional elements of the reproduction of the system of production and the relations of power that sanction it."[30]

27. Ibid., p. 9.

28. William Cronon, *Nature's Metropolis: Chicago and the Great West* (New York: Norton, 1991).

29. Michel Foucault, *Technologies of the Self: A Seminar with Michel Foucault*, ed. Luther H. Martin, Huck Gutman, and Patrick H. Hutton (Amherst: Univ. of Massachusetts Press, 1988), p. 18.

30. Jean Baudrillard, *For a Critique of the Political Economy of the Sign*, trans. Charles Levin (St. Louis: Telos Press, 1981), p. 85.

For the megamachines, the liberation of technically imagineered fictions like "wants" or "needs" is often fixated on commodities hitherto inaccessible to them. Liberating these needs, then, will be matched by mobilizations of need fulfillments in commodities. Consumer goods can be supplied once new subjects are recognized as having the will demanded of good consumers.[31] Subjectivity is refined into material needs, and subjection can be defined in the absolution of commodities designed to satisfy them. Disciplinary objectivities define disciplined subjectivity because, as Jean Baudrillard observes: "The *consumption* of individuals mediates the *productivity* of corporate capital; it becomes a productive force required by the functioning of the system itself, by its process of reproduction and survival. In other words, there are these kinds of needs because the system of corporate production needs them. And the needs invested by the individual consumer today are just as essential to the order of production as the capital invested by the capitalist entrepreneur and the labor power invested in the wage laborer. It is *all* capital."[32] A crude functionalism is not necessarily at play here; instead, one simply sets the sites of those elective affinities drawing technologies of the self (consumer decisions to exercise purchasing power) together with technologies of production (producer choices to organize adding value) in megamechanical ecologies. Ideologies of competitive progress are inscribed on each commodity delivered to consumers as tokens of their collective liberation; bizarre ideologies of individual empowerment arise out of each act of product appropriation.

Consummativity is the operational summation of industrial democracy. It represents the first principle of the megamachines sustaining the development of a global human ecology: "Everything has to be sacrificed to the principle that things must have an operational genesis. So far as production is concerned, it is no longer the Earth that produces, or labor that creates wealth... rather, it is Capital that *makes* the Earth and Labor *produce*. Work is no longer an action, it is an operation. Consumption no longer means the simple enjoyment of goods, it means having (someone) enjoy something—an operation modeled on, and keyed to, the differential range of sign-objects. Communication is

31. Stuart Ewen, *Captains of Consciousness: Advertising and the Roots of Consumer Culture* (New York: McGraw-Hill, 1976).

32. Baudrillard, *For a Critique of the Political Economy of the Sign*, p. 82.

a matter not of speaking but of making people speak. Information involves not knowledge but making people know."[33] In this setting, the megamachinery of second nature becomes "the environment." The third law of ecology is "nature knows best," and the logics of consummativity ironically affirm that this second nature also knows best.[34] Or, at least, the technocratic New Classes in charge of making and managing them know best. Maybe, to paraphrase Marshall McLuhan, who saw all technologies as media providing "extensions of man,"[35] people become psychic and physical media in second nature, impersonating extensions of these technologies. As the populists of the 1890s feared, the material coercion of consummativity is to be found within its authoritarian confinement of local choice and totalitarian denial of global alternatives. Through commodified freedoms, consummativity can "increase subjected forces" and "improve the force and efficacy of that which subjects them"[36] in the circulation of its commodified artifacts.

The "values and ways of living" embedded in the welfare states are predicated on this ecology of complex megamachines designed and managed by New Class experts to create clientalistic dependencies. When General Electric exclaimed that "we bring good things to life," it captures the essence of these vast global ecologies that bring huge bureaucratic machines of production and consumption into life by dropping their goods and services into the lives of consumers for whom "the good life" is "good things." Goods and services are produced, packaged, and purchased to bring the power of those good things to life for corporate capital.

The transition to intensive production over the past century also transforms the logics of governmentality, coordinating the administration of people, political economy, and government. Increasingly, "the instruments of government, instead of being laws, now come to be a range of multiform tactics."[37] Unlike classical sovereignty, which

33. Jean Baudrillard, *The Transparency of Evil: Essays on Extreme Phenomena*, trans. James Benedict (London: Verso, 1993), pp. 45–46.

34. Commoner, *Making Peace with the Planet*, p. 11.

35. Marshall McLuhan, *Understanding Media: The Extensions of Man* (New York: Signet Books, 1964).

36. Michel Foucault, *History of Sexuality*, vol. 1, *An Introduction*, trans. Robert Hurley (New York: Vintage, 1980), p. 104.

37. Michel Foucault, "On Governmentality," trans. Pasquale Pasquino, in *The Foucault Effect: Studies in Governmentality*, ed. Graham Burchell, Colin Gordon, and Peter

expresses directly the privileges or prohibitions determined by some powerful sovereign, modern governmentality works through things and people's interactions with them as "public" and "business" administration. "To govern," Foucault writes, "means to govern things" in accordance with the claim that "government is the right disposition of things, arranged so as to lead to a convenient end."[38] Both services and commodities provide a wide range of tactics for corporations, state bureaucracies, and experts to dispose of things and thereby also people, arranging them to lead to useful ends that both advance their interests and satisfy their clients.

As Simon Patten envisioned the system of mass production/individual consumption in the 1890s, "The standard of life is determined, not so much by what man has to enjoy, as by the rapidity with which he tires of any one pleasure. To have a high standard means to enjoy a pleasure intensely and to tire of it quickly."[39] What the populists once advocated as deep organic relations to others, communities, or the land, which the old nature myths once dictated to society, must be revalued. Such commitments imply husbanding resources, preserving nature on its own merits, and respecting networks of mutual aid in close-knit communities. Rapid destruction of resources in the pursuit of intense satisfaction from professionally imagineered commodities, only to push on relentlessly to new experiences with others, is the mark of "the highest standard of living." Frugality, stability, and durability, by definition, become tawdry signs of inferior "lower forms of life."

Federalism and Populism

As many Victorians observed in the 1900s about the course of their own lives during the nineteenth century, most people at that time still lived in first nature, much as they had for centuries. Rural life in 1830 was not all that unlike life in 1030 or 30. Urban life was somewhat different, mostly because of the rise of urban capitalism in the late Middle Ages. Even so, city living in most towns had not changed very much since 1780 or 1330. By the time the last Victorians passed away, however, almost everything had changed. Entirely new ideologies emerged along

---

Miller (Chicago: Univ. of Chicago Press, 1991), p. 95.

    38. Ibid., pp. 94–95.

    39. Simon N. Patten, *The Consumption of Wealth* (New York: Lippincott, 1892), p. 51.

with immense new technologies for producing and consuming the macroenvironments of second nature. By generating its corporate vision of the good life, "American business, after 1890, acquired such power and, despite a few wrenching crises along the way, has kept it every since."[40] As the populists anticipated in the 1890s, this shift has been a major revolutionary change, introducing new values and institutions, as well as obliterating many of the old beliefs and fixed ways of the past.

Postmodern populist movements today confront tremendous obstacles as they deal with the effects of this revolution. The artificial environment, global webs of trade, and basic ecologies, as they now are structured, all embody the agendas and prerogatives of state bureaucracies or corporate enterprises that have worked for over a century to reduce individual autonomy and communal freedom to a minimum in order to bolster the centralizing federal government and Fortune 500 companies. But this project seems to have reached its limit. Today, states and firms are shedding responsibilities and services in waves of restructuring that create new opportunities for postmodern populist innovations. With industrial democracy, corporate capitalism decisively defeated both American populism and European socialism. Yet these victories were won only to the degree that new macroenvironments with special ideologies of power, subjectivity, and value could articulate their ends and expectations in the realm of artificial commodities. Advanced standards of living mean more than affluence; they also imply living in accordance with normalizing standards presupposed by industrial democratic citizenship, i.e., the acceptance of the imperatives behind the design, operation, and possession of consumer goods. These material possessions bind individuals and communities, if only in part or merely for a while, to the megamachineries constituting such systems of material acquisition. At each nexus of consumption, complex alliances elicit all those normalized subjectivities, expectations, and subjugations perpetuating the megamechanical ecologies of industrial democracy.

In the mid-1850s, federalism became redefined in centralizing bureaucratic terms, shifting power and authority away from localities, counties, and states toward Washington. These developments occurred rapidly: (1) to acquire all or most of the territory on the North American continent in what became the trans-Mississippi West; (2) to control

40. Leach, *Land of Desire*, p. xiii.

the development of free wage and unfree slave labor in the entire federation, ultimately leading to the Civil War (as the extractive agrarian economies of the southern states practiced a more orthodox vision of federalism against Washington both before and after their secession); (3) to reconstruct the South after the Civil War in order to impose the victorious federal reading of law and order as well as northern terms of trade on the defeated Confederacy; (4) to pacify the indigenous peoples through warfare and resettlement, as well as to determine the economic development of the territories in the trans-Mississippi West in accord with federal policies; and (5) to foster the sustained industrialization of the entire nation through new policies for railroadization, easy immigration, colonization, naval expansion, inflation, and military conquest. Federalism in the 1890s was something far different than had been envisioned in the 1790s by either Hamilton or Jefferson, Madison or Washington, Jay or Adams, as federal state power moved with and against corporate capitalism to construct an industrial democracy capable of Americanizing millions of immigrants, normalizing millions of consumers, and disciplining millions of workers to accept strange forms of commercial reacculturation, political disempowerment, and economic dependency as a progressive way of life. What little sense of federalism's separation, division, and balance of powers or subsidiarity of powers remained after the crushing of most populist resistance by World War I typically boiled down to internal squabbles by different factions of New Class experts over how to divide the goodies in pork-barrel federalism from 1933 to 1975 or allocate blame in shift-and-shaft federalism from 1975 to 1995.

Arguably, the key problem in American federalism since the mid-1970s has been the impact of the global economy on communities and citizens. Caught within the territorial domain of Washington's rule, there are smaller economies tied to competitive capital that remain capable of besting everyone or anything in the global marketplace. Yet there also are smaller economies bound up with much less flexible monopoly capital or military support systems that cannot compete nationally, much less globally. Of course, the able wish to secede from the federation, and in many ways they already have, as members of the privileged classes build private telecommunication systems, patronize private schools, trade globally, live in gated communities, employ private security guards, and tax themselves in various systems of protective covenants. The less able are left seeking new entitlements from a weakened federal regime still coasting on the momentum of its Cold War authority, which rests upon the power to tax, borrow, and spend and the prerogatives of territorial sovereignty.

Yet, since the 1990s, these instruments have become increasingly inefficient as the New World Disorder, a four-trillion-dollar deficit, and post-Fordist informationalism make a mockery of Washington's former ability to control world events, regulate its currency, steer the economy, and police its own ideological frontiers, geographic boundaries, or technological domains. A revitalized federalism centered on people rather than central authority, the locality rather than the nation, the states rather than the federal government, and the sharing rather than the concentration of powers might well be what is needed to adapt to the realities of post-Fordist informationalism for both the able and the less able segments of society. It is clear that Washington does not have the answers. In struggling to solve these problems, it has nearly bankrupted the treasury, corrupted many local communities, and disrupted regional economies in maintaining the macroenvironments of industrial democracy long after it lost its ability to pay for it out of the current cash flow. The benefits of suburban consumerism have been retained only by robbing the future and ransacking the biosphere to keep the myth of industrial democracy alive, the New Class in power, and corporate America strong, as President Trump exclaims, to "Make America Great Again." Postmodern populism assumes instead that Americans can do better, but not within the context they have been forced into during the past century.

New Class managerialism, bureaucratic state interventionism, and transnational corporate capitalism all have become coaligned in a corruption of federalism, creating a peculiar ecology that binds atomized individual consumers to complex global chains of commodity production. Every product increasingly depends on matter, energy, and information outsourced from everywhere in order to operate anywhere. Consequently, almost no one can act autonomously as an independent producer without considerable dependence on outside sources of supply. New Class experts generate a host of social theories to justify these ecological insecurities as economic efficiency or instrumental rationality.[41] Large state bureaucracies create demand for their services by coordinating these exchanges through legal, fiscal, institutional, and regulatory mechanisms. Big corporate concerns continue to control markets, technologies, and resources by embedding more and more buyers in their networks of supply and demand. One must survey all these ties to grasp how these forces now bind people to their total environment, increasingly vended through "the clouds" digitally by Facebook, Amazon, Apple, Netflix, and Google. Unless and until these ecologies break down or redirect themselves, new populist forms of federalism cannot fully develop. Moreover, just as political federalism assumes that the forms of rule will work at the level and on the scale to which they are most suited, so too must a new sense of ecological subsidiarity begin to pervade today's political economies. New Class expertise, bureaucratic statism, and transnational corporate capitalism are centralizing, disempowering, and atomizing forces that can further erode communal autonomy, bioregional complexity, and local decision-making unless populist movements can vindicate the prerogatives of subsidiarity against their overweening authority.

Ecology and Populism

Of all the fragmentary positive sciences, ecology remains the only one with considerable subversive potentials, since it can comprehensively and critically examine the totality of relations between people and all other organisms in their inorganic and organic environments. The megamachines of transnational corporate capitalism, aided and abetted by the liberal welfare state, have reordered both the urban-industrial and rural-agricultural ecologies underpinning ordinary everyday life. In turn, a populist reconstitution of these economies and societies must disrupt the existing ecologies of such state-corporate macroenvironments, even as they search for alternative kinds of independent producership in local microecologies.

Huge corporate bureaucracies have been constructed since the 1880s on a regional, national, and global scale to produce the goods and services needed for survival. Consequently, a few vast monoculture, monoprod-

---

41. Timothy W. Luke, "Community and Ecology," *Telos* 88 (Summer 1991): 69–79, reprinted in this volume.

uct, monoservice networks now supply most of the matter, energy, and information needs of millions of people at virtually unsustainable and ungeneralizable levels of output. Without these megamachines, life itself, in its urban-industrial or suburban-consumer forms, is impossible. Yet as the Cold War has ended, the welfare state liberalism and consumer capitalism that emerged along with these megamachines during the Second Industrial Revolution are clearly in crisis. Today many people are asking the same questions raised by populists a century ago, challenging the viability of interventionist welfare states and transnational corporate capitalism as the social contract of industrial Fordism is being broken or ignored in the 1990s.

There is little discussion concerning what will replace these megamachineries. If the welfare state is dismantled, will its regulatory apparatus, which has underpinned the monocultures and monoproducts of modern ecology, also be closed down? Will the state accept alternative forms of rule to end deficits, reduce regulation, and control costs? If corporate capital downsizes, will its organization of production, which has determined product design, service delivery, quality control, and behavioral norms be eliminated? Will it tolerate alternative webs of production and consumption to reduce payrolls, rationalize product lines, and revitalize profitability?

There is no definitive program for postmodern populism that articulates what needs to be done. Populism does not provide a fail-safe recipe for the future. It does, however, outline possible strategies by pointing out what to undo. The notion of an industrial democracy was deployed by small groups of New Class professionals working for bureaucratic and technical interests in the welfare state or transnational firm. Its concerns usually focus on policies of damage control or codes for technical legitimation. By taking the ideas of federalism away from these narrow interests and integrating subsidiarity into a political critique of domination, postmodern populist forces may be able to reconstitute contemporary consumerist ecologies, removing them from their present context, as an initial step toward reconstructing the destructive exchanges of advanced industrialism with the environment.

Populists today may be caught within the system, but they can refuse to submit to its entrapment. Postmodern populism arises out of advanced industrialism but does not have to be for it. As in the 1890s, postmodern populists in the 1990s are about finding alternatives to serve more people more fairly and more locally. Even the most system-affirming corporate technologies contain self-subversive moments. Postmodern populism seeks to exhume and exploit that subversive potential by revealing the unseen flexibility, unknown possibilities, and untested alternatives that contemporary technologies contain for developing an ecologically sound economy. The society of bureaucratically controlled consumption, as a whole, can be undone. Yet its revolutionary "undoing" will be attained only by destructively reconstituting pieces and parts of its institutions, technologies, and values in a new ecological "doing"—reorganized on a small-scale, nonhierarchical, non-centralized basis in new forms of federalism outside the megamachines.

Any effort to embed ecological constraints in a populist society must enhance the accessibility of tools and economies to ordinary individuals, who for nearly a century have been denied individual autonomy as producers by artificial skill monopolies and corporate-driven regimes of capital accumulation. Likewise, what is, in fact, an extremely simple and fairly brittle transnational commerce in food, fuel, and fiber, tied to a few monoproduct output networks or monocrop extraction systems, needs to become much more diversified in many more complex regional and flexible local economies. Forgetting how to provision most parts of a basic everyday life in their own microecologies in favor of producing a few things for cash to buy everything else produced elsewhere and sold everywhere for immense profits in the urban-industrial macroenvironments has disempowered the many by empowering the few who control the megamachines forming this strange macroenvironment.

Systems of cultural normalization, which now underpin a transnational trade in the same hamburgers, automobiles, movies, and shoes, could well succumb to new zones of particularity where populist communities define and satisfy their own material wants at home. Biodiversity should mean more than protecting insects and fungi in the Brazilian rainforest; it could also imply safeguarding diverse forms of life in different economies, cultures, and societies tied to microecologies mostly apart from the transnational circulation of suburban consumer goods. Independent producership also suggests a production of independent relations with sufficient complexity, diversity, and density to generate alternative kinds of civilization. This ecological outcome, however, is to be expected and even applauded as people define their own communities in their own bioregions to sustain their own cultures, free from the colonizing governmentalities that have defined global Fordism. A federal system of populist commonwealths, then, would not involve, like New Class managerialism from the past century, a forcible reorganization of industrial capitalism to make it allegedly better serve the collective choicelessness of the powerless masses.[42] Rather, these complex federalist transformations can begin only when ecologically informed independent producers undo the consumerist dependencies in everyday life that reinforce their mass powerlessness.

Toward an Ecological Populism

As the populists of the 1890s so intensely argued, the technical advances of the Second Industrial Revolution have progressively robbed individuals and communities of their rights to self-definition, self-determination, and self-direction. This rationalization without representation has engendered new modes of personal and community domination. The authority of technical experts and specialized knowledge exerts itself through the material artifacts and organization processes of corporate culture, benefiting its anonymous controllers and designers in the technologically competent ranks of the New Class. It is this anonymous authoritarianism that needs to be attacked by postmodern populism. Grounded in a modern welfare state that tends toward total administration, any meaningful ecological critique must also recognize that transnational capital inescapably works to moderate, limit, and define such revolutionary thrusts.

New tools now can be developed that are simple, durable, useful, and manageable in individual, household, or community use to redirect the megamachines toward more micro- or mesomechanical styles of operation. By disengaging technology from corporate control, populist technologists could easily develop the renewable, inorganic energy sources needed to sustain a downsized but satisfying standard of living. A populist ecotechnics, then, would presume the displacement of current corporate capitalist production. The once inaccessible sciences of

---

42. Paul Piccone, "Federal Populism in Italy," *Telos* 90 (Winter 1991–92): 3–18.

corporate- and government-funded professionals can be reconstituted as a vernacular knowledge accessible to nonspecialists.

Thus, once cheap inputs of fossil fuels are removed from the scientific equations of agricultural production or engineering formulas for shelter construction, new habitat-specific rules of crop cultivation and housing development could reassert themselves. Those new bodies of technical knowledge would involve local experience, communal custom, collective goals, and formal design to develop agricultural and engineering techniques that suit the particular needs of definite communities in specific habitats. Rather than growing only a handful of different grains on a massive scale through energy-intensive monocultures or building minor variations of the same single-family dwelling for state-guaranteed suburban mass markets, each household in many diverse communities could produce foods and shelter suited to its particular social needs and environmental locale. Under communal rather than corporate control, knowledge could acquire a much greater craft quality, melding everyday practices with theoretical insights. Ultimately, within these craft-centered bodies of knowledge (reminiscent of the old artisanal framework) de-skilled individuals might re-skill themselves. Where and how might these post-megamechanical ecotechnics emerge in populist forms? At first, it must be with the work of immediate producers in intentional communities. One rudimentary start toward reconstruction can be found in today's immense underground or shadow economies, which through gifts, barter, and nonmonetary trade already may comprise over twenty percent of the GNP in the United States. A second source can be found in "self-service," or the growing production of goods and services for use only in the household, neighborhood, or community, which would account for another substantial percentage of the GNP if translated into dollars. It is also beyond the control of national corporate and government planners. By stressing reasonable exchange, durability, and renewability, these devolutional practices could be the beginning of a more ecotechnical organization of production.

Additional outlines for a genuine ecotechnics should emerge in populist communities, where communal relations would require new means of production to anchor everyday exchange. This ecotechnics would include many populist characteristics antagonistic to the megamachines of suburban consumerism. First, ecotechnics would produce goods to satisfy needs on a materially comfortable level—habitat-centered shelter, biome-based nutrition, environmentally suitable apparel, renewable resource use, and durable artifacts. Second, the mechanical implements and managerial organization of production should be accessible, useful, and understandable to all. These new processes create not only different goods but also new autonomous, competent persons, who along with others might wholly own, manage, and control their entire socioeconomic system in their locality. Third, energy sources would be renewable; materials would be recyclable (i.e., mainly organic, innocuous, and nonpolluting); labor would revolve around utility, quality, and accessibility; and management would tend to be democratic, non-centralized, and non-authoritarian, which would be encouraged by populist norms of production. These microecologies would define limits and find ways to live comfortably within them.

This does not imply that high technology, modern medicine, complex engineering, or grand science will be destroyed. On the contrary, those processes must be used to their fullest, first, to keep ecology vital and honest as a positive science of critical analysis and, second, to guide populism as an effective alternative. Technoscientific processes, however, could be downsized, disconnected, and dismantled within their current corporate capitalist frameworks to be reconstituted within populist contexts of communally created and democratically managed relations of citizenship and producership. Without additional scientific research, many new necessary ecologically viable energy sources would probably not be developed. Thus, small-scale microcomputer technology represents a crucial contribution to an ecotechnical mode of production. Once it becomes completely user-friendly and ultra-miniaturized, computer technology will contribute significantly to the creation of a more nonhierarchical, local, and ecological economy. Coupled with the latest telecommunications networks, computer technologies will also help make the present late-industrial city even more obsolete than it already is. As a technology for concentrating communication, energy, and information, conventional urbanism divorced itself from rural nature to dominate it. Microcomputer systems and localist telecommunication networks may make possible the deconcentration of communication, energy, and information in a spatial system of organization blending the urban and the rural outside of the reach of megamachines.

Ecotechnics and postmodern populism should also encourage lifestyles grounded in "voluntary simplicity." This does not imply a gleefully embraced austerity, which would mystify the falling rate of material satisfaction in contemporary industrial civilization. Instead, it suggests the self-definition of needs in local communities independent of corporate capital's "coercive complexity." By voluntarily accepting membership in the ecological community of competence made possible by ecotechnics, postmodern populists might move their society beyond the irrational pitfalls of the modern marketplace.

This new populism implies making the transition to a spatial setting that fuses the rural and urban into a new mode of "rurban" living. Rurbanism could deconcentrate urban resources, bringing "urban" commerce, art, society, and letters into balance with "rural" crafts, culture, community, and customs. Intensive modes of agriculture mixed with habitat-centered housing tied into windmill centers, solar ponds, household gardens, or community woodlots could begin to rehumanize nature and renaturalize humanity by resituating people in nature. The anthropocentrism of orthodox urban leftists and the nature chauvinism of traditional romantic rebellion, in turn, could be transcended in a new rurban culture that would redefine the human–nature relation along populist lines.

Rurbanized living would not tolerate the mindless obliteration of arable land, renewable resources, or fossil fuels in the technical nexus implied by suburban malls, tract housing, and perimeter beltways. The benefits of rural and urban life must be unified into a new mode of life, which could lessen the personal costs of rural isolation and urban giganticism with the advantages of informationalized communications and populist public life. Some of this could be achieved through architecture; some of it would be attained by a new federalist governance. Rurban institutions should promote popular participation and accountability in the management of the local economy and community in keeping with the logic of subsidiarity. Rurbanized settlements would fit a new postmegamechanical ethic of natural cooperation, close affinal association, and the practice of skilled crafts by situating people in nature and by reintroducing nature's needs to society. An ecological subsidiarity should follow closely from these political federalist arrangements.

Politics, Ecology, and Populism

For nearly a century, large state bureaucracies and major corporate enterprises have organized and operated the economic, political, and social environments by moving away from independent producership, toward dependent consumerism, out of free markets and into administered systems of commerce, beyond individual self-reliance and within statist regimes of clientalistic entitlement. What the populists opposed did come to pass in the forms of Fordist industrialism. Yet, in succeeding, the loose alliances of liberal welfare states and managerial corporate firms have apparently so abused the environment, social institutions, and common culture that their authority has been delegitimated. The Anthropocene debate only accentuates this sense of systemic failure. In the aftermath of the welfare state's collapse and the modern corporation's fragmentation, new populist movements are mobilizing people and resources to cope with a declining quality of life in the microecologies and macroenvironments generated by post-Fordist informationalism. Flexible modes of production, disorganized regimes of accumulation, and post-Fordist systems of regulation all foster entrepreneurialism because big government and big business either have failed to make advanced industrial society work rationally or have chosen to spin off their social control functions in numerous deficit reductions, personnel RIFs, organizational downsizing, or company restructuring campaigns during the past fifteen years. The writing has been on the wall for industrial democracy's new industrial state and affluent society since 1973, but the instructions were actually read only after 1989. With the end of the Cold War and the last gasp of the socialist specter (which Otto von Bismarck's welfare state and Frederick W. Taylor's managerial firm were built to contain in the 1880s and 1890s), the basic *raison d'être* of modern bureaucratic society faces new questions. In the same way populism did in the 1890s, postmodern populism in the 1990s is trying to provide answers by probing notions of social subsidiarity, community commonwealth, and personal producership for new solutions. The new gig economy, social media networks, digital cryptocurrency, and cognitive capitalism made possible by consumers buying "smart phones" and moving to "smart cities" are not proving to be the good answers that are needed.

However, the collapse of public and private sector bureaucracies threatens to take with it the macroenvironments of modern life as well as the massive megamachines of production and consumption that sustain everyday life. Clearly, the exhaustion of welfare state interventionism, as well as the bureaucratic paralysis engendered in corporate behemoths like GM, IBM, or Exxon over the past ten to fifteen years, is behind many experiments with both independent producership and populist politics. On the one hand, government downsizing is going to reduce the level and number of statist government redistributive programs. Often what is being done now is inefficient and frequently ineffective, and populist institutions will need to supplant some of the state's responsibilities. Moreover, corporate cuts are forcing many workers back into independent producer status as consultants, small businesspersons, or temp workers. A standard of living higher than the present can be realized out of the microecologies that populists want to reclaim from the clientism of today's existing systems of material and virtual macroenvironments, rooted in state-corporate industrial Fordism, fiscal Keynesianism, and cultural Sloanism.

Populism today is a complex, variegated, multidimensional phenomenon that no one analysis can fully articulate—much of it stands on the right, some of it veers left, a bit of it is a step back, a piece of it strikes out ahead. One might aver that the ecology nexus is insignificant in the scheme of things. In fact, one kind of relation with the environment presumes micrologies of independent producership, regionalistic communitarian exchange, and personal citizenship, while another entails a macroenvironment of dependent consumerism, global corporate exchange, and personal clientism. For postmodern populism to successfully reorder economy and society, another social ecology, radically different than the one that has prevailed for over a century, must be developed from within today's failing modernity.

7

Re-Reading the Unabomber Manifesto

T O THE EXTENT that his now infamous manifesto, "Industrial Society and Its Future," covers cultural, economic, and political issues
that *Telos* has addressed for over a quarter century, the odd story of Ted
Kaczynski and the particularities of his strategic bombing campaign
against "the system" warrants reexamination.[1] Unabombs killed three and

---

* Originally published in *Telos* 107 (Spring 1996): 85–108.

1. David Kaczynski turned his brother, Ted, over to authorities after noting some
disturbing parallels in Ted's personal letters, which espoused radical antiestablish-
ment positions, and the manifesto published in the *Washington Post* on September 19,
1995. Because he was not caught in the act and did not confess to any of these crimes,
Kaczynski's prosecution rests exclusively on forensic and circumstantial evidence. See
Serge F. Kovaleski and Pierre Thomas, "U.S. Had Substantial Evidence before Arresting
Kaczynski," *Washington Post*, June 14, 1996. The "Unabomber" tag is a product of the
FBI's investigation, which described the elusive bomber by his attacks on universities
("un") and airlines ("a") as "Unabombs." Nonetheless, government press releases to the
media indicate that Kaczynski's small cabin in the Montana woods has yielded a considerable cache of potentially damaging evidence. The Justice Department also alleges
it found lists of actual and potential bombing victims, as well as a secret numerical
code used by the Unabomber to verify his identity in communicating with authorities. Kaczynski's DNA—as detected from saliva testing—correlated positively with
traces extracted from the postage stamps affixed to mail bombs dating back to 1978.
Additionally, observers at hotels, restaurants, and bus terminals have put Kaczynski in
or around Sacramento, California, a location frequently used to post the bomb packages, when mail bombs were either mailed or detonated. See "Files Show Clues Tying
Suspect Held in Montana to Unabomber," *New York Times*, June 14, 1996.

wounded twenty-three others in a string of sixteen bombings from 1978 to 1995. Many of the victims, however, were individuals not usually associated with targets of terrorist activities: comparatively poor, obscure, or powerless academics whom the Unabomber saw as the key personnel supporting the operators of "the system."

Immediately following Kaczynski's arrest, *Newsweek* pointed out his "essentially "left-wing orientation"[2] and placed him in a line of famous American oddballs who, beginning with Henry David Thoreau, often take up "a grubby, lonely existence in one of the most rugged regions of the North American outback." In the case of the Unabomber, this pattern of life suggests such a profound alienation that "it makes Thoreau, with his two-year sabbatical at Walden Pond, look like a social butterfly."[3] Kirkpatrick Sale, by contrast, saw the Unabomber's activities as those of "a rational and serious man, deeply committed to his cause, who has given a great deal of thought to his work and a great deal of time to its expression of it."[4] And, of course, analyses indulging in psychobabble were not lacking. Thus, Maggie Scharf claimed that "the diagnosis of Narcissistic Personality Disorder seems to be the most illuminating explanation of the Unabomber's seemingly incomprehensible behavior." Allegedly, Kaczynski is "deeply injured at the core and suffering from sorely depleted supplies of self-esteem...with a sense of inner emptiness and painful feelings of unworthiness, despair and desolation."[5] Whether or not Kaczynski is mad or reasonable, narcissistic or selfless, evil or virtuous is not particularly interesting. More relevant are the relations between Kaczynski's life, his reputed manifesto, and the whole cultural context from which they emerged.

While the Unabomber's manifesto is a flawed document, crudely reducing a complex society to "the system," it contains interesting insights. There are no signs that the Unabomber followed any of the *Telos* debates

2. Joe Klein, "The Unabomber and the Left," *Newsweek*, April 22, 1996, p. 39.

3. "Probing the Mind of a Killer," *Newsweek*, April 15, 1996, pp. 32–33.

4. In his eagerness to promote his then forthcoming book on the Luddites, Sale wrote that "the Unabomber stands in a long line of anti-technology critics" who share a great many views with himself as well as "a number of people today who might be called neo-Luddites—Jerry Mander, Chellis Glendinning, Jeremy Rifkin, Bill McKibben, Wendell Berry, Dave Foreman, Langdon Winner, Stephenie Mills and John Zerzan among them." See Kirkpatrick Sale, "Is There a Method in His Madness?," *Nation*, September 25, 1995, p. 311.

5. Maggie Scharf, "The Mind of the Unabomber," *New Republic*, June 10, 1996, p. 22.

over the years or pitched his arguments to today's burgeoning populist movements. A quick survey of the footnotes suggests that its author did not have access to materials much more sophisticated than what one might find in second-hand bookshops or a public library in small western towns. Not unlike Paul and Percival Goodman's *Communitas* and their analysis of how "the means of livelihood" structure "ways of life," the Unabomber's violent destruction of those "man-made things" of "engineering and architecture" that are "the heaviest and biggest part of what we experience"[6] indicates that he recognizes how freedom is constrained by the categorical imperatives embedded in ordinary things.

Written in a disorganized series of short numbered paragraphs and running some 35,000 words in length, the Unabomber's manifesto begins with radical sentiments that many have shared for nearly 200 years: "The Industrial Revolution and its consequences have been a disaster for the human race," inasmuch as what is identified as the workings of "the industrial system" have "destabilized society, have made life unfulfilling, have subjected human beings to indignities, have led to widespread psychological suffering (in the Third World to physical suffering as well) and have inflicted severe damage on the natural world" (¶1).[7] The essay outlines a vision of "what must be done," allegedly from the perspective of a burned-out ex-academic living in Montana's backwoods. Because of this predicament, the bombings became a ploy to capture public attention.[8] But how lasting was this impression? The Unabomber killed three people in the course of seventeen years, and the message in his manifesto was mostly tossed away with the rest of the September 19, 1995, newspaper, although he continues his tirades under lock and key in the United States Penitentiary Administrative Maximum Facility outside of Florence, Colorado.

6. Paul and Percival Goodman, *Communitas: Means of Livelihood and Ways of Life* (New York: Vintage, 1960), p. 3.

7. All subsequent references to the manifesto will be cited parenthetically in the text, using the paragraph numbers of the published text. See "Industrial Society and Its Future," in "The Unabomber Trial: The Manifesto," *Washington Post*, September 19, 1995, https://www.washingtonpost.com/wp-srv/national/longterm/unabomber/manifesto.text.htm.

8. If the Unabomber had not committed any terroristic acts, he reasons, "and had submitted the writings to a publisher, they probably would not have been published." In order to get the message "before the public with some chance of making a lasting impression, we've had to kill people" (¶96).

The Unabomber concedes that the manifesto is not comprehensive: it examines "only some of the negative developments that have grown out of the industrial system," particularly those that "have received insufficient public attention or in which we have something new to say" (¶5). What he believes has received inadequate attention, or to be "new," are attempts to register how and why technology as "a means of livelihood" deprives people of their dignity and autonomy while imposing a sense of inferiority and powerlessness. Although this may be dismissed as another exercise in red-green confusion along the lines of Sale's "New Luddites,"[9] there is more here than this superficial critique lets on.[10] The Unabomber's belief that technology increases life expectancy and everyday ease as it decreases life enjoyment and freedom parallels Herbert Marcuse's reading of technology.[11]

What has garnered too little attention is the deadening impact of capital, research, and technology in market-mediated choices—how an allegedly emancipatory technology can, even within capitalist liberal-democratic regimes, result in a rational totalitarian order. The Unabomber approaches this question in several ways, but the concept of "oversocialization" captures much of his distaste. He sees human dignity and freedom bleeding away into preprocessed modes of subjectivity: "We are socialized to conform to many norms of behavior that do not fall under the headings of morality. Thus the oversocialized person is kept on a psychological leash and spends his life running on rails that society has laid down for him. In many oversocialized people this results in a sense of constraint and powerlessness that can be a severe hardship" (¶26). Ironically, he sees this condition afflicting leftists even

9. See Steven Marcus, "Rage against the Machine: The New Luddites, the Old Luddites, and Some Very Bad History," *New Republic*, June 10, 1996, pp. 30–38.

10. See Kirkpatrick Sale, *Rebels against the Future: The Luddites and their War on the Industrial Revolution* (New York: Addison-Wesley, 1996), pp. 261–79.

11. According to Marcuse, the daily mechanism of the industrial system "provides the great rationalization of the unfreedom of man and demonstrates the 'technical' impossibility of being autonomous, of determining one's own life. This unfreedom appears neither as irrational nor as political, but rather as submission to the technical apparatus which enlarges the comforts of life and increases the productivity of labor." While technology/industry/business pose as mediations of cultural liberation and humanitarian progress, they also generate "the legitimacy of domination" that opens out upon "a rationally totalitarian society." See Herbert Marcuse, *One-Dimensional Man: Studies in the Ideology of Advanced Industrial Society* (Boston: Beacon Press, 1964), p. xvi.

more acutely than most people because the prevailing blocs of power and wealth limit modern leftism mostly to acting out its resistance as artificial negativity with no relation to actual revolution (¶26–30).[12]

To compensate for lost power, the system not only provides for but also endorses "surrogate activities" that industrial peoples "set up for themselves merely in order to have some goal to work toward... for the sake of the 'fulfillment' that they get from pursuing the goal" (¶39). Because "only minimal effort is necessary to satisfy one's physical needs" (¶39), most of what preoccupies anyone is a surrogate: art, science, athletics, literature, as well as acquiring money, participating in corporatism, engaging in social activism, and pursuing celebrity. These surrogates are "less satisfying than the pursuit of real goals.... One indication of this is the fact that, in many or most cases, people who are deeply involved in surrogate activities are never satisfied, never at rest" (¶41). The Unabomber states that "the effort needed to satisfy biological needs does not occur AUTONOMOUSLY, but by functioning as parts of an immense social machine" (¶41). When meeting real needs takes only trivial effort and satisfying surrogate desires is given such latitude, the stage is set for individual marginalization on many interrelated levels. Thus, a very fine line divides "Sensible Sam the Smart Consumer" from "Crazy Kaczynski the Alleged Founder of the Freedom Club."

The Unabomber's interpretation again parallels Marcuse's account of technology as "instruments of social and political control." For Marcuse, all individuals' sense of their current needs takes place through the scientific organization of labor and leisure, "which operate beyond and outside the work process and condition the individuals in accord with the dominant social interests."[13] Autonomy under these conditions is difficult to attain because the individual's power is preempted by the highly rationalized social regime, which also, in turn, redefines rationality to

---

12. As the Unabomber observes, "the system couldn't care less what kind of music a man listens to, what kind of clothes he wears or what religion he believes in as long as he studies in school, holds a respectable job, climbs the status ladder, is a 'responsible' parent, is nonviolent and so forth" (¶29). Conceding that his analysis is very rough, he argues that the rational totalitarianism represented by oversocialization causes "low self-esteem, depressive tendencies, and defeatism" because this regime "tries to socialize us to a greater extent than any previous society" (¶32).

13. Herbert Marcuse, *Soviet Marxism: A Critical Analysis* (New York: Vintage, 1961), p. xii.

suit the profit targets of its "merchants of desire."[14] As Marcuse notes, "the apparatus to which the individual is to adjust and adapt himself is so rational that individual protests and liberation appear not only hopeless but as utterly irrational. The system of life created by modern industry is defined in terms of expediency, convenience and efficiency.... Rational behavior becomes identical with a matter-of-factness which teaches reasonable submissiveness and thus guarantees getting along with the prevailing order."[15]

Even though his resistance was futile, and perhaps irrational, Kaczynski acted against expediency, convenience, and efficiency in a life that would seem sociopathic even before he was indicted as the Unabomber. To live normally for him would have further interdicted his already tenuous freedom. As he emphasizes, this question of autonomy is decisive: "For most people it is through the power process—having a goal, making an AUTONOMOUS effort and attaining the goal—that self-esteem, self-confidence and a sense of power are acquired" (¶44). Industrial society destroys these conditions for autonomous action by embedding people in weak, unfree roles in every amorphous aspect of market-mediated social reproduction. This is why this system is in crisis and has to be destroyed by a popular revolution: "When one does not have adequate opportunity to go through the power process the consequences are (depending on the individual and on the way the power process is disrupted) boredom, demoralization, low self-esteem, inferiority feelings, defeatism, depression, anxiety, guilt, frustration, hostility, spouse or child abuse, insatiable hedonism, abnormal sexual behavior, sleep disorders, eating disorders, etc." (¶44).

To crush the regime of oversocialization and revitalize the power process, the Unabomber touts the merits of violent revolt, which is seemingly assumed to work as billed. His obviously poor sense of unintended consequences, however, pops up in this celebration of revolution, which must be "immediate" (¶166), "total" (¶179), "ecocentric" (¶183), "technoscientific" (¶193), "global" (¶195), and "communitarian" (¶199). The preservation of wild nature and individual autonomy depend on

14. William Leach, *Land of Desire: Merchants, Power, and the Rise of a New American Culture* (New York: Pantheon, 1993).

15. Herbert Marcuse, "Some Social Implications of Modern Technology," *Studies in Philosophy and Social Sciences* 9, no. 3 (1941): 421.

dismantling "the system." Yet, with complete naiveté, he somehow believes that his revolutionary program is antithetical to the visions of the future espoused by those technocrats, leftists, or politicians who keep the present system running so smoothly. In positing that "the single overriding goal must be the elimination of modern technology, and that no other goal [e.g., social justice, material equality, or popular participation] can be allowed to compete with this one" (¶205), he argues that everything else should be examined through an open-ended "empirical approach" (¶206). Not seeing how his revolutionary analysis mimics the industrial system's elitist managerialism, the Unabomber merely reasserts the enlightened self-empowerment co-opted by the captains of industry, inventors of tomorrow, or scions of commerce. In accord with the Enlightenment schema, he asserts that "[h]istory is made by active, determined minorities, not by the majority, which seldom has a clear and consistent idea of what it really wants" (¶189). Therefore, the coming revolution will follow an ideology written in two versions: a "more sophisticated" version that "should address itself to people who are intelligent, thoughtful and rational" (¶187) and another version that "should be propagated in a simplified form that will enable the unthinking majority to see the conflict of technology vs. nature in unambiguous terms" (¶188).

The revolutionaries of the Unabomber's Freedom Club must follow the classic Bolshevik strategy of energizing committed radicals and sensitizing the uninformed masses to ready themselves to coproduce their inevitable future under a visionary vanguard's lead: "Until the time comes for the final push toward revolution, the task of revolutionaries will be less to win the shallow support of the majority than to build a small core of deeply committed people. As for the majority, it will be enough to make them aware of the existence of the new ideology and remind them of it frequently; though of course it will be desirable to get majority support to the extent that this can be done without weakening the core of seriously committed people" (¶189). This peculiar vision of the transition is decisively negative: "We have no illusions about the feasibility of creating a new, ideal form of society. Our goal is only to destroy the existing form of society" (¶182). The possibility that there are such big majorities of people to mobilize only because of how technological society works seems to elude the Unabomber's allegedly intelligent, thoughtful, rational elite.

Of course, Kaczynski does not buy into the redistributive millenarianism of nineteenth-century socialism. He warns against "leftists of the most power-hungry type" (¶217) because ultimately "leftism is a totalitarian force" (¶219) "characterized by arrogance or a dogmatic approach to ideology" (¶230). Therefore, social justice as a revolutionary goal is forbidden because it tends to attract leftist do-gooders with power-hungry arrogance. It would compel revolutionaries to preserve large-scale, organization-dependent technology and would dilute the ecocentric focus of the revolution. In short, "it must not be allowed to interfere with the effort to get rid of the technological system" (¶201). Despite efforts to anticipate the possible consequences of mounting a revolution whose "focus will be on technology and economics, not politics" (¶193), there are no guarantees that this blow against technological progress would not self-destruct. In many ways, the Unabomber seems committed only to replacing technocratic New Class managers with small groups of green leaders, who would rule by wise ecological fiat. What guarantees are there in his designs that anti-systemic ecological technophobes, like the industrial system's technocrats, would not lead "all on an utterly reckless ride into the unknown" (¶180)?

The Unabomber embeds his critique in a fateful choice between two kinds of technology: "small-scale technology" and "organization-dependent technology" (¶208). Pursuing a line of attack that basically concludes by celebrating the collapse of Rome and the rise of medieval feudalism, he observes that the Roman Empire's organization-dependent technology (roads, aqueducts, urban sanitation, large buildings) did regress as the empire collapsed, while its small-scale technology survived in many households and villages. Since "[s]mall-scale technology is technology that can be used by small-scale communities without outside assistance" (¶208), it must play a major role in any post-revolutionary scenario. Prior to the Industrial Revolution, "[p]rimitive INDIVIDUALS and SMALL GROUPS actually had considerable power over nature; or maybe it would be better to say power WITHIN nature" (¶198). Therefore, "one should argue that the power of the INDUSTRIAL SYSTEM should be broken, and that this will INCREASE the power and freedom of INDIVIDUALS and SMALL GROUPS" (¶199).

Following the Goodmans, Marcuse, and Mumford, the nub of the Unabomber's protest is found in these questions: How does complex

technology, defined as large-scale or organization-dependent, determine life by eliminating freedom and substituting empty surrogate activities for personal power? What must be done to escape the destructive
consequences—on an individual, social, or global level—of this industrial system? The destruction of the system depends on the disruption of
the system's propagation of empty surrogates or false needs. If the mechanisms of such organizational dependence could be broken down by violent revolution, terrorism, or popular disinterest, then the networks
needed for operating them "would quickly be lost" (¶210). As the Unabomber articulates this possibility, he anticipates the necessary advent
of a new "dark age," arguing that "once this technology had been lost for
a generation or so it would take centuries to rebuild it, just as it took centuries to build it the first time around. Surviving technical books would
be few and scattered. An industrial society, if built from scratch, without outside help, can only be built in a series of stages. You need tools to
make tools.... A long process of economic development and progress in
social organization is required. And, even in the absence of an ideology
opposed to technology, there is no reason to believe that anyone would
be interested in rebuilding industrial society" (¶210).

Organization is where power actually ebbs and flows, rather than in
technology or the state or any individual alone. According to the Unabomber, all people need power; it is what defines autonomous human
beings. However, the Industrial Revolution was about the concentration of power in abstract social machines. As a result, these industrial
megamachines are where power for a few persists as powerlessness for
everyone else. "Modern man as a collective entity, that is—the industrial
system—has immense power over nature" (¶197). But, even more evil is
the fact that "modern INDIVIDUALS and SMALL GROUPS OF INDI-
VIDUALS have far less power than primitive man ever did," because "the
vast power of 'modern man' over nature is exercised not by individuals
or small groups but by large organizations" (¶197). For an individual to
wield the power of technology occurs only "under the supervision and
control of the system," as "you need a license for everything and with the
license come rules and regulations," so the individual has *only* "the technological powers with which the system chooses to provide him" (¶197).

Here, too, is the source of an intriguing level of operational sur-
vivability in organization-dependent technology; its codes of authority,

legitimacy, or use are embedded in the artifacts needed for its application. Consequently, the Unabomber is unequivocal about his immediate revolutionary program: "Until the industrial system has been thoroughly wrecked, the destruction of that system must be the revolutionaries' ONLY goal.... [I]f the revolutionaries permit themselves to have any other goal than the destruction of technology, they will be tempted to use technology as a tool for reaching that other goal. If they give in to that temptation, they will fall right back into the technological trap, because modern technology is a unified, tightly organized system, so that in order to retain SOME technology, one finds oneself obliged to retain MOST technology, here one ends up sacrificing only token amounts of technology.... Never forget that the human race with technology is like an alcoholic with a barrel of wine" (¶¶200, 203). Fortunately for the Freedom Club, this tendency toward breakdown is already occurring on a global scale due to the excesses and inherent flaws in the large-scale disorder of organization-dependent industrial systems. When all is said and done, the "industrial system will not break down purely as a result of revolutionary action," because its vulnerabilities are a product of the regime evolving such that "it is already in enough trouble so that there would be a good chance of its eventually breaking down by itself anyway" (¶167).

Beyond the more obvious difficulties of constructing an anti-technological revolution, the Unabomber employs a simplistic construction of "nature" as the fount of indisputable objective reason that revolutionists should contrapose to the sullied irrationalities of technology. While his references suggest he has not perused the works of Arne Naess, Bill Devall, or George Sessions, this reading of "nature" is straight out of deep ecology. With no sense of irony, the Unabomber asserts that "the positive ideal that we propose is Nature" (¶183) and that it is "not necessary for the sake of nature to set up some chimerical utopia or any new kind of social order" (¶184). This might be true, but could not nature itself, particularly when constructed along such deep ecological lines, become a new kind of social order for some chimerical utopia?

The Unabomber's categories of nature basically play ineffectually with Georg Lukács's two senses of nature.[16] "First nature," or "WILD

---

16. Georg Lukács, *History and Class Consciousness: Studies in Marxist Dialectics*, trans. Rodney Livingstone (Cambridge, MA: MIT Press, 1971), pp. 83–110.

nature; those aspects of the functioning of the Earth and its living things that are independent of human management and free of human interference and control" (¶183), is set up against technology as "second nature," or "an immense social machine" (¶41) composed of "technology that depends on large-scale social organization" (¶208). Human nature is the battleground between first and second nature because "with wild nature we include human nature, by which we mean those aspects of the functioning of the human individual that are not subject to regulation by organized society but are products of chance, or free will, or God" (¶183). Destroy second nature, and first nature will be redeemed and reclaimed, allowing human nature to flourish amid its tests of authentic power processes in the wild, not with artificial surrogate activities. In addition to healing the scars left on nature by the Industrial Revolution, "getting rid of industrial society will accomplish a great deal.... It will remove the capacity of organized society to keep increasing its control over nature (including human nature).... [I]t is certain most people will live close to nature, because in the absence of advanced technology there is no other way that people can live. To feed themselves they must be peasants or herdsmen or fishermen or hunters, etc.... [L]ocal autonomy should tend to increase, because lack of advanced technology and rapid communications will limit the capacity of governments or other large organizations to control local communities" (¶184).

These radical interpretations of nature, however, are no less artificial and no more certain than the positive ideologies of technology that the Unabomber opposes.[17] Instead, he simply conventionalizes a series of fashionable ecocentric assumptions about nature and transforms them into constant timeless truths, like so many others who naively sign on to the good ship "deep ecology" without thinking about where its admirals might sail them. On this account, Joe Klein's dismissal of the Unabomber for his "essential left-wing orientation" is laughable.[18] The Unabomber's contempt for modern leftism seconds deep ecology's criticisms of modern socialism's trust in big science, complex technology, and vast organizations to create limitless material abundance. Nonetheless, his commitment to "wild nature" does not lead all the way into

---

17. Timothy W. Luke, "Community and Ecology," *Telos* 88 (Summer 1991): 69–79, reprinted in this volume.

18. Klein, "The Unabomber and the Left," p. 39.

a biocentric Gaia worship; indeed, he razzes such ecospiritualist devotions as frivolous playacting, even though he admits that nature often inspires quasi-religious reverence.

Rather than singing from Marxist hymnals, the Unabomber merely recycles questionable assumptions cribbed from primers on wild nature philosophies: nature is the opposite of technology, nature is beautiful, nature is popular, radical environmentalists must exalt nature and oppose technology, nature takes care of itself, nature is a spontaneous creation, humans once coexisted with nature without doing any damage to it, only industrial societies really devastate nature (¶184). Most if not all of these points cannot be defended because they are by-products of skewed misinterpretations. Yet, within this utopia, the Unabomber draws his certitudes for a new social order constrained materially by this prime directive: nature's attributes make it necessary to destroy technology so that small groups of autonomous individuals can coexist with it in ways that do not devastate nature and thereby let it take care of itself. Clearly, this image is appealing, but it also necessitates the destruction of a global web of interrelated, complex organization-dependent technologies that provide a vital habitat for billions of people. Without such technologies, nature will take care of itself and let these immense populations die to the extent that their members cannot live autonomously like primitive man or "find and prepare edible roots...track game and take it with homemade weapons...protect [themselves] from heat, cold, rain, dangerous animals, etc." (¶198).

Maybe Kaczynski began to approach this ecological ideal in Montana, but unlike primitive man he also received a monetary allowance from his aged mother and perplexed brother. Many of his tools (a bicycle, his shack, the typewriters, various explosives, etc.) were also artifacts salvaged from industrial society. Moreover, mail-bombing computer store owners, timber industry lobbyists, and research university professors will not contribute to the collapse of a vast social machine that sustains billions of human beings. Living autonomously in small groups might turn out well on the level of Rousseau's noble savages, but it also could turn sour on the scale of the Road Warrior's ceaseless quest for petrol.

Basically, the Unabomber's manifesto is an essay on the origins of inhumanity, inequality, and insensitivity. The compounding of architecture/

engineering/utility/transportation/communication infrastructures with natural environments now produces such circumambient constraints on human beings that second nature is actively selecting autonomy, power processes, and small-group intimacy out of the human species.[19] The industrial system is animated not by conventional political ideologies "but by technical necessity" (¶119). The survival of mechanical networks of human and inhuman actors in these vast arcologies robs once free individuals of their autonomy and power,[20] because the individual's fate now "MUST depend on decisions that he personally cannot influence to any great extent," as "production depends on the cooperation of very large numbers of people" (¶117). These biopowered populations accept their daily disciplinary directives. Plainly, the autonomy of local communities disappears as these formations "become more enmeshed with and dependent on large-scale systems like public utilities, computer networks, highway systems, the mass communications media, [and] the modern health care system," as it becomes more obvious "that technology applied in one location often affects people at other locations far away" (¶118).

Here the Unabomber grasps a key populist complaint: the colonization of everyday life by industrial society is becoming virtually irresistible and irreversible as New Class symbolic analysts rob everyone of their autonomous power potential.[21] Inasmuch as each new technical device appears to advance life in a desirable fashion, technological systems "as a WHOLE narrow our sphere of freedom" (¶128) and success in resisting it "can be hoped for only by fighting the technological system as a whole; but that is revolution, not reform" (¶130). The Unabomber sees reform as the existing regime's most false promise, claiming that all efforts to make any room for "a sense of purpose and for autonomy within the system are no better than a joke" (¶120). Reformers ask how personal freedom and small-group autonomy might be mixed with the benefits of high technology. The needs of the technical order, however,

---

19. Lewis Mumford, *The Myth of the Machine* (New York: Harcourt, Brace and Jovanovich, 1970).

20. Timothy W. Luke, "The Politics of Arcological Utopia: Soleri on Ecology, Architecture, and Society," *Telos* 101 (Fall 1994): 55–78, reprinted in this volume.

21. Bruno Latour, *We Have Never Been Modern*, trans. Catherine Porter (London: Harvester Wheatsleaf, 1993).

will eventually overrule any true efforts to make reforms, as the system's demands impose inhumane consequences.[22] Ultimately, the existing order works much better without the uncertainties or lack of focus humane values would introduce into its operations. As the Unabomber fears, "it is NOT in the interest of the system to preserve freedom or small-group autonomy. On the contrary, it is in the interest of the system to bring human behavior under control to the greatest possible extent" (¶139).

At one level, Kaczynski's reading of technology and industrial society might be interpreted as a crude misinterpretation of Marcuse's "great refusal," being carried on as a real revolution by a true "outsider." Indeed, his rehash of Cal-Berkeley activists assailing "the system" at times sounds like the 1968 zeitgeist echoing back from the Montana Rockies. Fearing absorption by modern technological civilization, Kaczynski simply dropped out, refusing to cooperate with most of the high-technology systems that have transformed everyday life since the 1880s. Living in a ten-by-twelve-foot shack with no indoor plumbing, electricity, telephone connection, gas, or municipal services, he eked out an intentionally frugal existence, his level of technological sophistication not exceeding 1896. With a woodstove for heat, a bicycle for transport, game animals for food, a manual typewriter for communication, and local library books for entertainment, the Unabomber appears to have met his "single overriding goal...the elimination of modern technology" (¶7) in his own daily existence. Yet few would forsake their surrogate activities in today's world and the ultimate convenience of modern living to accept growing and eating their own turnips outside a shack in the woods as their version of an authentic power process.

One need not condone what Kaczynski has done to comprehend the logic of his actions. As marginalized as he was throughout his own life, much of what he did after leaving Berkeley in 1968 amounts to a one-man resistance movement. In a society that celebrates group conformity on the job and at home, he militantly chose a strictly feral existence. He does not claim that the end of industrial society is near; indeed, it can persist for many more decades simply racking up greater levels of ecological destruction and social anomie. Industrial society has a future,

---

22. Christopher Lasch, *The Revolt of the Elites and the Betrayal of Democracy* (New York: Norton, 1995).

albeit a bleak one that offers solitary, nasty, brutish, and short lives. So Kaczynski attempted to capitalize on its bleakness to leverage a revolution among subjects who can still act and think on their own.

The conditions of association that bring human beings into coexistence with machines are rarely, if ever, discussed. The Unabomber's manifesto focuses on this concern. Just as Gramsci asked how "Fordism" combined capital, technology, labor, markets, and culture in a determinate new social assembly line—"Americanism"[23]—so too does the Unabomber ask how this industrial system is forging a new psycho-physical nexus for power, science, freedom, and organization that is dehumanizing, disempowering, and decommunalizing everyday life. The answer he provides—technical necessity or organizational momentum—is not always all-inclusive. Other forces also structure the conditions of association. But because the Unabomber is so averse to "modern leftism," he neglects such additional factors as market rationality, class bias, ideological expectations, or bureaucratic imperatives in his examination of how collectives of people and machines actually become associated.

Telos has considered these questions in the past, and it continues its lines of investigation into the present.[24] In many ways, the phenomenon of populism is the political problematic that most directly focuses on questions of "who, whom" in organization-dependent, large-scale technology. Believing that new associations of autonomous individuals on a more than local but less than national level can work as viable alternatives to the surrogacies of industrial democracy, militarized nationalism, and personal consumption within the industrial system of developed nation-states, populists—old and new—advance their visions for alternative conditions of associating ordinary people with new arrangements of machines, which would accentuate personal competencies, familial cohesion, and communal ecologies. These modes of forging technical collectives also could stand against industrial society and for sane environmental practices, but they do not stand for going "back to the future"

23. Antonio Gramsci, *Selections from the Prison Notebooks*, ed. and trans. Quintin Hoare and Geoffrey Nowell Smith (New York: International, 1971), pp. 272–318.

24. See Paul Piccone, "Postmodern Populism," *Telos* 103 (Spring 1995): 45–86; Timothy W. Luke, "Searching for Alternatives: Postmodern Populism and Ecology," *Telos* 103 (Spring 1995): 87–110, reprinted in this volume; and Emory Roe, "Critical Theory, Sustainable Development, and Populism," *Telos* 103 (Spring 1995): 149–65.

to revitalize the power process with neolithic hunting-and-gathering lifestyles.

In fact, even the Unabomber admits that power processes in societies as developed as those of nineteenth-century America most likely were quite satisfying (¶¶56–57). Hence, there may be no need to eradicate those forms of industrial metabolism simply to abolish the hypertrophied disorder of corporate consumerism and warfare/welfare statism as it has evolved since the 1880s. Myths of living in or for "wild nature" cannot eliminate the docile domination of existing arcologies' second nature; instead, its organization-dependent, large-scale systems, with all of their surrogate activities and technological controls, need to be transformed from within to create workable populist communities. What is amiss here is not technologies that create domination but rather inhumane systems of corporate control and statist domination that misinform and disorganize technologies. Populist thinkers such as Christopher Lasch or Amory Lovins have attempted to disembed these insights from their current conditions of inarticulation and to derive answers from knowledge available in their own communities, economies, and technologies.[25] Because of these face-to-face or small-group modes of economic interaction, even the Unabomber could envision frontier societies in nineteenth-century America as ones in which the power process worked well: "[T]he 19th century frontiersman had the sense (also largely justified) that he created change himself, by his own choice. Thus a pioneer settled on a piece of land of his own choosing and made it into a farm through his own effort.... [He] participated as a member of a relatively small group in the creation of a new, ordered community.... [I]t satisfied the pioneer's need for the power process" (¶57). Bearing in mind the associated but unaddressed questions of dispossessing Mexican and Native American communities in the process, the result was that "19th century American society had an optimistic and self-confident tone, quite unlike today's society" (¶56). These are the traces that America's nineteenth-century populists struggled to keep, and what contemporary populists aspire to regain.

---

25. Christopher Lasch, *The True and Only Heaven: Progress and Its Critics* (New York: Norton, 1991); and Amory B. Lovins, *Soft Energy Paths: Toward a Durable Peace* (San Francisco: Ballinger, 1977).

Real autonomy for the Unabomber comes from broadening human freedom. By "freedom" he means "the opportunity to go through the power process, with real rather than artificial goals of surrogate activities, and without interference, manipulation or supervision from anyone, especially from any large organization" (¶94). Reiterating *Telos*'s articulation of the authentic message of populism, he defines freedom as "being in control (either as an individual or as a member of a SMALL group) of the life-and-death issues of one's existence; food, clothing, shelter and defense against whatever threats there may be in one's environment" (¶94). Freedom is not the meaningless freedom of consumer choice. It means, rather, "having power; not the power to control other people but the power to control the circumstances of one's own life" because, as most savvy populists observe with regard to big business and big government, "one does not have freedom if anyone else (especially a large organization) has power over one, no matter how benevolently, tolerantly and permissively that power may be exercised" (¶94). The "freedom to choose," as celebrated in advertising, is merely "an element of a social machine and has only a certain set of prescribed and delimited freedoms; freedoms that are designed to serve the needs of the social machine more than those of the individual" (¶97). Autonomy is more than political rights, economic discretion, or cultural liberation; it is also an ecological condition in which someone has the ability and latitude to determine the totality of their material interconnections in both nature and society.

Despite the Unabomber's celebration of nineteenth-century simplicities, his remarkably bleak reading of industrial society suggests no appreciation for the communities of that time. While many of his insights parallel those of populism, his lack of any grounding in community life is reflected in his angry loner analyses of the power process. In the wastelands of postwar suburbia, the Cold War research university, and backwoods Montana, Kaczynski missed the rootedness and direction provided by close cooperative and conflictual community life. It is not too surprising, therefore, that the Unabomber's manifesto calls for a return to small groups of humans struggling with "nature, red in tooth and claw," to revitalize feelings of individual identity, authentic autonomy, or close community. Populism must be integrated within the community life of those groups seeking to create workable conditions for their cultural, economic, and political freedom. Most importantly, these groups need a much keener sense of culture than the narrow, almost crabbed sociological aberration of culture permeating the manifesto. Without the cultural particularity of an aesthetics or ethics grounded in stable communities, populism makes no sense. Culture is much more than "leftist psychology" or "surrogate activities in the industrial-technological system." Seeing culture as the Unabomber does, only as the conduits of oversocialized bondage, washes away all of the exciting contradictions and cross-purposes of living communities.

Kaczynski never led a "normal life," and his personal experiences with the system appear to have done much to aid and abet his slide into socially abnormal ways. The subtext of media reporting on these tendencies is that his own arrogance and intelligence got in the way of "fitting in," so he opted out and finally decided to strike back. This is Kaczynski's key point: the routines of existing society are the heart of its inhumane reproduction. Strike at them successfully, and destabilization of everything in industrial society will be realized. His life seems to have been one of scholarly promise, followed by a consciously embraced internal exile. Yet his manifesto makes so many valid criticisms against industrial society that it cannot be ignored. Simply dismissing this philosophical statement with all of its flaws as a demented screed from a wacko ex-professor who turned to terrorism and a hermit's life to cope with his failures as a human being, which has been the mass media's recurring spin on Kaczynski since his arrest on April 3, 1996, dodges all of the interesting issues of this sad affair.

8

A Harsh and Hostile Land:
Edward Abbey's Politics
and the Great American Desert

MUCH OF CONTEMPORARY American environmental thought, implicitly or explicitly, circles around the literary corpus of Edward Abbey in search of its most radical aesthetic, ethical, and political perspectives. Whether this inspiration is drawn from *Abbey's Road, The Monkey Wrench Gang, A Fool's Progress, Desert Solitaire, Good News, Down the River, Black Sun,* or *Hayduke Lives!*, Abbey's fictional work holds the collective life of modern suburban America up against the discipline of surviving alone in the desert. In the extremes of that harsh and hostile land, he finds sublime inspiration rather than bleak desolation. Consciously anarchistic, extremist, and individualistic in his vision, Abbey propounds an aesthetic vision of "the desert" that implies a certain ethics and politics.

Yet these implications have divergent interpretations. Whether it is Sierra Club conservationism, Wilderness Society preservationism, or Earth First! activism, the tropes and tones of the southwestern American desert in Abbey's texts have motivated many to join environmental causes in the United States. Some see him as the patron saint of an "ecological antimodernism," which leads, in turn, to allegedly radical forms of resistance against industrial life as we know it.[1] However, Abbey's

---

* Originally published in *Telos* 141 (Fall 2007): 5–28.

1. Arthur Versluis, "Antimodernism," *Telos* 137 (Winter 2006): 96–130.

thought is far more complex, nuanced, and clever than this caricature. It would be fair to say that he has, first, "abmodernist" impulses, or a desire to simply be away and apart from industrialism, especially when he decries the edifices of the Glen Canyon Dam or the sprawl around Phoenix, Arizona, as cancerous growths on the land. Yet, at the end of the day, he also has, second, an "anamodernist" side, with a fresh vision for another more satisfying modern way of life, since he admits to enjoying immensely a cold beer, a good ethics book, a reliable pickup truck, and an accurate handgun. His thoughts, then, clearly are more "altermodernist" musings, meant to make modernity better by letting humanity become greater.[2] This study begins to explore Abbey's complicated and conflicted musings about wastelands and deserts in order to outline his unique evocation of another way of being, and it then asks how his aesthetic accounts of harsh and hostile land are meant to reshape everyday Americans' subjectivity and identity for pursuing strategies of political change.[3]

I. Abbey's Road

Since the details of his life are not widely known, it is worth recounting them, if only briefly. Edward Abbey was born January 29, 1927, near Indiana, Pennsylvania, deep in Appalachia, and died March 14, 1989, near Oracle, Arizona, at a place called Fort Llatikcuf. In between, he lived his life in a fashion that perhaps only Appalachian hollow-living mountaineers and Arizona desert rats might ever truly understand, namely, one grounded in ways of thinking and acting that too many describe inadequately as "anarchism." After growing up amid the demands of hardscrabble rural life in his improbably named hometown of Home, Pennsylvania, Abbey rode the rails out west in 1944, where he became fascinated by the spaces of its land and sky.

---

2. Timothy W. Luke, "Alterity or Antimodernism: A Response to Versluis," *Telos* 137 (Winter 2006): 131–42.

3. For additional views of Abbey, see Ann Ronald, *The New West of Edward Abbey* (Reno: Univ. of Nevada Press, 1988); Walter H. Clark, "Aesthetics and the Lived-in," *Journal of Aesthetic Education* 23, no. 4 (1989): 99–103; Daniel G. Payne, "Talking Freely around the Campfire: The Influence of Nature Writing on American Environmental Policy," *Society & Natural Resources* 12, no. 1 (1999): 39–48; and Jonathan Levin, "Coordinates and Connections: Self, Language, and World in Edward Abbey and William Least Heat-Moon," *Contemporary Literature* 41, no. 2 (2000): 214–51.

Graduating high school in 1945, he spent two years in the U.S. Army, serving in Alabama, Italy, and New Jersey. At twenty, he enrolled at the University of New Mexico on the G.I. Bill and worked at becoming a writer. His first novel, *Jonathan Troy*, was published in 1954. His first commercially successful novel, *The Brave Cowboy*, came out in 1956, and he continued writing until his death in 1989. His nonfictional work *Desert Solitaire* firmly anchored his reputation as a writer, since that book has come to be regarded as a classic work in "American nature writing."[4] *The Monkey Wrench Gang* from 1975, about a cadre of eco-saboteurs creating chaos in the Four Corners region, became another classic Abbey novel as well as an inspiration for the ethics and politics of Earth First! and then the Earth Liberation Front (ELF), the Animal Liberation Front (ALF), and other eco-activists for the past three decades.[5] Since the early 1970s, these works also earned him the odd nickname of "Cactus Ed" and the reputation of being the ultimate "southwestern writer."

Over thirty-five years, he published a tremendous range of work that some regard as classic, others as polemic, and still others as dyspeptic. Abbey himself often characterized his work as just plain comic. He admitted that a bit of it was erotic, some of it melodramatic, but much of it also can be read as tragic. His novel *The Monkey Wrench Gang* probably best sums up these contradictions, in that Abbey admitted he wrote the book to "entertain and amuse," but it also depicts the unrelenting despoliation of the Four Corners region in the Southwest by automobile tourism, federal bureaucrats, land development, and coal companies. Dubbed "the desert anarchist," Abbey did love the desert, and he had a wide and deep anarchist streak.[6] Yet no label easily defines his life or

---

4. See Timothy W. Luke, *Ecocritique: Contesting the Politics of Nature, Economy, and Culture* (Minneapolis: Univ. of Minnesota Press, 1997).

5. See Timothy W. Luke, "The Dreams of Deep Ecology," *Telos* 76 (Summer 1988): 65–92, reprinted in this volume; Rick Scarce, *Eco-Warriors: Understanding the Radical Environmental Movement* (Chicago: Noble Press, 1990); L. J. Pickering, *The Earth Liberation Front: 1997–2002* (New York: Arissa Publications, 2002); and Charles Rosebraugh, *Burning Rage of a Dying Planet: Speaking for the Earth Liberation Front* (New York: Lantern Books, 2004).

6. James Bishop, Jr., *Epitaph for a Desert Anarchist: The Life and Legacy of Edward Abbey* (New York: Atheneum, 1994).

work: it is often what this anarchist moniker connotes, but it also remains far more than words can define.

On February 7, 2007, about forty years after its writing, Abbey's *Desert Solitaire* (1968) had sales figures on Amazon.com that ranked it at 3,105 out of all the website's books; Amazon.com also noted that 94 percent of those who viewed the product listing for *Desert Solitaire* bought either "the item" or the January 12, 1985, Ballantine reissue edition of Abbey's classic 1968 book. Nearly four decades later, then, many still cannot resist the compelling first three sentences of *Desert Solitaire*:

> This is the most beautiful place on earth. There are many such places. Every man, every woman, carries in heart and mind the image of the ideal place, the right place, the one true home, known or unknown, actual or visionary.[7]

Once hooked, the writer teases the reader with glimpses of this yet unknown image, which the next 350-plus pages sketch out:

> For myself I'll take Moab, Utah. I don't mean the town itself, of course, but the country which surrounds it—the canyonlands. The slickrock desert. The red dust and the burnt cliffs and the lonely sky—all that which lies beyond the end of the roads.[8]

Here irony and metaphor mingle. Abbey writes in a desert to exalt its beauty and tout its ultimate expression of *Heimat* for himself and others, while spinning up this apparent reverie about nature into an aggressive critique of society.

The fantasy of living footloose and free in the desert is another part of the Abbey myth, but it is an obvious feint. The material realities of Abbey's road in the American Southwest are always on the page and frequently discussed by Abbey, but few readers see its hard truth. That is, he neither lived from the desert nor appreciated how rich its ecology actually was for those who could. When out in the desert, Abbey typically was just passing through, on temporary assignment, under a retainer or supplied from without by his writing, a federal job, local government

---

7. Edward Abbey, *Desert Solitaire: A Season in the Wilderness* (New York: Ballantine, 1968), p. 1.
8. Ibid.

work, or day labor tied to the apparatus of industrial tourism.[9] Always a drifter, occasionally a tenant, never a native, Abbey did not truly tie himself to living in, by, and from the desert until late in his life. He wistfully speculates about those Native Americans who did, whether they are the Anasazi, Navajos, Hopi, or Utes, and he grudgingly admires old Mormon towns, whose daily life stays close to nature itself as their residents earn their daily bread from farming, ranching, or timbering. The realities of scratching out a living in the desert were obscured in the dust of his dreams. Abbey goes searching the desert for "life" and evading "death," but always on some idiosyncratic *haj*, still tethered materially to the "contemporary techno-industrial greed-and-power culture" that he decries.[10]

While gaggles of greens today continue to clutch their copies of *Desert Solitaire*, convinced that Abbey is a fervent fellow-traveler, as the Ecology Hall of Fame website attests,[11] Abbey himself foreswore pious political allegiances. Many ecological crusaders have seized upon his writings because both booksellers and local activists pigeonhole Abbey as the quintessential "western environmentalist writer," but Abbey shrugged off their devotion.[12] He only wished to write and then attain beyond any doubt the status of "an artist." As he admitted to James Hepworth in February 1977, in an interview at the University of Arizona, "I never wanted to be an environmental crusader, an environmental journalist. I wanted to be a fiction writer, a novelist."[13] Abbey's politics and ethics flow from his aesthetics, yet his aesthetics are not "about the desert." They instead are impressionistic, evocative, or alluring forays in, from, and around the spaces surrounding many desert cities in the

9. Edward Abbey, *One Life at a Time, Please* (New York: Henry Holt and Company, 1988).

10. Edward Abbey, *A Voice Crying in the Wilderness (Vox Clamantis in Deserto)* (New York: St. Martin's Press, 1989), p. xiii.

11. See the Ecology Hall of Fame website, http://ecotopia.org/ecology-hall-of-fame/.

12. See Mark Mossman, "The Rhetoric of a Nature Writer: Subversion, Persuasion, and Ambiguity in the Writings of Edward Abbey," *Journal of American Culture* 20, no. 4 (1997): 79–85; and Nathanael Dresser, "Cultivating Wilderness: The Place of Land in the Fiction of Ed Abbey and Wendell Berry," *Growth and Change* 26, no. 3 (1998): 350–64.

13. James Hepworth and Gregory McNamee, eds., *Resist Much, Obey Little: Some Notes on Edward Abbey* (Salt Lake City: Dream Gardens Press, 1985), p. 37.

American Southwest.[14] Even though many environmentalists hear environmentalism in his words,[15] Abbey did not shrink from exclaiming, "I am not an Environmentalist." Facing these facts is important because Abbey's writing should not be sent away to the taxidermy shop of literary theory, only to return as America's finest "western environmentalist writer," when so much of his art addresses more than just the American West, the desert environment, and nature writing.

II. Space: Shadows from the Black Sun

The thinking of Henri Lefebvre can be invaluable when approaching Abbey's writing. Both Lefebvre and Abbey recognize that spatiality should not be left to be discovered, preserved, or safeguarded as if it could be seen as a preexistent externality always unknown or untrammeled apart from human action. On the contrary, space must be recognized, as Lefebvre asserts, as "social." Whether it is "the American Southwest," our "environment," "locality," or "community," space always "manifests itself as the realization of a general practical schema" rooted in socially fabricated orders of homogeneity, fragmentality, and hierarchy that give rise "to multiple tactical operations directed towards an overall result."[16] These problematic realities begin with historical appearances, conceptual frameworks, or mental maps. As Lefebvre suggests, few critical works, even those on environmental resistance, recognize:

> At this moment, a representation of space—which is by no means innocent, since it involves and contains a strategy—is passed off as disinterested positive knowledge. It is projected objectively; it is affected materially, through practical means. There is thus no real space or authentic space, only spaces produced in accordance with certain schemas developed by some particular groups within the general framework of a society (that is to say, a mode of production).[17]

14. See James I. McClintock, "Edward Abbey's 'Antidotes to Despair,'" *Critique: Studies in Contemporary Fiction* 31, no. 1 (1989): 41–54.

15. See Frances K. Foster, "Recommended: Edward Abbey," *English Journal* 70, no. 6 (1981): 65–66; Reed F. Noss, "Sustainability and Wilderness," *Conservation Biology* 5, no. 1 (1991): 120–22; and Michael D. Yates, "The Ghosts of Karl Marx and Edward Abbey," *Monthly Review* 56, no. 10 (2005).

16. Henri Lefebvre, *The Critique of Everyday Life*, vol. 3, *From Modernity to Modernism: Towards a Metaphilosophy of Daily Life*, trans. John Moore (London: Verso, 1981), p. 134.

17. Ibid., p. 135.

Despite whatever well-meaning mystifications are wrapped around the deliberative projects of collaborative governance, collective self-management, or communal eco-resistance, today those tactics always remain entangled in the stealthy schematics of homogenized, fragmented, and hierarchical spatial practices of contemporary capitalism.

Therefore, as a product, space still "is made in accordance with an operating instrument in the hands of a group of experts, technocrats who are themselves representative of particular interests but at the same time of a mode of production, conceived not as a completed reality or an abstract totality, but as a set of possibilities in the process of being realized."[18] Here it is important to ask: who sets the possibilities, what is the realm of the possible imagined to be, and how are they to be realized? Abbey's works plainly use the American Southwest to question these modernizing conditions in spatial constructs.

Spatiality, as a social product of sites, settings, and symbols, is still charged with coded meanings, no matter how integrated into operational systems they become. In many ways, it is this place-based space of being, as Abbey asserts, that must be recovered. To focus upon the environment, ecology, or the earth, as Abbey's writing does, is to preoccupy oneself with specific spaces and all the particular aspects, elements, and moments of relevant social practice associated with their social practices.[19] Discursive appropriations of desert spaces, for example, have particular implications inasmuch as thinking about and/or acting with the American Southwest in the late twentieth century is a grounded practice. For Abbey, as it is for Lefebvre, it is one in which:

1. it represents the political (in the case of the West, the "neocapitalist") use of knowledge. Remember that knowledge under this system is integrated in a more or less "immediate" way into the forces of production, and in a "mediate" way into the social relations of production.

2. it implies an ideology designed to conceal that use, along with the conflicts intrinsic to the highly interested employment of a supposedly disinterested knowledge. This ideology carries no flag, and for

18. Ibid., p. 134.
19. See Paul Lindholdt, "Writing from a Sense of Place," *Journal of Environmental Education* 30, no. 4 (1999): 4–10; and Belden C. Lane, "The Desert Imagination of Edward Abbey," *Christian Century* 102 (1989).

those who accept the practice of which it is a part it is indistinguishable from knowledge.

3. it embodies at best a technological utopia, a sort of computer simulation of the future, or of the possible, within the framework of the
   real—the framework of the existing mode of production. The start-
   ing-point here is a knowledge which is at once integrated into, and
   integrative with respect to, the mode of production. The technological utopia in question is a common feature not just of many science-
   fiction novels, but also of all kinds of projects concerned with space,
   be they those of architecture, urbanism, or social planning.[20]

Each of these spatial disjunctures can be found in American environmental politics today, and their real effects, which are only partly explicit,
are troubling enough to anchor much of Abbey's literary project. That
"everyday life in the U.S.A." can implicitly constitute a technological
utopia, a biased ideology, and a quite destructive political economy simply as spatiality is a reality that Abbey's writings acknowledge but never
accept as necessary.

The ethical impulses driving many environmental political programs
today are said to be grounded in spaces of nature, even though they are
disappearing into a diverse array of professional discourses, developments, and disciplines. Despite many ecologists' obsession with nature's
alleged moral privilege, as Lefebvre notes, "everyone wants to protect
and save nature; nobody wants to stand in the way of an attempt to re-
trieve its authenticity. Yet at the same time everything conspires to harm
it."[21] Abbey's defense of "the desert" sees, and then questions, the multiple senses of spatiality that American politics, economics, and cultures
give to it. Southwestern spaces are social products, and all that conspires
to acclaim their authenticity, or needlessly harm them, is entangled in
conventional illusions about nature's opacity and transparency.

Spatiality as both social production and a social product can be
gauged in its fullest particularity only by indicating "the extent that it
ceases to be indistinguishable from mental space (as defined by the philosophers and mathematicians) on the one hand, and physical space (as

20. See Henri Lefebvre, *The Production of Space*, trans. Donald Nicholson-Smith
(Oxford: Blackwell, 1991), pp. 8–9.

21. Ibid., pp. 30–31.

defined by practico-sensory activity and the perception of 'nature') on the other."[22] Even though it is a social product, space is not a collection of things, an aggregation of sense data, an emptiness packed with things, or a formless veil draped over phenomena, events, or sites. Its creation as social product operates instead through "a double illusion, each side of which refers back to the other, reinforces the other, and hides the other," creating simultaneously "the illusion of transparency" and "the illusion of opacity."[23] Abbey's meditations on the rivers of the Southwest, the desert itself, and tourists loving the West to death play on these twin illusions.

A great deal of rational preparation must transpire to create the illusion of transparency in which "space appears as luminous, as intelligible, as giving action free rein," even as the illusion of opacity veils most analyses of the environment "chiefly because of its appeal to naturalness, to substantiality."[24] Devotees of spatial transparency regard what happens in space as giving

> a miraculous quality to thought, which becomes incarnate by means of a *design* (in both senses of the word). The design serves as a mediator—itself of great fidelity—between mental activity (invention) and social activity (realization); and it is deployed in space. The illusion of transparency goes hand in hand with a view of space as innocent, as free of traps or secret places. Anything hidden or dissimulated—and hence dangerous—is antagonistic to transparency, under whose reign everything can be taken in by a single glance from that mental eye which illuminates whatever it contemplates.[25]

On the one hand, Abbey's cautious reflections about deserts, and what they should mean to us, support this analysis. On the other hand, the illusion of opacity is rooted in epistemic conventions about realist essences "from which the proper and adequate word for each thing or 'object' may be picked," and thus the "illusion of substantiality, naturalness, and spatial opacity nurtures its own mythology."[26] Here, of course, Abbey would eschew his "Cactus Ed" persona: the desert is always far more than

22. Ibid., p. 27.
23. Ibid.
24. Ibid.
25. Ibid., p. 28.
26. Ibid., p. 30.

Desert Solitaire ever could portray. The sober realism of social analysis, therefore, adduces both its substantive foci and its transparent frames for their examination in spatial investigations. Ironically, "each illusion embodies and nourishes the other.... The rational is thus naturalized, while nature cloaks itself in nostalgias which supplant rationality."[27]

The explicit, or sometimes merely implicit, problem of too many environmentalists, intent upon making concrete in practice their "defending the desert" discourse, is their acceptance of some "basic sophistry whereby the philosophico-epistemological notion of space is fetishized and the mental realm comes to envelop the social and physical ones."[28] That some concrete mediation between these two realms is needed to demystify this fetishism and that one cannot move back and forth between the mental and social at will are the conceptual caution signs that one easily finds in most of Abbey's writings.

Lefebvre claims the analysis of space must scrutinize all "spatial practice" because this process "secretes that society's space; it propounds and presupposes it, in a dialectical interaction," and in today's neocapitalist order, spatial practice "embodies a close association, within perceived space, between daily reality (daily routine) and urban reality (the routes and networks which link up the spaces set aside for work, 'private' life and leisure)."[29] Arguably, with technonature/technoculture, these materialities are foundational in each one of Abbey's discussions of the desert. As Lefebvre claims, these connections embrace

> production and reproduction, and the particular locations and spatial sets characteristic of each social formation. Spatial practice ensures continuity and some degree of cohesion. In terms of social space, and of each member of a given society's relationship to that space, this cohesion implies a guaranteed level of *competence* and a specific level of *performance*.[30]

Urban technostructures, both propounded and presupposed in the secretion of such space, will work only if urbanized people are accustomed to performing rightly or wrongly in them. Cities are environments in

27. Ibid.
28. Ibid., p. 5.
29. Ibid., p. 38.
30. Ibid., p. 33.

which urbanity's amicable compliance is derived from individual competence and collective performance at particular locations with certain spatial settings. None of these projects can be changed without remaking spatial practices.

Lefebvre is right about cities. They generate strong normative agendas through everyday spatial codes, like liberal amicality or modern convenience, because metropolitan life, especially as Abbey sees it at work in "the New West," is much more than a means of interpreting space and its practices. It is simultaneously a site of living in this space and a strategy for concretizing the means of living beyond that space, making it difficult to always be clear about how to understand it. Every engineered system of embedded materiality that now services America's accidental normality, then, is concretized normativity.[31] Whether it is leveraged daily as an element for governance actions, either where it sits or when it is deployed to other sites, spatial formations are the ongoing "in-formationalization" and/or "de-formation" of the conventions for social practices in action. This fact is true of material structures as well as any agents that serve as their caretakers, managers, or vendors.

Living in societies of bureaucratically controlled consumption on a transnational scale, as Lefebvre suggests, can disclose that consumption is a normative cluster of conduct. It directly enables modes of bureaucratic control and control by corporate, government, and technoscientific bureaucracies. To examine "everyday life in the modern world" is to realize how much "the modern world" is an imagined, embedded, and engineered community that normatively delimits, defines, and directs "everyday life" as a mode of global governance via technified space. This reality is ignored by far too many, but Abbey finds this trail in all of his writings. His ruminations about desert mesas, flooded canyons, and river running call these occluded systems and their dangers to our attention, lest this destructive urban revolution spread out to every last butte and box canyon in the American Southwest.

For Abbey, "the desert" recedes as "the Southwest" expands, and this leads only to the growth of real "wastelands." On this point, he too would have little use for the materiality of today's global "empire." That is, "certainly we continue to have," as Michael Hardt and Antonio Negri

31. See Henri Lefebvre, *The Urban Revolution*, trans. Robert Bononno (Minneapolis: Univ. of Minnesota Press, 2003).

argue, "crickets and thunderstorms…and we continue to understand our psyches as driven by natural instincts and passions; but we have no nature in the sense that these forces and phenomena are no longer understood as outside, that is, they are not seen as original and independent of the civil order."[32] Abbey's thinking concurs with Hardt and Negri, but he does it far more caustically.

As he writes of what lies beyond "the end of the road," Abbey rips into all that rests behind and beside where the road begins as it winds out into the spaces of his "most beautiful place on earth." Amazon.com, in the site's editorial review of *Desert Solitaire*, misses these subtleties, like so many others before it, remarking: "With language as colorful as a Canyonlands sunset and a perspective as pointed as a prickly pear, Cactus Ed captures the heat, mystery, and surprising bounty of desert life. *Desert Solitaire* is a meditation on the stark landscapes of the red-rock West, a passionate vote for wilderness, and a howling lament for the commercialization of the American outback."[33] The book is this in part, but only in a very small part. Why it is, how it is, when it is, where it is, and what it is remain caught in the ironies of displacement and diversion split forth as Abbey depicts the heat, mystery, and surprising bounty of desert life in *Desert Solitaire*'s pages. Writing in this desert about its beauty, however, also gets the reader thinking of how much the book really is about another desert whose harsh and hostile lands lie not at the end, but rather at the start, of the roads leading to Moab, Utah.

Clearly, the American Southwest in Abbey's writing evolves into an excellent example of absolute space found, fixed, and finalized as a fragment of potential transcendence by the grids of abstract spatial practices. As Lefebvre asserts:

> The cradle of absolute space—its origin, if we are to use that term—is a fragment of agro-pastoral space, a set of places named and exploited by peasants, or by nomadic or semi-nomadic pastoralists. A moment comes when, through the actions of masters or conquerors, a part of this space is assigned a new role, and henceforward appears as transcendent, as sacred (i.e. inhabited by divine forces), as magical and

---

32. Michael Hardt and Antonio Negri, *Empire* (Cambridge, MA: Harvard Univ. Press, 2003), p. 187.

33. See the product listing for *Desert Solitaire* at the Amazon.com website, https://www.amazon.com/Desert-Solitaire-Wilderness-Edward-Abbey/dp/0345326490.

cosmic. The paradox here, however, is that it continues to be perceived as part of nature. Much more than that, its mystery and its sacred (or cursed) character are attributed to the forces of nature, even though it is the exercise of political power therein which has in fact wrenched the area from it natural context, and even though its new meaning is entirely predicated on that action.[34]

Such clusters of contingencies sit in absolute space, and their dependence on abstract space for natural givenness and historical significance comes together well in Abbey's celebration of America's southwestern deserts. Abbey's work also tussles close to the ground with a personal subjectivity in which "time contained the spatial code" that suddenly faces absolute spaces and those moments in which the modern industrial tourist makes day trips into the edges of deserts for "'reading' or 'decoding' the prospect before him in terms of his feelings, knowledge, religion, or nationality."[35]

Many episodes in Abbey's work illustrate this tension. However, one from *Black Sun* is quite suggestive. Will Gatlin, the book's main character, works as a fire lookout at the Grand Canyon. He becomes defined by his conscious awareness of the time spent hiking in the wilds of the canyon as the space itself spent as time itself:

> The sun, touching the horizon, burned for a few minutes directly into his face. He paused to rest, turning his back on the glare, and gazed with weary, aching, blood-flecked eyes at the world of the canyon. He was alone in one of the loneliest places on earth. Above him rose tier after tier of cliffs, the edge of the forest barely apparent on the rim of the uppermost wall; around him the gray desert platform where nothing grew but scrub brush and cactus sloped toward the brink of the inner gorge and the unseen river. From the river to forest an ascent of over five thousand feet; from rim to rim ten miles by airline at the most narrow point; from canyon head to canyon mouth two hundred and eighty-five miles by the course of the river. In all this region was nothing human that he could see, no sign of man or of man's work. No sign, no trace, no path, no clue, no person but himself.[36]

34. Lefebvre, *The Production of Space*, p. 234.
35. Ibid., p. 241.
36. Edward Abbey, *Black Sun* (New York: Avon, 1982), p. 150.

This unity of absolute space pervades Abbey's description of Gatlin's daily routine, place of work, and site of shelter in the desert highlands. His fire lookout tower is a human construct, as is the national forest he oversees from it, but the spatiality Abbey celebrates is that of timeless essential organic being:

> This world is very quiet. Almost silent. The clear song of the hermit thrush exaggerates the stillness, makes it seem only more stark. If he were listening the man could hear the murmur of the fire in the stove, the creak of the metal roof expanding slightly in the first sunlight, the fall of a spruce cone on the ground outside. But nothing else. Later in the season—soon enough—will come other sounds: the thunder of lightning splitting the sky, spiraling like a snake in flame down the trunk of a tree, driving a cannonball of fire through the forest's carpet of dust, duff, debris—the sigh of burning trees, the roar of chaos. But now nothing....
>
> The tower is surrounded by the forest. In all directions lies the sea of treetops, a seemingly unbroken canopy of aspen and conifer rolling toward deserts in the dawn, toward snow-covered mountains far to the south and west, and on the remaining side toward something strange, a great cleft dividing the plateau from end to end, an abyss where the pale limestone walls of the rim fall of into a haze of shadows, and the shadows down into a deeper darkness.[37]

The river, the canyons, and the desert for Abbey explode the age-old colonization of *habitus* and *intuitus* by *intellectus*. It is difficult, but in the badlands of the Southwest, and on its rivers of life cutting through their rocks of death, Abbey suggests, like Lefebvre, that as long as "time and space remain inseparable, the meaning of each was to be found in the other, and this immediately (i.e., without intellectual mediation)."[38] Augustine's claim that "mundus est immundus" again makes some sense in this context.

Abbey's West, then, is one of a certain monumentality, but it is a popular monumentality for America—one in which this nation is still regarded as a rich collective project full of real individual possibility. Clabbering around the hoodoo rocks of the Canyonlands or hiking at midday in desert barrens combines Abbey's aesthetic appreciation for

37. Ibid., pp. 12–13.
38. Lefebvre, *The Production of Space*, p. 241.

spatiality with lived existential fulfillment. Desert lands, as monumental spaces, collect "the perceived, the conceived, and the lived; representations of space and representational spaces; the spaces proper to each faculty, from the sense of smell to speech; the gestural and the symbolic.... [They offer] each member of a society an image of that membership, an image of his or her social visage."[39] Still, unlike so many other celebrants of the Southwest, Abbey does not make his representation of space a basis for reducing lived experience to a primordial imperative. Instead, his art is a series of qualified, and then qualifying, forays into the desert to explore and then exult "the fragmented and uncertain connection" between representations of space and representational spaces as objects that imply and explain to subjects a finer array of spatial practices, as that ideal subject confronts "the desert" and becomes "a *subject*—that subject in whom lived, perceived, and conceived (known) come together within a spatial practice."[40] While nature may not have made the Southwest so expressive, it is the sign of Abbey's art that he can recast nature as being capable of becoming so communicative.

III. Politics, Ethics, Aesthetics: Down the River

With regard to politics, Abbey's playful anarchistic writings have inspired countless wilderness lovers to engage in low-level sabotage long enough to provoke serious counterreactions from local, state, and federal authorities. Monkeywrenching activities typically are instances of property crime, ranging from disabling construction equipment, destroying billboard signs, and disrupting suburban development to burning ski lodges, breaking power transformers, and busting livestock corrals. While playful, they were also felonious in nature, serious in monetary damage, and obvious in their intent.

Consequently, the followers of "Cactus Ed," whether they were freelancing saboteurs or dedicated Earth First!ers, were classified as "eco-terrorists" as early as the 1980s. FBI infiltrators, state authorities, and local officers continuously sweep the back roads and survey the wild canyons on watch against monkeywrenching crime. *Desert Solitaire,* ironically, documents how a U.S. government park ranger acted as a truly public servant in the late 1950s, working as a handyman, nature

39. Ibid., p. 220.
40. Ibid., p. 230.

guide, and occasional constable in the pursuit of simply conserving the Arches National Monument outside of Moab, Utah.

Since America itself has changed in the past fifty years, a national security state mentality now prepares park rangers for riot control, anti-terrorist strikes, and SWAT sweeps as much as it does their traditional service as nature guides, land curators, or just plain old park custodians. Politically, "the authorities" would argue that such preparations actually were made necessary by Abbey and other "monkeywrenchers" preparing for, and then continuously conducting, a low-intensity guerrilla war against "the American way of life" in the Southwest as it manifests itself in industrial tourism and suburban sprawl. Abbey's influence, of course, has not been this pervasive or profound, but his writings and antics do provide a more than suitable scapegoat for justifying a quasi-military mobilization in the nation's wildernesses and wastelands since the 1970s.

Otherwise, Abbey's political influence arguably has been quite negligible. Few immigrants to the New West agree with his cantankerous protests against their presence, and fewer still are those native westerners still remaining who might join together in any common cause inspired by his writings. Abbey has been gone from the scene for nearly two decades, and no one has taken his place as a voice for the American West. A few Earth First! activists have become even more hard-core ELF cadres, but they mostly do not much more than burn a Ford Excursion here and there or a trophy log home now and then. George Hayduke would approve.[41] Still, these actions alone have enabled the FBI to classify the ELF, the ALF, and Earth First! leftovers as the most serious threat to America's domestic tranquility next to al-Qaeda. Such counterreactions are both absurd and authoritarian, but quite real.

Ultimately, the super-excessive growth of Southwest suburbanism in the 1970s and 1980s has morphed into the hyper-growth of the 1990s and 2000s. Abbey's dystopian tract *Good News* might prove prophetic in another decade or sooner, particularly as the realities of peak oil and climate change make Sun Belt living more and more untenable in the Southwest.[42] In the meantime, however, Abbey's political impact is more theoretical than tangible. Such influence is not insignificant. As Nikolai Chernyshevsky's *What Is to Be Done?* showed with Russia's *narodniki*,

41. Edward Abbey, *Hayduke Lives! A Novel* (Boston: Little Brown, 1990).
42. Edward Abbey, *Good News* (New York: E. P. Dutton, 1980).

novels can have political influence. Nothing of this magnitude, however, is building now in the United States—especially with the DHS, the FBI, and other police forces constantly on the lookout for "eco-terrorists" across the nation.

In this respect, Abbey is not unlike many anti-industrial critics before him. His entertaining romances of rural wilderness center upon sketching an alluring alternative to urban settlement as his ecological transformation. What is right with America for Abbey are its southwestern deserts, but ironically what is wrong with America are, first, its desert southwesterners and, second, the larger articulated apparatus of techno-industrial culture in which most southwesterners are simply the most proximate, destructive, and unappreciative bunch of unthinking agents in a corrupted system. Abbey carefully cultivated his image as the cantankerous "Cactus Ed," the sage philosopher of desert wilderness, because, in large part, most of this figure's preoccupations actually are those of an even more elusive "Concrete Ed," the savage prophet of industrial collapse.

Ann Ronald's *The New West of Edward Abbey* (1988) captures, and then concentrates, this wrongheaded exotic reading of Abbey. Strangely, her work is still the only sustained analysis of Abbey's writings, and it is now nearly twenty-five years old. In her view, "entering Edward Abbey's world, the reader steps inside a western landscape carefully reshaped and repainted by a master.... Foremost among Southwest writers, this observant, articulate author paints a vivid scene."[43] Even though Ronald is astute about Abbey's commitment to picturing "a world painstakingly designed to expose contemporary values in conflict," she gets trapped by the tropes of Abbey's writing that pose "questions crucial to anyone who has seen the frontier shrink and the American dream begin to fade."[44] Abbey, in fact, is far more ironic than her depiction of him as "Cactus Ed," the anarchist romantic writer of America's New West. Abbey writes from his southwestern desert homes about the desert, and many read only within this frame. Yet he does this work to write on what occurs beyond the Southwest, beside the desert, and behind the New West, in order to express his wrath about more tragic misdeeds elsewhere that are ruining the world in general and the Southwest in particular. This

43. Ronald, *The New West of Edward Abbey*, p. 1.
44. Ibid., pp. 1–2.

preoccupation directly runs against how Abbey has been typecast by so many readers, but it is the real core of his writing.[45]

Indeed, this counterintuitive current streaks through Abbey's fiction, from *The Brave Cowboy* to *Hayduke Lives!* At the end of his life, in *A Voice Crying in the Wilderness (Vox Clamantis in Deserto)*, which he finished two weeks before his death in March 1989, Abbey cuts to the chase in the book's introduction:

> The *Deserto* in the title, therefore, denotes not the regions of dry climate and low rainfall on our pillaged planet but, rather, the arid wastes of our contemporary techno-industrial greed-and-power culture; not the clean outback lands of sand, rock, cactus, buzzard, and scorpion, but, rather, the barren neon wilderness and asphalt jungle of the modern urbanized nightmare in which New Age man, eyes hooded, ears plugged, nerves drugged, cannot even get a decent night's sleep.[46]

Seconding this thought continuously throughout the book, Abbey took pains to praise the civilization often found in urbane cultures, but he does not equate the urban with the urbane. As he observes about America's fifth largest city, "Phoenix, Arizona: an oasis of ugliness in the midst of a beautiful wasteland."[47]

In making these judgments about contemporary America, Abbey can be equally dyspeptic about major world cities and minor wide spots in the road. Whether it is New York ("New Yorkers like to boast that if you can survive in New York, you can survive anywhere. But if you can survive anywhere, why live in New York?") or Page, Arizona ("Shithead capital of Coconino County: any town with thirteen churches and only four bars has got an incipient social problem. That town is looking for trouble."), Abbey assumes the role of curmudgeon, raging against the urbanizing chaos of techno-industrial life.[48] It is a role he loves as well as one he believes too many others are unwilling to play. Hence, Abbey turns his gaze to the non-urbanized, non-industrialized, non-mechanized spaces of the earth to find meaning and value: "I come more and

45. Lewis P. Hinchman and Sandra K. Hinchman, "Should Environmentalists Reject the Enlightenment," *Review of Politics* 63, no. 4 (2001): 663–92.

46. Abbey, *A Voice Crying in the Wilderness*, p. xiii.

47. Ibid., p. 97.

48. Ibid., pp. 110, 107.

more to the conclusion that wilderness, in America or anywhere else, is the only thing left that is worth saving."[49]

Behind his hotly hyped public persona, Abbey also was more aware than most writers that he did not exist as he came to be, and still remains, known by his readers. As so many bloviators who boost his books have blurbed, Abbey *was* "the Thoreau of the American West" (Larry McMurtry), "the original fly in the ointment" (Thomas McGuane), and "the next literary guru to the nation's campus readers" (*New York Times*). Arguably, one can claim that Abbey was, and was not, these figures as well as the many other characters that his readerly texts permitted him to personify. At the end of the day, however, Abbey was quite certain about the nature of his "author" function: "I write to entertain my friends and to exasperate our enemies. To unfold the folded lie, to record the truth of our time, and, of course, to promote esthetic bliss."[50] When those friends or enemies read his work, or read other writings about his work, he still knew that he could never exist as he was read, or written about, as "Cactus Ed," because the author always is "an imaginary person who writes real books."[51]

In this regard, Abbey also recognized that he wrote books "classified by librarians as 'nature books,' [but to him] they belong to the category of personal history rather than natural history."[52] Disdaining with wisecracks the titles of "naturalist," "sportsman," and "nature writer"— "so much for the mantle and britches of Thoreau and Muir. Let Annie Dillard wear them now"—he admits that he was merely a displaced person, a wanderer, a redneck, a loafer, and an anarchist.[53] Very few liberal environmentalists who have embraced Abbey as their truest hero, believing that he is a soulful western blend of Thoreau and Dillard, actually would have liked him. He liked women but detested feminists; he loved guns but gave up on hunting; he enjoyed Mexico but thought Mexicans should stay home behind a big, high border fence; he developed a learned and critical mind, but he had little use for university academics and literary critics; he realized that many regarded him as

49. Ibid., p. 82.

50. Ibid., p. 65.

51. Ibid.

52. Edward Abbey, *The Journey Home: Some Words in Defense of the American West* (New York: E. P. Dutton, 1977), p. xiii.

53. Ibid.

an authentic western hero, but he admitted that he was an immigrant Appalachian redneck.

Not too surprisingly, he shocked, repelled, and threatened those admirers who got close enough to see him in action, because he was very plainspoken about his root disposition, namely, "extreme intransigence...because I am—really am—an extremist, one who lives and loves by choice far out on the very verge of things, on the edge of the abyss, where this world falls off into the depths of another."[54] While Abbey lived life that way, few of his admirers truly do, or even ever would, take up this way of living. Abbey is no Annie Dillard. On the contrary, he took pride in tending "to go off in a more or less random direction myself, half-baked, half-assed, half-cocked, and half-ripped."[55] Abbey admirers will admit that their dear "Cactus Ed" also was, or at least could seem to be, a male chauvinist, a gun nut, a crude drunk, a serious racist, a crazy survivalist, or a nasty clown. Some call all of this ecological antimodernism, but it could just as easily be seen as green modernism.

As the mythic author of *Desert Solitaire* recounts, that book was written on the run, completed in a Nevada whorehouse, failed to sell as a hardback, but found great legs as a paperback that was widely read by college students in the 1970s. The author's comment on "the real book" is that "I haven't had to turn my hand to an honest day's work since 1972....I don't much like the book myself...but as to that, who cares but the author himself? Let the poor scrivening wretch sink ever deeper into his delusions."[56] Obviously, the writer of the real book does seem to be far more interesting than its now highly imaginary author, but his loyal readers prefer Abbey mythologies. Even his final acrid words of epigrammatic musing bear these blots, as the publisher opines to its readers on the last page that Edward Abbey

> worked for a time as a forest ranger and was a committed naturalist and a fierce environmentalist; such was his anger, eloquence, and action on the subject that he has become a heroic, almost mythic figure to a whole host of environment groups and literally millions of readers.[57]

54. Ibid., p. xiv.
55. Ibid., pp. 17–18.
56. Edward Abbey, *Down the River* (New York: E. P. Dutton, 1982), p. xiii.
57. Abbey, *A Voice Crying in the Wilderness*, p. 111.

Anyone who actually reads one or two of Abbey's books should recognize that such posthumous puffery would make him cringe. Still, like the ending of the film *The Man Who Shot Liberty Valance*, one must remember that in the commercial culture that Abbey despised, when faced with reporting the truth or repeating the legend, one always prints the legend.

The legend, of course, has been fascinating enough for thousands, as the politics of Earth First! or the ELF attest. Nevertheless, the real clincher with Abbey is the extent to which the actual truth of his writing is so much more interesting. For those hectoring environmentalists intent upon proving themselves greener than thou, Abbey admits:

> I love America because it is a confused, chaotic mess—and I hope we can keep it this way for at least another thousand years....Who gave us permission to live this way? Nobody did. WE did. And that is the way it should be—only more so. The best cure for democracy is more democracy.[58]

Abbey plainly is more than a wilderness lover for the sake of wilderness with its many intriguing species of flora and fauna. Wild places count for him as the ultimate site for the democratic pursuit of life, liberty, and happiness by human beings. His wilderness love is fundamentally anthropocentric, on the one hand, and unabashedly libertarian, on the other. Abbey knows that wilderness areas are out-and-out human constructs, but such bureaucratic constructions are vital: "once inside that line you discover the artificiality beginning to drop away; and the deeper you go, the longer you stay, the more interesting things get—sometimes fatally interesting....To be alive is to take risks; to be always safe and secure is death."[59] Most importantly, then, wilderness is a site where death can await people, and Abbey regarded a rigorous test against death as the most humanizing experience that each person can face. In every sense of the word, he was a humanist rather than a naturalist. In *Desert Solitaire*, he makes his stance plain: "I am a humanist; I'd rather kill a man than a snake."[60]

58. Abbey, *The Journey Home*, p. 230.
59. Ibid. See also Edward Abbey, *Beyond the Wall: Essays from the Outside* (New York: Henry Holt and Company, 1984); Abbey, *Down the River* (New York: E. P. Dutton, 1982); Abbey, *Abbey's Road* (New York: E. P. Dutton, 1979); Abbey, *Cactus Country* (New York: Time-Life Books, 1973).
60. Abbey, *Desert Solitaire*, p. 20.

His pointed defense of liberty also is anchored to wilderness because of his anarchist political leanings, which were plain and simple. Ultimately, he doubted that Americans as individuals and as a people could survive without wilderness. He is quite somber on this point:

> As I see it, our own nation is not free from the danger of dictatorship. And I refer to internal as well as external threats to our liberties.... [S]ome of us may need what little wilderness remains as a place of refuge, as a hideout, as a base from which to carry on guerrilla warfare against the totalitarianism of my nightmares.... Could I survive in the wilderness? I don't know—but I do know I could never survive in prison.[61]

Abbey, the mythic environmental hero, is, in many ways, also the realistic revolutionary strategist. He is no postanthropocentric green; he instead dreams of some undefined steady-state economy with a democratic, wide-open community. Abbey had a hard-nosed tactical attitude here:

> I see the preservation of wilderness as one sector of the front in the war against the encroaching industrial state. Every square mile of range and desert saved from the strip miners, every river saved from the dam builders, every forest saved from loggers, every swamp saved from the land speculators means another square mile saved for the play of human freedom. All of this may seem utopian, impossibly idealistic. No matter. There comes a point at every crisis in human affairs when the ideal must become real—or nothing.[62]

IV. Conclusion: Beyond the Wall

Those first affected by Abbey, but then driven further out into nature to become today's "nature writers," still attempt to fill his shoes as authors. Unfortunately, they are all too often "the naturalists" that Abbey was not, and they never rise to the level of astute political observation that he could not avoid. Whether it is Craig Childs reporting on *The Secret Knowledge of Water*, *The Desert Cries*, and *Soul of Nowhere*, or Terry Tempest Williams rhapsodizing about *Red: Passion and Patience in the Desert*, *Desert Quartet: An Erotic Landscape*, and *An Unspoken Hunger:*

---

61. Abbey, *The Journey Home*, p. 232.
62. Ibid., p. 236.

Stories from the Field, there is no one writing about the American desert who equals the intensity of Abbey. In part, his imitators lack his philosophical acumen, social outrage, and ironic disposition about what "the desert" really is. And, in part, they are content simply churning out red-rock romances to valorize what once made the Southwest so alluring to all those millions who were lured there only to despoil the attractions that these scribblers now romanticize as naturalists.

Their work, however, is not insignificant. In fact, its readers openly or tacitly are heeding Abbey's "Survival Hint #1 on the Great American Desert," which is:

> Stay out of there. Don't go. Stay home and read a good book, this one for example. The Great American Desert is an awful place. People get hurt, get sick, get lost out there. Even if you survive, which is not certain, you will have a miserable time. The desert is for movies and God-intoxicated mystics, not family recreation.[63]

Childs and Williams, then, are useful to the degree that they provide riveting entertainment, or at least enough edifying diversion, to get millions more to stay home, keep out the badlands, and enjoy their desert walkabouts vicariously.

Irony always suffuses Abbey's writings about America's desert. Having become so identified with the hot, empty spaces of the Southwest, he came to the end of his life as the persona of a *vox clamantis in deserto*. In his small book about this role, he asserts: "[M]y sole purpose has been a private and egocentric one. I have no thought of serving others; such ambition is beyond both my intention and my powers. I am myself the substance of the book."[64] The ruse of the curmudgeon, passing his days as a desert rat spitting sarcasm, continued to serve him well in this text. His *vox clamantis in deserto* echoes from Fort Llatikcuf, Arizona, on the edge of the Sonoran Desert, but it actually cries in the wilderness about the cancerous sprawl of Sun Belt suburbia, on behalf of the truly barren emptiness of wild lands that its malls, power lines, cul-de-sacs, freeways, and canals were ruining. Far south of Phoenix, and north enough of Tucson, he saw the starlit desert skies washing out in the nighttime glow of those vacuous urban wastelands. The voice really cries here about the

---

63. Ibid., p. 13.
64. Abbey, *A Voice Crying in the Wilderness*, p. xiv.

deadening desert of Phoenix/Tucson/Mesa/Glendale/Peoria, and what this dead zone is doing to the living wilds of Arizona. Having such freedom of speech was a meaningful privilege to Abbey, and he knew he had to "make the most of it or betray both thy neighbors and thyself."[65]

Of course, the figure of "Cactus Ed," a.k.a. Edward Abbey, is revered by millions as an ardent environmentalist and true advocate of a postanthropocentric biocentrism open to the survival of all beings. While this belief is not entirely false, its spare truth-value obscures the real center of Abbey the thinker and man. In *The Journey Home*, which he regarded as a much better book than *Desert Solitaire*, he speaks plainly:

> Science is not sufficient. "Ecology" is a word I first read in H. G. Wells twenty years ago and I still don't know what it means. Or seriously much care. Nor am I primarily concerned with nature as living museum, the preservation of spontaneous plants and wild animals. The wildest animal you know is you, gentle reader, with this helpless book clutched in your claws. No, there are better reasons for keeping the wild wild, the wilderness open, the trees up and the river free, and canyons uncluttered with dams. We need wilderness because we are wild animals. Every man needs a place where he can go crazy in peace.... Because we need brutality and raw adventure, because men and women first learned to love in, under, and all around trees, because we need for every pair of feet and legs about ten leagues of naked nature, crags to leap from, mountains to measure by, deserts to finally die in when the heart fails.[66]

Such thoughts are not those of a pale Dillard-reading pilgrim coming to the banks of Tinker Creek and thirsting for communion with nature's trees, bees, and rippling water as "Otherness" for its own sake. They are those of an intense ethico-political partisan of "humanity," placing heavy anthropocentric claims on the wild to help make humanity more civilized. He is a radical, but he is hardly an ecological antimodernist. To reduce his work to the simplicities of ALF or ELF activists does both a severe disservice.

At the end of the day, "Cactus Ed" was not an ecologist, not much of an environmentalist, and surely not even close to being a green. Abbey is instead "Ed the Cactus"—a hard, spiny, tough, sharp critic of all those

65. Ibid.
66. Abbey, *The Journey Home*, pp. 228–29.

odd green hypocrites that revere red-rock canyons and desert sunsets by driving out across them in huge 4x4 trucks, polluting the pure skies in pursuit of western fantasies that he sadly recognizes he continuously fueled with his literary work, either unintentionally or intentionally, in slick coffee-table books about "the West."

Abbey loves the West. Yet as he admits on the first page of *Desert Solitaire*, the most beautiful place on earth is not Moab, Utah (the town that now serves as a backcountry boutique for outdoors enthusiasts of every stripe, with all of their high-tech apparatuses for machinic leisure), but the wild land around it. Although not an Aldo Leopold follower by profession, he implicitly espouses a credo for citizenship of the land, for the land, and by the land's limits against all those who would stand in the land, against the land, and beyond the land's qualities. In this stance, Abbey worked as a real writer, and with this work, the fictional guerrilla movements of eco-activists, which he romantically invented to recount in his novels and short stories, can live on as long as the desert-defending spirit of George Hayduke, or another Abbey persona, lives.

Abbey is a critic of modern industrial society, but to reduce the richness of his writing to "ecological antimodernism" is far too simplistic. Industrial products, industrial processes, and industrial production, he realizes, form a complex system of conducting conduct by managing fear, insecurity, and desire. The New West of Edward Abbey is far from natural, but it is not yet wholly artificial. Rather "the Southwest" is a manifold of engineered, embedded, and imagined spaces in which the quality, pace, substance, and opportunity that define material and mental life derive from decisions made elsewhere by unknown others without popular participation, deliberation, or even awareness. Abbey simply protests these exploitative acts against society and its spaces much more artfully than most. In other words, as the perceived, conceived, and lived spaces of the Great American Desert unfold as an accidental normality, Abbey artfully decries how America's spatiality has become an economic and political order founded upon purposeful abnormality; and then he calls for its "monkeywrenching" to make it more open, free, and satisfying for those who endure its corruptions.

9

Hashing It Over:
Green Governmentality
and the Political Economy of Food

The Starter Course: Food and Green Governmentality

THIS ANALYSIS IS a cautious, provisional exploration of one aspect of the new green economy. At best, it serves as a prelude to more elaborate critiques of today's growing economic inequalities and their close ties to the industrial food system and its ecology. The nexus of human food and ecological degradation has been a leitmotif in the contemporary American environmental movement since at least 1962, when Rachel Carson traced some of the detrimental effects of DDT contamination in North America's food chains. Consequently, efforts to trace the ties between "a vibrant food politics" that explores why "what we choose to eat" as well as how "the production, distribution, and consumption of food affords—as individuals, societies, and a species—both power and privilege over others"[1] are vital to a more complex economic critique of the present. In probing the economies and cultures of industrial food production today, it seems clear "that an increased

---

* Originally published in *Fast Capitalism* 10, no. 1 (2013): 39–48. The initial efforts to articulate this argument were made at the conference on "Ecological Inequalities & Interventions: Contemporary Environmental Practices," held at George Mason University on September 22–23, 2011, and at the annual meeting of the Western Political Science Association, held in Portland, OR, on March 22–24, 2012.

1. Chad Lavin, "The Vegetarian Lesson," *Chronicle Review*, August 14, 2011, http://chronicle.com/article/the-vegetarian-lesson/128562/.

attention to political economy is a sine qua non for a revived cultural studies."[2] As an exploratory exercise in ecology as critique and self-critique, this study digs into the political economy of food to unearth a handful of its economic inequalities and how environmental activism can both assail and assuage them.

In that spirit, this exploration also surveys a few of the deepening economic and social inequalities that local activists, community agriculture enthusiasts, and neighborhood revitalizers have opposed with a diverse array of policies and practices. By using food ecologies as the spearhead of broader social transformations, these social forces have sought to redirect the production, distribution, and consumption of food. Yet this analysis also considers how some of today's well-intentioned interventions, which have been aimed at the reform of food policies, could appear to articulate contradictory policy assemblages embedded in the controlling logics of green governmentality.[3]

In particular, one must reexamine the mixed record of purportedly alternative, communitarian, or emancipatory practices, namely, those tied to attaining more economic autonomy and cultural authenticity in self-produced, locally distributed, and quickly consumed foods from "locavorist" urban agriculture. Such food stocks are produced by a bevy of loosely organized initiatives, from officially endorsed CSA (community-supported agriculture) groups to semi-illegal "guerrilla gardening" circles. Often, these popular interventions seem radical, populist, or anti-systemic. Under the right conditions, their subversive, transformative, or postmodern potential for change could spark to life. At the same time, one wonders if these developments can be a marker of how contemporary capitalist modernity's retrograde limits and contradictions oddly can manifest themselves in what are allegedly progressive practices. Indeed, the significance of such developments seems far more mixed and murky than the bright burnish their enthusiasts have given to them.[4] Michael Pollan is now famous for noting that "the way we

2. Paul Smith, introduction to *The Renewal of Cultural Studies*, ed. Paul Smith (Philadelphia: Temple Univ. Press, 2006), p. 6.

3. Timothy W. Luke, "On Environmentality: Geo-Power and Eco-Knowledge in the Discourses of Contemporary Environmentalism," *Cultural Critique* 31 (Autumn 1995): 57–81.

4. David Kennedy, *21st Century Greens: Leaf Vegetables in Nutrition and Sustainable Agriculture* (Berea, KY: Leave for Life, 2011); Peter Bane, *The Permaculture Handbook*

eat represents our most profound engagement with the natural world"[5] and then setting off in search of ideal examples of ethically self-sourced, cultivated, and/or foraged meals that actualize certain food experiences as authenticity. Something like greater "food justice"[6] can develop from such initiatives, but then so too might greater food injustice. While the supporters of heavily authenticated eating economies highlight the bright liberational opportunities for realizing greater nutritional health or personal freedom for all who engage in authentic food-getting activity,[7] is it just as plausible to see instances of locavore food politics as the darker necessities of an austerity intent upon coping with broader institutional systemic crises that already have begun?[8]

Out on the Ground: One Intriguing Intervention

Following these lines of flight in the world economy, a recent news story comes from the Virginia Cooperative Extension (VCE) service as an instructive insight. In reviewing its report, one wonders if its accounts reveal a few of the operators of institutionalized domination, working to support, reinforce, and multiply each other in a blur of green good intentions that ensure how "society must be defended"[9] today. Facing broken families, obese citizens, underemployed workers, and vacant land, the VCE news release recounts how Henrico County's board of supervisors recently approached the Extension Service to deal with high infant mortality, poor nutrition, and family stress in one district of the county. As the VCE horticulture agent in Henrico County observed, "We knew that if we improved the nutrition and physical activity of the people in that district, we might be able to make a difference. Encouraging people to grow their own fruits and vegetables would provide a physical activity

---

(Bloomington, IN: Permaculture Activist, 2012).

5. Michael Pollan, *The Omnivore's Dilemma: A Natural History of Four Meals* (New York: Penguin Press, 2006), p. 10.

6. Robert Gottlieb and Anupama Joshi, eds., *Food Justice* (Cambridge, MA: MIT Press, 2010).

7. *Permaculture Activist* 81 (2011): 1–64.

8. Thomas Homer-Dixon with Nick Garrison, eds., *Carbon Shift: How Peak Oil and the Climate Crisis Will Change Canada (and Our Lives)* (Toronto: Random House of Canada, 2009).

9. Michel Foucault, *"Society Must be Defended": Lectures at the Collège de France, 1975–1976*, trans. David Macey (New York: Picador, 1997).

that they could do together as a family and provide them with access to fresh and nutritious food."[10]

Starting with two acres, VCE mobilized seven families to work twelve plots during 2008. In 2010, the acquisition of another nearby property allowed more families to join in this experiment, and now over twenty families are tilling twenty-seven plots in 2011. While the VCE explicitly targets low-income families, anyone can join this community gardening campaign as long as they follow VCE's handbooks, take VCE classes, adhere to VCE rules regarding general safety, personal responsibility, and group activity, and then adopt VCE approaches to organic methods for the cultivation, preservation, and preparation of their family-grown produce. On the one hand, many people appear to be eating differently. And, on the other hand, their changed food practices are articulating a mode of green governmentality through this VCE program for "Gardens Growing Families," which is proving to be quite effective. The VCE horticultural agent reports that "77 percent of gardeners indicated that they saved money by growing their own fruits and vegetables in 2010. And 94 percent of the gardeners said their family diet improved as a result of the vegetables or fruit grown in their garden."[11]

When they were surveyed by VCE experts, the Gardens Growing Families participants indicated that they believed their members cooperated together better as domestic units, cultivated a stronger work ethic, and improved their daily diet, while keeping to a tighter household food budget. The willingness to waste money on the less fresh, less healthy, and less economical products of the fast-food industry was sharply curtailed. And apparently the importance of personal effort and economy became far more evident as moral tasks to the participants when they began tilling the earth.

The VCE concluded that such local urban agricultural initiatives should be embraced and expanded as important new policy practices that put "food on the table and bring families together." This recent effort is only one small experiment. Nevertheless, it proves instructive amid today's deepening inequalities to the extent that the VCE approach to food as economy perhaps has begun, in turn, to test new tactics by

10. "Garden Program Puts Food on the Table, Brings Families Together," *Spotlight on Impact*, Virginia Tech website, August 15, 2011, http://www.vt.edu/spotlight/impact/2011-08-15-local-food/henrico.html.

11. Ibid.

which "society must be defended" by mobilizing, first, the underclass and then, next, other willing participants to re-socialize themselves as cultivators, consumers, and collaborators in a community garden.

Pollan has observed that eating is "an ecological act, and a political act, too. Though much has been done to obscure this simple fact, how and what we eat determines to a great extent the use we make of the world—and what is to become of it."[12] His criticism of omnivorous humans essentially pivots upon the industrial food chain's massive substitution for renewable carbohydrate energies drawn from plants, and then burned by animals and humans to sustain themselves on complex carbon molecules from photosynthesis, with new toxic and dirty nonrenewable hydrocarbon fossil fuels. That is, "industrial agriculture has supplanted a complete reliance on the sun for our calories with something new under the sun: a food chain that draws much of its energy from fossil fuels instead."[13] These fossil-fueled modes of industrial agrarian life in America are the greatest expression of its population's excessive waste, or general affluenza, or quest for easy money to be spent unwisely.[14]

While fossil fuel has generated agricultural abundance in the United States for both America and the world, this newfound plenty is one of immense waste. Every acre of corn takes at least a barrel of oil to produce; each beef cow takes nearly a barrel of oil to grow, feed, and bring to market, with each pound of beef usually taking seven pounds of corn to grow; and many fast-food lunches for four (usually eaten in a car) take about 1.3 gallons of oil to produce.[15] Humans are indeed omnivores, but actually those at the top fifth or third of the global food chain are, in some real sense, essentially monivorous. Their ultimate food source is oil, making them to a very real extent "petrovores."

Petrocomestibles, however, are the epitome of capital, energy, labor, and material waste. Hence, many of today's new food politicizers, like the VCE or guerrilla gardeners, make it their imperative to bring a new economy of food into being at least for some significant number of people. It is one that depetroleumizes, deruralizes, and perhaps even

12. Pollan, *The Omnivore's Dilemma*, p. 11.

13. Ibid., p. 10.

14. Wendell Berry, *Bringing It to the Table: On Farming and Food* (Berkeley, CA: Counterpoint, 2009).

15. Pollan, *The Omnivore's Dilemma*, pp. 45–46, 83–84, 115, 117.

deindustrializes the modern food chain by localizing, slowing, and de-diversifying the array of foods available to such omnivorous humans. Indeed, today's most spirited proponents for civic agrarianism see urban agriculture as having a long-term crisis mitigation utility. Consequently, they assert, "One of the shortest routes from passive consumer to active food-system designer is through the community garden."[16] With 48 million people ages 18 to 64 in the United States not working even one week a year in 2010, and 45 million in the same fix during 2009, the community garden perhaps is now part of the new social safety net.[17] Fifteen percent of the entire population, and nearly twenty-five percent of all children live below the official poverty level,[18] so becoming "active food-system designers" may be one of the best legal options that many individuals have available to survive everyday life in contemporary America.

To attain this new food economy, however, all must twist down, and then slowly almost turn off, the petropower spigot. Are Henrico County's poor neighborhoods arguably one of its prefigurations? Visiting an organic farm in California, Pollan is shocked that "growing, chilling, washing, packaging, and transporting [each] box of organic salad to a plate on the East Coast takes more than 4,600 calories of fossil fuel energy, or 57 calories of fossil fuel energy for every calorie of food."[19] His amazed calculations capture the centrality of the industrial food chain's energy-intensitivity. Nonetheless, if communities move in disgusted awe from this level of wasted fossil fuel calories into a new food economy grounded on more locally sourced, organism-powered, or personally grown comestibles, then the world we make around and out of our food must change radically by returning to small-scale, labor-intensive, and locally based modes of cultivation.

With world demand for oil rising 25 billion barrels a year, with the American dollar becoming less desirable to price global oil purchases, and with oil prices rising in real terms to perhaps $150 a barrel (as they did briefly during 2008–2009) or maybe $200 or $300 a barrel in

16. David Tracey, "Urban Agriculture—Depaving Paradise," *Permaculture Activist* 81 (2011): 9.

17. Sabrina Tavernise, "Soaring Poverty Casts Spotlight on 'Lost Decade,'" *New York Times*, September 14, 2011.

18. Connor Doughtery, "Income Slides to 1996 Levels," *Wall Street Journal*, September 14, 2011.

19. Pollan, *The Omnivore's Dilemma*, p. 167.

the near future, the United States as a whole will not be able to afford $8.00 a gallon gasoline or $300 a barrel crude. Of course, fracking oil and gas reserves captured in certain rock formations across the nation could slightly postpone these dire developments. Postponements, however, are not permanent solutions. Hence, many CSA activists believe "of necessity, Americans will return to a simple way of life....One way this can happen is by having massive unemployment in those sectors of the economy that do not generate exportable goods and services, such as residential construction and real estate. Unemployed people will use less gasoline and buy less stuff at Wal-Mart. Trade *will* ultimately balance. The fact is that we can get by on a lot less than we have been."[20]

A new kind of politics, then, is implied by reordering who does what, when, and how when there is a lowering of all fossil fuel caloric inputs into food caloric outputs. It is not shocking, as the VCE indicates, that people with lots of time, energy, and labor to spare will be brought first into the daily routines of Gardens Growing Families if there are no better economic alternatives. Still, without more due deliberation, these shifts undoubtedly could result in new more inequitable arrangements for pushing trends toward "degrowing" big industrial food chains as well as supercharging other smaller upscale postindustrial food markets around today's unequal class divides.

Dilemmas in the Dirt: Omnivores or Petrovores

Does the trope of omnivores "facing the dilemmas" of choosing carnivorousness, herbivorousness, or at least less omnivorousness, as Pollan's writings assert, occlude a bigger structural imperative embedded in the industrial food chains? Modern American society's reliance upon a non-renewable legacy resource drawn from 500 million years of fossilized solar energy in coal, gas, and oil deposits[21] makes an organic salad from California available in Maryland at everyday low prices as petrovory extremely problematic. While coal and gas along with oil now constitute 85 to 90 percent of human energy use, it still is petroleum that drives much of today's industrial food chain.[22] Renewable sources of energy

20. Kenneth D. Worth, *Peak Oil and the Second Great Depression (2010–2030)* (Denver: Outskirts Press, 2010), p. 30.

21. Homer-Dixon with Garrison, *Carbon Shift*, p. 65.

22. Alfred W. Crosby, *Children of the Sun: A History of Humanity's Unappeasable Appetite for Energy* (New York: Norton, 2006).

have increased during the past 150 years, but the typical global consumer on average uses the same amount of such energy—percentage-wise annually—as one did in 1850. Fossil fuel use, on the other hand, has risen eightfold per capita since 1850,[23] so typifying this food economy and ecology as one rooted in oil-burning makes analytical sense.

The miracles of modern industrial agriculture rest upon "mining" rather than "minding" the earth's resources—a depredation that has been clearly recognized by many critics for decades. Pollan and others in the new sustainable food movements of the twenty-first century are only rediscovering worries expressed by Scott and Helen Nearing in the 1930s, Barry Commoner in the 1960s, and Wendell Berry in the 1980s. Despite decades of criticism, however, petrocomestibility has only grown more elaborate, excessive, and extreme. It is not clear that real change can come now, but many more people are considering it as a more viable option. In its bright promise phase, more locavory appears in the guise of ethical awareness, ecological concern, or economical sensibility; but, in fact, its darker realities are very clear. As Pollan suggests, eating is a political act. A major element in the politics of this new eating assemblage is adapting large groups of once affluent, but now increasingly impoverished, people to irreversible climate change, worsening economic inequality, collapsing industrial economies, and eroding urban landscapes[24] by keeping them fixed in place as post-consumerist cultivators living in dying automobile suburbs or stressed big cities as their access to oil-burning globovore food ecologies closes.

A few individuals with serious financial means undoubtedly will continue to enjoy the bounty of many diverse and intensive food chains from their specialized niches in the widening two-tiered economy of the present;[25] but, at the same time, many others will lose out. Food deserts already exist, and their emptiness is spreading. To combat food desertification, the increasingly superfluous or obsolete majorities of most industrial-era factory and farm workers shall be left by necessity and design to live, at least in part, more deeply in new deindustrial-

---

23. Homer-Dixon with Garrison, *Carbon Shift*, p. 66.

24. Jacob S. Hacker and Paul Pierson, *Winner-Take-All Politics: How Washington Made the Rich Richer—And Turned Its Back on the Middle Class* (New York: Simon & Schuster, 2010).

25. Bill Vlasic, "Detroit Sets Its Future on a Foundation of Two-Tier Wages," *New York Times*, September 13, 2011.

ized, depetroleumized, deglobalized, denationalized, and demechanized food ecologies. These webs of economy are pushing them in the direction of Gardens Growing Families, which includes tactics to mobilize their labor time, animal energy, and personal property in order to feed themselves and their neighbors. Rather than advancing slow food, soft energy paths, and simple living as superior forms of human emancipation, as many of their original advocates have stressed during the last forty or fifty years of fossil-fueled excess, are these alternative political economies being valorized in today's lingering Great Recession sensible survival strategies for mitigating economic stagnation or adapting to technological decline as petropowered civilization becomes less sustainable? Arguably, yes. Food transfer payments are one of Washington's highest social welfare expenditures, and anything that can reduce them is welcome news in President Obama's second term

Of course, large-scale global economic disruptions cascade into almost all urban neighborhoods and suburban tracts, and they can cause what their residents experience as "the city's social issues of homelessness, addiction, prostitution, and crime."[26] When a city lot or a few abandoned homes' backyards are turned into gardens for community supported agriculture where the local residents will do much of the daily work, a very convenient relation of people to things, or people without things to their environment, can come into force. David Tracey, for example, comments upon the residents of Vancouver's Downtown Eastside neighborhood:

> Some did not have homes themselves, which may be why the site turned into a farm that resembled an outdoor living room. All kinds of neighborhood people would drop in. Nurses would visit on breaks from the only legal facility in North America where addicts can use heroin under medical supervision. Sometimes sex-trade workers would stroll in to pick up a few raspberries off the vine, perhaps the only fresh organic food they would eat that day. Others would come in just to sit for 20 minutes away from the chaos of the street. Urban agriculture is all about the food, but it can also be about much more than that.[27]

26. Tracey, "Urban Agriculture," p. 10.
27. Ibid., pp. 9–10.

CSAs plainly are about much more than the food; they are, as this activist's idyll reveals, about agriculture supporting community. To grow food where people live is significant; but keeping people where they live, no matter how destitute, getting them engaged in productive and rewarding, albeit unpaid, labor to promote healthy survival, and organizing more secure, stable, and safe neighborhoods within the limits of this alternative agrarian commonwealth are decisively useful tactics to cope with the contemporary crisis.

Rather than perhaps creating a true cultural advance through collective social and economic transformation to prefigure another better form of modernity, as their original deep green advocates asked, are these reformist locavores more often than not also picking piecemeal over earlier green radical designs for survivalistic tactics to mitigate the unintended demodernizing consequences of neoliberal financialization? Without justifying what have been, and are, fixed relations of global inequality, the collapse of once wealthy national economies (as well as their more prosperous and stable core cities, neighborhoods, and towns) seems to be reducing many locales to a more peripheralized status plagued by huge brownfields, dead zones, and obsolescent areas.

Out of such spaces, the inhabitants of once prosperous states face life up against growing food deserts, service cutbacks, job deserts, security deficits, housing losses, and population migrations as spatiality itself remediates the full spectrum of complex economic and social decline.[28] Too many accounts of "food deserts" focus only on inner-city neighborhoods.[29] In fact, the vast expanses of petropowered agriculture have monoculturalized rural America through petrovory to the point that many farmers also live on monivorous food deserts even more dire than those of inner-city consumers.

Space, as Henri Lefebvre argues,[30] is more than the naturalized expanses, surfaces, and volumes of ordinary physical matter. It is, more importantly, the material articulation and activation of social relations. The West's relentless drive to conquer uninhabited, or only sparsely settled, lands and waters in the grand rush to attain economic, industrial,

28. Robert Brenner, *The Boom and the Bubble: The U.S. in the World Economy* (New York: Verso, 2002).

29. Matt Chittum, "Food Deserts," *Roanoke Times*, July 24, 2011, pp. 1, 12–13.

30. Henri Lefebvre, *The Production of Space*, trans. Donald Nicholson-Smith (London: Blackwell, 1991).

social, and urban development during the Industrial Revolution from the 1720s through the 1970s has been called "development." Its waves of modernization occupied and ordered space with the social interactions of modern urbanization, organization, and administration of a commercial world system that reified multiple spatialities in the cruel fusion of statist empires and business emporia, which one might designate as the creatively fused emporium of capital and power. Working around the classic capitalist antinomies of capital/labor, urban/rural, industry/agriculture, city/country, and settlement/wilderness, the industrial food chain is one of modernity's most reified spatial articulations.[31] In many ways, petropowered agricultural path dependencies developed out of centuries of struggle over land, labor, and capital after World War I. In some places, the apparatus of industrial agriculture will still persist for the few, but its relations of organization, order, and operation plainly have been splintering for the many since the late 1990s and early 2000s.[32]

When seen in this light, today's diverse celebrations of agro-ecology, green cities, agro-urbanism, and community agriculture on a local, small-footprint, and frugal scale, which have worked in a variety of once so-called Third or Fourth World settings, are a somewhat mixed blessing. A "plant's-eye view of the world"[33] is in part only one in which a desire for basic botanical skills boosts nutrition, life chances, and social capital stocks as much or more than machinic aplomb.[34] The spreading sprawl of these underdeveloped sites also is renowned for its destitution. Other sociological studies fretting about the earth's future identify it as the definitive marker of a "planet of slums."[35]

Poorer people can be prepared and equipped to till nearby brownfields to feed themselves and their families. Are what once might have been Liberty Gardens, Victory Gardens, or Whip Inflation Now Gardens only unfree patches, defeated plots, or deflationary diggings? Of course, each one "draws from sun and earth,"[36] but with an array of im-

31. Michael Pollan, *Food Rules: An Eater's Manual* (New York: Penguin Press, 2008).

32. Christian Marazzi, *The Violence of Financial Capitalism*, new ed. (New York: Semiotext(e), 2011).

33. Michael Pollan, *The Botany of Desire: A Plant's-Eye View of the World* (New York: Random House, 2002).

34. Ibid.

35. Mike Davis, *Planet of Slums* (London: Verso, 2008).

36. Shawna Morrison, "Drawing from Sun and Earth," *Roanoke Times: NRV Current*, July 26, 2011, pp. 4–5.

mobile, underpaid, and unfree labor practices adopted out of necessity along the way. In some sense, Pollanesque food politics are a new ethical consumerism;[37] but, in other more insidious developments, these clean, lean, or green styles of being also can express a highly re-engineered post-consumerist politics for underemployed cultivators of bankrupt businesses' green space, foreclosed-upon homes' front lawns, or failed subdivisions' street medians.

Overcooked Economies: Adaptations and Mitigations

The contemporary need for new environmental practices, such as sustainable community agriculture, emerges from a specific set of conditions. Those particularities can best be mapped, first, in the recent crises of the Great Recession and, second, in the systemic decay of economic and social equality in the United States since the 1970s. Both of these tendencies deserve some extended discussion. An overview of how long-term trends toward economic collapse set the stage for new adaptation and mitigation strategies tied to new food ecologies, therefore, is worth mapping.

A recent report from the Pew Research Center confirms the worri-some significance of these broader trends toward economic inequality by reassessing American household income and wealth. During the recent housing crisis, more and more regions in the United States seem to be sliding off toward the "planet of slums" after decades of neoliberal policies of dispossession. In 2005, the median household net worth of all American households was $96,894. For white households, this figure stood at $134,992, black households stood at $12,124; Hispanics at $18,359; and Asians at $168,103. Yet, after the Great Recession, the 2009 net household worth figures were severely worse. All households' net worth had fallen during four years to the figure of $70,000; white households at $113,149; black households at $5,677; Hispanics at $6,235, and Asians at $78,066.[38] These still-burning losses have now led to the greatest wealth disparities in the United States since twenty-five years ago. Indeed, the median worth of white households is 20 times greater

---

37. Chad Lavin, "The Year of Eating Politically," *Theory & Event*, 12 no. 2 (2009), http://muse.jhu.edu/journals/theory_and_event/vo12/12.2.lavin.html.

38. Sabrina Tavernise, "Recession Study Finds Hispanics Hit the Hardest," *New York Times*, July 26, 2011.

than blacks and 18 times greater than Hispanics.[39] Hispanics are 16 percent and blacks are 12 percent of the U.S. population, but one-third (35 percent) of all black and Hispanic households (31 percent) had a zero or negative net worth in 2009, as opposed to only 11 percent of white households.[40] While things have improved moderately since 2012, the positive trend lines here are the weakest since 1945.

Over the past generation, one out of every three Americans who grew up in a middle-class household has dropped back into the lower classes, and this finding is drawn from data only from 1979 to 2006. Another Pew Charitable Trust study examined teenagers in 1979 who were between 39 and 44 years old in 2004 and 2006. Remaining in the middle class was marked by steady income in a range between the 30th and 70th percentiles of income distribution, or living, for example, in a family of four with $32,900 to $64,000 of income annually in 2010 dollars.[41] One out of three people experienced downward mobility in the United States, which was marked by falling below the 30th percentile of income, falling 20 percentiles or more than their parent's household income, or earning annually 20 percent or more less than their parents.[42]

Major Fortune 500 firms in the United States have noticed this deterioration in middle-class living standards. Procter & Gamble, for instance, in 2011 launched its first dish soap since 1973 for the downmarket "bargain" niche. Because it has products in 98 percent of all U.S. households, and it wants to keep them there, P&G is tracking how the middle class—or all households in the $50,000 to $140,000 annual income range—is shrinking overall, while its members endure constant distress every month. P&G's marketing experts have determined the median income in the United States in 2009 was lower after inflation than in 1998.[43] The big dips in family income came in the 1970s, the early 1990s,

39. Rakesh Kochar, Richard Fry, and Paul Taylor, "Wealth Gaps Rise to Record Highs between Whites, Blacks, Hispanics: Twenty-to-One," July 26, 2011, p. 1, available at Pew Social & Demographic Trends: Pew Research Center, https://www.pewresearch.org/wp-content/uploads/sites/3/2011/07/SDT-Wealth-Report_7-26-11_FINAL.pdf.

40. Ibid., p. 2.

41. "Study: Many Americans Fall Out of Middle Class," *Roanoke Times*, September 7, 2011, p. A8.

42. Ibid.

43. Ellen Byron, "As Middle Class Shrinks, P&G Aims High and Low," *Wall Street Journal*, September 12, 2011.

and since 2006, which all have left the United States with a Gini index of 0.468. This coefficient indicates a 20 percent increase in income inequality in the United States since the end of the Cold War, leaving the United States with about the same Gini index for overall social inequality as Mexico or the Philippines.[44] Although it is not a welcome development for P&G executives, they recognize their long post–World War II run of successfully selling more, and gradually more expensive, household products to middle-class market segments is ending.

To survive in the United States, the company now targets consumers with systemically "falling" or "stagnating" incomes. As its vice-president for consumer marketing in North America notes, "This has been the most humbling aspect of our jobs. The numbers of middle America have been shrinking because people have been getting hurt so badly economically that they've been falling into lower income."[45] Similarly, Federal Reserve records on household wealth indicate that Americans held about $6.1 trillion in home equity in March 2011. That figure was only half the 2006 level; and all households' net assets grew only 2.4 percent from 2001 to 2007, only to tumble over 26 percent from 2007 to 2009.[46]

Still, at the other higher end of the income distribution, whites in the top 10 percent of all such households saw their share of wealth increase from 46 percent in 2005 to 51 percent in 2009. Among Hispanics, this disparity is even greater, as this figure rose from 56 percent in 2005 to 72 percent in 2009.[47] For 90 percent of American households, however, falling net worth, increasing amounts of free time, and the wasting opportunity of unused land in many cities and towns all combine as an opportune conjuncture to adapt many communities to these systemic crises by going all out green in the garden.

Petrovorous living obviously reshaped urban space, and this shift in the overall social context is crucial for understanding these food politics. In 1920, about 50 percent of the U.S. population lived in rural areas on a farm or ranch, and only 7 percent of the nation's population lived in the suburbs. By 1950, after waves of automobility, two-thirds of Americans

44. Ibid.
45. Ibid.
46. Ibid.
47. Kochar, Fry, and Taylor, "Wealth Gaps Rise to Record Highs," p. 8.

lived in cities or suburbs, and this figure hit 75 percent by 1970 as suburban populations eclipsed the number of inner-city residents.[48] For example, Detroit, the "Motor City," expanded in area from 40 square miles in 1910 to 139 square miles in 1950, as its boundaries filled with workers and factories making all of the automotive apparatuses of petropowered prosperity.[49]

Yet, as the percentage of its industrial workforce fell from over 39 percent in 1951 to less than 19 percent of total population in 2010, Detroit crashed.[50] It has devolved into a vast capital, food, jobs, and technology desert. A million people left the city from 1950 to 2000; and by 2009, 44,000 of its 65,000 homes that were in foreclosure were vacant, the unemployment rate was officially near 30 percent, and 62,000 vacant lots or abandoned properties littered its landscapes.[51] Just the vacant land in Detroit amounts to an area almost equal in size to Boston, but Detroit still is the eleventh largest metropolitan region in the nation. It is, however, also full of many underemployed, less skilled, and dispossessed people. Now a test case for "the shrinking city,"[52] Detroit is bulldozing down many of its vacant abandoned buildings. In turn, "acre upon acre of once useless vacant lots are being turned into vibrant urban farms."[53] Such recultivated lands are, in turn, now occupied differently. Working the soil there is more typically depetroleumized, highly localized, and essentially deindustrialized, as it pulls underemployed residents into a new agrarianism amid industrial ruination. By substituting bigger amounts of time spent on small plots to grow food for hours of paid labor to manufacture industrial goods or provide complex services in big lots for collective benefit, the larger social and spatial relations of the population are experiencing and expressing major changes.

Coevolving with these dismal realities of structural economic stagnation, one finds strangely cheerful hopes for "the third sector" of nongovernmental organizations tied to urban agro-ecology. The belief is that

48. Richard Florida, *The Great Reset: How the Post-Crash Economy Will Change the Way We Live and Work* (New York: Harper Collins, 2010), p. 35.

49. Ibid., p. 34.

50. Ibid., p. 72.

51. Ibid., pp. 72–74.

52. Belinda Lanks, "The Incredible Shrinking City," *Metropolis Magazine*, April 17, 2006, http://www.metropolismag.com/story/20060417/the-incredible-shrinking-city.

53. Florida, *The Great Reset*, p. 80.

they can rescue most people trapped in essentially hopeless conditions of economic collapse now manifest in these complicated spatial deformations. Urban agriculture, because it is not unlike the leisure activities of home gardening, is an easy sell because it promises people better food, greater health, household improvement, ecological virtue, and food security. Some will be saved, but can everyone improve their lot by community gardening?

Left underemployed, facing foreclosure, and needing to survive, people often look to their neighborhoods for solutions. Frequently, the houses there have some spare outside square footage and/or neighborhoods of these homes have vacant lots of sufficient size to make cultivating the earth a viable proposition for cash-starved, if not truly undernourished, homeowners and tenants. Returning to the private plot, community garden, or city lot to grow food is not a grand vision of an ever more powerful modern society; but these options can put food on the table that otherwise would not be there. Moreover, some cities now pay people with cash internships, minimum wage jobs, or monetary incentives to adapt to economic stagnation through such microscale reagrarianization schemes.

With regard to community gardens, Tracey suggests that they are local sites for normative engagement but that they also serve as points of organized normalization:

> A community garden is not just about vegetables. It can be a farm, a playground, a school, a temple, a gym, a stage, a refuge, a wildlife habitat, and more—all on the same day. At best, it derives its strength from and serves as a model for the community around it. Community gardens teach and celebrate values we cherish, including cooperation, volunteering, appreciation for diversity, and ecological awareness.[54]

Certainly, these virtues are worth preserving. With their preservation and the level of home foreclosures in 2011 exceeding 2010's record levels,[55] one also sees strategies for protecting housing stock, bank capital, and private equity simply by people cooperating to feed each other beyond the conventional cash nexus.

---

54. Tracey, "Urban Agriculture," p. 9.

55. "2011 to Top 2010 Record of 1 Million Home Forecloses," *Roanoke Times*, January 14, 2011, p. A8.

In a Stew: Eating as Authenticity or Austerity

Again, the purpose of this preliminary study is to question cautiously the new politics of food in an era of considerable scarcity. Celebrants of the third sector, such as Jeremy Rifkin,[56] see such efforts to enhance the everyday economies of food as the best path out of "a commodified future in which all of life becomes a series of paid-for performances, entertainments, and fantasies" and into an alternative green order with "emphases on connectivity, embeddedness, and relatedness...punctuated by a newfound sense of oneness and participation with others."[57] Since it is not clear that the choices before the denizens of the planet's degraded urban sprawl are this certain, one must worry about why such fabulations for authenticity and food are also being presented to the underemployed, underpaid, or even unemployed residents of areas that once were the so-called First World.[58]

As the Virginia Cooperative Extension service teaches, using food to anchor a new moral, political, and urban economy is indeed an exciting new recipe for enforcing social order. It points toward a two-tiered economy anchored by two unequal poles: one smaller tier will have secure high-paying careers, and the other much larger tier will feature mostly unstable low-paying or nonpaying jobs.[59] For those less affluent citizens with a more hunter-gatherer disposition than an agrarian one, it is possible for those in the declining tiers of fixed, fallen, or fractionalized incomes to forage successfully on already in place urban landscapes, plots of random wild growth, or just what appear to be weeds.

Rachel Kaplan, for example, notes, "In my small city, fruit literally falls off of the trees and onto the streets. Some people harvest their backyard trees, but many people let the fruit fall and rot....Foraging and gleaning are ways to eat local, save money, and practice our resourceful relation to place."[60] Noting that many people have fruit trees but lack the

---

56. Jeremy Rifkin, *The Age of Access: The New Culture of Hypercapitalism, Where All Life is a Paid-For Experience* (Boston: Putnam, 2000).

57. Ibid., p. 212.

58. Pollan, *Food Rules*.

59. Vlasic, "Detroit Sets Its Future"; Catherine Rampell, "At Well-Paying Firms, a Low-Paid Corner," *New York Times*, May 23, 2011.

60. Rachel Kaplan, "Foods from the Wilds of the City," *Permaculture Activist* 81 (2011): 38.

time for or interest in harvesting their crop, the enterprising forager can pick that fruit, leave a good measure on the owners' porches, and glean a surplus. Tons of food that would otherwise go to waste thereby become, once again, agriculture supporting a community.

Similarly, civic agrarians point out how edible plants on public property can be mapped for personal and group foraging sessions. Such produce certainly will be wasted unless it is gleaned, so new urban agrarians would do well to identity, inventory, and then intercept this usufruct lest it go to waste. Gathering such crops, whether they are found on private property or public lands, is important to managing "food insecurity" inasmuch as food that "otherwise would have gone to waste and rotted on people's lawns was foraged and distributed to people who need it."[61] The truly inventive new urban agrarian also can exploit the never obliterated biodiversity of naturally occurring perennial plants, or "weeds," that grow almost anywhere all the time. Knowing what parts are edible, where weeds will (or will not) get sprayed with herbicides, and if they grow on private property is important. Yet, once those facts have been determined, foraging wild and weedy food stocks, from blackberries, burdock, chickweed, chicory, and dandelion to mint, mustard, nasturtium, raspberries, and sorrel, "is a most essential and beautiful skill to cultivate however you choose to practice it."[62]

At the other end of the class continuum, however, property developers are recalibrating suburbia's designs for a shrinking top tier with good solid incomes. That is, "in a movement propelled by environmental concern, nostalgia for a simpler life and a dollop of marketing savvy, developers are increasingly laying out their cul-de-sacs around organic farms, cattle ranches, vineyards and other agricultural ventures."[63] Edible landscaping and community orchards, along with zoning in cattle ranchettes, organic farms, or boutique vineyards instead of strip malls, 24-hour minimarkets, or tennis courts, are key ingredients of this new twist in mobilizing food as economy. To sell upmarket suburban homes, the key amenity is no longer a golf green beyond the rear fence; it is salad greens in the backyard.[64]

61. Ibid.

62. Ibid., p. 39.

63. Stephanie Simon, "An Apple Tree Grows in Suburbia," *Wall Street Journal*, September 12, 2011, p. R3.

64. Ibid.

These ideas weakly echo the aesthetics and economics of William Morris or Paul Goodman, as their proponents anchor new conceptions for the townscape in visions of what Quint Redmond "calls 'agriburbia,' where suburbs aren't just built around a farm; they support food production at every turn."[65] Where the underclass is left to forage from the lawns of the remaining affluent, inner-city homeowners, Redmond's design would plant almond, apple, or avocado trees along all the agriburbia's streets. He would embed kale, corn, or grains in golf course roughs. He would seed shrubbery beds with cabbage, carrots, or currants and edge lawns when they are necessary with chives or herbs.[66] Some in the upmarket demographic may remain uninterested in this potential, but such new homes with their solar panels, super insulation, or embedded efficiencies also could spark other agriburban economies. For those buyers seeking CSA-oriented attractions, Redmond maintains that "many homeowners could earn half their mortgage payment by converting lawns into gardens and selling the bounty to restaurants or at farmer's markets. 'Organic basil is like growing gold,' he says. 'You can net $26,000 an acre.'"[67]

Globalization in its financialized neoliberal forms today is devalorizing key links in world commodity chains. This move is leaving some populations, regions, and settlements behind with no reliable source of continued growth, while preserving the energy-intensive traditional order for the upscale end of the class hierarchy. In various households and neighborhoods, along within certain towns and cities, alternatives for the maintenance of everyday life must be found—even if it leads to gradual deindustrialization, demechanization, and depetroleumization, where foraging for free weeds or waste fruit is cast as a beautiful essential skill for liberation.

Community agriculture is a plausible response for people living in food deserts or low-income census tracts where a major fraction of the population is a mile away from its nearest supermarket in an urban setting or ten miles away in a rural area. But it is crucial to see how and why accessible food-buying outlets deserted them. Low-income spaces indicate that there also are job deficits, housing degradation, income

65. Ibid.
66. Ibid.
67. Ibid.

deserts, health deterioration, and skill declines sweeping across major concentrations of these same populations. The increasing degree of precarious living in all these registers reveals a new hollowed-out spatiality. Pushing this initiative is an intervention in favor of building a material alternative in which the dispossessed "build real wealth, increase food and energy security, reduce the need for income, [and] create a home-based livelihood."[68] The great cost and scarcity of oil already is tracing its constricting effects in such urban-industrial desertification.[69] The waning of public goods and services is both mystified and made obvious by the mapping of food deserts. One must ask: if the state is left only to go about mapping its food deserts, then what can it do about such economic desertification? Apparently, Proctor & Gamble will identify these zip codes, track them and their surrounding urban locales as they become more like Mexico or the Philippines, and then develop more "bargain" down-market goods to sell their residents.

Green critiques of modern industrial society have had highly progressive agro-ecological elements at their strategic core for decades as the potentially liberating basis for new cultural alternatives. Whether it is home-based solar power, collective neighborhood gardens, or autonomous "off-the-grid" homes, such as New Mexico's "Earth Ship" houses, once revolutionary designs to reorder everyday life in Fordist or post-Fordist urban industrial economies from the 1960s through the 1990s have been essentially ignored. Yet, after being neglected for all this time, they are being (re)discovered as remediations of green governmentality.[70] As they are discovered, bits and pieces of them are also repurposed as adaptive interventions for coping minimally with the aftermath of the same excessive patterns of helter-skelter urban industrialization at the center of those same green critiques. Rather than grounding some major transformational experiment for more emancipatory human existences, too many green populist agro-ecologies are being hashed over for measured expedients needed to adapt to economic decline and ecological degradation, which have been engineered by cognitive capitalism

68. *Permaculture Activist* 81 (2011), inside front cover.

69. Michael C. Ruppert, *Confronting Collapse: The Crisis of Energy and Money in a Post Peak Oil World* (White River Junction, VT: Chelsea Press, 2009).

70. Timothy W. Luke, *Ecocritique: Contesting the Politics of Nature, Economy, and Culture* (Minneapolis: Univ. of Minnesota Press, 1997).

to aid the reproduction of plenty for the few and destitution in the dirt for the many.

Eating now is clearly, and even more ironically, a very political act. Warm green mythologies about getting back to the garden will have a hard time legitimating food authenticity alone as the path to a truly progressive future. Too many serious questions remain unanswered because eating as authenticity can cloak hard new command, control, and communication campaigns for enforcing more austerity in the regimen of green governmentality. Is this new green economics being imposed in the ruins to sustain the spirit of a society that must be defended, but only after it has been roundly defrauded?

10

On the Politics of the Anthropocene

I. Overview

E VEN THOUGH THIS new scientific term has been kicking around
for fifteen years, "the Anthropocene" suddenly has drawn immense
attention. The multidisciplinary Association for Environmental Studies
and Sciences (AESS), for example, confidently anchored its 2014 annual
meeting's call for papers with the title "Welcome to the Anthropocene:
From Global Challenge to Planetary Stewardship," which succinctly
captures much of contemporary environmentalism's enthusiasm for this
idea, following its endorsement by the *Economist* in 2011.[1] This study,
however, is a more cautious exploration of this new label for "Geology's
New Age."

* Originally published in *Telos* 172 (Fall 2015): 139–62. Parts of this essay draw from
my "The Anthropocene and Freedom: Terrestrial Time as Political Mystification," *Platypus Review* 60 (October 2013), available at http://www.platypus1917.org/2013/10/01/
anthropocene-and-freedom, as well as from "Urbanism as Cyborganicity: Tracking
the Materialities of the Anthropocene," *New Geographies 06: Grounding Metabolism*,
ed. Daniel Ibañez and Nikos Katsikis (Cambridge, MA: Harvard Univ. Press, 2014),
pp. 38–53. Both of these papers are derived in part from my "The Holocene-Anthropo-
cene Extinction Event: Ecocritique as Probing the Impact of Urbanistan," presented at
the annual meetings of the Western Political Sciences Association, March 28–30, 2013.
This paper won the 2014 Award for the Best Paper on Environmental Political Theory
by the Western Political Science Association in April 2014.

1. See "2014 AESS Conference," Association for Environmental Studies and Sciences
(AESS) website, https://aessonline.org/wp-content/uploads/2016/01/AESS-2014-PRO-
GRAM_25_FINAL.pdf; and "Welcome to the Anthropocene, Geology's New Age," *Econ-
omist*, May 28–June 3, 2011.

It reassesses the ongoing ideological reprocessing of this taxonomic term by environmentalists, naturalists, philosophers, and scientists, whose efforts are being paralleled elsewhere by intellectual clarifications of this idea for stratigraphers, paleontologists, geologists, and other earth scientists. Following the lead of conservation biology, applied climatology, and atmospheric chemistry, some stratigraphers are gripped by fears aroused by "ecological catastrophism" with respect to the dire impact "humanity" is having on the planet.[2] This impact, in turn, is also being reconceptualized as the cause of a major biotic event (the "sixth extinction") as well as the advent of a new geological era, the Anthropocene, whose disruptions are "resulting in profound alteration of the planet's climate, serious threats to a large array of species and critical ecosystems, and the conversion of fertile lands to desert."[3]

The widespread celebration of "the Anthropocene" as an operational scientific notion constitutes an intriguing intellectual and political puzzle.[4] Its proponents appear as vigilant scientific sentries, declaring

2. See Andrew Biro, "Good Life in the Greenhouse? Autonomy, Democracy, and Citizenship in a Warmer World," Western Political Science Association, March 22–24, 2012, pp. 1–3. A version of this paper appears in *Telos* as "The Good Life in the Greenhouse? Autonomy, Democracy, and Citizenship in the Anthropocene," *Telos* 172 (Fall 2015): 15–37.

3. Ibid. In pursuit of its thematic call to assume the role of global stewards, the AESS asks itself, and, of course, highlights for policy-makers and the general public, "What are the roles of the humanities, social sciences, and natural sciences in helping to confront planetary threats posed by anthropogenic activities and to develop a sustainable future?" (2014 AESS Conference, call for papers).

4. Paul Crutzen and Eugene F. Stoermer in 2000 asserted that humanity has become a geological and ecological force in nature of sufficient magnitude to modify the collective understanding of geological time: "To assign a more specific date to the onset of the 'anthropocene' seems somewhat arbitrary, but we propose the latter part of the 18th century, although we are aware that alternative proposals can be made (some may even want to include the entire Holocene). However, we choose this date because, during the past two centuries, the global effects of human activities have become clearly noticeable. This is the period when data retrieved from glacial ice cores show the beginning of a growth in atmospheric concentrations of several 'greenhouse gases,' in particular CO_2 and CH_4. Such a starting date also coincides with James Watt's invention of the steam engine in 1784." Paul Crutzen, and Eugene F. Stoermer, "Have We Entered the 'Anthropocene'?," International Geosphere-Biosphere Programme, *Global Change* 41, October 31, 2010, http://www.igbp.net/news/opinion/opinion/haveweenteredtheanthropocene.5.d8b4c-3c12bf3be638a8000578.html. The Anthropocene essentially has become a concept in a state of continuous manufacture after being popularized by Crutzen and others after 2000. Like most facts, it is being made rather than discovered as more peak science

their alarm, hoping to mobilize nation-states "to do something" about today's ecological state of emergency on new "planetarian" policy scales about the destruction that "Man" has wrought in the environment for 250 years.[5] On the one hand, a growing shadow of mass depoliticization is cast by such scientific studies of the Anthropocene as various networks of scientific and technical experts once again position themselves to administer from above and afar any collective efforts to mitigate or adapt to rapid anthropogenic climate change. On the other hand, the Anthropocene idea is at the center of a serious theoretical dispute in the biological, geophysical, and stratigraphical scientific communities. They must judge if humanity's growing civilizational products and by-products are indeed now a world-historical episode of ecological degradation, and especially whether or not their joint impact even registers significantly on a geological time scale. If it does, then what cultural, economic, or political significance should their conceptual confirmation carry for corporate interests, government agencies, and lay publics concerned about the environment?

Paul Crutzen, as Elizabeth Kolbert notes, "wants to focus our attention on the consequences of our collective actions—on their scale and permanence. 'What I hope,' he says, 'is that the term "Anthropocene" will be a warning to the world.'"[6] Crutzen and his warning unfortunately turn up far more than a day late and a dollar short. The world has been repeatedly warned for over 150 years to practically no avail.[7] Indeed, George

---

networks are mobilizing the term. As *Smithsonian* magazine observed in 2012, "This year, the word has picked up velocity in elite science circles: It appeared in nearly 200 peer-reviewed articles, the publisher Elsevier has launched a new academic journal titled *Anthropocene* and IUGS (International Union of Geological Sciences) convened a group of scholars to decide by 2016 whether to officially declare that the Holocene is over and the Anthropocene has begun." Joseph Stromberg, "What Is the Anthropocene and Are We in It?" *Smithsonian*, January 2013.

5. Timothy W. Luke, "Developing Planetarian Accountancy: Fabricating Nature as Stock, Service, and System for Green Governmentality," in *Nature, Knowledge, and Negation*, ed. Harry F. Dahms (Bingley: Emerald Publishing, 2009), pp. 129–59.

6. Elizabeth Kolbert, "Enter the Anthropocene: Age of Man," in *Making the Geologic Now: Responses to Material Conditions of Contemporary Life* (Brooklyn, NY: Punctum Books, 2013), p. 32.

7. Terms approximating the meaning of the Anthropocene have been tossed around with little notice for many decades. Crutzen and Stoermer, however, brought "the Anthropocene" into rapid circulation as the most widely accepted term in 2000. Just as the Pleistocene era had to be "invented" over a period of many years, so too can one now

Perkins Marsh was already making comparable claims about humanity in 1864, which anticipated this Anthropocenic turn, but little serious notice was given to his alarm except by would-be geoengineers.[8] The historical origins of this idea's intellectual genesis and political problematization, then, cannot be ignored. As Michel Foucault notes, one must ask hard questions about concepts when they develop. That is "why a problem and why such a kind of problem, why a certain way of problematizing appears at a given point in time."[9] By pushing to ratify the Anthropocene as a valid scientific benchmark, the disciplinary agitation its advocates create forces one to reconsider "the way in which things," such as the addition of the Anthropocene to geological taxonomies, "become a problem."[10]

From one perspective, applied ecocritique must probe if such new concepts do capture carefully the material challenges at hand, and if they point toward pragmatic rules of behavior that truly are an improvement. From another perspective, do Crutzen's Cassandra-like conceptualizations of the particularities in today's current climate change crisis leave him and other scientists in the role of taxonomic traffic cops, who are left letting the accelerating juggernaut of nearly out-of-control global economic development off with a warning about how fast the world is speeding into a cluster of irreversible ecological catastrophes? Plainly, the creation and circulation of the new analysis swirling around in the Anthropocene debate must be approached, conceptually and discursively, as more than academic squabbles over paleontological stratigraphy. These professional-technical tussles also appear to demarcate "a history of the present: what are we and what are we today."[11]

---

witness the Anthropocene being fabricated. Still, it is only during the 1990s, amid rising anxieties about rampant biodiversity loss and rapid climate change, that this idea gained traction. See Lydia V. Pyne and Stephen J. Pyne, *The Last Lost World: Ice Ages, Human Origins, and the Invention of the Pleistocene* (New York: Viking, 2012).

8. See George Perkins Marsh, *Man and Nature* (Cambridge, MA: Harvard Univ. Press, 1998 [1864]). For a review of how atmospheric chemists and geophysicists anticipated the Anthropocene and then proposed grand designs for its management, see Timothy W. Luke, "Geoengineering as Global Climate Change Policy," *Critical Policy Studies* 4, no. 3 (2010): 111–26.

9. Michel Foucault, *The Politics of Truth*, trans. Lysa Hochroth and Catherine Porter (New York: Semiotext(e), 2007), p. 141.

10. Ibid.

11. Ibid., pp. 136–37.

Until recently, most social, political, and cultural theorists interpreted the growth of settled urban centers as the "rise of civilization"
instead of the "center of catastrophe" on planet Earth.[12] Complex processes of bringing together bigger populations concentrated at sites that
blend architectures and ecologies into "arcologies," in turn, advanced
the spread of "citification" and created "the citificate" outputs of both
work and waste from the social-ecological systems (SES), knitting together many domiciles into cities.[13] There is no dramatic intervention
that can be identified as a cause, but this shift becomes a watershed
event:

> The changes brought over the past 10,000 years as agricultural land-
> scapes replaced wild plant and animal communities, while not so
> abrupt as those caused by the impact of an asteroid at the Cretaceous-
> Tertiary boundary some 65 million years ago or so massive as those
> caused by advancing glacial ice in the Pleistocene, are nonetheless
> comparable to these other forces of global change. Though the "ag-
> ricultural revolution" exhibits some basic similarities to the major
> "natural" forces of global change, it differs dramatically in being a
> uniquely human creation, and, unlike these natural changes, it can-
> not be traced to a single causal event or process.[14]

The materiality of arcological formations, and their embeddedness in
multiple life zones, acquire tremendous anthropogenic force over generations in stable settlements:

> Such settlements were continuously occupied for thousands of years,
> and their remains often provide detailed archaeological records of
> the expanding complexity and scale of agricultural societies. Villages
> turned into towns, cities and city states gained control of growing

12. See Lewis Mumford, *The City in History* (New York: Harcourt Brace Jovanovich,
1934); John M. Meyer, *Political Nature: Environmentalism and the Interpretation of
Western Thought* (Cambridge, MA: MIT Press, 2001); and Roger A. Carras, *A Perfect
Harmony: The Intertwining Lives of Animals and Humans throughout History* (New York:
Knopf, 1996).

13. Paolo Soleri, *The Urban Ideal: Conversations with Paolo Soleri*, ed. John Strohm-
eier (Berkeley, CA: Berkeley Hills Books, 2001); Lewis Mumford, *Technics and Civilization* (New York: Harcourt Brace Jovanovich, 1934).

14. Bruce D. Smith, *The Emergence of Agriculture* (New York: Scientific American
Library, 1998), p. 16.

agricultural landscapes, and empires emerged as our ancestors became more and more successful at organizing agricultural production
and the populations it fed.[15]

As cities came to constitute Lewis Mumford's urban megamachinic clusters of concentrated arcological innovation, their metabolism intertwined natural habitats with artificial structures in many different places
and times on other continents, until they collectively remixed the planet's artificial and natural ecologies as "neo-nature," "socio-nature," "technonature," or "urbanatura."[16]

A major pulse in global warming signaled an end to the last Ice Age.
It began around 20,000 years ago, but it was preceded by slightly rising levels of carbon dioxide in the earth's atmosphere.[17] The advent of
intensive citification and agrarianization in a few human communities
from 11,000 to 4,000 years ago also coincides with the first major leap
in the rates of atmospheric greenhouse gassing, not matched until the
past decade.[18]

More material signs of the Anthropocene are found in the growing concentrations of "carbon dioxide in the atmosphere" as it has risen
"41 percent since the Industrial Revolution began in the 18th century."[19]
Fossil fuel consumption intensifies this effect, so rapid climate change
will be more pronounced than it has been to date—more intense heat
waves, extreme precipitation events, altered growing seasons, and flooded coastal regions. As Jeremy Shakun, a Harvard research scholar, observes, "We're just entering a new era in earth's history.... It will be
an unrecognizable new planet in the future."[20]

15. Ibid., p. 15.

16. Timothy W. Luke, "Property Boundaries/Boundary Properties in Technonature
Studies: Inventing the Future," in *Environments, Technologies, Spaces, and Places in the
Twenty-First Century*, ed. Damian F. White and Chris Wilbert (Waterloo: Wilfrid Lau-
rier UP, 2009), pp. 173–213.

17. Justin Gillis, "Study of Ice Age Bolsters Carbon and Warming Link," *New York
Times*, March 1, 2013.

18. Ibid.

19. Justin Gillis, "Global Temperatures Highest in 4,000 Years," *New York Times*,
March 8, 2013.

20. Gillis, "Study of Ice Age." See also Richard Manning, *Against the Grain: How Agriculture Hijacked Civilization* (New York: North Point Press, 2005).

II. Arcology and the Anthropocene

The missing human links in the Anthropocene thesis are crucial: which specific human groups created these new environmental effects with such geological import where, when, and how on this Anthropocenic scale? At some point between 11,500 BCE and today, humanity's anthropogenic changes to the planet's environments did become perceptible, undeniable, and considerable during the Holocene, but what social forces generated these changes? Arguably, as Paolo Soleri observes, where large agglomerations of permanent human shelters in cities lead to the spread of agriculture on a large scale, one finds arcologies.

Taking the same extraterrestrial perspective as today's planetarian ecomanagerialists, Soleri observes that "there are two things that are apparent on this planet in terms of the presence of humanity, even from outer space. One is agriculture and the other is habitat. Those two domains are essential, and in any absence of them, we do not exist. If we cannot feed ourselves, evidently, we do not exist. If we cannot shelter ourselves it is the same; shelter is mandatory."[21] While he does not use the terms, Soleri is clearly an architect with an awareness of the technonature at the heart of his arcological design projects; and, in the final analysis, anthropogenic environmental changes are "urbanthropogenic" phenomena. The embedded reproduction of cities as artificial networks of human habitats rests upon enduring material formations as habitats to store and distribute the huge reserves of food energy farmed by citified human and nonhuman beings. This technical turn, as Mumford maintains, brings into action the world's first highly productive, and quite polluting, megamachineries in states, cities, and markets.[22]

Soleri's far more utopian vision of arcology called for smaller, compact, and megastructured three-dimensional shelter systems for cities to combat the automobile-based, flat, urban sprawl of the twentieth century. The single-family, four-bedroom, two-bath, and three-car-garage suburban home—built by the hundreds of thousands every year, further and further away from some historic city center or a planned urban service core in the "actually existing arcology" of Western liberal democracies—is the epitome of urbanthropogenic ecological disaster.

21. Soleri, *Urban Ideal*, p. 38.
22. Mumford, *Technics and Civilization*.

Consequently, Soleri's project continuously emphasized architecture and planning as imperative: "Because of all the activities of mankind, the bulkiest, most expensive, the most demanding, and the most necessary is sheltering. We have to shelter ourselves, our families, our society, and the institutions that society needs. So sheltering is really an immense imposition, an immense transportation of nature...the most consuming, the most wasteful, the most polluted, the most segregating kind of shelter we can devise is the suburban home."[23]

Wringing all of the excess energy, materials, labor, and information out of this abuse of energy, materials, and labor in wasted space became the main aspiration for his ideal arcologies. The megalopolis of endless sprawl is the ultimate environmental threat to the biosphere. Soleri's green sense of arcology was definitive: "[T]here must be an acceptance of limits which are defined by its physical limits.... [I]t is a necessity to make the city package small enough so that both the man-made and the natural are at your disposal. There is a limit to the size of any organism, whether biological or para-biological. The city is no exception to this imperative."[24]

Crutzen's somewhat obtuse application of ideas like the Anthropos, Man, or humanity as the key agent behind, responsible for, and in charge of today's environmental crises overlooks Soleri's better sense of the social, material, historical, and cultural nuances in citification. In fact, it is not "Man" as such but rather only some men, in a few places at different times, who have structured the evolving urbanthropogenic changes of the earth in such ways that its arcological spatiality now is more degrading, toxic, and unsustainable. Many suffer considerably, while only a few benefit tremendously.[25] These relations of unequal

23. Soleri, *Urban Ideal*, p. 57. For a discussion of the limits to his vision, see Timothy W. Luke, "The Politics of Arcological Utopia: Soleri on Ecology, Architecture, and Society," *Telos* 101 (Fall 1994): 55–78, reprinted in this volume.

24. Soleri, *Urban Ideal*, pp. 94, 99.

25. The depredations of fossil-fueled capitalist exchange, which is conceptually occluded or flattened out by the Anthropocenic turn, mark the ecological degradation of the earth in an ecological and economic estrangement in which "Life itself appears only as *a means of life*" (Karl Marx, "Economic and Philosophic Manuscripts of 1844," in *The Marx-Engels Reader*, 2nd ed., ed. Robert Tucker [New York: Norton, 1978], p. 76). The unreal universality of the Anthropocene hides the profane practices of degraded capitalist individuality in the detritus left by the machinic means of personal lives defined by the alien powers of commodification. These new Anthropocenic chronicles also

arcological exchange are historically regarded as the basis of "human progress." Yet they rely upon the proliferation of new markets for more capital, energy, labor, and materiel whose by-products are proving increasingly destructive at the local, regional, and global level. Ironically, the source of the best possible solution to the present predicament is the origin of the worst obvious problems, namely, the arcologies driving this citification of the planet. Seven billion people can survive now on earth only because of the these arcologies' logistical capabilities (albeit very unequally distributed by class, region, and neighborhood), but the by-products of these operations are degrading this urbicolous capability and the survival of terrestrial life itself.[26]

Some radical environmentalists urge us to return to the Pleistocene, which a few hundred thousand or a million humans perhaps could try, while billions would die.[27] Some urge us to simply do more of the same to ecomodernize ourselves out of the pervasive side effects of modernization, which has led at best to today's sustainable degradation of the biosphere and the "hard green" realist response.[28] Only a few urge us to look not at nature but at society (and most specifically at the city) for the radical alterity that today's malignant arcologies need.[29] While he is not systematic in his reasoning, Soleri astutely notes that too many environmentalists essentially ignore today's forms of urban living:

> [T]here has been no hint in the environmental movement, as far as I
> know, about the connection between our presence in terms of habitat,

---

estrange Man from nature, himself, and species-being. Indeed, "first it estranges the life of the species and individual life, and secondly it makes individual life in its abstract form the purpose of species, likewise in its abstract and estranged form" (ibid., p. 75). Making other men and nature a means to serve as playthings of such alien powers happens continuously, but then it is hidden. Once hidden by crossing out the Holocene, it makes the purposive control over more men and material as mere means for these alien powers' purpose of life for the human species taking command-and-control of the planet as a "social-ecological system" to manage them all as the playthings of the Anthropocene in close to a permanent global emergency with earth system science.

26. Timothy W. Luke, "'Global Cities' vs. 'Global Cities': Rethinking Contemporary Urbanism as Public Ecology," *Studies in Political Economy* 71, no. 1 (2003): 11–22.

27. Bill Devall and George Sessions, *Deep Ecology* (Layton, UT: Peregrine Smith Books, 1985).

28. John Barry, *The Politics of Actually Existing Sustainability: Human Flourishing in a Climate-Changed, Carbon Constrained World* (Oxford: Oxford Univ. Press, 2012), pp. 17–25.

29. Luke, "Developing Planetarian Accountancy," pp. 129–59.

> and the environment.... [T]he salvation of the environment is in the
> city. Should we ignore the city, forget it, the environment is going to
> be a shambles.... So the salvation of the biosphere as the environmen-
> tal movement wants should be geared to the presence of the city.[30]

Unless and until the degrading dynamics of today's arcologies are cor-
rected, the city cannot be saved, and new human habitats cannot be
geared to the presence of their multiple environments—artificial and
natural, machinic and meteorological, social and biological.

III. Tracking the Not Yet Recognizable

Natural and social reality does not just exist as such for human beings.
Its tones and textures must be made and then remade in use through
discursive cultural development. In all of the ways that everyday language captures and contains meaning, its textual totalities stabilize what
people believe actually "is" and ideally "ought to be" through the discursive representations of such ontological groundwork. Who makes these
ontographic representations? For whom? Deploying what processes of
production? Any means that can be found to shake, shock, or stop the
logic of their workings would disclose a great deal about the ontopoliti-
cal reach of thought and action.

To renegotiate these cognitive contracts, semantic subversion can
prove helpful. Excess will shock the consensual conventions of concep-
tualization, which loosely underpin ordinary representational schemas
for the world. This analysis of the Anthropocene immerses its critique in
etymological excess and subversive semiosis. Otherwise, the constraints
of already in-use diction will enforce the existing terms from language's
cognitive contracts in an older, more fixed fashion. This often prevents
more fluid (pre)cognitive manners of making more meaningful contact with yet-to-be-signified referents in the emergent fullness of new
presences.

The utopian and realist notions of arcology presented here anticipate the profound socio-spatial transformations of urbanthropogenesis
unfolding around the world—as marked *in extremis* by the Anthropocene concept—in which, as Neil Brenner and Christian Schmid argue,
there are many curiosities: new scales of urbanization, a blurred reart-
iculation of urban territories, the disintegration of the hinterland, and

---

30. Soleri, *Urban Ideal*, p. 44.

an end to wilderness. They agree that "[w]e need first of all new theoretical categories through which to investigate the relentless production and transformation of socio-spatial organisation across scales and territories. To this end, a new conceptual lexicon must be created for identifying the wide variety of urbanisation processes that are currently reshaping the urban world and, relatedly, for deciphering the new emergent landscapes of socio-spatial difference that have been crystallising in recent decades."[31] To some extent, this ecocritique of the Anthropocene responds to such analytical and conceptual needs by exploring the promise of arcological criticism.

What lies behind us in the distant past probably is less significant than what is being produced and consumed today, because the scale, scope, and severity of change in the arcologies arising with planetary urbanthropogenic change are unprecedented. Efforts by social-ecological system (SES) managers to calibrate them to return to a set of mapped-and-measured coordinates in the spatialities of 1990, 1970, or 1950 are likely to fail, even if there were trustworthy tools to use for making that return.[32] Whatever is not fully detected, manipulated, and understood as society, ecology, or a system cannot be managed; yet, at the same time, much of it cannot become more discernible without answering the appeal by Brenner and Schmid for new concepts. New terrains are always uncertain, but they feature familiar Anthropocenery in which hybrid life-forms, cyborganic ecological systems, and technonatural urban sprawl fuse together new ranges to be managed. Coyotes and falcons may inhabit urban office parks and robotic drones follow waterfowl in their migratory flyways while inventorying foliage densities in the suburban sprawl ingesting wilderness to produce jobs, homes, and shops for the human denizens of this technonature.

IV. Touring the Anthropocenery

The Anthropocene, even if its professional-technical proponents prevail in their disciplinary squabbles over its categorization, might simply

---

31. Neil Brenner and Christian Schmid, "Planetary Urbanization," in *Urban Constellations*, ed. Matthew Gandy (Berlin: Jovis, 2011), p. 13.

32. Eckart Ehlers and Thomas Krafft, *Earth System Science in the Anthropocene: Emerging Issues and Problems* (Berlin: Springer Verlag, 2010). For a hint of the range management techniques that ESS can foster, see Peter Kareiva and Michelle Marnier, "What is Conservation Science," *BioScience* 62, no. 11 (2012): 962–69.

be only the late Holocene. Perhaps it merely indicates the turn toward times whose citification and arcological traces rapidly emerge in many more geophysical registers, as the urbanthropogenic changes to the planet grow under oil power in scope and intensity under late capitalism. Citification produces civilizational progress as well as municipal waste. Both appear in material citificates, and they pile up as the innumerable detrital and developmental flows of urban living are produced day in and day out by metrometabolic processes. Citificates accumulate as successive strata of human settlement at various sites that leave their detrital traces in soil sediments, ice layers, rock formations, plant concentrations, atmospheric chemistries, animal populations, hybridized biota, and terrestrial topographies. In the vastness of geological time, their advent is quite recent. Yet this evidence is quite perceptible, and citificate incidence is becoming more frequent as their output diversity and level get much more intense, to the extent that human transportation, agriculture, metallurgy, irrigation, stonework, and organization all grow in scale and complexity. Crutzen exaggerates and mystifies these changes by pinning them all on steam engines from 1780 until today; the changes are far deeper, much longer, and more complex.

Whether there also is an early, middle, and late Anthropocene, or some other logic of subdivision for such times, remains an argument for anthropologists, geologists, paleobotanists, and stratigraphers to hash out.[33] If they conclude it does exist, and its existence is typified by this or that set of characteristics, it is a methodological quarrel that will continue for those sciences.[34] Yet how and why the idea of the Anthro-

33. Will Steffen et al., "The Anthropocene: From Global Change to Planetary Stewardship," *Ambio* 40, no. 8 (2011): 739–61; Frances Westley et al., "Tipping toward Sustainability: Emerging Pathways of Transformation," *Ambio* 40, no. 7 (2011): 762–80; Will Steffen, Paul J. Crutzen, and John R. McNeill, "The Anthropocene: Are Humans Now Overwhelming the Great Forces of Nature?," *Ambio* 36, no. 8 (2006): 614–21.

34. Paleolithic human cultures (2.6 million to 10,000 BCE) already were capable of altering the biosphere dramatically on a regional, and then more global, basis. As they spread out of Africa from 100,000 to 130,000 BCE, the first *Homo sapiens* clearly beset the world's large populations of prehistoric avian and mammalian megafauna. Many species were quickly hunted to extinction, and fire was used on landscapes as an environmental management technology to facilitate human hunting-and-gathering in pursuit of those fauna that survived. *Homo erectus* had been thriving for nearly 2 million years, using stone tools to hunt animals and fire to create better hunting grounds. By 30,000 BCE, *Homo sapiens* were dispersed nearly all around the world, and a systematic adoption of various methods to maintain agrarian settlements had become more

pocene is being touted now by other scientific communities, such as atmospheric chemistry, conservation biology, soil science, physical geography, applied climatology, or public administration, is a more political question. To the extent that Anthropocene theory is being trumped up into a writ of empowerment to preside over the declaration, and then implementation, of an ecological state of emergency, it matters. "Letting go" of ecological catastrophism has many political dimensions, and the Anthropocene is one of them. Instead of disaster, it represents an opportunity in which "the deciders," adapting to climate change, may "right-size" carbon intensity, growth prospects, and economic globality for the few in the planetary omnipolis, while ecomanagerialist geoengineering schemes might firmly decarbonize, degrow, and deglobalize life for the many.[35]

The invention and popularization of the Anthropocene as a chronotope for the current crisis, then, is politically significant. It redirects a scientific system of geological time measurement, or stratigraphy, to run as a legitimation engine for those seeking to generate new knowledge as well as to acquire greater power to combat the crisis that "Man" in the Anthropocene supposedly causes.[36] Constituting this chronotope

---

common between 15,000 and 8500 BCE. In Mesopotamia, Jericho was flourishing with a population of a few thousands around 6500 BCE, while Sumer sustained nearly 50,000 residents by 3500 BCE. As the Mesolithic era gave way to the Neolithic Revolution, it is apparent that "the beginning of sedentary modes of food production—the intensified domestication of plants and animals—was a momentous occurrence in human prehistory.... 10,000 years ago almost all human societies lived by hunting and gathering; 8,000 years later, hunter-gather societies were a distinct minority." Franz J. Browswimmer, *Ecocide: A Short History of the Mass Extinction of Species* (London: Pluto Press, 2002), p. 30. Also see Fred Pearce, "Humans' Indelible Stamp on Earth Clear 5000 Years Ago," *New Scientist*, April 30, 2013.

35. See Paul Virilio, *Open Sky*, trans. Julie Rose (London: Verso, 1997); and Virilio, *The Art of the Motor*, trans. Julie Rose (Minneapolis: Univ. of Minnesota Press, 1995).

36. The "Anthropos" of the Anthropocene is a strange reified, sophistical, or tentative construct. Just as Marx mapped the trope of "Man" in his "On the Jewish Question" (in *The Marx-Engels Reader*, pp. 26–52) and Engels probed in *The Condition of the Working Class in England* (in *The Marx-Engels Reader*, pp. 579–85), its subjectivity is anchored in the same political economy that Engels characterized as that "science of enrichment born of the merchant's mutual envy and greed" rooted in "despicable immorality" (cited in Robert Tucker, introduction to *The Marx-Engels Reader*, p. xxviii). Marx's vision of Man, then, triangulates itself against the duplicities of seeking personal enrichment in the realm of civil society and global markets along with collective empowerment of the bourgeois class in the domain of the state. The Anthropos, or "Man," is a social being

also keeps an uneasy sense of considerable peril in the air to justify declarations of ecological emergency; but this idea also could normalize these changes, recasting them as yet another survivable episode in the chronicles of time. On this point, for example, the chair of the National Committee on Global Change Research in Germany, Wolfram Mauser, asserts:

> The term Anthropocene has been suggested to mark an era in which the human impact on the Earth System has become a recognizable force. Presently there are no signs for a deceleration or reversal of this development. Coping with the consequences of Global Change therefore becomes a challenge of prior unknown dimension for human societies. It goes far beyond the analysis of changes to the global climate system and rather compromises the Earth System in its physical, bio-geochemical and societal processes as a whole.[37]

Earth system science (ESS) is one title given to the analysis of all of these changes, and its partnership with the many scientific and policy players co-aligned in the IGBP (International Geosphere-Biosphere Programme), IHDP (International Human Dimensions Programme), WCRP (World Climate Research Programme), and DIVERSITAS (International Programme of Biodiversity Science) produces more clusters

---

enfolding in very recent times framed by states and civil societies with all their mythic qualities. The egoistic existence of all men is tied to the axial forces animating "Man." Marx asserts that the double-dealing of modernity comes into full play: "Where the political state has attained to its full development, man leads, not only in thought, in consciousness, but in reality, in life, a double existence—celestial and terrestrial. He lives in the *political community*, where he regards himself as a *communal being*, and in *civil society* where he acts simply as a *private individual*, treats other men as means, degrades himself to the role of a mere means, and becomes the plaything of alien powers" (Marx, "On the Jewish Question," p. 34). Unexpectedly and ironically, species-being for humans in the Holocene appears as this categorical "Man." Crutzen and Stoermer, as they date the most noticeable effects of human activities globally in their Anthropocenery, are addressing the humans caught in these same containers of agency—the state and civil society—in which their relations as communal beings and private individuals are the egoisms of a doubled existence pitched at treating other men as means. That is, those social formations in which "man is the imaginary member of an imaginary sovereignty, divested of his real, individual life, and infused with unreal universality" (ibid.).

37. Cited in Ehlers and Krafft, *Earth System Science*. For an even more celebratory statement of the Anthropocene, see Mark Lynas, *The God Species: How the Planet Can Survive the Age of Humans* (London: Fourth Estate, 2011).

of new expert initiatives intent upon defining and then developing ESS as a new discourse of truth for surviving in the Anthropocene.

Without saying it as critically or directly as Marx, the "Man" at work in these networks of earth scientists is not all of humanity as such but instead a familiar, more mystified face. That is, he/she is basically the technological, scientific, modern, commercial, and acquisitive men/women at work, and/or enduring the pressures, in the projects of Western nation-building, empire-expansion, and capitalist-development leaping out of the past 250 years in Crutzen's Anthropocenic instant in geological time. The Anthropocene concept becomes, in part, an urbanthropocentric exercise that simultaneously bemoans and celebrates the agency of these displaced chronocentric and ethnocentric figurations of "Man" in the world's rapid citification.

The discourse of truth, operating on the basis of these Anthropocenic applications for ESS, appears ready to serve as a directory of planetarian management by generating policy-ready findings for new waves of allegedly sustainable development.[38] As Eckart Ehlers and Thomas Krafft maintain, this project is immense, important, and imperative. Although it will be global in scope and authority, they assure everyone that "Earth System Science has to provide place-based information by analyzing global and regional processes of Global Change and by translating the research findings into policy relevant results."[39]

To date, ESS has been busy at the research bench as well as at international conferences, and an immense amount of scientific work is revealing more about how such experts want to understand what "is" happening with rapid climate change, biodiversity loss, and growing urbanization. Yet this patchy knowledge is not leading to many clearly decisive programs for "what ought to be done," because those engaged in this research still tend to consign those decisions to policy-makers. Green public intellectuals, such as Al Gore, Thomas Berry, or Bill McKibben, recommend improbable and hasty reductions of energy, material, and land-use levels to match those 1990, 1970, 1950, or even some earlier point in time. Most realize that the politics of sacrifice being pushed by these individuals, however, is not a very workable set of policy recom-

38. Timothy W. Luke, "Neither Sustainable nor Developmental: Reconsidering Sustainability in Development," *Sustainable Development* 13, no. 4 (2005): 228–38.

39. Ehlers and Krafft, *Earth System Science*, p. 10.

mendations.[40] Meanwhile, applied climatologists work away at creating more international research programs and projects, which spin up an appearance of doing something, but few reductions in the putative threat levels have been attained. More careers are made, CVs become more impressive, conferences are attended, and collaborations are created, but species keep disappearing, coastlines are being flooded, carbon dioxide levels are rising, and global temperatures are increasing.

As lame as it is, the most prevalent normative injunction for living better in the Anthropocene is, bizarrely enough, to encourage more "sustainable development." Despite their lean, green, or clean pretensions, most sustainable development practices are centered on sustaining economic development rather than developing ecological sustainability. Development is at the root of the planet's degradation, but it also is at the heart of urban culture. *Our Common Future* propounded directives to enjoy the benefits of development up to the point that it will not compromise the ability of future generations to have that same opportunity.[41] The best science on this generation of greenhouse gases, for example, suggests that 350 ppm of carbon dioxide is the tipping point for stabilizing global warming. Regrettably, this threshold was tagged in 1987–88. In turn, this point was passed in 1990 by 4.35 ppm with regard to carbon dioxide greenhouse gas emissions, which once was considered the safest limit, as James Hansen testified before Congress in 1988. Rather than abiding by the WCED's quarter-century-old moral injunctions about denying equal ecological opportunity to future generations, too many communities of scientists still are quarreling with even more policy-makers who dispute their findings or who reject their recommendations *in toto*. What once was a sincere appeal to radically restructure industrial civilization by developing slowly and sustainably has, in turn, become a corporate chamber of commerce homily for lean and clean growth. And carbon dioxide levels in the atmosphere at Mauna Loa Observatory in Hawaii were 395.5 ppm in January 2013.[42]

40. Michael Maniates and John M. Meyer, eds., *The Environmental Politics of Sacrifice* (Cambridge, MA: MIT Press, 2010).

41. World Commission on Environment and Development (WCED), *Our Common Future* (1987), http://www.un-documents.net/our-common-future.pdf.

42. "Trends in Atmospheric Carbon Dioxide," U.S. Department of Commerce, National Oceanic and Atmospheric Administration, NOAA Research, http://www.esrl.noaa.gov/gmd/ccgg/trends.

Centering discourse and practice on attaining fundamental changes in the energy economy of human culture now rests at the core of ESS, which is also rooting itself in the Anthropocene concept for scientific and political legitimation.[43] Reexamining today's "liberal democratic capitalism" returns one, at the same time, to the "archaeological and genealogical study of practices envisaged simultaneously as a technological type of rationality and as strategic games of liberties" as they play out in global governmentality's systems of systems.[44] These grids create some purportedly right disposition between people and things embedded in large capital-intensive technologies with their own embedded environmentalities.[45] These urbanthropogenic industrial ecologies, run on oil, gas, and coal energy, engineered for lives of material consumption, and imagined around attaining ever greater, faster, and deeper levels of mass consumption—the conditions of how "development" actually might become sustainable—are all tied to hydrocarbon fossil fuels.[46]

V. Energy and the Anthropocene

Braden Allenby's analysis of the Anthropocene stresses these same measures of energy intensity by reconsidering its industrial and protoindustrial origins and implications, although he does not date it like

43. Luke, "Geoengineering as Global Climate Change Policy."

44. Michel Foucault, "What Is Enlightenment?," in *The Foucault Reader*, ed. Paul Rabinow (New York: Pantheon, 1984), p. 46.

45. Timothy W. Luke, *Ecocritique: Contesting the Politics of Nature, Economy, and Culture* (Minneapolis: Univ. of Minnesota Press, 1997).

46. Humans willingly degrade themselves, becoming mere means for the fossil-fueled and steam-powered depredation of those alien powers of capitalist exchange. As they consume more and more resources in the narrow profane worlds of civil society, the political state stands over them in civil society to acknowledge, reinforce, and then dominate its order on temporal, terrestrial, and technoeconomic levels of practice. Is Man, or the Anthropos, therefore, only mystified as "species-being" or a socially authentic living agent? In Crutzen's views of "Man," can we see an essentially bourgeois consciousness—or the Anthropocenic subject—colonizing history and humanity to estrange men and women from their humanity, their individual being, and nature? For Marx, all of humanity's time on earth is, in a sense, the Anthropocene inasmuch as Man's history "makes all nature his *inorganic* body—both inasmuch as nature is (1) his direct means of life, and (2) the material, the object, and instrument of his life activity....Man lives on nature—means that nature is his body, with which he must remain in continuous intercourse if he is not to die. That man's physical and spiritual life is linked to nature means simply that nature is linked to itself, for man is part of nature" (Marx, "Economic and Philosophic Manuscripts," p. 75).

many others at being 250 years old. Paul Dukes pegs 1763 as the birth year of the Anthropocene, tying it to James Watt's perfection of his reciprocating steam engine design—as a "mere mechanician" improving upon the Newcomen engine of the time.[47] Allenby takes a longer view:

> The Earth has become an anthropogenic planet. The dynamics of most natural systems—biological, chemical, and physical—are increasingly affected by the activities of one species, ours.... Although this process has been accelerated by the Industrial Revolution, "natural" and human systems at all scales have in fact been affecting each other, and coevolving, for millennia, and they are more coupled than ever. Copper production during the Sung dynasty as well as in Athens and the Roman Republic and Empire, are reflected in deposition levels in Greenland ice; and lead production in ancient Athens, Rome, and medieval Europe is reflected in increases in lead concentrations in the sediments of Swedish lakes. The buildup of carbon dioxide in the atmosphere began not with the post–World War II growth in the consumption of fossil fuel, but the growth of agriculture in, and thus deforestation of, Europe, Africa, and Asia over the past millennia. Humanity's impacts on biota, both directly through predation and indirectly through the introduction of new species to indigenous habitats, have been going on for centuries as well.[48]

Others push the metric of centuries out into the scale of millennia, because carbon dioxide began building perceptibly around 8,000 years ago, and methane at about 5,000 years ago, as humans started their more intense agricultural and pastoral economic activities to create permanent settlements.[49] Anthropogenic qualities could be found in global environmental changes back to the dawn of the Holocene, but it is the quantitative amplification of them since 1763 that has led to the recalibration of, or the extensive renegotiation over, the dating of the Pliocene, Pleistocene, Holocene, and now Anthropocene eras.[50]

47. Paul Dukes, *Minutes to Midnight: History and the Anthropocene Era from 1763* (London: Anthem Press, 2011).

48. Braden Allenby, *Reconstructing Earth: Technology and the Environment in the Age of Humans* (Washington, DC: Island Press, 2005), pp. 9–10.

49. William F. Ruddiman, *Plows, Plagues, and Petroleum: How Humans Took Control of Climate* (Princeton, NJ: Princeton Univ. Press, 2005).

50. See Pyne and Pyne, *The Last Lost World*.

Crutzen's key indicator of Anthropocenic change is the steam engine, but he takes a slight misstep in attributing importance to the apparatus per se rather than its economic and social applications.[51] Watt's innovations (his design enabled it to become about five percent efficient) on the steam engine technologies introduced by Newcomen, which was often only one percent efficient, centered on that apparatus in order to improve its thermal and mechanical efficiency. Together, this ensemble of men and machines is "the most important event in the Industrial Revolution" because Watt's improvements sparked the concentrated but widespread applications of steam power throughout a few wealthier, more powerful economies and societies.[52]

Watt's steam engine improvements allowed the carbohydrate energy regime of living biomass to be eclipsed by a hydrocarbon energy regime tied to coal, petroleum, and gas from fossil stocks of solar energy that had accumulated over eons. Watt's improved steam designs in 1800 might produce twenty kilowatts of power, and many engines by 1900 were thirty times more powerful than units from 1800.[53] Hence, coal production alone grew exponentially per annum from 15 million tons in 1800 to over 700 million tons in 1900.[54] Petroleum-fueled steam engines became common with high-pressure steam systems, but internal combustion engines (burning kerosene, gasoline, or diesel fuels) after 1880 fully embedded hydrocarbon energy in the basically imperialist articulation of an increasingly capitalist global economy.

With the attendant rise of electrification in the 1880s and 1890s, global energy use "increased fivefold in the nineteenth century…and then another sixteenfold in the twentieth century," such that the Anthropocene also truly could be tagged as "the Etheranthracene" (recent hydrocarbon epoch) inasmuch as "in the 100 centuries between the

51. Paul J. Crutzen, "The 'Anthropocene,'" in *Earth System Science in the Anthropocene: Emerging Issues and Problems*, ed. Eckart Ehlers and Thomas Krafft (Berlin: Springer Verlag, 2010); and Crutzen and Stoermer, "Have We Entered the 'Anthropocene'?"

52. Ben Marsden, *Watt's Perfect Engine: Steam and the Age of Invention* (Cambridge: Icon, 2002).

53. J. R. McNeill, *Something New under the Sun: An Environmental History of the Twentieth-Century World* (New York: Norton 2000).

54. Vaclav Smil, *Energy in World History* (Boulder, CO: Westview, 1994), p. 186; and Carlo Cipolla, *The Economic History of World Population* (Harmondsworth: Penguin, 1978), p. 56.

dawn of agriculture and 1900, people used only about two-thirds as much energy as in the twentieth century."[55] The use of this fossil fuel energy at the same time is extremely inequitable, and highly concentrated, because it is capital-intensive, complex, and reserved for rich urban-thropocentric economies sustaining developed commercial exchange. This extravagant historical use of fossil fuels is still with us in the growing carbon loadings of the world's air, soil, water, and ice, but few are ready or willing yet to relabel the Anthropocene as the Carboniferous Age Redux.

Crutzen is quite clear about this agenda: "existing but also difficult and daunting tasks lie ahead of the global research and engineering community to guide mankind toward global, sustainable, environmental management into the Anthropocene."[56] Intent upon building transition towns or resilience redoubts, these social forces ignore how it is essentially already too late to restore the planet quickly to conditions that prevailed in 1990, 1970, 1950, or 1900. Even if this return were possible, it would not lessen, mitigate, or end the Anthropocene. Arguably, the entire Holocene has been already the Anthropocene, and its start date at approximately 12,000 BCE to 1763 BCE was only its "early" era, and perhaps 1763 to 1945–2000 was its "middle" or "later" era. Nonetheless, between 1763 and 2013, the entire planet essentially has become a business park, and its environmental artifices have mainly exploited and enhanced conservation initiatives to camouflage contemporary capitalism's "sustainable degradation."[57] Moreover, applied climatology, sustainability science, resilience studies, or social-ecological systems management embedded in ESS are the latest manifestations of knowledge as power, or power calling for knowledge, to further enhance and exploit the arcological environments of the earth as a happier and healthier "business park."

VI. The Anthropocenery of the Past, Present, and Future

Stratigraphers' assessments of the Anthropocene surpass the hard biocentrism and soft anthropocentrism of deep ecology in seeking comparable goals, namely, "an overriding vital need for a healthy and high-quality

---

55. McNeill, *Something New under the Sun*, pp. 14, 15.
56. Crutzen, "The 'Anthropocene,'" p. 17.
57. Luke, "Neither Sustainable nor Developmental," pp. 228–38.

natural environment for humans, if not for all life, with minimum intrusion of toxic waste, nuclear radiation from human enterprises, minimum acid rain and smog, and enough free flowing wilderness so humans can get in touch."[58] Deep ecology has pretended this is a hard biocentric line, but it has been, in practice, a soft anthrocentrism that now tags benchmarks for those who cling to the nature/culture, society/ecology, history/biology divide in complex coupled social-ecological systems. The Anthropocenics of ESS big science networks, however, efface this division with their stratigraphically legitimated ecological state of emergency. From 1763 to 2013, "Man" putatively has become an awesome geomorphic power, and his destructive power now expresses a deeper, if not the deepest, ecology of hard anthropocentrism to shelter what little life remains in this sixth great extinction event for the benefit of a soft biocentrism worried about the remnants of Creation.

Crutzen's Anthropocene uncritically recycles Enlightenment-based ontographies for nature/culture, humanity/technology, subject/object, man/environment relations as stratigraphic operational assumptions. Ironically, he takes Kant's "man of nature, of exchange, or of discourse," always presented as "the foundation of his own finitude,"[59] and transforms him/her into the Anthropos of modern exchange pitted against nature. In the discourses of stratigraphy, Man's putatively Promethean powers play into an *illusio* of infinitude by recasting anthropogenic change as a geophysical force, which now leaves its mark on time in the soil, waters, air, and rocks of the planet. Crutzen's attempts to awaken and think anew, however, only manifest new disturbances to Kant's "anthropological sleep," which still remain misguided about where humanity is destined to go, why Man is no longer the measure of all things, and when we hope to be human in a time when humanity no longer is. By mobilizing paleontology for this Anthropos to theorize and fabricate a politics of planetary ecomanagerialism, earth system science deploys its new applied Anthropocenarios to reinvent its needs to control nature all the way down into the existing geological record. Yesterday's carboniferously excessive anthropogenesis is transmuted into today's ecologically correct anthropocentrism.

58. Devall and Sessions, *Deep Ecology*, p. 262.
59. Michel Foucault, *The Order of Things: An Archaeology of the Human Sciences* (New York: Vintage, 1970), p. 341.

VII. The Etheranthracene: Policy Anthropocenarios

Earth system science, as a knowledge formation, implies, in turn, new power articulations, matching, making, and massing its epistemic and directive capacity to propound planetarian governance capabilities.[60] As one all-too-willing volunteer puts the problem, planetarian knowledge regimes constitute "a single earth system," which they characterize as perched "on the edge of chaos" that necessitates managerial interventions working "in a way that secures the sustainable development of human society" and "the co-evolution of human and natural systems"[61] to rationalize various Anthropocenian designs for what is, in fact, the dawn of Etheranthracene era (marked by its dirty hydrocarbon metabolisms), growing now on a global scale. Thomas L. Friedman's "hot, flat, and crowded" world could continue, while ESS elites manage the patchwork adaptations of human and nonhuman life to spreading ecological catastrophe by refining sustainable degradation.

The political implications of ESS Anthropocenarios are plenty, but also problematic. In addition to mystifying the materiality of the Etheranthracene era as it actually has been developing in the capitalist world system, as well as juicing up the mythos of the Anthropocene, the figurations of a man-made geophysical era support the recruitment campaigns for a green vanguard of right-minded experts to move from today's ecological catastrophism, with its vernacular/spontaneous/unintended stance toward Anthropocenic evolution, to a far more planned/organized/intended approach to arcologizing the planet even more ruthlessly. The answer to the ultimate political question—"Who, Whom?"—is already being advanced by the green vanguard of earth system science or sustainability science. They rule, and all others will follow their rules. As many green vanguardist cadres at work in many disciplines openly assert, the Anthropos has realized that now is not a time merely to monitor, interpret, or explain earth systems; rather, the point is to change them under their self-certain enlightened command.

60. Westley et al., "Tipping toward Sustainability," pp. 762–80.
61. Frank Biermann, "Earth System Governance as a Cross-Cutting Theme of Global Change Research," *Global Environmental Change* 17, nos. 3–4 (2007): 326–37. Also see Peter Kareiva, Robert Lalasz, and Michelle Marvier, "Conservation in the Anthropocene: Beyond Solitude and Fragility," *Breakthrough Institute* 2 (Fall 2011): 29–37.

The ratification of the Anthropocene as a valid term of stratigraphic analysis, as well as a reliable theorization for greater geophysical interventions in the biosphere, also should provide ideological justification for limited and/or extensive efforts at geoengineering. Moral injunctions to burn less oil, adopt the Kyoto Protocols, enter carbon trading markets, and embrace green engineering are not stopping rapid climate change (due apparently to greater greenhouse gassing as the Etheranthracene persists). Hence, the contrivances of geoengineering should perhaps be unleashed, if only experimentally, to mitigate greenhouse gas effects on the atmosphere, cryosphere, hydrosphere, and lithosphere. What techniques are chosen, who will stand at the controls, what signs of success are sought, and who controls "the thermostat," of course, are all questions "TBD," even though their answers could determine the who, where, what, when, and why that shall continue to be.[62]

To validate its planetary significance and then tie their terraformative force to science and technology, the networks of earth system science are implicitly "taking charge" as planetarian ecomanagerialists with very little collective discussion, deliberation, or decision-making about equity, justice, or representation—beyond their own limited scientific findings—to guide them.[63] Their climatological conception of history is basically a depoliticized program grounded in their reified assessments of earth itself and then ratified by sedimentology, paleontology, geophysics, zoology, dendrology, oceanography, and other sciences.

The demographic transition of the world around 2000 to being more urban than rural will accelerate until at least 2040, and the impact of urbanthropocenic built environments with their omnipolitanizing effects are mostly hidden in the shadows of the Etheranthracene. The degradation of soil, water, air, and biodiversity by omnipolitanization is occurring globally, but its most concentrated effects are being felt in the megalopoli of the planet. As machinic modernity dawned in Europe in the nineteenth century, urban life often was sophisticated, liberating, civilized, and attractive. Today's new urbanthropocenic life in Africa, Asia, or the Americas is frequently crude, oppressive, dehumanizing, and atrocious.

62. Luke, "Geoengineering as Global Climate Change Policy," pp. 111–26.
63. David Schlosberg, *Defining Governmental Justice: Theories, Movements, and Nature* (New York: Oxford Univ. Press, 2009).

While there are fresh Anthropocenic myths of utopian arcologies, floating cruise ship cities, and super skyscraper developments still being circulated in the pages of the *Economist*, the *Wall Street Journal*, or the *Financial Times* as the fantasies of global starchitects, it is only a tiny variant subspecies of the Anthropos, or "Davos Man," who does (or maybe will) inhabit such new hyperurbs in the urbanthropocenery where the good life in the greenhouse made by greenhouse gassing will continue. Even so, they will hide behind physical and electronic walls in such planned urban developments (PUDs), where community is strongly gated, subjectivity is heavily guarded, and identity is continuously graded.[64] Elsewhere the world sprawls out as a planet of slums that can be policed from an empire of bases from which drone wars, *Zero Dark Thirty* special-ops strikes, and perpetual cyberwar can be rationally staged and then ruthlessly conducted.[65]

At one level, the geopolitics of planetary ecomanagerialism will perhaps leap up to the fabulous terrain of futuristic geoengineering; however, on another level, a grubbier and more familiar geopolitics of planetary policing will undoubtedly continue in the meantime. Democracy can cash out as votes to decarbonize most personal transport with municipal bike-sharing systems, and citizenship might mean support for degrowing fast capital to rest in slow cities. In any event, this warmer world will be hotter, flatter, and more crowded. Most of it will be like Baghdad from 2003–2011, Gaza through the intifadas, Homs in the Syrian Civil War, Mumbai in its BRIC-clad globalization, Detroit's slow-motion degrowth since 1973, or Ciudad de Juárez/El Paso during its "narco guerras."

Again, the Anthropocene rarely highlights these microenvironments for planetarian ecomanagerialists to ponder, but then the Anthropocenic turn also tends to ignore the swelling gyres of plastic detritus with which omnipolitanization is saturating the Pacific, Atlantic, and Indian Oceans. Another expression of the Etheranthracene at work, the new tidal deposits, suspended microparticles, floating tangles, and food-chain-invading molecules of various plastics from "the 5 gyres" are becoming normalized by the media as the viewing public tends to regard

---

64. Daniel Brooks, *A History of Future Cities* (New York: Norton, 2013).
65. Mike Davis, *Planet of Slums* (London: Verso, 2008).

such phenomena as another fascinating dimension in the rich webs of life evolving in the Anthropocenery of the twenty-first century.[66]

The Anthropocene's key conceit is to celebrate the centrality of anthropogenic changes in the many polyvalent directions of biotic evolution on the earth, while at the same time mystifying how completely the planet is now an extreme monoculture dedicated to the survival of one cultigen, namely, humanity, people, ourselves, that "We" ourselves, people, humans, supposedly have propagated. Meanwhile, ESS continues to demonstrate why and how, "if we are to comprehend, let alone move toward grappling with, the world we are continually remaking, we must get behind the idea that we are imposing our intent, our purpose, on the future. Religion may be the opiate of the masses, but 'cause and effect' is the opiate of the rational elite."[67]

To conclude, the planetarian project of earth systems science ecomanagerialism plainly pushes Paul Virilio's dour visions of the omnipolis and Paolo Soleri's hopeful designs for arcology to their logical limits by making them geophysically official with this ideological dawn of the Anthropocene. Standing out amid the spreading desertification, coastal flooding, and rising temperatures of rapid climate change, sustainability science makes precisely the appeal needed to see the planet as an omnipolis ready to be geoengineered. In the anthropocentric arias being scored by today's Anthropocenarists, the earth's inhabitants are being urged to start thinking of themselves as defined by the newest folds in time—now known as the Anthropocene. Going back is impossible, stopping now improbable, and expanding even more inexorable; the Anthropocene allegedly lies ahead but is also already around us. As long as scientific experts peer at these turbulent currents of planetary transformation through the taxonomies and terms of Victorian science, the arcologies of the earth will continue to destructively omnipolitanize the planet-state, but in strong accord with peer-reviewed Anthropocenarios from ESS labs and their panels of expert authority.

---

66. See "The Plastic Problem," 5 Gyres website, http://www.5gyres.org/the-plastic-problem/; and the NOAA's Marine Debris Program, http://marinedebris.noaa.gov/.

67. Braden Allenby and Daniel Sarewitz, *The Techno-Human Condition* (Cambridge, MA: MIT Press, 2011), pp. 70–71.

11

On the Road to Marrakesh:
A Politics of Mitigation or Mystification
for Global Climate Change?

THE NUTS AND BOLTS of global climate change negotiations rarely are as riveting as other major world events, like the electoral victory of Donald Trump in the United States, the Syrian Civil War, or the Brexit vote in the United Kingdom, but they can lead to long-term outcomes of tremendous importance. In this vein, the full implementation of the Paris climate change accords on November 4, 2016, on the eve of the COP 22 meetings in Marrakesh, represented a significant step toward climate change mitigation, albeit one taken decades later than needed. The conditions of its approval, however, have thrown its completion into doubt, given how approval by the United States came by presidential executive order from President Obama. On the other hand, President-elect Trump has sworn to negate Obama's directive after his January 20, 2017, inauguration as well as nominate Myron Ebell, an infamous climate change doubter, who chairs the Cooler Heads Coalition of nonprofit organizations that opposes many current energy policies. Trump promises to reorganize the Environmental Protection Agency as an independent bipartisan regulatory commission. At this juncture, then, it is apparent that the Paris Agreement will be intensely contested by a number of climate change deniers, clean coal advocates, and carbon-intensive industries. Even so, this multilateral UN-organized

* Originally published in *Telos* 177 (Winter 2016): 209–18.

compact solidifies a generally united effort by over one hundred countries to mitigate the accelerating ill effects of climate change.

At the same time, the Paris Agreement also has mystified how difficult meeting its goals will be. Its success pivots upon a bizarre combination of loose national pledges by some nations "to begin doing everything differently," a few countries touting the merits of "green capitalism," and many other states trapped in the wasteful practices of "business as usual" in their daily global commerce. Indeed, the Paris Agreement already can allow the world climate to increase 3°C (5.4°F) above pre-industrial levels, while most scientific authorities continue to believe 2°C (3.6°F) is the ultimate outer limit for further global warming. The next few years will soon tell if these measures are enough to induce necessary improvements in overall climatic conditions or prove only to be yet another set of global accords that do too little, too late.

The first worldwide celebration of Earth Day by over 200 million people in 141 countries on its twentieth anniversary in April 1990 created a consensus to convene a UN-backed Earth Summit in Rio de Janeiro two years later. In turn, the United Nations Framework Convention on Climate Change (UNFCCC) came into operation with its adoption as part of the concluding agreements from the Rio Earth Summit during June 1992. The UNFCCC plays off the relatively successful 1987 Montreal Protocol, which regulated the production and use of chlorofluorocarbons (CFCs). Due to their corrosive effects on the earth's ozone layer, the Montreal Protocol forged a complex multilateral agreement between most nation-states to regulate the corporate production and sale of these chemical refrigerants. Following this precedent, the UNFCCC then sought to organize the same intergovernmental institutional mechanisms in efforts to slow and then stabilize anthropogenic climate change. A few smaller states quickly complied, but the largest countries with the most pollutant-ridden economies equivocated for nearly two decades, evading the UNFCCC's scientific guidance or eluding its legal dictates in the quest for greater material prosperity.

Although it is colloquially labeled "global warming," the dynamics of rapid climate change since the 1940s and 1950s entail far more deleterious alterations in the planet's atmosphere. Indeed, the unintended consequences of fossil fuel use makes regulating greenhouse gas (GHG) emissions through every plausible combination of local, national, and international policies imperative. Scientists from different countries and disciplines in various ways had puzzled provisionally through the connections between changing atmospheric temperatures and rising terrestrial GHG emissions during the nineteenth century, especially as new anthropogenic outputs of carbon dioxide rose from burning more peat, wood, and fossil fuels to drive steam-powered machinery. Measuring these gases systemically with a rigorous monitoring regime, however, did not begin until the American–Soviet arms and space races intensified during the 1950s. Even then, GHG measurement began haphazardly only with wider surveillance initiatives to detect radioactive isotopes from nuclear weapons testing in the atmosphere.

At Rio, the parties to the UNFCCC agreed to create stronger reporting and verification practices, find workable market-based GHG governance solutions, and define verifiable systems for compliance during the next five years. Yearly meetings for the nation-states making up the "conference of the parties" (COP) began in 1995 at Berlin to evaluate the range of different policy options and their likely effectiveness.[1] Those deliberations quickly led to a series of binding national emissions targets that required an average 5 percent reduction of GHGs from 1990 levels for the first commitment period (2005–2012) and an 18 percent reduction for the second commitment period (2013–2020), as tracked by the UN Climate Secretariat in Bonn, Germany. Ratified December 11, 1997, at the COP 3 in Japan, the Kyoto Protocol was questioned repeatedly in many countries for its severe emission-reduction goals aimed directly at 37 richer industrialized countries and the European Community. The Protocol pushed for varied phases of national implementation, and it required all parties to recognize the larger role of richer industrial economies in producing current GHG volumes along with responsibilities for their historical legacy emissions since the 1760s. This resolution underscored how all signatories acceded to the regulative ideals of "common but differentiated responsibility" for countries trying to mitigate climate change. At the same time, this principle has worked as an invid-

---

1. See the United Nations Framework Convention on Climate Change website, https://unfccc.int/. For consideration of the evolving tools for governing the global environment, see Timothy W. Luke, "Developing Planetarian Accountancy: Fabricating Nature as Stock, Service, and System for Green Governmentality," in *Nature, Knowledge, and Negation*, ed. Harry F. Dahms (Bingley: Emerald Publishing, 2009), pp. 129–59.

ious distinction that branded successful economic development by its privileged production of greater GHG emissions. The developed nations conceded this fact, but the underdeveloped countries then demanded their own rights to pollute as a fast path to attaining economic growth.

For the most part, even this loose agreement to comply with common goals was widely disparaged by many countries, even as their respective national records often overstated, and then underperformed, their national GHG controls to maintain political stability, economic growth, and cultural pride during the crisis-ridden first years of the twenty-first century. The material circumstances, priorities, and capacities in many national capitols to battle climate change might have been relatively favorable. Yet turning moral resolve into economic facts as "nationally determined contributions" (NDCs) to climate change mitigation was hard going. When the Protocol came into force in 2005, its requirements were not met fast enough, or at all, because many nations fought to avoid deeper economic losses amid the Great Recession. Bad economic times stalled climate actions for years, and few decisive advances were made until 2015 with the Paris Agreement.

Prior to the opening of the G-20 summit in Hangzhou, China, however, Presidents Xi Jinping of the PRC and Barack Obama of the United States affirmed on September 3, 2016, that both nations would ratify the Paris Agreement of the UNFCCC. As the two nations are the largest GHG-producing countries, which together produce 35 percent of all current emissions, this declaration immediately accelerated many other adoptions of the Paris Agreement, since up to that point only 24 countries—which together emitted only around 1 percent of world GHG emissions—had actually ratified this document, even though 197 formally had signed it. Once any group of countries with 55 percent of the world population and 55 percent of GHG emissions ratified the treaty, however, all COP states agreed it would come immediately into force. With Canada's, India's, Nepal's, and the European Union's formal ratification after the jointly announced Chinese and American approvals, the Paris Agreement became active on November 4, 2016—thirty days after the required participation triggers were pulled for the COP's ratifying signatory countries.

On November 4, 2016, then, the global community of nation-states collectively boarded—in a diplomatic and poetic way—the Marrakesh

Express to convene COP 22 in Morocco from November 7–18, 2016. By punching their tickets from the COP 21 Paris meetings and beginning to coordinate their NDCs, the participant countries deliberated over putting climate change mitigation programs in place worldwide.[2] This momentous shift, of course, largely was ignored as the increasingly divisive U.S. presidential election eclipsed almost all other news during 2016. Indeed, not one question about climate change was ever raised at any of the three nationally televised election debates between Hillary Clinton and Donald Trump, largely due to the GOP's openly negative views on the UNFCCC's activities. Meanwhile, the 170 countries that had adopted the 1987 Montreal Protocol to eliminate the use of CFCs (chlorofluorocarbons) hammered out a crucial amendment to that agreement in Kigali, Rwanda, during October 2016 to eliminate the use of HFCs (hydrofluorocarbons) in refrigeration systems. Created to replace CFCs in the 1980s, HFCs have proven to be extremely dangerous GHGs (ranging from 100 to 3,000 times more destructive than carbon dioxide). In reducing their use alone by 90 percent, the world should slow global temperature increases through 2050 by 0.5°C.[3]

As with the Paris accords, however, the Kigali negotiators mystified the full promise of these negotiations as they engineered too many degrees of national freedom into HFC reductions country-by-country in order to forge a minimum winning global coalition of nations to adopt the convention. The Kigali agreement to limit HFCs exemplifies some merits of flexible schedules for different countries to begin limiting HFC use and/or to fully phase out their utilization. Yet it also underscores other demerits of such variable terms, which freely prolong the use of extremely pernicious compounds on a global scale in very populous nations that are only now adopting widespread uses of industrial refrigeration. The agreement directs the United States, Japan, and the European Union to begin quicker HFC phase-outs in 2019. Many developing countries can wait until 2024, and a few, like India and Pakistan,

2. See "Marrakech Climate Change Conference: November 2016," United Nations Framework Convention on Climate Change website, https://unfccc.int/process-and-meetings/conferences/past-conferences/marrakech-climate-change-conference-november-2016/marrakech-climate-change-conference-november-2016.

3. John Vidal, "Kigali Deal on GFCs Is Big Step in Fighting Climate Change," *Guardian*, October 15, 2016, https://www.theguardian.com/environment/2016/oct/15/kigali-deal-hfcs-climate-change.

will not start until 2028.[4] If the biggest users act first, the negotiators reasoned, then the smaller ones will follow up later to ease their transitions more equitably. Yet, in ten to fifteen years, smaller users will become bigger, and there is no assurance they will maintain their current resolve to junk HFC-dependent technologies. Once again, the less-developed countries condemned the legacy pollution of the richer economies, while claiming their right to pollute just as much as a sovereign prerogative and economic necessity for national development.

As promising as the COP 21 agreements are, these understandings remain trapped within a "climatological nationalism" that has shadowed the UNFCCC's "methodological nationalism" for global GHG emission calculations since their inception. The main GHG dangers lie in the rising levels of water vapor, carbon dioxide, nitrous oxide, CFCs/HFCs, and methane associated with fossil fuel burning. Before 1991, the industrial, urban, and capitalist countries in the West had produced and consumed these energy sources for many more decades than the less industrial, urban, and capitalist countries in the East and South. Since the end of the Cold War, however, these one-time pollution leaders have been rapidly matched, or overtaken, by one-time pollution laggards, such as China, India, Brazil, Indonesia, and Russia.

The metrics of methodological nationalism, which conventionally track emission levels within the boundaries of the existing nation-states at the 1992 Rio summit, also have hatched these nationalist counter-methodologies for condemning historical pollution leaders of the "Global North" for their overburden of legacy GHG emissions as well as excusing historical pollution laggards in the "Global South" without such legacy emissions to catch up by allowing them higher pollution levels. The colonialism, imperialism, and neoimperialism that shaped global exchange from the fifteenth century to 1991—when the last large Eurasian empire collapsed in Moscow—all rested upon fossil-fueled imperialism, especially after 1900. But those one-time imperial legacy emissions operationally now are chalked up only against the former colonial metropolitan territorial domain rather than the full sweep of each empire. Hence, the national accounts of England, France, Spain, the Netherlands, Germany, Portugal, Russia, or the United States carry these debits, even though nontrivial amounts of their legacy GHG

4. Ibid.

emissions were accumulated integrating what are now African, Asian, Australasian, or Latin American territories into the world economy up to the present day.

Consequently, many conflicts developed faster between these new climate change blocs of carbon-intensive countries. Exercising the right-to-pollute in the name of rebuilding once colonized societies with greater economic growth has been a major stumbling block on the road to attaining GHG reductions, despite all of the talk in the Global South about clean, green, or lean energy. When fossil fuels are burned, real growth often has not occurred or its benefits are not equally distributed. And some wealthy economies are beneficially off-shoring GHG pollution to their advantage as those costs now fall on the Global South. Yet these lesser-developed countries have stalled broader negotiations on new restrictions to allow them to grow (and pollute) and/or lobbied as a group to have later and lighter emissions targets to fuel their economic progress. Hence, as the years pass, overall GHG levels around the world continue to rise despite so many pious good intentions to check their increase. Unfortunately, the UNFCCC's loosely monitored and managed GHG emission scheme tolerates, if not legitimates, the global deterioration of the planet's atmosphere by putting the lipstick of official regulative performativity on the pig of loosely controlled destructive pollution.

At the same time, more developed economies, such as the United States, Australia, Canada, and the United Kingdom, have rigid fossil fuel lock-ins. These realities have made shifting to alternative fuels, finding energy efficiencies, adopting renewable fuel sources, and making growth reductions very difficult for political reasons as well as technological ones. Climatological nationalism also has occluded how transnational corporate networks have rapidly decamped from the deindustrializing zones in the pollutant leader countries, such as the United States, the United Kingdom, Japan, or France, while they off-shore new facilities to the newly industrialized regions in one-time pollution laggards. In 2015, for example, the top ten GHG-emitting countries in declining order were the core G-7 and BRIC nations: China, the United States, the European Union, India, the Russian Federation, Indonesia, Brazil, Japan, Canada, and Mexico.[5] Due to the climatological nationalism of the UNFCCC, waves of largely export-driven industrialization in these

5. See the UNFCCC website, http://unfccc.int.

pollution laggard countries effectively have transferred, then, many links in fossil-fueled commodity chains to the Global South. This shift there has fostered new production sites. Still, their transnational outputs mostly have benefited pollution leaders with cheaper goods, less pollution, and new innovations, while creating more economic precarity, environmental degradation, and commercial fragility in many one-time pollution laggard countries.

The ideological canopy of turning to market-driven solutions to manage GHG emissions in the COP process, like the international emissions trading, the Clean Development Mechanism, and joint implementation offsets, allows this shift to appear largely as progressive, innovative, and beneficial for all concerned. In many respects, however, the prices and costs of fossil fuel capitalism are merely being redirected globally into different national accounts through these market-based responses for carbon release, sequestration, and trading, even as global climatological conditions continue degrading. Planetary-scale ecomanagerialism basically has shifted the loose operational logics of environmental protection mechanisms from the G-7 countries, which are the pollution leader states, through UN-sanctioned deliberations to the G-77 nations in the Global South. These agreements also dispersed the policy assumptions and goals of climatological nationalism as systems of resource development and range management for the Global North all around the world. Destruction of the environment has not stopped, or indeed even slowed that much. Instead, cadres of professional-technical environmental experts in global networks manage more layers of elaborate legal and technological tools for a transnational regimen of deliberative ecological deterioration in the Global North and South. UNFCCC regulations perhaps decreased some of the most egregious and spectacular episodes of environmental destruction unfolding around the planet, but it has utterly failed to stop their occurrence. This sophisticated system of sustainable degradation, in turn, has morphed into a deeper lock-in. It constitutes "our common future" as more countries have adopted UN-endorsed policies for "sustainable development" that are neither developmental nor sustainable.[6]

6. See Timothy W. Luke, "The System of Sustainable Degradation," *Capitalism Nature Socialism* 17, no. 1 (2006): 27–36; and World Commission on Environment and Development, *Our Common Future* (Oxford: Oxford Univ. Press, 1987).

COP 21, then, is the latest institutional articulation of the rules and regulations needed to enforce climatological nationalism on a global scale by means of nationalist climatologies playing back and forth between the G-7 and G-77 states through these UNFCCC fora. The Brundtland Commission's designs for "our common future" still serve global purposes as the projection of good faith to not advance development in "the present" in any manner that compromises the same opportunities of others in "the future," while displacing emotionally and intellectually the hard realities of how much "our common past" has already overshot the natural resource stocks that once made such pledges plausible. Because Brazil, Russia, India, and China, for example, have developed economically by some measures compared to their respective conditions three decades ago, it seems now less probable that much of Africa, the Mideast, or other reaches of Asia can ever attain the same degrees of freedom or levels of success enjoyed elsewhere in the world due to environmental constraints.

On the plus side, these multilateralist global accords, no matter how symbolic and incomplete, are stimulating some cost-saving, less carbon-intensive, more renewable energy investments in agriculture, housing, industry, and transportation at the local and/or regional levels. By prototyping and installing low-carbon, energy-saving, and climate-minded infrastructure, there are significant demonstration effects, technology transfer opportunities, and energy equity innovations beginning to happen both domestically and internationally, often at the neighborhood, town, or city scale. Turning away from one-size-fits-all environmental policy approaches also should allow different localities to develop culturally attuned climate change adaptation strategies.[7]

On the minus side, many regions are trapped deeply in hard technological lock-ins with very energy-intensive urban growth patterns, such as major urban areas in China, Russia, India, Mexico, Indonesia, Malaysia, or Brazil, in strategies to boost national economic growth. Most of the carbon gigatonnage of imperative future GHG reductions must come from these countries, but both their older twentieth-century legacy energy systems and new twenty-first-century development

---

7. See Harriet Bulkeley, Matthew Paterson, and Johannes Stripple, eds., *Towards a Cultural Politics of Climate Change: Devices, Desires and Dissent* (Cambridge: Cambridge Univ. Press, 2016).

showcases entail leaving larger carbon-intensive footprints. Not surprisingly, their NDCs to the Paris accords will undoubtedly arrive later, be smaller, and remain unmonitored, because the byzantine ratification procedures of the Kyoto Protocol delayed their entrance into force until February 2005. Its continuation only was agreed upon, despite bitter opposition in many countries and poor compliance procedures, in December 2012 with the Doha Amendment, as the number of countries committing to the Kyoto Protocol rose to seventy by September 2016 in a "second commitment period" running from 2013 to 2020.

Beyond the dictates of UNFCCC conventions, one of the unanticipated, and yet most beneficial, reductions of GHG in the United States, for example, has been an unanticipated interactive result of climate change, economic stagnation, and technological efficiency. From January to June 2016, the United States polluted less as a nation than at any time during the past quarter-century. An El Niño winter coupled with higher average winter temperatures allowed the United States to use 9 percent less energy than during this same period in 2015, and 18 percent less coal, which meant the number of 2016 heating days for American households matched those of 1949, when there were 180 million fewer people living in the country. When coupled with only 1 percent growth in GDP and a 9 percent increase in renewable energy sources, the carbon footprint of the United States for 2016 probably will equal that of 1992.[8] Such trends also are to be found elsewhere in the Northern Hemisphere as temperatures rise over its colder landmass; and, by the same token, trends in new electricity generation installed capacity favors using renewable sources. In 2015, industry reports indicate as much as 50 percent of all new capacity then being built was powered by wind, water, or solar.[9] And 2016 will mark the eclipse of coal by natural gas in electricity generation across the United States at 35 versus 30 percent, with renewables rising up to 8 percent.[10]

8. Ellen Knickmeyer, "Fossil Fuel Emissions Are Lowest since 1991," *Arizona Republic*, October 14, 2016, p. 4A.

9. Andrew Ward, "General Electric Pays $1.65bn for LM Wind Power," *Financial Times*, October 11, 2016, https://www.ft.com/content/0c6e9808-8fbd-11e6-8df8-d3778b55a923.

10. Bobby Magill, "U.S. Energy Shakeup Continues as Solar Capacity Triples," *Climate Central*, October 20, 2016, http://www.climatecentral.org/news/us-energy-shake-up-continues-solar-triples-20802.

After November 4, 2016, the UNFCCC's COP 21 accords—as agreed upon by the conference of parties during December 2015 in Paris—will mobilize worldwide climate change mitigation campaigns to keep the world's average temperature from rising no more than 2°C/3.6°F, and then push to keep the increase to only 1.5°C/3.4°F in the hopes of attaining global net-zero emissions levels between 2050 and 2100. These ambitious goals, however, are already obsolete. In 2016, the world crossed the once unacceptable level of 400 ppm carbon dioxide in the atmosphere during January. As a result, the first quarter of 2016 saw temperature increases of 1.4°C in January, 1.55°C in February, and 1.4°C in March, compared to averages from a century ago, leaving the planet right at the margin of its agreed-upon limit of a 1.5°C increase over the 1880–1910 baseline months before the Paris agreements come into force in November.[11] Three months in any given year do not add up to yearly or decades-long trends, but it does suggest the permanently dangerous increase in major GHGs has not slowed, and the maximum allowable global temperature averages will arrive by 2025–2030, as opposed to the 2045–2050 time frame that other groups had predicted, using their 1985–2005 baseline global average. This 2°C redline perhaps was reliable when originally advanced during the 1990s. Unfortunately, in the meantime, environmental monitoring indicators reveal global average temperatures already have risen 1°C. Hence, 1.5°C is the newest outer limit on temperature rises, as all parties at COP 21 agreed in Paris during December 2015. The upper limit on all new carbon releases for all sources to stop world temperature increases at 2°C is 800 gigatons, but the known reserves of all exploitable oil, gas, and coal equal 942 gigatons.[12] Moreover, the upper limit on carbon release to halt temperature increases at 1.5°C is 353 gigatons, which means all coal mines and most oil/gas wells would have to be closed almost immediately to keep nearly 500 gigatons of carbon in the ground.[13]

While unity of purpose would be displayed at COP 22 in Marrakesh, and the Morocco summit will be celebrated widely as a watershed event

---

11. See "Flirting with the 1.5°C Threshold," *Climate Central*, April 20, 2016, http://www.climatecentral.org/news/world-flirts-with-1.5C-threshold-20260.

12. Bill McKibben, "Recalculating the Climate Math," *New Republic*, September 22, 2016, https://newrepublic.com/article/136987/recalculating-climate-math.

13. Ibid.

whose putative success is vital for the survival of the earth's biosphere, current scientific analysis suggests the provisos of the Paris Agreement will not let the world meet the agreed upon targets of only 2°C/3.6°F greater than pre-industrial global temperatures by 2100. Business-as-usual practices will lift temperatures to 4.5°C/8.1°F, and these activities regrettably continue to roll along almost undisturbed in too many economies. Yet, even if the Paris accords are observed scrupulously, global temperatures probably will hit 3.5°C/6.3°F by 2050, overshooting the ideal target temperatures by 70 percent.

The largest known unknown here is the new round of NDCs to be defined and implemented by each country between 2015 and 2030. Switzerland, for example, has already presented the first national plan and pledged to reduce its overall GHG emissions by 50 percent in 15 years. This target might be attainable by Zurich, but most other countries express great frustration over the short time frames and high reduction targets they must meet by 2030. By the same token, it is unlikely that the NDC packages discussed in Marrakesh will be implemented as they have been designed as quickly as promised by most of the Paris Agreement signatory countries—a fact that the Poodwaddle Earth Clock openly tracks on the COP 22 website.[14]

Having COP 21 in force on November 4, 2016, is preferable to having no institutional mechanisms in place to constrain global GHG omissions. Even weak agreements are better than no agreement at all. Still, mystifications outnumber the mitigations here. The benchmark for judging success in the Global North and South should not boil down to either attaining almost no change ever at all or perpetuating multilateral cultures for agreeing weakly to insincere worldwide "nationally determined contributions" to postpone GHG reductions at some point five, ten, or fifteen years out. The known knowns of rapid climate change today, such as the Arctic Ocean becoming nearly ice free all year, deepening droughts in once very wetter regions, serious sea rise issues in many coastal areas, and the collapse of biodiversity in more biomes, are

---

14. See "Marrakech Climate Change Conference: November 2016." Also see the Poodwaddle Earth Clock for rough tracking estimates of the rates of sustainable degradation being incurred in real time by the planet, http://www.poodwaddle.com/worldclock/.

quite real now.[15] Their collective momentum is pushing the planet faster toward starker unknown challenges for radical climate adaptation to irreversible changes that are beyond any mitigation. How to adapt robustly to these many disruptions by the new lights of environmental resilience is becoming more and more unknown. In the meantime, all the conferring parties that traveled to Marrakesh for COP 22 sadly encountered no longer clear Moroccan skies as they looked at a degraded world in the sunset of our eyes.

15. Ibid. The World Meteorological Organization affirmed at Marrakesh that 2011–2015 have been the five warmest years for which there are accurate records in modern history. Likewise, Arctic Sea ice during this period is about 30 percent less than it was from 1981 to 2010, and these more open waters are sparking resource races between the United States, Canada, the European Union, and Russia across these polar expanses.

Seven Days in January:
The Trump Administration's
New Environmental Nationalism

D URING 2016, TWO remarkable events took place: Donald J. Trump
was elected president of the United States of America, and the
earth's overall temperature rose for the third year in a row. Two days
before Trump's inaugural events in 2017, both the National Aeronau-
tics and Space Administration (NASA) and the National Oceanic and
Atmospheric Administration (NOAA) reported the entire earth during
2016 had experienced its highest global temperatures as documented by
credible scientific records dating back to 1880. The year 2016 eclipsed
2015, the previous hottest year, and with 2014's high temperatures, scientists marked three straight years of rising global temperatures, which
has occurred only once before in the modern scientific record, in 1939,
1940, and 1941.[1]

Some calculations indicate the entire planet has warmed 2 to 2.16
degrees Fahrenheit from 1750 to 2016, but the most extraordinary rises
during the twenty-first century are unfolding all across the Northern
Hemisphere and the Arctic Ocean region, with many autumn temper-

---

* Originally published in *Telos* 178 (Spring 2017): 197–201.

1. Seth Borenstein, "Globe on a Blistering Hot Streak," *Roanoke Times*, January 18,
2016; Henry Fountain, "Global Temperatures Are on Course for Another Record This
Year," *New York Times*, July 19, 2016, https://www.nytimes.com/2016/07/20/science/
nasa-global-temperatures-2016.html.

atures in the Arctic 20 to 30 degrees higher than prior decades. These rapid and radical increases were a central focus of the Obama administration, and they remain a major policy concern in the European Union, China, India, and Japan, as well as for the United Nations.

The old "environationalist" policies of the United States, France, the United Kingdom, Germany, the Soviet Union, and Japan mystified how their "natural resource" policies were truly just "national resource" development schemes to fuel carbon capitalist or statist sustainability projects. The leaders of these governments, as they fixated upon greater growth to give "Man" control over "Nature," endowed their respective nation-states with these powers, but they actively denied them to "Humanity" per se to evince their respective nationalist geopolitical powers.[2] People in these societies therefore became most of the "Humans" who dominated "Nature" and its resources, which boosted their countries' national power and the prosperity of their citizens. Since 1992, however, an ethos of ecomanagerialism on a planetary scale, under the aegis of the United Nations, has worked to mitigate the more negative externalities of this phase of history. With the earth's growing human populations, biodiversity loss, water quality degradation, and soil contamination, rapid climate change is becoming the world's largest negative externality with the greatest ill effects. Because such nationally caused damage creates degradation globally, many members of the UN concurred weakly during the 1990s that precautionary principles warranted some minimal collective efforts at shared regulation of this increasingly worrisome damage.

While some economic interests in larger countries have resisted such linkages, the global community, at the behest of most nation-states collaborating with the UN, has pursued the thin "cap and review" policies of the Kyoto Process for nearly a generation. Yet some experts have regarded even minimal regulatory advances as coming at a high price for too many industries, localities, and regions without mitigating much ecological damage. In the United States, voters and business interests incurring these costs have looked to the Republican Party to end their losses since 1998. The election of President Trump in the United States undoubtedly will begin a major repudiation of the National

2. Timothy W. Luke, "The Wilderness Society: Environmentalism as Environationalism," *Capitalism Nature Socialism* 10, no. 4 (1999): 1–35.

Environmental Policy Act's conservationist ideals (ironically launched with enthusiasm by President Nixon nearly five decades ago). Presidents Clinton, Bush, and Obama generally had sustained a delicate balance between America's traditional environationalist growth paradigm and the world community's post-1992 eco-globalist programs for mitigating climate change, but Obama in particular strongly backed the UN-sponsored Paris Agreement in 2015 and 2016 to take decisive immediate action on climate policy.

As he promised on the campaign trail, President Trump dismissed global climate change policies as a "hoax" and then gave his whole-hearted support to a new all-out environmental nationalism that always will put "America First." Indeed, climate science is dismissed in the Trump White House as a foreign plot to weaken the powerful, impoverish the rich, and cripple private enterprise. In its place, the "alternative facts" of right-wing populist politics are anchoring a new unilateralist American approach to environmental policy that is anti-statist, pro-business, and growth-centered. Initially, the radical shift made here appears to be one that lessens state intervention and highlights private enterprise. Actually, state agencies mostly have worked with private businesses since the first days of the U.S. Forest Service in 1905 under President Theodore Roosevelt. President Trump instead has simply changed the tone and tenor of state intervention in a manner that, once again, privileges all enterprises willing to advance energy independence, rapid resource extraction, greater economic growth, and quicker access to natural resources by, in, and for the United States. In its most extreme expression, "America First" quickly could lead, as President Trump continues down this path, to a more economically autarkic and ecologically isolationist American economy and society.

In the first hours after his inauguration, President Trump's administration pivoted abruptly toward this new environmental nationalism. The new White House website (www.whitehouse.gov) flashed up with hardly any references to global environmental policy cooperation, climate change issues, or decarbonizing the economy. Likewise, his close advisors promised a larger purge of any public information about anthropogenic climate change, as it has been accumulated for policy purposes at the Departments of Defense, Energy, and the Interior, as well as at the Environmental Protection Agency (EPA), for many years. Of course, on one level, these changes are routine. President Bush endorsed different positions on climate change policy than President Clinton, and President Obama quickly shifted away from the more skeptical outlook of the Bush White House when he was inaugurated in 2009. Trump's "America First" unilateralism, however, turned these actions, on another level, into moves of much greater magnitude. Indeed, this nationalist push was matched rapidly in other U.S. policy domains related to diplomatic, economic, and military issues with China, Russia, Mexico, and the UN, as well as how the nation's daily procedures for border protection, fighting terrorism, immigration control, military appropriations, energy infrastructure, national security, and health care need more nationalistic spin. After one week in the White House, Kellyanne Conway, counselor to the president, summed up these seven days in January on Twitter: "High-energy, high-impact POTUS. Washington still adjusting."[3] While many in Washington are adjusting to the changes Trump made during his first days on the job, the world also now must consider how to adapt over the coming decades to the deeper ecological consequences of this single-minded unilateral pursuit of economic and environmental nationalism in Washington, DC, to get as much as possible for "America First."

For Trump, economic and environmental nationalism are fully intertwined, as the first round of his Republican nominees for key cabinet and senior agency heads from major corporations, prominent gubernatorial positions, and congressional delegations starkly underscores. Near-term prospects for traditional forms of fossil fuel capitalism look very promising with the recently retired CEO of Exxon Mobil, Rex Tillerson, as secretary of state. With Texas Governor Rick Perry's nomination to lead the Department of Energy (the agency he pledged to shutter during his 2016 presidential campaign) and Georgia Governor Sonny Perdue as secretary of agriculture (a former veterinarian and small business owner with strong ties to America's chemically intensive industrial food system), both nominees have climate change denier to skeptic leanings that closely complement President Trump's new environmental nationalism.

3. Charles Savage, Peter Baker, and Michael Haberman, "Trump's First Week: Misfires, Crossed Wires, and a Satisfied Smile," *New York Times*, January 27, 2017, https://www.nytimes.com/2017/01/27/us/politics/president-donald-trump-first-week.html.

In addition, Montana's newly reelected congressman Ryan Zinke's nomination to chair the Department of the Interior was troubling, given his history of running hot-and-cold about climate change during his political career. As President Trump's prospects for success rose during 2016, Zinke became much cooler about the science supporting anthropogenic climate change analysis out on the campaign trail. As the sole congressman from Montana, which has respectable levels of coal, gas, and oil production, he also has taken large campaign contributions from fossil fuel companies. His record of erratic performance in office proved problematic, and he resigned in December 2018. David L. Bernhardt, Zinke's deputy secretary, replaced him in April 2019. The Trump nomination for administrator of the EPA, Oklahoma Attorney General Scott Pruitt, however, was more chilling. In addition to having brought fourteen lawsuits against the EPA as Oklahoma's attorney general, Pruitt opposed stricter regulation of agribusinesses, oil companies, and firms that contaminate the environment. As he prepared to face the Senate, Pruitt also enjoyed support on January 12, 2017, from many prominent political pressure groups. Grover Norquist's Americans for Tax Reform, the Club for Growth Political Action Committee, the American Energy Alliance, Freedom Works, the Energy and Environment Action Team, and the Competitive Enterprise Institute all hailed Pruitt's small-government, states' rights, business-friendly beliefs that "the federal government is not the end-all, be-all solution" in backing "his commitment to upholding the Constitution and ensuring the EPA works for American families and consumers."[4] Barely eighteen months later, however, Pruitt also was left to resign this position due to a number of personal scandals while in office. His successor, Andrew R. Wheeler, a well-known coal industry lobbyist and fossil fuel advocate, took office in February 2019 and is more daunting to many environmentalists.

Again, economic nationalism in strict dollars-and-cents terms has obscured other options beyond the always false choice between "the economy" and "the environment." Better-funded and stronger environmental protections, for example, might do much more toward protecting America's (and other nations') families and consumers at this

---

4. See "CEI Joins Coalition Letter Supporting Pruitt Nomination for EPA," January 12, 2017, Competitive Enterprise Institute, https://cei.org/content/cei-joins-coalition-letter-supporting-pruitt-nomination-epa.

critical conjuncture in the world community's mitigation of rapid climate change. By ignoring this choice, at the same time, the White House has sparked resistance inside and outside of government. The larger scientific community quickly mobilized efforts to download endangered scientific information in federal archives, which government officials feared could be erased or censored, to safer storage sites. Likewise, many environmental agency staffers ignored requests to report on their activities to a new administration of prospective nominees rather than legally confirmed officials.

The nation's public health sector also felt this chill. Fearing sanctions, or perhaps severe censorship, the Centers for Disease Control and Prevention (CDC) cancelled its Climate and Health Summit planned for February 2017 in Atlanta.[5] Even though Al Gore's Climate Reality organization quickly worked with the Harvard Global Health Institute, American Public Health Association, and the Turner Foundation to stage the meetings with other funds at the Carter Center in Atlanta, Trump's agendas for stressing greater energy production from fossil fuels in the United States over advancing climate change protection for Americans with the rest of the world are giving form and substance to how "America First" policies will develop. As *Energy & Environment News* noted, "Trump has made no secret of his opposition to climate change policy. He has called climate change a "hoax," and former White House Chief of Staff Reince Priebus said the president believes warming is "a bunch of bunk," which will make it imperative for the new administrative leadership of the EPA "to dismantle 'harmful and unnecessary' climate change policies."[6]

Whether it means ignoring how the Zika virus will spread more rapidly northward as temperatures in the United States rise with rapid climate change, or downplaying why the pollutant-laden dirty coal reserves in long-ago shuttered mines will not provide many jobs to the forgotten white working class of Appalachia, the promise to serve "America

5. Brady Dennis, "CDC Abruptly Cancels Long-Planned Conference on Climate Change and Health," *Washington Post*, January 23, 2017, https://www.washingtonpost.com/news/energy-environment/wp/2017/01/23/cdc-abruptly-cancels-long-planned-conference-on-climate-change-and-health/?utm_term=.091e4064f806.

6. Scott Waldman, "CDC Quietly Cancels Long-Planned Climate Summit," *Energy & Environment News*, January 23, 2017, http://www.eenews.net/climatewire/2017/01/23/stories/1060048779.

First" is destined to deliver harsh downsides from such ill-considered moves to Americans first as well. Progressive environmental initiatives once had been a traditional commitment of GOP presidents from Theodore Roosevelt to Richard Nixon. More recently, Presidents Clinton and Obama supported such policies in backing, albeit weakly, the global ecomanagerial designs of the 1997 Kyoto Protocol and the 2016 Paris Agreement.[7] Now, however, the environmental backsliding launched by President George W. Bush in 2001 clearly did begin anew under Donald Trump as this essentially isolationist new environmental nationalism is implemented by a "high-energy, high-impact POTUS," whose dysfunctional administrative style, as affirmed by the continuous personnel turnover at the White House and in his cabinet since 2017, closely matches this destructive policy direction.

7. Timothy W. Luke, "On the Road to Marrakesh: A Politics of Mitigation or Mystification for Global Climate Change?" *Telos* 177 (Winter 2016): 209–18, reprinted in this volume.

13

Science at Dusk in the Twilight of Expertise:
The Worst Hundred Days

O<small>N</small> A<small>PRIL</small> 30, 2017, President Trump had 1,361 days on the clock of his presidency, and many experts from academia, mass media, and policy think tanks searched for insights into how this time might unfold from his initial 100 days in office. Since Franklin Delano Roosevelt's first inauguration in 1933, "the First Hundred Days" of governance by victorious first-term presidential candidates have become the benchmark of success for new administrations. In his first 100 days, FDR swore in his entire cabinet on day one, passed fifteen major acts of legislation with Congress, and reassured the nation with his "fireside talks" on the radio as the United States tackled the Great Depression. During the 1960s, John F. Kennedy's first 100 days did not prove to be a huge success as he spent many hours deriding the shortcomings of the Eisenhower administration. After the televised spectacle of his inauguration, JFK slowly organized his cabinet, met with the poet Robert Frost, and then signed the executive order to set up the Peace Corps.

Yet, during April 1961, JFK and the United States were deeply shaken by the Soviet Union's successful launch and recovery of cosmonaut Yuri Gagarin, who became the first human being safely put into orbit and then returned to earth. More tragically, JFK also suffered through the humiliating failures around the CIA-planned Bay of Pigs invasion

---

* Originally published in *Telos* 179 (Summer 2017): 189–94.

of Fidel Castro's Cuba, which Eisenhower doubted would succeed. Of course, President Lincoln's first 100 days brought the opening shots of the Civil War, but old government hands in the Democratic and Republican Parties saw few gains and many losses for President Kennedy in 1961 despite the aura of Camelot. Nonetheless, within a month, JFK called upon the nation's scientists and technicians to accomplish an incredible goal by 1970, namely, flying American astronauts to the moon and back in the name of all mankind, as well as for a Cold War victory over the Soviet Union.

The erratic collapse of President Trump's grandiose 2016 campaign promises during his first 100 days, however, has eclipsed JFK's troubles. With each passing day, Trump's divisive approach to governing the nation only worsened many serious issues at home and abroad. A feeling of illegitimacy took hold soon after November 8, 2016, when 54 percent of the electorate voted against him, while the evidence mounted that his victory in the Electoral College, in part, was due to elaborate "active measures" in Moscow, including social media agitprop campaigns planned in the Russian Institute for Strategic Affairs to discredit Hillary Clinton and the Democrats.[1] Beyond pushing hard for the confirmation of Judge Neil M. Gorsuch on April 7, 2017, to fill Antonin Scalia's seat on the U.S. Supreme Court, executing a "wag the dog" cruise missile strike on Syria after Damascus attacked one of its villages with outlawed nerve gas, signing a presidential memorandum withdrawing the United States from the Trans-Pacific Partnership (TPP) agreement that nullified President Obama's 2015 executive order to enter the TPP, replacing his National Security Advisor, General Michael Flynn, after only twenty-four days at his post due to improperly disclosed contacts with Vladimir Putin and the Russian Federation, announcing his desire to renegotiate the NAFTA pact with Canada and Mexico, issuing a "buy American, hire American" jobs creation policy that his own real estate empire evades daily, and avoiding a nasty snit with President Xi Jinping at their Palm Beach summit in early April, Trump has few points on the scoreboard. Signing decrees is not the demanding work of passing laws. Trump and his entourage of alt-right ideologues, neoliberal grifters, and

1. Ned Parker, Jonathan Landay, and John Walcott, "Exclusive: Putin-Linked Think Tank Drew up Plan to Sway 2016 U.S. Election-Documents," *Reuters*, April 20, 2017, http://www.reuters.com/article/us-usa-russia-election-exclusive-idUSKBN17L2N3.

economic nationalists still have not recognized the importance of this crucial distinction in their everyday governance of the United States.

In late April, as his 100 days ran down, Trump himself remarked with no deadpan inflection, "It's a different kind of a presidency."[2] Of course, in his unending quest for great television ratings, Trump claimed at a rally in Kenosha, Wisconsin, on April 18, 2017, that while "the 100 day" standard was meaningless, "no administration has accomplished more in the first 90 days," which he reemphasized with another campaign-style rally—funded by his 2020 reelection committee—at the Pennsylvania Farm Show Complex & Expo Center in Harrisburg, PA, on day 100.[3]

After pledging huge reforms on the campaign trail, Trump was at a near standstill legislatively after his first 100 days, while running rhetorically at 100 mph in a rush of one-page quick-and-dirty tax reform, foreign trade, and foreign policy plans. Along with failing to repeal and replace the Affordable Care Act, not sanctioning China for currency manipulation, triggering a military face-off on the Korean peninsula over Pyongyang's strategic nuclear weapons program, not defeating the rogue Islamic caliphate in Iraq after pledging in Iowa "to bomb the SHIT out of ISIS," failing to ignite rapid economic growth with new business-friendly tax and labor laws, not forcing Mexico to pay for massive new border walls from San Diego, California, to Brownsville, Texas, refusing to release his own tax returns while proposing major tax cuts for the

2. Julie Pace, "President Trump Nears 100-day Mark," *Roanoke Times*, April 25, 2017. Strangely enough, Trump admitted in an interview on day 99 how totally unaware he was of what lay ahead for him: "I loved my job. I had so many things going. This is much harder than in my previous life. I thought it would be easier." See Stephen J. Adler, Jeff Mason, and Steve Holland, "Exclusive: Trump Says He Thought Being President Would Be Easier Than His Old Life," Reuters, April 29, 2017, http://www.reuters.com/article/us-usa-trump-100days-idUSKBN17U0CA.

3. See Glenn Kessler, "Trump's Claim That 'No Administration Has Accomplished More in the First 90 Days,'" *Washington Post*, April 20, 2017, https://www.washingtonpost.com/news/fact-checker/wp/2017/04/20/trumps-claim-that-no-administration-has-accomplished-more-in-the-first-90-days/. When checked against his own "Contract with the American Voter," Trump comes up short. He issued press releases, picked fights, and gave speeches, but virtually nothing of legislative weight was accomplished in his first 100 days. See "Donald Trump's Contract with the American Voter," Donald J. Trump website, https://assets.donaldjtrump.com/_landings/contract/O-TRU-102316-Contractv02.pdf. For more on Trump's summation, see Mark Landler, "Trump Savages News Media at Rally to Mark his 100th Day," *New York Times*, April 30, 2017, https://www.nytimes.com/2017/04/29/us/politics/trump-rally-pennsylvania.html.

wealthy that are sure to benefit him and his family, and not being connected directly by the FBI to Kremlin dirty tricks in the 2016 election, the high hopes for Trump's first 100 days are unfulfilled—except in the domains of climate science and environmental policy, where too many of his promises are being kept. As a result, this legacy is starting to inflict lasting damage that is another loud and clear Anthropocene alert.

His relatively quick wins, however, are largely another outcome of the institutional dysfunctionality in executive and legislative branch relations since the 2010 Tea Party rebellion. Unable to enact legislation using regular means, President Obama increasingly resorted to the use of executive orders and memoranda to prod the government into action. Likewise, with the stroke of a pen, the executive orders, executive memoranda, and proclamations Trump has issued for 100 days make good TV but not much policy and no law. Trump's edicts mostly override Obama's prior executive actions, just as those issued by Obama largely replaced directives signed by President Bush after 2001.

Yet Trump's proposed cuts to most federal science and technology funding for climate change research, as well as his suspension of environmental executive orders signed by President Obama, are creating troublesome turmoil. On the one hand, these actions are suspending important environmental research across many federal agencies. On the other hand, they are eroding public trust in science and technology, which has been widely fostered in Washington since the Kennedy administration. Inspired by the tactics of the massive Women's March around the country on January 21, 2017, to defy Trump's derogation of women, the members from dozens of professional academic, scientific, and technology organizations staged the March for Science in Washington, DC, as well as in over five hundred other satellite locations around the country and across the world, on April 22, 2017—Earth Day 48— to reaffirm the importance of scientific expertise in public policy. This action opened a week of events aimed at defending the legitimacy of science, which culminated in the People's Climate March on April 29, 2017—Trump's 100th day in office.

In his March 2017 "skinny budget" proposals for FY 2018, President Trump revealed his plans for deep cuts in federal science spending. With regard to climate change and environmental research, his office proposed a 31 percent reduction in Environmental Protection Agency

(EPA) spending as well as layoffs of 3,200 of its 15,000 employees, with overall research spending dropping from $483 million to $250 million in FY 2018 along with around a 20 percent cut in climate research across all federal agencies from the Department of Energy (DOE) to the National Oceanic and Atmospheric Administration (NOAA).[4] The only new scientific research increases are slated for next generation nuclear weapons developments started under Obama. These startling moves are a radical retreat from the active advance of national science policies begun in the 1960s during the Kennedy, Johnson, and Nixon administrations.

In July 1969, the United States made good on JFK's promise to go to the moon and back by 1970. That same year, however, after months of news about oil spills, burning rivers, and smog alerts from across the country, the citizenry called upon scientists to turn their research tools to solve problems back on the planet that its astronauts saw from their base on the moon's Sea of Tranquility. The United States needed "science for the people" to improve the lives of all human beings. On April 22, 1970, over 20 million Americans participated in a "national teach-in" about the nation's environment, which was planned, organized, and co-chaired by Democratic Senator Gaylord Nelson of Wisconsin and Republican Congressman Paul Norton "Pete" McClosky of California. Their bipartisan campaign mustered immediate attention in Washington for scientific experts to overcome environmental and public health challenges with the newly created EPA and later with extensive legislation, such as the Clean Air, Clean Water, and Endangered Species Acts.

Popular engagement with Earth Day has waxed and waned over nearly five decades, but the anti-environmental programs of newly elected President Donald Trump are reigniting interest in this event as his administration attacks basic scientific research. Earth Day's original appeal to science was urgent and direct: fix unresolved ecological problems, like "oil spills, polluting factories and power plants, raw sewage, toxic dumps, pesticides, freeways, the loss of wilderness, and the

---

4. Sara Reardon, Jeff Tollefson, Alexandra Witze, and Chin Ross, "Science under Fire in Trump Spending Plan," *Nature* 247 (March 23, 2017): 471–72. For climate change research, White House Budget Director Mick Mulvaney said on March 16, 2017, "We're not spending money on that anymore. We consider that to be a waste of money." See Justin Worland, "President Trump's Budget Is a Blow to Fighting Climate Change. And It's Not Just the EPA," *Time*, March 16, 2017, http://time.com/4703569/trump-budget-epa-climate-change/.

extinction of wildlife,"[5] which all remain just as pressing today. Regrettably, the Trump era is turning to dusk for such science in the public interest. His government's intent is to defund and dismiss well-trained experts, scientific findings, and seasoned researchers, inside and outside of government, whenever their research contradicts Trump's gut instincts about "the truth." This new campaign is one of the most unsettling forces at loose in American politics today.

As Rhea Suh, president of the Natural Resources Defense Council, wrote to NRDC members before his inauguration, "Donald Trump has vowed to withdraw America from the landmark Paris Climate Accord...approve the disastrous Keystone XL Tar Sands pipeline...throw open our last wild places to rampant oil development...kill President Obama's Clean Power Plan...scale back support for wind and solar...and unleash big polluters from environmental regulations."[6] Most mainstream journalists did not take candidate Trump seriously during his 2016 campaign, but President Trump has delivered on almost every one of the campaign promises identified by the NRDC during his first 100 days in office. Having installed Scott Pruitt as EPA Administrator, the Trump White House is bobbing across these troubled waters as the jagged tip of an "America First" ideological iceberg. A noxious blend of climate denial, romanticized industrialism, corporate deregulation, and renewed neoliberalism, its rhetorical run-off feeds the cold currents in Trump's angry electoral coalition that assault the legitimacy of science itself. Now former EPA Administrator Pruitt's refusal, on March 29, 2017, to uphold a ban of the dangerous insecticide chlorpyrifos for all agricultural uses, which was presented to him by EPA scientists with recent lab evidence from Columbia University, highlights the administration's disregard of careful scientific research. Two major environmental groups petitioned him to uphold the ban to protect farm workers and rural residents. Pruitt quickly rebuffed their request, however, on the word of the insecticide's manufacturer, Dow Chemical.[7]

5. See "The History of Earth Day," Earth Day Network, http://www.earthday.org/about/the-history-of-earth-day/.

6. See Rhea Suh, "Dear NRDC Member," *NRDC: A Force for Nature*, National Resources Defense Council, January 2017.

7. Eric Lipton, "E.P.A. Chief, Rejecting Agency's Science, Chooses Not to Ban Insecticide," *New York Times*, March 29, 2017, https://www.nytimes.com/2017/03/29/us/politics/epa-insecticide-chlorpyrifos.html.

By weaving together the current styles of outsider protest with the skills of some Washington insiders, the 2017 March for Science on Earth Day and the People's Climate Movement might only be staging fresh productions of tame, if not co-opted, political street theater to appeal to disgruntled Democratic and independent voters. Its leaders pitched their criticism against the widely acknowledged policy disarray of the Trump White House, which even many Republicans admit is more and more evident. At the end of the day, the agenda of the Marchers for Science maximally defended the contested integrity of law, logic, and rationality against Trump's cuts in key science-based government agencies. Minimally, in fighting for these substantive values, the Marchers could be an attempt to restore scientific research funding with dramatic doses of "artificial negativity."[8] Either way, the Marchers for Science and the People's Climate Movement have focused their pushback on Trump's self-serving elitism, which still poses as a public-spirited populism rooting out suspicious scientific work that supposedly kills jobs and destroys freedoms that Americans want.

Before 1973, some believed that the EPA could have worked like the Federal Communications Commission (FCC) or National Labor Relations Board (NLRB) by using specific congressional legislation to support its actions, but distrust between the White House and Capitol Hill during Watergate, as well as a lack of will during the 1970s oil crises, created constant partisan conflict over exploiting more domestic oil sources regardless of cost versus the need to protect the environment. Caught in this "energy versus environment" stalemate, both Congress and the president usually kicked the can down the road to be managed by oil industry experts and pubic interest lawyers in the courts and regulatory agencies. This outcome has not been good for either the environment or the energy industry, but it has meant job security for many attorneys and consultants in Washington for over forty years as they largely have mustered factual scientific evidence in support of their environmental lawsuits.

Trump's corrosive style of governance is quite clear in his "war on facts," as the Earth Day 2017 protests underscored. His administration

---

8. See Paul Piccone, "The Crisis of One-Dimensionality," *Telos* 35 (Spring 1978): 43–54; and Timothy W. Luke, "Culture and Politics in the Age of Artificial Negativity," *Telos* 35 (Spring 1978): 55–72.

eagerly is violating the basic trust in science at the foundation of the National Environmental Policy Act (NEPA), namely, "to use all practicable means and measures, including financial and technical assistance, in a manner calculated to foster and promote the general welfare, to create and maintain conditions under which man and nature can exist in productive harmony, and fulfill the social, economic, and other requirements of present and future generations of Americans."[9] Even President Nixon proclaimed in 1970 "that each person should enjoy a healthful environment and that each person has a responsibility to contribute to the preservation and enhancement of the environment."[10] President Trump, however, regards such promises as empty rights and faux responsibilities, hiding behind the job-killing mystifications of climate change science.

Ironically, many competitive American businesses now favor "sustainability," and their managers welcome reliable scientific research and tolerable environmental regulations. These interests, however, are not big players on Trump's team, because former White House advisor Steve Bannon aspires "to deconstruct the administrative state." This inward-looking economic nationalism has pushed Trump's EPA to end the Renewable Fuel Standard program, cut federal subsidies for solar and windmill-generated electricity, relax strict automobile emissions guidelines, and neutralize urban ozone rules despite good science that supported Obama-era plans for quickening the nation's transition to a cleaner energy regime.

While President Trump did ease strict carbon dioxide emission guidelines for coal-burning power plants, he has not yet withdrawn from the Paris climate change accords after the entreaties from former Secretary of State Rex Tillerson and President Xi Jinping of China to stick with the climate pact in order to avoid the possibility of international carbon tariff trade wars.[11] Nonetheless, this decision is not final, as he assured his base supporters in Harrisburg on Day 100, and he did not formally prepare to withdraw until October 2019. This repudiation

9. National Environmental Policy Act, 1969, https://www.epa.gov/NEPA.

10. Ibid.

11. Coral Davenport, "Policy Advisers Urge Trump to Keep U.S. in Paris Accord," *New York Times*, April 18, 2017, https://www.nytimes.com/2017/04/18/us/politics/trump-advisers-paris-climate-accord.html.

of science to guide policy, at the same time, leaves Trump drifting on the ideological tides in the White House flowing between climate change deniers, such as Steve Bannon or Myron Ebell, and climate change pragmatists, such as Ivanka Trump or Jared Kushner, who continued to tussle over Washington repudiating the 2015 Paris Agreement.

By removing one bloc of technocratic green statists and replacing them with a cadre of radical anti-statists with different legal agendas, Trump still pretends to affirm the EPA's original mission while they scale back its regulatory reach. Even in the age of Citizens United, public opinion polls in many American states show that voters acknowledge the reality of global warming, over-allocated watercourses, widespread desertification, and biodiversity loss. Trump's populist followers, on the other hand, are now also questioning how state and local departments of environmental quality are using science.

The billowing blowback against scientific rationality in favor of "alternative truths" taken from Fox News programs or Internet social media was troubling enough that the March for Science on Earth Day 2017 required a pledge from its participants:

> We, the peaceful, passionate, and diverse members of the March for Science, pledge…to ensure that scientific evidence plays a pivotal role in setting policy in the future.…On April 22, we take a decisive step toward ensuring a future where the fullness of scientific knowledge benefits all people, and where everyone is empowered to ask new scientific questions. We march for countless individual reasons, but gather together as the March for Science to envision and sustain an unbroken chain of inquiry, knowledge, and public benefit for all.[12]

Even though it is short and simple, this statement recalls seventeenth- or nineteenth-century struggles in Europe against royal or religious restrictions on science itself. That such a pledge to guarantee the integrity of science seems necessary in 2017 highlights the damage being incurred by federally funded scientific and technical networks simply for Trump to say that "something is being done" to drain the swamps in Washington of elitist experts.

---

12. "Marcher Pledge," March for Science website, https://www.marchforscience.com/marcher-pledge/.

Despite the uproar of the March for Science, the politicization of Earth Day in 2017, and Trump's poor showing in his first 100 days, many valued scientific programs, including several in medical research, public health, and industrial safety, are fading into the dusk under Trump. The dismantling of the EPA was well prepped before the inauguration, and many people in the White House Council on Environmental Quality under Obama simply resigned or retired before Trump could force them out. He is, however, not refilling many of these posts, while his aides are cutting those agency budgets. Enforcement of executive orders often falls upon named cabinet posts, like the Department of the Interior or the EPA, but Trump has filled those jobs with officials who are skeptical of most environmental scientists and climate change research.

Moreover, the Office of Information and Regulatory Affairs (OIRA) coordinates new executive memoranda and orders. Obama used this office extensively to enforce his executive orders, and Trump is expected to do the same. His nominee, Neomi Rao, who was Justice Clarence Thomas's law clerk and a Bush White House special assistant and who is now a professor at the Scalia School of Law at George Mason University and director of its Center for the Study of the Administrative State, was to implement tactics that suit the Trump White House. Instead, in 2019 Trump named Rao as judge of the United States Court of Appeals for the District of Columbia Circuit and left OIRA with a weaker acting administrator. That being noted, Trump's progress on making his campaign promises good on the environmental front has been considerable, but only relative to a general lack of progress where the economic and political costs are much greater as Washington's political gridlock deepens.

The embedded system of executive branch/judicial branch/non-profit policy group "shared environmental management" is now wholly compromised by Trump's defunding and destaffing of environmental executive agencies, as the Marchers on Science and the People's Climate March were protesting. Dozens of empty federal attorney and judge positions needed for the process to operate are not being filled quickly. In addition, former Attorney General Sessions and his successor, William P. Barr, along with the GOP committees in the Senate, are unfriendly to green causes. On the other hand, the full panoply of major environmental non-governmental organizations are now being forced to defend, or trying to retake, ground they held securely in 2009, or even in 1989. In turn, the more settled Nixon/Reagan/Clinton-era compromise of allowing environmental directives to be managed as technocratic regulatory decisions has also been shaken. This regime for managing resource conservation and environmental regulation at times has been self-serving, but it typically relied upon science to guide its findings for enforcing managerial directives. Without these checks and balances, Trump's aspirations to allow energy exploration in fragile ecological zones, such as the Arctic, national parks, or the coastal Atlantic, is now simply likely to be granted to the first takers.

In this respect, Trump's ever-changing cabinet and Judge Rao also support Bannon's program of dismantling large pieces of the existing administrative state, regardless of their possible proven benefits. Rao hopes to revisit the 1984 *Chevron v. NRDC* Supreme Court decision, which anchors much of the current system, and backs enforcement of the "non-delegation" laws of Congress that were ignored as this new regulatory regime came into force in the 1970s and 1980s. All of these counteroffensives coming so close together will likely bog down the major non-governmental environmental policy organizations in self-defense actions rather than free them to continue their already limited, and not always effectual, enforcement and implementation work.[13] Add to this shifting ground fresh cultural conflict over alternative facts, greater visibility for climate realism, doubts over climate alarmism, and Trump's minimalist construction of the EPA's institutional mission, and much of the important science that has been funded by Washington since the days of the Space Race during the 1960s will grind to a halt. Not only will climate change research slow, but the funding for the satellites and sensors used to collect data for such investigations will be curtailed, or ended, leaving other countries to conduct such studies, unless they too come under the control of new nationalist, populist, or austerity-minded governments with no interest in scientific research.

Consequently, it now appears that all three elaborate fronts on the post-1970 iron triangle for environmental defense in the United States—executive branch environmental protection agencies, federal judicial

13. See Theodore Lowi, *The End of Liberalism: The Second Republic of the United States*, 2nd ed. (New York: W. W. Norton, 1979).

benches charged with reviewing government's natural conservation regulatory responsibilities, and national environmental action groups—are
being undermined. These changes could lead to broader, more localized, and possibly participatory civic networks to protect the earth's environmental integrity. Some struggles for environmental justice, climate
conventions, and biodiversity defense have been pointing in these directions since 2001, but their gains thus far are limited.

Meanwhile, as once settled policy boundaries are breached, many
scientific networks and expert panels are being drawn away for their
own perimeter defense, and they will slide into the bureaucratic bogs
of budget battles over declining appropriations, changed administrative
law procedures, and scientific summits about missing data. With these
once well-respected environmental protection agents distracted by other threats in Washington and state capitals, small commercial cliques can
then battle each other out in the wild to grab what is being made free
for the taking by Trump's string of new executive orders. Trump's green
light for the Keystone and XL pipeline projects and the lifting of the 2025
fuel efficiency targets for automobiles are two immediate cases in point.
In turn, big corporate coalitions intent on getting more access in hitherto protected lands and waters for quicker resource extraction will get
what they want in this twilight for once trusted government science and
technical expertise. As earth-imaging satellite feeds are turned off, data
is not collected, and research labs are shuttered by a government and an
electorate convinced their money was being wasted on a hoax that prevented "Making America Great Again," the efforts to mitigate and adapt
to rapid climate change will lose years at a pivotal point they cannot
afford to have wasted in these ill-considered attacks on science and the
Republican Party's traditional support for environmental causes.

Now the GOP at large, Trump's voters from the 2016 election, and
the Republican-controlled House and Senate own this legacy as much as
the president. How bad his first 100 days have been was sharply accen-
tuated by Trump's inept firing of FBI Director James Comey on May 9,
2017, who learned of his dismissal from cable TV news reports while he
addressed FBI agents in the bureau's Los Angeles office. Trump's contempt for expertise with respect to science and environmental policy
seemingly is the flip side of his disdain for legality and constitutional rule. Indeed, Comey's unwillingness to pledge personal loyalty to

Trump over his oath to uphold the Constitution, as well as his refusal to suspend the FBI's investigations into General Flynn's interactions with Russian officials before and after Trump's inauguration, apparently triggered his removal as director, sparking a bipartisan political uproar in Washington. The appointment within a week of former FBI Director Robert Mueller as special counsel by Deputy Attorney General Rod Rosenstein to probe independently into potential Russian meddling in the 2016 presidential election briefly restored calm. Yet prima facie signs of possible legal obstruction, dereliction of duty, or abuse of office in the White House all reaffirm how these tense times in 2017 became the worst 100 days as well as a very clear indicator of President Trump's executive style up to the present—making his leadership record as good a backdrop as any for the Dark Enlightenment.

The Dark Enlightenment and the Anthropocene: Readings from the Book of Third Nature as Political Theology

Introduction

TUNING INTO THE cacophony of social media or the blogging world, another Anthropocene alert sounds in the appeals of the "accelerationism" movement, whose followers celebrate today's apocalyptic ecological disasters. This chapter critically examines several aspects of this small but strangely attractive network of thinkers, who also fashion themselves as the core circle of *nouvelle philosophes* behind a "Dark Enlightenment" that has surfaced during "The Great Acceleration." With their links to contemporary alt-right politics, its supporters merit harder scrutiny because they also maintain close ties to many Silicon Valley–centered venture capitalists, cyber-libertarian thinkers, and corporate entrepreneurs. The writings of these thinkers often are contradictory, convoluted, and confusing, but one should not ignore the remarkable number of elective affinities between their strange political agendas and odd ideological alliances at the advent of the Anthropocene.

Arguably, this movement is yet another twist in the so-called "California Ideology," which some once saw bringing "cyber-communism" to America through the Internet economy during the 1990s.[1] After three

*   An earlier version of this paper was delivered at the 2019 Telos-Paul Piccone Institute Conference on "Political Theology Today as Critical Theory of the Contemporary," held on February 15–17, 2019, in New York City.

1. Richard Barbrook, "Cyber-Communism: How the Americans are Spreading Communism in Cyber-Space," *Science as Culture* 9, no. 1 (2000): 5–40.

decades of economic booms and prolonged economic busts, however, this putative transition to cyber-communism went off its rails. Instead, a strange reactionary modernism now has gripped the imagination of many thinkers spinning in Silicon Valley's circles of influence today.[2] The Dark Enlightenment and its accelerationist ties perhaps are two of its more prominent developments.

Materially, the ideological, political, and sociological turns taken by the Dark Enlightenment are unusual. In a country without an established church, a feudal aristocracy, or a once well-entrenched peasant economy, Dark Enlightenment followers proudly claim to be "neo-reactionaries." Yet they show little awareness of how "paleo-reactionaries" historically arise from political alliances between these missing social forces and traditional ruling institutions. Moreover, from within high technology industries made profitable by sustained heavy government investment and regulation, the neo-reactionaries, or "NRx," claim to be radical libertarian anti-statists, presuming that it was their STEM degrees or software coding skills that made them rich by dint of spending all-nighters in front of their computer screens. In addition, for a constitutional republic allegedly devoted to the sustainable capitalist development of an egalitarian industrial democracy for millions of hard-working consumers striving to acquire the electronic goods and cybernetic services these same high-tech firms produce, one finds a deep disdain in NRx thought for such generous commercial goals. Instead, NRx thinkers now often denounce democratic equality, the masses, and individual choice, fearing that such once popular forces and political ideas are prodding governments to raise taxes on the highest flyers among America's entrepreneurial elites. As standout performers in these elites, many among Silicon Valley's digiterati also see big government in failing states frittering away these tax monies on the undeserving poor in minority underclass households.

"For the hardcore neo-reactionaries," according to the accelerationist thinker Nick Land, "democracy is not merely doomed. It is doom itself."[3] In blunter language, the neo-reactionary movement is:

---

2. Jeffrey Herf, *Reactionary Modernism: Technology, Culture, and Politics in Weimar and the Third Reich* (Cambridge: Cambridge Univ. Press, 1984).

3. Nick Land, "The Dark Enlightenment" (2012), the Dark Enlightenment website, http://www.thedarkenlightenment.com/the-dark-enlightenment-by-nick-land/.

Predisposed, in any case, to perceive the politically awakened masses as a howling irrational mob, [and thus] it conceives the dynamics of democratization as fundamentally degenerative: systematically consolidating and exacerbating private vices, resentments, and deficiencies until they reach the level of collective criminality and comprehensive social corruption. The democratic politician and the electorate are bound together by a circuit of reciprocal incitement, in which each side drives the other to ever more shameless extremities of hooting, prancing cannibalism, until the only alternative to shouting is being eaten.[4]

Land's appraisal of modern democratic ideals is clearly negative; but it also underscores the opposing choices made after the eighteenth century between the progressive aspirations of the, so to say, "bright Enlightenment" in many European countries versus the reactionary perspectives now in favor during the twenty-first century's "Dark Enlightenment" around the Pacific Rim.

For Land and those inspired by him,

Where the progressive enlightenment sees political ideas, the Dark Enlightenment sees appetites. It accepts governments are made of people, and that they will eat well. Setting its expectations as low as reasonably possible, it seeks only to spare civilization from frenzied, ruinous, gluttonous debauch. From Thomas Hobbes to Hans-Hermann Hoppe and beyond, it asks: How can the sovereign power be prevented—or at least dissuaded—from devouring society? It consistently finds democratic "solutions" to this problem risible, at best.[5]

The fact that earlier public figures identified with "the progressive enlightenment" in America, such as James Madison, John Jay, Alexander Hamilton, Benjamin Franklin, and John Adams, also shared these elitist suspicions of "democracy," of course, is ignored. Moreover, the "systems engineering" embedded by Madison in the arcane architecture of the U.S. Constitution, as explained in the pages of *The Federalist Papers* and explicated further in the Bill of Rights, to counterbalance such energies of popular passion, also is downplayed in NRx thinking. To enhance the drama of their new narratives about collective social decline under

4. Ibid.
5. Ibid.

modernity, Land and other neo-reactionaries basically ignore the complicated details of actual practices in order to tout the radical principles they believe will accelerate capitalism's inhumane degradations.

On the one hand, this simplistic political stance perhaps is to be expected from the historically uninformed, morally unfocused, and politically naive streams of STEM-centered education that too many high-tech workers have endured on their way to some IPO bonanza. Such training leaves many of them stringing together their own autodidactic "liberal arts" education from alt-right online bloggers, science fiction mythologies, and gothic horror tales in a manner that lacks the rigor of classical core curricula to foster greater sensitivity to political uncertainty, freedom, and choice. Hence, many ironically see themselves as not unlike the electro-existentialists and cyber-warriors celebrated in *The Matrix* film trilogy.

This cinematic worldview, in turn, justifies the accelerationists' raw epistemic elitism, since they fashion themselves among those special few choosing the "red pill" and its "Wonderland" over the "blue pill" of clueless unawareness.[6] On the other hand, as they revel in Wonderland's workings, many conflate their personal success and hard work with the productive mass media celebrations of today's high-tech illiberal corporatocracy. Indeed, they often toil away their days for FAANG (Facebook, Amazon, Apple, Netflix, and Google) capital or its expanded network of consultants, outsourcers, and suppliers. While holding solid personal stock positions in the FAANG sector and/or closely related IPO firms, the bigger visionaries also are diversified into good old-fashioned material holdings in FIRE (Finance, Insurance, and Real Estate) assets in the United States and abroad. For even greater peace of mind, others who fear the envious masses latch onto more secure assets: silver bullion, gold shares, blockchain currency, or New Zealand boltholes. Immense wealth frequently is matched to libertarian values, but today's billionaires are deeply committed to their narrow self-interests, not unlike most robber barons during the Gilded Age before state trustbusting broke up the big bank, oil, railway, and steel monopolies of that era.

---

6. Mencius Moldbug [Curtis Yarvin], *Unqualified Reservations*, https://www.unqualified-reservations.org/. See also Scott Aikin, "Deep Disagreement, the Dark Enlightenment, and the Rhetoric of the Red Pill," *Journal of Applied Philosophy* 36, no. 3 (2019): 420–35.

The Accelerationist Creed

These new masters of the universe on Wall Street, in downtown Seattle, or scattered around the San Francisco Bay Area admire Hans-Hermann Hoppe's philosophical aspirations for "getting libertarianism right" on their cybernetic common ground of true freedom, believing it lies somewhere between Thomas Hobbes and Friedrich Hayek. Once there, they spin up cyber-sagas grounded in fringe ideological lore beyond Hoppe's libertarianism. In fact, for most NRx followers, there are many substantively compelling ideological alternatives beyond autocracy and democracy, which all lean toward anarchistic "alt-right" thinking.[7]

Surveying Mencius Moldbug's writings, for example, the moral ambiguity in his thoughts is high and the conceptual aporia in his writing is deep, given the amazing ideological affinities he recounts running through human history. As a result, it is difficult at times to infer what Moldbug actually means and then decide where his project stands. Nonetheless, Moldbug is, according to Land, "the supreme Sith Lord of the neo-reactionaries," and he often is regarded as clairvoyantly correct in his many sociological short takes. Since the state, or the academic/scientific/bureaucratic formations that Moldbug calls "the Cathedral," cannot be abolished, its current addiction to democracy must be cured by cleansing its "systematic and degenerate bad government" through "neo-cameralism."[8]

Looking to his root corporate ideals, Moldbug's neo-cameralist formulae are plain: "a state is a business which owns a country."[9] Believing more in the generative animal spirits of greed and fear behind the S&P 500 than in the degenerative afflictions of contemporary democracy, Moldbug's statal design would mimic the structure of an IPO:

7. See Hans-Hermann Hoppe, *Getting Libertarianism Right* (Auburn, AL: Mises Institute, 2018); Christopher Chase Rachels, *White, Right, and Libertarian* (CreateSpace Independent Publishing Platform, 2018); and Murray N. Rothbard, *What Has Government Done to Our Money?*, 5th ed. (Auburn, AL: Mises Institute, 2005); along with Nick Land, *Fanged Noumena: Collected Writings 1987–2007*, 5th ed. (Falmouth: Urbanatomy Electronic, 2011); Land, *Calendric Dominion* (Falmouth: Urbanatomy Electronic, 2013); and Land, *Templexity: Disordered Loops through Shanghai Time* (Falmouth: Urbanatomy Electronic, 2014).

8. Land, "The Dark Enlightenment," pt. 1.

9. Mencius Moldbug, "Against Political Freedom," *Unqualified Reservations*, August 16, 2007, https://www.unqualified-reservations.org/2007/08/against-political-freedom/.

> A state should be managed, like any other large business, by dividing logical ownership into negotiable shares, each of which yields a precise fraction of the state's profit. A well-run state is very profitable. Each share has one vote, and shareholders elect a board, which hires and fires managers. The business's customers are its residents. A profitably managed neo-cameralist state will, like any business, serve its customers efficiently and effectively. Misgovernment equals mismanagement.[10]

Governments espousing liberty, equality, and fraternity, then, are fraudster scams. Neo-cameralist states, however, should be regarded as exemplars of managerial perfection in which governance would whip up efficient, effective, and entrepreneurial miracles. Moldbug graciously admits that he too is "a corporate serf," his great manor itself, the United States, "is nothing but a corporation," but "it's not too crazy to say that all options—including restructuring and liquidation—should be on the table."[11]

While working as young computer coders or pre-IPO business moguls, such grumpy "corporate serfs" apparently acquire a taste for executive autocracy, a love of status, and a passion for futuristic transhuman fantasies. Since many ordinary American citizens regard the "brand" of the Trump Organization as more credible than the legitimacy of the U.S. Constitution, this narrative about contemporary politics cannot be downplayed. In today's world, everything is being produced as, or soon is reduced to, "big data." For the masters of big data, there is, in turn, an increasingly less visible line between their epistemic sophistication and racial supremacy, philosophical neo-reaction and actual neo-fascism, technocratic elitism and national chauvinism, anti-multiculturalism and xenophobic nationalism, or cybernetic futurism and scientific elitism. Given these ideological elective affinities in accelerationist thought, the proponents of Dark Enlightenment definitely should not be downplayed.

Unlike 1990s cyber-communism, the neo-cameralism of NRx thought would not be as well known without endorsements by accelerationist

---

10. Ibid. Also see Rosie Gray, "Behind the Internet's Anti-Democracy Movement," *Atlantic*, February 10, 2017, https://www.theatlantic.com/politics/archive/2017/02/behind-the-internets-dark-anti-democracy-movement/516243/.

11. Mencius Moldbug, "A Formalist Manifesto," *Unqualified Reservations*, April 23, 2007, https://www.unqualified-reservations.org/2007/04/formalist-manifesto-originally-posted/.

philosophers like Land. He has become more positive about how, first, Dark Enlightenment thought describes the general conditions under which accelerationism emerges at the advent of the Anthropocene. And, second, he admires the neo-reactionary readings of the economy and society that would permit an accelerationist program to succeed. Success, however, for the accelerationists amounts to hastening the rapid transformative and total collapse of contemporary advanced industrial society as well as global capitalist exchange, which also was the agenda, according to Robin Mackey and Armen Avanessian, of Karl Marx, "the first accelerationist."[12] In this regard, "Accelerationism is a political heresy; the insistence that the only radical political response to capitalism is not to protest, disrupt, or critique, nor to await its demise at the hands of its own contradictions, but to accelerate its uprooting, alienating, decoding, abstractive tendencies."[13]

Like Marx, accelerationists regard the demise of capitalism as necessary to make any new beginnings rather than the end of all that exists; but their new beginning simply is not yet well understood. As Mackey and Avanessian observe, "The general reasoning is that if modernity= progress=capitalism=acceleration, then the only possible resistance amounts to deceleration, whether through a fantasy of collective organic self-sufficiency or a solo retreat into miserabilism and sagacious warnings against the treacherous counterfinalities of rational thought."[14]

In surveying its advocates' fantasies of collective organic self-sufficiency, and other more solo condemnations of the rational scientific thought praised by the existing order, it is clear the Dark Enlightenment is intellectually diverse. Still, many NRX supporters offer harsh rejections of their existing comfortable accommodations, namely, "liberal

12. Robin Mackey and Armen Avanessian, eds., *#Accelerate: The Accelerationist Reader*, 2nd ed. (Falmouth: Urbanomic Media, 2017), p. 9; Andy Beckett, "Accelerationism: How a Fringe Philosophy Predicted the Future We Live In," *Guardian*, May 11, 2017, https://www.theguardian.com/world/2017/may/11/accelerationism-how-a-fringe-philosophy-predicted-the-future-we-live-in. Ted Kaczynski would agree. Trapped in "technological slavery," humanity ignores how much technology itself is a disaster. Indeed, he claims that "only the collapse of modern technological civilization can avert disaster." See Theodore J. Kaczynski, foreword to *Technological Slavery: The Collected Writings of Theodore J. Kaczynski, a.k.a. "The Unabomber"*, intro. David Skrbina (Port Townsend, WA: Feral House, 2010), p. 13.

13. Mackey and Avanessian, *#Accelerate*, p. 4.

14. Ibid., pp. 5–6.

capitalist democracy." With their highly stylized *Hunger Games*, *Harry Potter*, *Star Wars*, and *Game of Thrones* political imaginaries, a heroic self-adulation behind the extraordinary political theology of neo-reactionary thinkers also allows them to give an equally warm reception to new organic collectives of self-sufficient city-states as well as vast mythic empires of wealthy grandeur somewhere far beyond the ambit of today's fast-failing capitalism.[15]

Unabloggers

The key *philosophes* of the Dark Enlightenment at this juncture are a curious assortment of individuals, including Curtis Yarvin (a.k.a. "Mencius Moldbug," a computer scientist in the San Francisco Bay Area), Justine Tunney (a Google software engineer), Michael Perilloux (a high-tech investor), Bruce Laiberte (a Catholic anarchist), and, more prominently, the accelerationist thinker Nick Land (a one-time professor of philosophy from the University of Warwick who now works as a writer in Shanghai after a series of personal crises). In some ways, their *élan vital* is not unlike the vision of Ted Kaczynski, another Bay Area visionary, who took his fight against "industrial society and its future" into direct action primitivism and mail-bombing terrorism from the Montana backwoods as the "Unabomber" a generation ago.[16]

Kaczynski also wanted to trash the forms of contemporary collective life, since he believed Silicon Valley and the American state had seized control of humanity's future in the 1980s and 1990s. By turning to direct individual violence, he believed he could crash "the system." That prediction was largely off target, but his prolonged low-intensity bombing campaign was strangely arresting in many media markets across America as a truly radical exemplification of the "propaganda of the deed." Today, however, he is followed by the "Unabloggers" of the Dark Enlightenment, waging high-intensity disinformation wars with a belief

---

15. Frédéric Nayrat, *The Unconstructable Earth: An Ecology of Separation* (New York: Fordham Univ. Press, 2019), pp. 121–30. Also see Safiya Umosa Noble, *Algorithms of Oppression: How Search Engines Reinforce Racism* (New York: NYU Press, 2018); and Cathy O'Neil, *Weapons of Math Destruction: How Big Data Increases Inequality and Threatens Democracy* (New York: Broadway Books, 2017).

16. See Timothy W. Luke, "Re-Reading the Unabomber Manifesto," *Telos* 107 (Spring 1996): 85–108, reprinted in this volume.

that their visions for crashing today's capitalist systems provide much better plans for the future.[17]

Proud to take the "NRx" tag for themselves, neo-reactionary thinkers are diverse, but their unablogging styles tend to be elitist and ethnonational in tone, with ample measures of the will to power, rhetorical grandstanding, and zealous eagerness to offend. This proclivity to embrace authoritarian, anarchist, and antihumanist ideals also draws from the ever-changing *Kitschkultur* of corporate futurism, science fiction cinema, and libertarian writing, which is much loved by nerdy teenagers and STEM majors at major research universities, who are awakened to such fables by Ayn Rand, Robert Heinlein, or Milton Friedman. Eloquence is not characteristic of Unablogger writings, because much of this discourse largely spins in the sentence fragments of born-digital blogs or floats on hashtags on social media. The archive of the Dark Enlightenment, therefore, is somewhat hermetic, but it also is voluminous, expansive, and aggressive. Moreover, it antedates the Great Recession of 2007–2009.[18] Many arcane points are made evasively, and this opens their authors to multiple mistaken interpretations. This result is not perplexing in light of the overall post-literate qualities of many fragments of communicative interaction moving through online media environments.

The contempt of NRx thinkers for almost all aspects of liberal democracy, progressive theories of government, and the notion of positive law working through the state is quite evident. In Moldbug's critique of today's current correlation of forces in the United States, for example, America has become a cohesive cluster of constant crises. He associates them all with the most reviled social formation: "the Cathedral." In Moldbug's assessment, its functionaries work under the guidance of what he sees as "the Left," or "the party of the educational organs, at

17. In Mackey and Avanessian, *#Accelerate*, see the following chapters: Sadie Plant and Nick Land, "Cyberpositive," pp. 303–24; CCRU, "Swarmachines," pp. 321–31; Reza Negarestani, "The Labor of the Inhuman," pp. 425–66; and Patricia Reed, "Seven Prescriptions for Accelerationism," pp. 521–36. On the power of the Cathedral in the Trump era, see Arthur Gordian, "The Rise of Cultural Anarchism," *Social Matter*, October 1, 2018, https://www.socialmatter.net/2018/10/01/the-rise-of-cultural-anarchism/.

18. George Hawley, *The Alt-Right: What Everyone Needs to Know* (New York: Oxford Univ. Press, 2018), pp. 88–89.

whose head is the press and the universities."[19] At his blog, *Unqualified Reservations*, he portrays the Cathedral strangely as "our 20th-century version of the established church," in which the "present system of government—which might be described succinctly as an atheistic theocracy—is accidentally similar to Puritan Massachusetts.... This architecture of government—theocracy secured through democratic means—is a single continuous thread in American history."[20]

Neo-reactionary thought in these registers of Dark Enlightenment reasoning exemplifies the tendencies that Carl Schmitt sees unfolding as political theology in the "social structure of an epoch," which always gropes toward a closer correspondence with "its metaphysical view of the world."[21] Moldbug's off-kilter NRx reading of Western civilization and Land's neo-Deleuzean saga of slouching toward some posthuman singularity in the times now branded as the Anthropocene share the same faith, if only to a degree, in digital machinic systems. For them, this social structure of our epoch is fragile, waiting to be crashed, hacked, or endlessly upgraded by them. Still, NRx thinkers are eager to disclose, as Unabloggers, how and why "what must be done" in the Dark Enlightenment should abide by their digital discourses.

From *Bildungsbürgertum* to *Bytesbürgertum*

The self-absorption of such digiteratarian commentaries starkly pushes the disruptive potential of apocalyptic texts, like those of Nick Land or Sadie Plant, "to propagate and accelerate the destitution of the human subject and its integration into the artificial technosphere" as a path to *"antihumanist catastrophism."*[22] The irony of this development amid "the Great Acceleration" of fossil-fueled globalization of the Anthropocene since 1945 is startling.[23] Likewise, the values of an enlightened

---

19. Mencius Moldbug, "A Gentle Introduction to Unqualified Reservations," *Unqualified Reservations*, January 8, 2009, https://www.unqualified-reservations.org/2009/01/gentle-introduction-to-unqualified/.

20. Ibid.

21. Carl Schmitt, *Political Theology: Four Chapters on the Concept of Sovereignty*, trans. George Schwab (Chicago: Univ. of Chicago Press, 2006), pp. 45–46; and Nick Land, "Teleoplexy: Notes on Acceleration," in Mackay and Avanessian, *#Accelerate*, pp. 509–20.

22. Mackay and Avanessian, introduction to *#Accelerate*, p. 20.

23. J. R. McNeill and Peter Engelke, *The Great Acceleration: An Environmental History of the Anthropocene since 1945* (Cambridge, MA: Harvard Univ. Press, 2016).

middle class whose greater education once enabled them in the nineteenth century to guide society in its collective *Bildung* have morphed bizarrely with today's floods of big data in the twenty-first century. In a world organized around digital information infiltrating all materiality to connect everything to the smart systems as "the Internet of Things," accelerationist thought is a thick tangle of cluttered confusion. As Andy Beckett observes, it contradicts almost every earlier politicized intellectual project, including "conservatism, traditional socialism, social democracy, environmentalism, protectionism, populism, naturalism, localism and all other ideologies that have sought to moderate or reverse the already hugely disruptive, seemingly runaway pace of change in the modern world."[24] Yet it intentionally also takes this turn.

The cyberian nihilist intellectuals pushing accelerationism largely tend to downplay how the messy details of growing human populations, mushrooming fossil fuel use, accelerating global climate changes, spreading piles of waste plastic, and collapsing nonhuman biodiversity, which come with rapid planetary urbanization, already are fulfilling their heresies as they speak. This tendency also casts more light on how "accelerationism now gleefully explores what is escaping from human civilization" during its "anastrophic collapse into the future."[25] Such "radical heretics," however, seem also to differ only slightly in temper and tone from well-established World Economic Forum enthusiasts, who celebrate "the Fourth Industrial Revolution."[26] Those Davos men and women are mapping out another great and glorious hypertechnified future for the existing Silicon Valley–based *Besitzbürgertum* from the activation of an even greater, newer, and quicker revitalized *Bytesbürgertum*, emerging with their patents for fifth-generation wireless networks, ubiquitous autonomous systems, and greater robotization in which cybernetic monopolies will anchor the next great transformations in capitalism.[27]

24. Beckett, "Accelerationism."

25. Mackay and Avanessian, introduction to *#Accelerate*, p. 20.

26. See Klaus Schwab, *The Fourth Industrial Revolution* (New York: Portfolio Penguin, 2017); and Andrew McAfee and Erik Brynjolfsson, *Machine, Platform, Crowd: Harnessing Our Digital Future* (New York: W. W. Norton, 2017).

27. James Bridle, *New Dark Age: Technology and the End of the Future* (New York: Verso, 2018).

The threads in this *bytesbürgerliche* accelerationism are complicated, but they are well worth untangling to find the political theology working this juncture in history. Many of its more audible voices are not entirely cranks, but their elective affinity for adopting value from a variety of reactionary movements from the nineteenth and twentieth centuries, ranging from aristocracy, eugenics, and fascism to autarchy, elitism, and racism, arises without much deliberation or only for political provocation. Still, this tendency might aid the effort to understand where they begin, who they are, when they operate, how they gain credibility, and what they want politically.

The Book of Third Nature

The immersion of NRx thought in the theories and practices associated with social media, cyberspatial networks, and artificial intelligence is not trivial, because this machinic nexus appears to be their origin point. Many adherents of the Dark Enlightenment have come to this philosophy through their everyday work with computer code and the networked subcultures it generates. With now billions of intelligent devices tied into global networks, and with many more coming with the growing Internet of Things, "the digital planet" is now a more concrete reality.[28] Most of the world's money, much of its communication, transportation, and distribution systems, and the majority of data analysis and information archiving now circulate in and out of cloud computing systems whose nebulous banks, fronts, and storms already are beyond complete individual comprehension. Out of the darkness of paleotechnic industrial obsolescence, an alluring future is illuminated by photon and electron pulses, and it brings a seductive transcendent rapture.[29] This spiritual charge is one that the Dark Enlightenment loves to champion. Consequently, it is crucial not to forget how and why algorithms, codes, and servers are the enabling material infrastructures constituting accelerationism's ideal modes of digital being.

---

28. Erik Brynjolfsson, *The Second Machine Age: Work, Progress, and Prosperity in a Time of Brilliant Technologies* (New York: W. W. Norton, 2014).

29. See Timothy W. Luke, *Screens of Power: Ideology, Domination, and Resistance in Informational Society* (Urbana: Univ. of Illinois Press, 1989); Fredric Jameson, *Postmodernism, or the Cultural Logic of Late Capitalism* (Durham, NC: Duke Univ. Press, 1991); and David Harvey, *The Condition of Postmodernity: An Enquiry into the Origins of Cultural Change* (Oxford: Blackwell, 1989).

Cyberspaces are, in one sense, one of many modalities being made manifest in nature's unfolding pluralization. After millennia of living in small bands in the spaces and places of the earth, or "first nature," the Neolithic revolution led to settled agriculture, permanent dwellings, the rise of cities, and the infamous emergence of "civilization." This new culture of cities amid "nature" opened the books of a "second nature" scrawled across the earth by human culture, history, and society. With the transformative infiltration of this second nature, fabricated from humans' far-flung industrial and agricultural activity over centuries, informational modes of living are now pushing its iterations beyond these pre-informatic technical artifices in second nature and opening hyperreal domains in cybernetic/telematic/digitalized "third nature." Thus, multiplex imbrications of biogeophysical first nature, along with the technified artifices of second nature, increasingly are reformatted, supplemented, or captured in the digital environments of a new third nature.[30]

Philosophers long have spoken about reading the Book of Nature (twisted into terrestriality) as well as the Book of Culture/History/Society (tethered to territoriality) as second nature for insights. Now the Book of Technology (tied to telemetricality) as third nature is cracked open for its revelations—revealed and renewed in binary code 24x7—as well.[31] Traditionally, the Nature of Creation has been pluralized, differentiated, and appropriated in terms of "firstness" and "secondness," while the *nomos* marking human presence has juxtaposed these interplays of nature's two modes in economy and society.[32]

In the Book of Third Nature, the Anthropocene is anticipated in the algorithms of cybernetic rationalization that morph "thirdness" through the cyberscape/infoscape/mediascape as the *telemetrical*. With this shift, the Dark Enlightenment denounces abiding by antiquated conceptual categories imposed by orthodox discourses of first and second nature's

30. See William J. Mitchell, *City of Bits: Space, Place, and the Infobahn* (Cambridge, MA: MIT Press, 1995).

31. Timothy W. Luke, "Placing Powers/Siting Spaces: The Politics of Global and Local in the New World Order," *Environment and Planning D: Society and Space* 12, no. 5 (1994): 613–28.

32. Georg Lukács, *History and Class Consciousness: Studies in Marxist Dialectics*, trans. Rodney Livingstone (Cambridge, MA: MIT Press, 1971); and Carl Schmitt, *The Nomos of the Earth in the International Law of the Jus Publicum Europaeum*, trans. G. L. Ulmen (New York: Telos Press Publishing, 2006).

cosmological idealism or political realism.[33] Divine revelation and classical antiquity are not their touchstone; instead, it is all connected to switching continuously between the binary of "0" and "1." Beyond the outer/inner reaches of the cybernetic technosphere, earlier epistemic visions of what is "real" do not hold fast. The Book of Third Nature is transcribed in accord with Jean Baudrillard's observations about informationalism and faith in the cybersphere, with its systems of simulation running through the endless lines of coded hyperreality.[34]

Here one must recall the framing of political theology by Schmitt. First, to what extent is it a political representation of past/future history through some transcendent aesthetic or ethico-political vision of a person and place in the context of the present, which can be tied to aesthetic judgment and spiritual affect along with more universal rational principles and reasoned argument.[35] And, second, whether it is Wonderland, toppling the Cathedral, accelerationist sagas, or other sci-fi/cli-fi/goth-fi fables, these representations can anchor political theology as they latch onto the "materiality" of first, second, and third nature (terrestriality, territoriality, and telemetricality) managed through new modes of cybernetic sovereign power and posthuman spiritual discourse. Most conveniently, third nature is virtual, hyperreal, and telemetrical, and its cyberspatiality amorphously fuses materiality and representation in virtual acts of intellect and will.

It is not as simple as Moldbug's "Cathedral," because those networks of power cling to territorial and terrestrial roots. Nonetheless, systems of hyperreal telemetricality spin in the bits in televisual/cybernetic changes that some believe are evaporating fixed representational differences between true and false, concept and object, real and representation. Accelerationism essentially accedes to seeing everything anew as third nature:

> No more mirror of being and appearances, of the real and its concept; no more imaginary coextensivity: rather, genetic miniaturization is

---

33. Land, "Teleoplexy," pp. 511–20.

34. Jean Baudrillard, *In the Shadow of the Silent Majorities*, trans. Paul Foss, John Johnston, Paul Patton, and Stuart Kendall (Cambridge, MA: MIT Press, 2007); and Baudrillard, *Simulations*, trans. Phil Beitchman, Paul Foss, and Paul Patton (Cambridge, MA: MIT Press, 1983).

35. Schmitt, *Political Theology*, pp. 36–50.

the dimension of simulation. The real is produced from miniaturized units, from matrices, memory banks and command models—and with these it can be reproduced an indefinite number of times. It no longer has to be rational, since it is no longer measured against some ideal or negative instance. It is nothing more than operational. In fact, since it is no longer enveloped by an imaginary, it is no longer real at all. It is a hyperreal: the product of an irradiating synthesis of combinatory models in a hyperspace without atmosphere.[36]

Third nature, then, appears as clusters of complex cybernetic simulacra, copies of domains for which there are no stable originals. Nevertheless, these zones retain very concrete, material, and powerful qualities as they nest within second and first nature. Looking to these domains, NRx thinkers have been imaginatively constructing visions for a new life organized within boundaries of bits, regimes on RAM, cultures from clouds, dominions of data, companies of code. A fascination with reading the Book of Third Nature ontopolitically has evolved along with the proliferation of complex networked communication and computer systems over the past three decades. These social implications have been anticipated for years by informational theorists, ranging from Hans Moravec to Nicholas Negroponte, who also spoke about humanity evolving from pushing "atoms" (matter) to generating "bits" (information).[37]

Representational imaginaries advanced by science fiction writers, such as William Gibson, shape fictive visions of history and culture around the contours of third nature to underscore the impact of cyberspaces upon contemporary society. In *Neuromancer*, he imagines cyberspace as "a consensual hallucination experienced daily by billions of legitimate operators, in every nation, by children being taught mathematical concepts.... A graphic representation of data abstracted from the banks of every computer in the human system. Unthinkable complexity. Lines of light ranged in the nonspace of the mind, clusters and constellations of data. Like city lights, receding."[38] Such language is spiritual, transcendent, and mysterious. Its creators and users circulate such

36. Jean Baudrillard, *Simulacra and Simulation*, trans. Sheila Faria Glaser (Ann Arbor: Univ. of Michigan Press, 1994), p. 71.

37. Hans Moravec, *Mind Children* (Cambridge, MA: Harvard Univ. Press, 1988); and Nicholas Negroponte, *Being Digital* (New York: Vintage, 1996).

38. William Gibson, *Neuromancer* (New York: Ace Books, 1984), p. 51.

liturgically charged lingo as new illuminati, and they often feel an om-nipresence, omnipotence, and omniscience of some rising spirituality in digitality. With readings from such cyberian psalms in the Book of Third Nature, the ideological carrier waves in telemetrical circuits easily carry content that is taken as almost theologically charged political rev-elations for the NRx movement.

Many advocates of Dark Enlightenment naturalize cyberspace, ac-cepting it as a given that can and will be accessed at will by anyone astute and equipped enough to gain entry through such Unablogger wisdom. Yet, for other NRx networks, it is an occult domain out-of-bounds for the "normies," who should never be granted the full access, authority, or acceptance already gained by the digiterati. Cybernetic control is their special realm of unique expertise, the grounds for their autocratic au-thority, and the foundation for a new political theology.

Few moments in history are afforded the possibility of pluralizing nature, and the power of firms and individuals to create entire realms of hyperreal estate online today has moved many to reimagine themselves and fellow computer users as possessing godlike attributes. Steward Brand, for example, sees this turn at the core of third nature: "Junior de-ities, we want to be. Reality is mostly given. Virtual reality is creatable."[39] With an ever-accelerating potential for generating billions a year out of bits, such god talk is to be expected. With the profits derived from such 24x7 turnover, cyberspatial theorists easily naturalize their net-worked connections, because money, at least for them, will be no object. Indeed, some imagine a new kind of immortality on the Internet in real-izing such power and profit. As John Perry Barlow claimed, "When the yearning for human flesh has come to an end, what will remain? Mind may continue, uploaded into the Net, suspended in an ecology of volt-age as ambitiously capable of self-sustenance as was its carbon-based forebears."[40] Heaven's gate is the screen, and paradise itself could be eternally online in the cloud.[41]

    39. Stewart Brand, *The Media Lab: Inventing the Future at MIT* (New York: Viking 1987), p. 116.

    40. Cited in Mark Slouka, *War of the Worlds: Cyberspace and the High-Tech Assault on Reality* (New York: Basic, 1995), pp. 11–12.

    41. Gregory Stock, *Metaman: The Merging of Humans and Machines into a Global Superorganism* (New York: Simon & Schuster, 1993).

Accelerationist Fables

Such tenets in Dark Enlightenment philosophies represent the basic vision of a new political theology.[42] Accelerationist teachings demand the unrelenting rapid change of everything, and they target anything standing in their way, like "the Cathedral" and its operatives. For NRx circles, the 24x7 performative intensity of global capitalist exchange chewing up the planet, its people, and life itself at the frenetic pace of Internet time is all to be desired:

> [T]echnology, particularly computer technology, and capitalism, particularly the most aggressive, global variety, should be massively sped up and intensified—either because this is the best way forward for humanity, or because there is no alternative. Accelerationists favour automation. They favour the further merging of the digital and the human. They often favour the deregulation of business, and drastically scaled-back government.... They often believe that social and political upheaval has a value in itself.[43]

This invidious intensification boosts NRx thinkers in their struggle to spark "end time" upheavals from nature's exhaustions, life's extinctions, and society's exclusions to bring their techno-theosophical vision of "the singularity" to pass.[44] Their antipathy for the Cathedral, its leftish *apparatchiki*, and the less technically inclined masses, who are all their enemy, justify in turn a politics of elite autocracy by, for, and of pure technology against mere humanity.

Meanwhile, back in the salons of the Dark Enlightenment, Moldbug pieces together other parts of the puzzle from the Atlantic Republican tradition from the English Civil War to the present, which he brusquely dismisses, suggesting that if this set of developments is what "has gotten us from the Stuarts to Barack Obama" then "[p]ersonally, I would like a refund."[45] Moldbug also asserts that the "leftward direction is, *itself*, the principle of organization," and it constitutes an ongoing scam on

42. See the Zeroth Position website, https://www.zerothposition.com/.

43. See Beckett, "Accelerationism."

44. Ray Kurzweil, *The Singularity Is Near* (New York: Viking, 2005); and Kurzweil, *The Age of Spiritual Machines: When Computers Exceed Human Intelligence* (New York: Penguin, 2000).

45. Moldbug, "A Gentle Introduction to Unqualified Reservations."

society.[46] Looking back over nearly four hundred years, he argues that there has been a "two-party democratic system, with Whigs and Tories, Democrats and Republicans, etc.," but that most importantly, "the intelligentsia is always Whig. Their party is simply the party of those who want to get ahead. It is the party of celebrities, the ultra-rich, the great and the good, the flexible of conscience. Tories are always misfits, losers, or just plain stupid—sometimes all three."[47] In this flat, chronocentric, reactionary reading, both left and right are defined in terms of political entropy: "Right represents *peace, order and security*; left represents *war, anarchy and crime*."[48]

Since he asserts that "values are inherently subjective, it is possible to argue that the left can be good and the right can be bad.... On the other hand, it is also quite easy to construct a very clean value system in which order is simply good, and chaos is simply evil. I have chosen this path. It leaves quite a capacious cavity in the back of my skull, and allows me to call myself a *reactionary*."[49] Speaking as the key NRx advocate at *Unqualified Reservations*, Moldbug suggests that "it is interesting to go back and read your Chomsky. What you'll see is that Chomsky is, in every case, demanding that all political power be in the hands of the Cathedral." The left, the Whig, the progressive, whom Chomsky favors, "is always the underdog in his own mind. Yet, in objective reality, he always seems to win in the end."[50]

These NRx ontographies recall, albeit from another time and context, other spiritual movements whose political theologies embraced gnostic intuitive personal encounters with divine wisdom. Typically, other esoteric knowledges, texts, or sagas anchor such theosophy, but its variants, not surprisingly, usually claim that some richer, larger, or deeper reality exists, which only their special wisdom can access at the hazy interface of first and second nature. At the same time, their belief in extraordinary esoteric knowledge comes with the presumption that only a small elite group of special devotees could appreciate this teaching, which brought greater spiritual, psychic, moral, and ethical power

46. Ibid.
47. Ibid.
48. Ibid.
49. Ibid.
50. Ibid.

to its followers. Many sects, such as Freemasons, Rosicrucians, Manichaeans, and Neoplatonists, have espoused such beliefs. So too did the Theosophical Society, which was organized in New York in 1875 by Helena Petrovna Blavatsky, Henry Steel Olcott, and William Quan Judge. Taken with so-called "Eastern religious wisdom" and its occult spiritualism, Olcott and Blavatsky moved to India (where the Theosophical Society still remains active) in 1878 after scandals over some phony encounters in high society involving staged conversations with the dead.[51]

Regardless, in their ethico-political moments, Dark Enlightenment and accelerationist thinkers put their digital pedal to new cybernetic metal. Some become neo-theosophical proponents for seizing ahold of technoscientific divinity, which could be developed digitally for them beyond death, or "the bionic horizon," by merging cells and code. As Meredith Broussard suggests, such values are the most extreme "techno-chauvinism," namely, "the belief that tech is always the solution" because it is radical, revolutionary, or revelatory.[52] Still, is this faith only another mystification of capital via marketing? The paladins of digital salvation, such as Land and Moldbug, overlook how "digital technology has been an ordinary part of scientific and bureaucratic life since the 1950s, and everyday life since the 1980s," even though "sophisticated marketing campaigns still have most people convinced that tech is something new and potentially revolutionary."[53]

Reading Moldbug's and Land's overwrought rhetoric, Broussard seems dead right, but the Dark Enlightenment goes further. For Land, "the Cathedral" that Moldbug savages must pit its dull leftish wallowing against sharp NRx wisdom in basic nature/nurture terms: "As the suppressive orthodoxy of the Cathedral becomes unstrung...a time of monsters is approaching."[54] Putting it in the crudest terms, "the right likes genes and the left likes culture," where "hereditarian determinism confronts social constructivism," unable to accept "*the culture of*

---

51. See Rudolf Steiner, *Spiritualism, Madame Blavatsky, and Theosophy: An Eyewitness View of Occult History* (Great Barrington, MA: Anthroposophic Press, 2002); and Julie Chajes, *Recycled Lives: A History of Reincarnation in Blavatsky's Theosophy* (New York: Oxford Univ. Press, 2019).

52. Meredith Broussard, *Artificial Unintelligence: How Computers Misunderstand the World* (Cambridge, MA: MIT Press, 2018), p. 8.

53. Ibid.

54. Land, "The Dark Enlightenment," pt. 4F.

practical naturalism, which is to say: the techno-scientific/industrial manipulation of the world."[55]

Nonetheless, some of these much-feted high-tech transformations have already happened, and their gadgets and gizmos already are routine and ordinary. They proliferate through standardized seriality: software updates to versions 1.0, 2.0, 3.0; mobile networks increase to 3G, 4G, 5G; new operating systems appear, such as iOS 11, 12, 13; chip capacity increases in KB, MB, GB, PB, etc. Technochauvinism is that "artificial unintelligence" behind the university administration's, marketing department's, and ordinary consumer's desire to relentlessly "Invent the Future" or "Put Knowledge to Work" for its own atavistic sake as well as that of technocapitalism.[56] Venture capitalists, start-up entrepreneurs, and major stockholders, however, also can cast these wares as sources of salvation, mistaking perhaps the miracles of monetary compound interest for the true signs of everlasting life.

This salvation also sells itself with yet greater future revelations, putting consumers' and producers' trained incapacities into play in Vegas at the Consumer Electronics Show, in Gotham on the NASDAQ, or from Seattle through Amazon. Such technochauvinism reverberates at the established frequency and amplitude of today's commercial culture, which trusts in capital as a godly power. The deepest belief here remains rock-solid—corporations, markets, entrepreneurs of "the system" are always "the solution." Regardless, these commercial myths are nothing new, quite conservative, and very compatible with the wide range of retrogressive NRx thought.

Conclusion

At the same time, apostles of Dark Enlightenment continue to read from the Book of Third Nature for even deeper revelations. Realizing that "nature and culture compose a dynamic circuit, at the edge of nature, where fate is decided," Land asserts that codes and cells will fuse together in a material transcendence beyond "our bionic horizon" and will become "the threshold of conclusive nature-culture fusion at which a population becomes indistinguishable from its technology."[57] Like the

---

55. Ibid.
56. Broussard, *Artificial Unintelligence*, pp. 8–9.
57. Land, "The Dark Enlightenment," pt. 4F.

"gene traders" of Octavia Butler's Xenogenesis trilogy, who have "no identity separable from the biotechnological program that they perpetually implement upon themselves, as they commercially acquire, industrially produce, and sexually reproduce their population within a single, integral process,"[58] the "artificial unintelligence" driving digitality can, and therefore must, reprogram animality.[59]

As the planet seems to be dying in the Anthropocene, new political theologies are being tested here. Such imperatives constitute a streak of divinity in radical political theology, even though such revelations betray kinship with even stranger cults. Such cyber-creeds indeed have been foreshadowed in the faith of earlier reactionary fellow-traveler sects, who have favored Ayn Randian meritocracy, cyborg technolibertarianism, machinic objectivity, biotic ultracomputerization, or artificial intelligence in the quest to "create a digitally enabled utopia."[60] Yet the darker final dystopia, which Land and other NRx thinkers propound in creating a New World Order for a reactionary modernist libertarianism, amounts to something not unlike high-tech "auto-Aryanization."

That is, beyond the "religious traditionalists of the Western orthosphere," the Dark Enlightenment envisions how "techno-scientific auto-production specifically supplants the fixed and sacralized essence of man as a created being, amidst the greatest upheaval in the natural order since the emergence of eukaryotic life, half a billion years ago."[61] In his new Genesis story, this historic change "is not merely an evolutionary event, but the threshold of a new *evolutionary phase*...the emergence of *Homo autocatalyticus*."[62] Consequently, one learns this techno-theosophy goes beyond "the concerns of identity politics (racial purity) or traditional cognitive elitism (eugenics)" because its proponents are merging "hard/software" with "wetware" to take an "altogether

---

58. Ibid.

59. Ibid.

60. Broussard, *Artificial Unintelligence*, p. 8.

61. Land, "The Dark Enlightenment," pt. 4F. For earlier visions of this turn, see Kevin Kelly, *Out of Control: The Rise of Neo-Biological Civilization* (Reading, MA: Addison-Wesley, 1994); and Bruce Mazlish, *The Fourth Discontinuity: The Co-Evolution of Humans and Machines* (New Haven, CT: Yale Univ. Press, 1993). Another variant is expressed by James Lovelock, *Novacene: The Coming Age of Hyperintelligence* (London: Penguin Random House UK, 2019).

62. Land, "The Dark Enlightenment," pt. 4F.

wilder and more monstrous bearing—towards *speciation*"[63] via "creative conscious evolution."

While "speciation talk" pretends to avoid racism, this reading of the Book of Third Nature parallels those made by the advocates of the Creative Conscious Evolution movement, and it rings in the tenor and tone of auto-Aryanization together with dreams about "*Homo autocatalyticus.*"[64] As John H. Campbell, a University of California, Los Angeles, biologist suggests, "We shall be able to redesign our biological selves at will." His followers see this claim as justifying "the abandonment of *Homo sapiens* as a 'relic' or 'living fossil' and the application of genetic technologies to intrude upon the genome...using a DNA synthesizer. Such eugenics would be practiced by elite groups, whose achievements would so quickly and radically outdistance the usual tempo of evolution that within ten generations new groups will have advanced beyond our current form to the same degree that we transcend apes."[65] Campbell's elective affinities are a bit expansive, but such new CRISPR-encoded posthuman beings could coexist with *Homo sapiens*. The latter species, however, will become, like the Neanderthals before the dominance of modern humans, essentially "Silizumthal" men and women, fated to fade away before the more boundless, seemingly divine *Homo autocatalytici* springing forth anew.

From whatever "technoplastic beings" recode them, these auto-Aryanizing humans will be well suited to "precise, scientifically informed transformations" that arise from humanity's subsumption into its own "technosphere, where information processing of the genome...brings reading and editing into perfect coincidence."[66] If the Anthropocene is to be a time of technospheric tumult, NRx thinkers are designing the posthumans ready to be the crown of man's own planetary creation.

63. Ibid.

64. See "Radical Intervention," Creative Conscious Evolution website, https://www.euvolution.com/eugenics/radical_intervention.html. While these turns seem beyond far-fetched, Silicon Valley–minded thinkers are already taming the radical posthuman aspirations at work here by rebranding this revolutionary acceleration as "design anthropology" to remix ethnonational elitism, biomedical experimentation, and technocratic oligarchy. See, for example, Travis Dumsday, "Transhumanism, Theological Anthropology, and Modern Biological Taxonomy," *Zygon: Journal of Religion & Science* 52, no. 3 (2017): 601–22.

65. See "Radical Intervention."

66. Land, "The Dark Enlightenment," pt. 4F.

Ironically, the human geoengineered modification of the earth's biosphere in deep time will coevolve with new bioengineered distinctly re-speciated transhuman beings whose posthuman bones soon will begin to accumulate in historical time to fossilize as another decisive marker of the Anthropocene's advent for intelligent biota and smart things to come in the future to assay as part of the de-Holocenation of the Dark Enlightenment

On this extreme point, Land is somewhat coy, but his favored source of such thinking, Campbell, is forthright: "I predict that human destiny is to elevate itself to the status of a god and beyond."[67] Likewise, Campbell, Moldbug, and Land are mute about which humans will elevate themselves, but Majorityrights.com, speaking for "Native European Nationalists in Alliance," stresses that "ethnic genetic interests," "ethnocracy," and "the Euro-DNA nation" must lead the way.[68] Campbell highlights how such paths toward "extradarwinian evolution," which must be "an elitist, self-referent, and generative process," will become tied to "private human evolution."[69]

Here the elective affinities in the Dark Enlightenment's political theology become remarkably bizarre. NRx leanings toward techno-theosophy are, on the one hand, high-tech visions; but, on the other hand, they are maps for high-handed insurrectionists intent upon burning down the Cathedral to bring forth a new era for its auto-Aryanizers' "technoplastic human beings."

67. John H. Campbell, "The Moral Imperative of Our Future Evolution," *National Vanguard*, July 12, 2012, https://nationalvanguard.org/2012/07/the-moral-imperative-of-our-future-evolution/.

68. See the Majorityrights.com website, https://majorityrights.com/.

69. Campbell, "The Moral Imperative." Such forms of "private human evolution," however, assume considerable capital will be required. Hence, as Marx extrapolates from his readings of Shakespeare, money once again mediates, "the visible divinity—the transformation of all human and natural properties into their contraries, the universal confounding and distorting of things: impossibilities are soldered together by it," in these moves toward "private evolution." Likewise, the accelerationist weakness for some extradarwinian techno-theosophical auto-Aryanization could be guaranteed, as Marx also would observe, to bridge from mere "human being" into extrahuman, posthuman, or posthuman being: "If *money* is the bond binding me to *human* life, binding society to me, connecting me with nature and man, is not money the bond of all *bonds*? Can it not dissolve and bind all ties? Is it not, therefore, also the universal *agent of separation*?" See Karl Marx, "The Power of Money," in *Economic and Philosophic Manuscripts of 1844* (Moscow: Progress Publisher, 1959), p. 61.

With this worldview, other NRx thinkers at the Neoreaction website (neoreaction.net) suggest that "modern history is an epic tale of social decay under chronically bad government, masked by increasing technological wealth." Consequently, they await some truly transformative "versteckte Anführer," since "the core of our solution is to find a man, and put him in charge, with a real chain of command, and a clear ownership structure." With this agenda before them, the upmarket opportunities for attaining "auto-Aryanization" may well prove to be the "patient new work on a new system" that serves at this juncture to declare that the "only viable path to restoration of competent government is the simple and hard way: (1) Become worthy; (2) Accept Power; (3) Rule."[70] Thus, industrial fascism from the twentieth century might be refitted to operate as biocybernetic fascism in the twenty-first century.

With the accelerationist, elitist, and separatist motifs woven through this apotheosis for alt-right auto-Aryanization, many among the Dark Enlightenment's NRx digiterati at least are forthright about how humanity might adapt to the Anthropocene. The "programmer ethic" behind accelerationism plainly points toward a very different "spirit of capitalism" than the one explored by Max Weber's studies of the arduous endless accumulationism behind the Protestant ethic.[71] They represent how, as Horkheimer and Adorno anticipated in *Dialectic of Enlightenment*,[72] the dynamics of Dark Enlightenment could lead directly to a dismal but digitalized, gene-edited, and technoplastic barbarism. After the global crash, NRx thinkers believe their highly anticipated new posthuman beings could arise and prosper beyond the reach of the de-Holocenated Cathedral in the truly New World of the Anthropocene. Such musings are dangerous and disturbing, but they set the stage for chapter 15 on how Adorno serves as the best accompaniment to the Anthropocene, given his cutting questions for those who name themselves worthy, acquire power, and seek to rule.

---

70. See the Neoreaction website, http://www.neoreaction.net.

71. Max Weber, *The Protestant Ethic and the Spirit of Capitalism* (New York: Scribner's, 1958).

72. Max Horkheimer and Theodor W. Adorno, *Dialectic of Enlightenment*, trans. Edmund Jephcott (Stanford, CA: Stanford Univ. Press: 2007). More directly, as others would claim, "in the end, an inhuman power rules over everything." See Marx, *Economic and Philosophic Manuscripts of 1844*, p. 159.

Reflections from a Damaged Planet:
Adorno as Accompaniment to Environmentalism
in the Anthropocene

F OR FIFTY YEARS, the current of debate in *Telos* has articulated as well as contested the critical theory of the contemporary. In many ways, 1968 was a decisive turning point for radical politics in the West, which the journal has chronicled over five decades. As the year of the now classic photograph of the earth taken from Apollo 8 while it orbited the moon during December, environmental thinkers and movements were given a brilliant new cultural imaginary to anchor all of their actions to save the planet and its environments. Nonetheless, the growing sense of loss behind these efforts often is overwhelming, and the environmental critiques advanced in *Telos* since 1969 all could be said to depart from Adorno in presenting their "reflections from a damaged planet."

During 1968, carbon dioxide levels in the earth's atmosphere were 325 ppm. Fifty years later, they now have dangerously increased almost fifty percent from the preindustrial levels of 280 ppm to over 410 ppm.[1] As a prime source of such greenhouse gases, human economies and societies are being reimagined as more than merely historical forces. Scores of geoscientists and biophysicists are lobbying to date these years

---

* Originally published in *Telos* 183 (Summer 2018): 9–24.

1. For data on the earth's rapid climate change and greenhouse gas levels, see "Current Carbon Dioxide Levels," Carbonify.com, http://www.carbonify.com/carbon-dioxide-levels.htm.

in the twentieth and twenty-first centuries as the advent of a new geological epoch, namely, "the Anthropocene." Hence, it seems apropos to recall how Adorno can serve as a sly but somber accompaniment for critical speculations about the economy and society in this unfolding new epoch.

The mixed jargons of authenticity and apocalypse spinning around in today's troubling discourses about the Anthropocene ironically are anticipated by Adorno's reflections in *Minima Moralia*, which rambled through the damaged life of humanity and nature during the mid-twentieth century.[2] Today's widely celebrated operational mystifications in Anthropocene studies, such as "the Great Acceleration," "the end of nature," or "planetary boundary maintenance," become more explicable when set against Adorno's piercing critique of the Enlightenment.[3] Adorno's phil-

---

2. Theodor W. Adorno, *Minima Moralia: Reflections from Damaged Life*, trans. E. F. N. Jephcott (London: Verso, 2005), and Dennis Redmond's more recent translation at http://members.efn.org/~dredmond/MinimaMoralia.html, which this essay cites. These connections also have been debated productively in *Telos* for decades. See Vincent Di Norcia, "From Critical Theory to Critical Ecology," *Telos* 22 (Winter 1974): 85–95; and Manussos Marangudakis, "Ecology as a Pseudo-Religion," *Telos* 112 (Summer 1998): 107–24.

3. Today's most informed scientific worries about the changing planet share some of the apprehensions of earlier thinkers, but earlier takes on this topic had more robust analytical goals than simply decrying the horrors of hyperobjects or learning how to die in a yet to be named geological epoch. Neither imperfection nor incompletion, however, should prevent anyone from reconsidering the importance of earlier accounts about humans transforming the earth before this radical turn was branded as "the Anthropocene." From a critical perspective, what is taken to be the Anthropocene is both simple and complex. Basically, it is understood as a moment in recent historical time that coincides with the explosive expansion of fossil fuel energy use, rapid population growth, machinic industrial innovation, worldwide trade, and greater urbanization over the past 75 to 250 years. See Paul J. Crutzen and Eugene F. Stoermer, "The Anthropocene," *Global Change Newsletter* 41 (2000): 17–18. For additional discussion, see also Bill McKibben, *The End of Nature* (New York: Random House, 1989); J. R. McNeill and Peter Engelke, *The Great Acceleration: An Environmental History of the Anthropocene since 1945* (Cambridge, MA: Harvard Univ. Press, 2016); Will Steffen et al., "Planetary Boundaries: Guiding Human Development on a Changing Planet," *Science* 347, no. 6223 (2015): 1259–65; Timothy Morton, *Hyperobjects: Philosophy and Ecology after the End of the World* (Minneapolis: Univ. of Minnesota Press, 2013); and Ron Scranton, *Learning to Die in Anthropocene: Reflections on the End of Civilization* (San Francisco: City Lights Books, 2015). For some experts, the rate, scope, and endurance of these ecological changes in historical time are now leaving permanent effects in the *longue durée* of geological time. The Working Group on the Anthropocene (AWG), operating as a

osophical project and his ethical sensibilities are very closely attuned to how the environment constrains life for human and nonhuman beings before, during, and after apocalyptic "end times." Affirming by happenstance Walter Benjamin's realization that "there is no document of civilization that is not at the same time a document of barbarism,"[4] Adorno's eclectic collection of reflections gathered together in 1951 is well worth revisiting.

As he suggested over sixty-five years ago in *Minima Moralia*, "the culture industry sanctimoniously claims to follow its consumers and to deliver what they want," like the climate change community in the Anthropocene; yet these desires are an unstable imaginary twisted in another well-integrated, slickly packaged green product line, whose message "not so much...adapts to the reactions of its customers, as that it feigns these latter. It rehearses them, by behaving as if it itself was a customer."[5]

This reflection, then, suggests how the incisive approaches to critical theory taken by Adorno, and developed by *Telos* debates since 1968, reveal many social, political, and economic contradictions in contemporary environmental thinking. Likewise, the Anthropocenarian chords, motifs, and tones that are used for composing many of today's socioenvironmental soundtracks clearly tend to harmonize with "sorrowful science." While Adorno might well agree that their dirge of telluric chaos

---

special task force within the Subcommission on Quaternary Stratigraphy, has pushed for an official adoption of the Anthropocene category in all sciences with a series of increasingly detailed and emphatic declarations since 2009. A preliminary August 2016 report issued in Cape Town, South Africa, also has pointed to the year 1950 as the plausible starting point for the Anthropocene. The report's evidentiary basis is a cluster of global spikes in particular materials observed around the world: (a) radioactive trace elements left by nuclear bomb tests; (b) the widespread use of plastics; and (c) an increase in garbage dumps of bones from domesticated avian food species for humans. See Jan Zalasiewicz et al., "The Working Group on the Anthropocene: Summary of Evidence and Interim Recommendations," *Anthropocene* 19 (September 2017): 55–60.

4. See Walter Benjamin, "Theses on the Philosophy of History," in *Illuminations*, ed. Hannah Arendt (New York: Schocken Books, 1969); and Slavoj Žižek, *Living in the End Times* (London: Verso, 2013), pp. 253–64. These debates about environmental conditions and politics also have preoccupied *Telos* for decades. For example, see Joel Whitebook, "The Problem of Nature in Habermas," *Telos* 40 (Summer 1979): 41–62; Timothy W. Luke, "Informationalism and Ecology," *Telos* 56 (Summer 1983): 59–73, reprinted in this volume; and John Zerzan, "Why Primitivism?," *Telos* 124 (Summer 2002): 166–72.

5. Adorno, "Customer Service," in *Minima Moralia*, pt. 3, no. 129.

could affirm where, when, and why living a good life for humanity is no longer possible, he also would wonder how "the inhuman world" gains so much heft in creating these impossibilities. Human history is now being rescored in the measures of geological deep time as a response to living in a "more human world," through "the oath of fealty to social powerlessness," since "the entire adjustment, which it claims to obey, is ideology," all implemented "to participate in power and to drive out equality, the more they attempt to make themselves resemble others and the whole."[6] Nonetheless, for many *Telos* readers after 1968, it has been important to reconsider Adorno's insights. Perhaps they can demystify how the "human enterprise" during the Anthropocene is busily counterfeiting its customers' reactions by promising them new modes of gaining total mastery over the earth along with melancholic modes of mourning about the failed efforts to mitigate rapid climate change.[7]

Thoughts on Living a Damaged Life

For those conversant with the Frankfurt School project and, in particular, *Dialectic of Enlightenment* by Horkheimer and Adorno, the Anthropocene thesis might seem to be little more than a banality.[8] Still, this idea obviously excites many groups of physical, natural, and biological scientists as well as literary critics, art scholars, and cultural theorists. For critical theory expressed in the discursive terms of the Frankfurt School tradition, however, this conceptual craze arguably is another trace of background radiation in a world remade by Auschwitz, the Gulag, and Hiroshima. As the Enlightenment project of instrumental reason, namely, "the disenchantment of the world," with its aspiration "to dispel myths, to overthrow fantasy with knowledge," became dominant in the twentieth century, *Telos* authors and audiences have documented and disputed how "the wholly enlightened earth is radiant with triumphant

---

6. Ibid. Also see Eileen Crist, "Beyond the Climate Crisis: A Critique of Climate Change Discourse," *Telos* 141 (Winter 2007): 29–55; Aaron Bell, "Life in Ruins: Ecological Disaster and Adorno's Idea of Natural History," *Telos* 179 (Summer 2017): 188–94; and Andrew Biro, "The Good Life in the Greenhouse? Autonomy, Democracy, and Citizenship in the Anthropocene," *Telos* 172 (Fall 2015): 15–37.

7. See *Telos* 172 (Fall 2015) and *Telos* 177 (Winter 2016) on the politics and ethics of life in the Anthropocene.

8. Anne Chin et al., "Anthropocene: Human Interactions with Earth Systems," *Anthropocene* 1 (September 2013): 1–2.

calamity."[9] That intense negative radiance of technocapitalist catastrophe has proved itself to be mostly uncontained by altering the world ecology of earth itself in 1945 at Alamogordo, Hiroshima, and Nagasaki with the Manhattan Project's nuclear technoscience.

As measured in geological deep time, prefigurations of this shift in the power of some humans over nature also echo much earlier critiques of capitalism by Marx and Engels. Capital is already during the nineteenth century a force of such power in historical and geological time worldwide that "the cheap prices of its commodities are the heavy artillery with which it batters down all Chinese walls," as it compelled all nations to adopt and adapt to "the bourgeois mode of production" that "creates a world after its own image."[10]

Horkheimer and Adorno were well aware of how these world-altering capacities played out in advanced industrial society's capitalist rationality. Its negative radiance constantly fulfills the greatest enlightenment goals of power, because "enlightenment is totalitarian."[11] Its goal for human beings is "to learn from nature," especially "how to use it to dominate wholly both it and human beings. Nothing else counts."[12] Given these deep centuries-in-the-making tendencies toward "the enslavement of men," it was not a major revelation when Paul Crutzen and Eugene Stoermer asked geoscientists fifty years later to relabel these days of the human domination of men and women to master nature as "the Anthropocene."[13] Bearing in mind all of these longer-running forces at play, it is useful to reconsider how Adorno's return to Germany in 1949—where he worked during the world's post-1945 economic boom and West Germany's *Wirtschaftswunder* until his death in 1969—provides a richly textured, if somber, accompaniment to the advent

9. Max Horkheimer and Theodor W. Adorno, *Dialectic of Enlightenment*, trans. Edmund Jephcott (Stanford, CA: Stanford Univ. Press, 2002), p. 1.

10. Karl Marx and Friedrich Engels, "The Manifesto of the Communist Party," in *Selected Works*, vol. 1 (Moscow: Progress Publishers, 1969), p. 16. Jason Moore affirms this point in "Capitalism as World Ecology: Braudel and Marx on Environmental History," *Organization & Environment* 16, no. 4 (2003): 514–17.

11. Horkheimer and Adorno, *Dialectic of Enlightenment*, p. 4.

12. Ibid., p. 2.

13. Ibid. Also see Crutzen and Stoermer, "The Anthropocene"; and Murray Bookchin, "Ecology as Politics," *Telos* 46 (Winter 1980): 177–90.

of the Anthropocene, as he experienced the initial phases of "the Great Acceleration."[14]

For some readers of *Telos*, it is easy to see why the Anthropocene idea has become almost narcotic, as the capitalist West and the socialist East perfected humanity's creative power of destruction during the post-1945 years of global change with the balance of thermonuclear terror and the rush of rapid economic growth. Given Adorno's alert appraisals of "damaged life" on earth after 1945, the awesome scope of capitalist instrumental rationality hints at how corporate planning and everyday subjectivity become fused in the way individuals manage their collective anxieties about the possibilities for atomic doom and the vicious realities of markets:

> The veiled tendency of calamity of society cons its victims in the false revelation, in the hallucinatory phenomenon. They hope, in vain, that its fragmentary obviousness will enable them to look at the total doom in the eye and withstand it. Panic breaks out once again after millennia of enlightenment on a humanity, whose domination over nature as domination over human beings surpasses in horror whatever human beings had to fear from nature.[15]

In this context, Adorno's *Minima Moralia* and other works are indeed an outstanding compendium of "reflections from a damaged planet," as well as a marvelous score of meditative moments to accompany the events of what is now renamed as the Anthropocene.

Adorno, as Steven Vogel indicates, could hardly be regarded as a strong believer in either humanism's effectiveness or its worth.[16] And as advanced industrial society accelerated greatly from 1949 to 1969, Adorno saw much at work in contemporary modernity—whether it was grounded in the West's liberal democratic capitalism or the East's authoritarian state socialism—that was totalitarian by nature. That human ingenuity was, quite ironically, producing noxious toxic by-products so profusely that the earth itself was being marred for eternity is not startling. Adorno would recognize how these twists and turns in techno-

---

14. See Jan Zalasiewicz et al., "The New World of the Anthropocene," *Environmental Science and Technology* 44, no. 7 (2010): 2228–31.

15. Adorno, "Theses against the Occult," in *Minima Moralia*, pt. 3, no. 151.

16. See Steven Vogel, *Against Nature* (Albany: SUNY Press, 1996), pp. 1–11.

capitalism befitted his sense of enlightenment as barbarism. Humanist philosophy failed to become truly realized within either liberal democratic or state socialist ideology. Adorno knew that because "it had merely interpreted the world," all philosophical discourse now "becomes a defeatism of reason after the attempt to change the world miscarried."[17]

Today's Anthropocene movement represents how reason underpins this dangerously miscarried unity that "cements the discontinuous, chaotically splintered moment and phases of history—unity of the control of nature, progressing to rule over men, and finally to that over men's inner nature."[18] In light of all the catastrophes left behind by modernity, "and in view of the catastrophe to come, it would be cynical to say that a plan for a better world is manifested in history and unites it."[19] Abiding by this recognition, *Telos* debates over the environment also have repudiated so-called special knowledge of nature. The Anthropocene's totalized flattening of all prior history is just another case in point, because this concept easily, if not proudly, stands for "our totally bourgeois society, which has forcibly been made over into a totality."[20]

Getting to the Damage of Life

Not fearing to face the contradictions of contemporary reality, like new materialists who talk about "vibrant matter," Adorno also would privilege neither society over nature nor nature over society.[21] Although what he knew as nature plainly is disappearing under the rising waves of reification that now constitute human history, Adorno also would not say that we live in a wholly artificial world simply because it is so deeply degraded and damaged. He opposed primacy for the social against and over the natural, knowing that markets always interlace the two.[22] The

---

17. Theodor W. Adorno, *Negative Dialectics*, trans. E. B. Ashton (New York: Continuum, 1973), pp. 362–63.

18. Ibid., p. 320.

19. Ibid.

20. Ibid., p. 25. For an excellent example of this epistemic and ethical view of earth's ecology, see Christian Schwägerl, *The Anthropocene: The Human Era and How It Shapes Our Planet* (Santa Fe, NM: Synergetic Press, 2014).

21. Jane Bennett, *Vibrant Matter: A Political Ecology of Things* (Durham, NC: Duke Univ. Press, 2009).

22. For more discussion, see Andrew Biro, *Denaturalizing Ecological Politics: Alienation from Rousseau to the Frankfurt School and Beyond* (Toronto: Toronto Univ. Press, 2005).

exchange values of the market rend both society and nature; indeed, commercial exchange is now "the standard social structure, its rationality constitutes people; what they are for themselves" in the final and full reification of nature.[23]

To consider how Adorno might assay these years of rapid climate change, one should recall his thoughts on poetry after Auschwitz in *Prisms.* As Anthropocenarian enthusiasts jockey for greater primacy in the chambers of earth system governance that earth system science calls forth, one can feel the dark shadows of total administration sweeping over today's ravaged citified terrains, where one sees and hears that daily events from shallow historical time are registering more enduringly in deep geological time. No rhetorical move should erase our collective memory to recall that "the more total society becomes, the greater the reification of the mind and the more paradoxical the attempt to escape reification of its own."[24]

Overwhelmed by gyres of plastic detritus in the planet's oceans, swirling together megatons of toxic fossil fuel extracts shaped for minutes or months to serve as beverage bottles, trawling nets, or cheap toys, this degraded dreck of global plastic exemplifies the crush of global reification of life itself. Now destined for refossilization in the ocean's sediments of washed-away soils, these plastic artifacts of polymerized fossil energy are fusing together through heat and pressure into "plastiglomerates" in countless trash middens for new archeologists in the ages to come. Far too many overwrought environmentalists are developing empty insights about today's crisis that prove Adorno right: "Even the most extreme consciousness of doom" all too often only will "generate into idle chatter," as the rising tides of minor geoscientific papers, ecological policy bulletins, or coastal science surveys illustrate today.[25]

Perhaps Adorno is correct. That is, "to write poetry after Auschwitz is barbaric," because poets and poetry festivals remain largely unaware of how they too only add to this "idle chatter."[26] The flood of ecopoetics,

23. Theodor W. Adorno, "Subject and Object," in *The Essential Frankfurt School Reader,* ed. Andrew Arato and Elke Gebhart (New York: Bloomsbury Academic, 1978), p. 501.

24. Theodor W. Adorno, *Prisms,* trans. Samuel and Shierry Weber (Cambridge, MA: MIT Press, 1982), p. 43.

25. Ibid.

26. Ibid.

environmental literary criticism, and green aesthetics notwithstanding, what is really being made lyrical in a society rendering itself and its detritus into stone? Is "the final stage of the dialectic of culture and barbarism" the commercial powers of ephemeral reification on our damaged planet celebrating their insane ability to transform so much of its energy and substance into such monstrously timeless petrification?[27] For Adorno, art's immediacy clearly has a downside, and thinking through poetry is problematic: "By upholding immediacy via mediation, instead of comprehending the former as something mediated in itself, thinking inverts into the apologetics of its own opposite, into the immediate lie. It serves all sorts of bad ends, from the obdurateness of the private things-are-just-so to the justification of social injustice as nature."[28] Thus, environmental literary critics and art school ecologists call upon nature to serve as the stage for their impassioned pleas for social changes that they believe will supposedly end environmental racism or technocapitalist waste as we know it, while they in fact deepen it daily, flying here and there to exotic locales to deliver these pathetic pleas to each other.[29]

Getting beyond Identity Theory in Environmentalism

Adorno would be the first to acknowledge how anyone can become completely misled by the totalizing identity of environmentalism as a concept. His project asks one to discern what is at play in the political agendas of so many privileged human environmentalists in Washington, DC, who invite all of us to embrace this deeply damaged world as "adapting to the Anthropocene" by loving what the global economy's toxic trash has made monstrously possible.[30] Beyond the dream worlds of deep ecology, environmental disaster does reduce human subjects to objects: "The signature of the epoch is that no human being, without any exception, can determine their life in a somewhat transparent sense,

27. Ibid.

28. Adorno, "Theses against the Occult." Also see Dipesh Chakrabarty, "The Climate of History: Four Theses," *Critical Inquiry* 35, no. 2 (2009): 197–222; and Jean-Claude Paye, "The 'End of History,' or Messianic Time," *Telos* 173 (Winter 2015): 181–90.

29. Timothy W. Luke, "On the Politics of the Anthropocene," *Telos* 172 (Fall 2015): 139–62, reprinted in this volume.

30. Michael Shellenberger and Ted Nordhaus, *Love Your Monsters: Postenvironmentalism and the Anthropocene* (Washington, DC: Breakthrough Institute, 2011).

as was earlier possible by gauging market relationships. In principle everyone, even the mightiest of all, is an object."[31]

Still, this recognition stands far beyond ultimate defeatism or domination. Given its insatiable quality, any resistance against petty satiety must reject "the foolish wisdom of resignation" because, at the end of the day, "open thinking points beyond itself" to the distance, to nonidentity and the negation needed for full individual autonomy.[32] Even with all of the types of environmental activism today, "the utopian image of the unrestricted, energetic, creative human being has been infiltrated by the commodity fetishism, which in bourgeois society brings with it inhibition, powerlessness, the sterility of monotony."[33] In today's damaged life, green politics still is mired in "the idea of unfettered doing, of uninterrupted creating, of chubby-cheeked insatiability, of freedom as intense activity [that] feeds on the bourgeois concept of nature, which from time immemorial has served to proclaim social violence as irrevocable, as a piece of healthy eternity."[34]

Sustainable development enthusiasts are celebrants of a complete and final transition to a fully processed world, which must be subjected to total administration to maximize efficiency and maybe even equity.[35] For them, the empiricities of the earth, in fact, are equal to any conceptually equivalent reduction of its qualities from geology, physics, or stratigraphy.[36] For Adorno, however, such totalizing arrogance can, and

31. Adorno, "All Rights Reserved," in *Minima Moralia*, pt. 1, no. 17. See Timothy W. Luke, "The Dreams of Deep Ecology," *Telos* 76 (Summer 1988): 65–92, reprinted in this volume; and Jon Wittrock and Richard Polt, "Introduction: The Nature of Nature and the Politics of Fate," *Telos* 177 (Winter 2016): 3–15.

32. Theodor W. Adorno, "Resignation," *Telos* 35 (Spring 1978): 165–68.

33. Adorno, "*Sur l'eau*," in *Minima Moralia*, pt. 2, no. 100.

34. Ibid. For more insight, see Eric S. Nelson, "Revisiting the Dialectic of Environment: Nature as Ideology and Ethics in Adorno and the Frankfurt School," *Telos* 155 (Summer 2011): 105–26.

35. See Timothy W. Luke, "Developing Planetarian Accountancy: Fabricating Nature as Stock, Service, and System for Green Governmentality," in *Nature, Knowledge, and Negation*, ed. Harry F. Dahms (Bingley: Emerald Publishing, 2009), pp. 129–59; and Emory M. Roe, "Critical Theory, Sustainable Development, and Populism," *Telos* 103 (Spring 1995): 149–62.

36. See Vaclav Smil, *Harvesting the Biosphere: What We Have Taken from Nature* (Cambridge, MA: MIT Press, 2013); and Colin Waters et al., "The Anthropocene Is Functionally and Stratigraphically Distinct from the Holocene," *Science* 351, no. 6269 (2016): 62–69.

must, be vigilantly "opposed by convicting it of non-identity with it-self—of the non-identity it denies, according to its own concept."[37] This technocratic identity-thinking is presently what enables them to "love their monsters."

In his accompaniments to the Anthropocene, then, Adorno recoils, as a philosopher and individual, from regarding any scientific finding first as total, irrefutable, or fixed. And, second, he notes how no contingent project of ongoing research into mutable irregular economic trends should ever anchor any system of sociological, political, or cultural dictates about how to adapt to, or possibly mitigate, its effects permanently for human beings' collective subjectivity. Adorno's intellectual vocation was directly opposed to such misadventures, since he struggled "to use the strength of the subject to break through the fallacy of constitutive subjectivity."[38]

Looking at zoos, he foresaw that humanity was preparing to harness the biosphere completely and to become a peak fossilizer itself by turning most of the living biomatter on the planet into energy, information, or waste.[39] As Adorno notes:

> The more that civilization preserves and transplants unspoiled nature, the more implacably the latter is controlled. One can afford to encompass ever greater units of nature and to leave the interior of such tracts seemingly intact, while previously the selection and domestication of particular pieces still testified to the necessity of conquering nature. The tiger which paces to and fro in its cage, mirrors back negatively through its confused state something of humanity, but not however those who frolic behind impassable trenches.[40]

Efforts to preserve, protect, and police large domains of land, sea, and air in order to safeguard the earth simply become the work of humans struggling to erect their own artificial cages around themselves to salvage patches of what once were their natural habitats.

---

37. Adorno, *Negative Dialectics*, p. 320.
38. Ibid., p. xx.
39. Vaclav Smil, "Harvesting the Biosphere: The Human Impact," *Population and Development Review* 37, no. 4 (2011): 613–36.
40. Adorno, "Mammoth," in *Minima Moralia*, pt. 2, no. 74.

Aesthetics for Adapting to the Inevitable

Adorno's project, then, serves as a fine accompaniment to the pragmatic environmentalists touting the Anthropocene inasmuch as its Holocene-ending detrital origins in the products and by-products of global capitalism sadly equal what philosophers have considered to be constitutive of today's "good life" for humanity. This processed domain of artificial activity, however, "has turned into the sphere of the private and then merely of consumption, which is dragged along as an addendum of the material production process, without autonomy and without its own substance," and thus anyone who wants "to experience the truth of immediate life, must investigate its alienated form, the objective powers, which determine the individual existence into its innermost recesses."[41] Those innermost recesses of objective power today are immediately evident in today's "carbon democracy," which sustains such material production processes and their unending colonization of everyday lifeworlds.[42]

The untruth of global capitalism's wholeness elides its dependence on technocratic expertise, because socio-technical development is so advanced that many functions are not that far beyond technical comprehensibility to most. In this fusion of production with consumption, industrial democracy promises that "membership in an elite appears achievable for everyone. One waits only for the cooptation."[43] In these puzzle pictures, the appearance of mobility, opportunity, equality, and equity is so potent, its allure soon causes "the fixity of economic social order to be forgotten" in the damaged life of the present.[44]

When confronting the ominous overwhelming order of the Anthropocene's iterations in the work of so many contemporary scientists, one is struck by the tough veracity of Adorno's insights in *Minima Moralia*. In particular, he is quite suggestive with regard to links between modernity and planetary damage. As Adorno recalls, "That which has most recently happened is always portrayed as if it had been destroyed

---

41. Adorno, "Dedication," in *Minima Moralia*.
42. Timothy J. Mitchell, *Carbon Democracy: Political Power in the Age of Oil* (London: Verso, 2013); and Adorno, "Puzzle-Picture," in *Minima Moralia*, pt. 3, no. 124.
43. Adorno, "Puzzle-Picture."
44. Ibid.

in a catastrophe."[45] The disruptions of rapid climate change are becoming pervasive and undeniable; but, at the same time, Adorno warns all, when considering such totalizing representations, that "the whole is the untrue" inasmuch as basic bureaucratic banalities still constitute the core of this catastrophe.[46]

Stark Reckonings in the Great Acceleration

As the overture to the Great Acceleration, the modernity of the Enlightenment brought to fruition a one-dimensional society whose most rational expressions perhaps are Auschwitz, the Gulag, and Hiroshima.[47] How many tons of coal, cords of wood, and gallons of gasoline were expended, leaving their carbon footprints to bring hundreds of thousands of victims to Auschwitz-Birkenau? How many millions of human bones are melding in the peaty mire of soggy bogs across all of Europe or flaking away in dusty clay pits in Latvia's forests, Russia's steppes, and Ukraine's meadows, becoming the fossils of tomorrow? This speculation is to mention just one death camp, but from the plumes of Auschwitz's ovens, how much more rapidly has climate changed as the fires carried millions of tons of carbon dioxide, as this Holocaust released from each corpse the 18 percent of a human body that is carbon?

We are barely past seventy-five years after *Die Endlösung*. Yet molecular particles from the Shoah still swirl in the stratosphere, and will float there for many decades more. Totalitarian state terror physically obliterated individuals and communities, manufacturing the chemical accelerants of rapid global warming in the processes of genocide. This horrifying geophysics also must be faced as a moment in "the final stage of the dialectic of culture and barbarism."[48] To that ledger, Horkheimer and Adorno would not shrink from adding the carbon costs of the Gulag's *zeks* being transported to the depths of Siberia by rail or the vaporized bodies of Hiroshima's and Nagasaki's men, women, and

---

45. Adorno, "Dwarf Fruit," in *Minima Moralia*, pt. 1, no. 29.

46. Ibid. Also see Timothy W. Luke, "Science at Dusk in the Twilight of Expertise: The Worst Hundred Days," *Telos* 179 (Summer 2017): 199–208, reprinted in this volume.

47. On the larger implications of this point, see Paul Piccone, "The Crisis of One-Dimensionality," *Telos* 35 (Spring 1978): 43–54.

48. Adorno, *Prisms*, p. 34.

children, stopped in mid-step in the searing heat of atomic bombs, flashing another victory for instrumental rationality.

Even when pulled into everyday technopolitical regimens aspiring to total control, ruthless dehumanization, and degradation of many aspects of what is, much of what has been, and perhaps most of what is to come with nature, it is clear that enlightenment cuts both ways.[49] Control is never total, no concept exhausts the pre-categorical fullness of life, humanity evinces its worthiness against domination, and degradation is not yet absolute destruction.[50] Still, *Minima Moralia*—as a meditation about damaged life on a damaged planet—partakes fully of Nietzsche's philosophy as melancholic science.

Environmentalist thinking about Anthropocene life is comprised of "reflections from damaged life" because living it unfolds now amid our damaged reflections on degrading rational monstrosity. To engage in reflection at all is inevitably an ordeal, and today it is wholly captured with more and more damaged lives entangled within the unending degradation of living beings, who still look to the hills and shores for nature. Yet "only the irrationality of culture itself, the nooks and crannies of the city, in which the walls, towers, and bastions of zoos are crammed, are capable of preserving nature. The rationalization of culture, which opens a window to nature, thereby completely absorbs it and abolishes along with difference also the principle of culture, the possibility of reconciliation."[51] Whether due to the products or by-products of enlightenment reason, every human being now living on the earth must endlessly incur, and then endure, devastating damage, knowing that this ordeal for each living being's endurance irreparably also damages other lives.[52]

Conclusion: Damage Assessments

In pushing beyond modernist metaphysics, neither divinity nor nature must be allowed to succor precepts holding "that hope is mistaken for truth; that the impossibility of living happily, or even living at all, with-

---

49. See Deborah Cook, *Adorno on Nature* (Durham: Acumen, 2011).
50. Alison Stone, "Adorno and the Disenchantment of Nature," *Philosophy & Social Criticism* 32, no. 4 (2006): 231–53.
51. Adorno, "Mammoth."
52. Adorno, *Negative Dialectics*, pp. 349–58.

out the thought of the absolute, does not vouch for the legitimacy of that thought."[53] The delusional deferments of taking decisive action against rapid climate change by global summit conferences until 2020, 2030, or 2050 rest, in part, on trust in the earth, divine providence, higher purpose, or randomly beating the odds. More to the point here, one soon realizes that most eco-activism is only another scam. As Adorno wonders:

> If society is truly one of rackets, as a contemporary theory teaches, then its truest model is precisely the opposite of the collective, namely the individual [*Individuum*] as monad. By pursuing the absolutely particular interest of every single individual, the essential nature [*Wesen*] of the collective can be most precisely studied, and it requires no great leap to decipher the organization of the various conflicting drives under the primacy of the reality-oriented ego from the beginning as an innervated band of robbers with a leader, followers, ceremonies, oaths, oath-breaking, interest-conflicts, intrigues and all the other paraphernalia. One need only observe outbreaks, in which the individual [*Individuum*] reacts energetically against the environment, as for example rage. The enraged always seem to be their own gang-leaders, whose unconscious has received the command to strike mercilessly, and from whose eyes gleams the satisfaction of speaking for the many, which they indeed are. The more someone is taken up with their aggression, the more perfectly they represent the repressing principle of society. In this sense, perhaps more than in any other, the rule applies: that which is most individual would be the most general.[54]

These activist alibis are addictive absolutions. In fact, they refine misplaced hopes into the synthetic rush of adaptation's, mitigation's, or even denial's addictions, which is one of today's most invidious rackets.

Each additional jet flight from Tokyo, London, or Chicago to Paris, Durban, or Bali by post-Kyoto climate change activists to hash out another comprehensive operational protocol that really will not "make a difference for the planet" looks like a racketeer's distorted dream of agency. Yet this article of faith is one that too many environmental activists wholeheartedly believe. Somehow their faith can endure, and

53. Adorno, "Court of Appeal," in *Minima Moralia*, pt. 2, no. 61.
54. Adorno, "*Plurale tantum*," in *Minima Moralia*, pt. 1, no. 23.

their rackets thrive, while more of Greenland melts, fewer corals survive ocean acidification, less of Kiribati stays above the waves, and fewer cacti thrive in the Mohave as the desert's aridity increases. The metaphysics of measured collective responses to unchecked embedded excesses only "attributes absolute potential," like today's "new environmentalists" and "breakthrough" devotees, "to the productive energies of human beings and their extension in technology."[55] For Adorno, these politics can only come up short: "'One fool makes many'—the abyssal loneliness of delusion has a tendency towards collectivization, which cites the picture of delusion into life. This pathic mechanism harmonizes with the socially determining one of today, wherein those who are socialized into desperate isolation hunger for togetherness and band together in cold clumps. Thus folly becomes epidemic: vagrant sects grow with the same rhythm as large organizations. It is that of total destruction."[56]

From stories about prehistoric fossils celebrated by U.S. newspapers in California during his exile there in the 1940s, Adorno anticipated the world's mass media celebrating humanity's fossilization in the present for tomorrow. He notes:

> *Mammoth.* Some years ago, the report circulated in American newspapers about the discovery of a well-preserved dinosaur in the state of Utah. It was emphasized that the specimen in question had outlived its species and was a million years younger than any hitherto known. Such reports, like the repulsively humorous craze for the Loch Ness monster and the King Kong film, are collective projections of the monstrous total state. One prepares for its horrors by getting used to giant images. In the absurd willingness to accept these, a humanity mired in powerlessness makes the desperate attempt to grasp the experience of what makes a mockery of every experience. But this does not exhaust the notion that prehistoric animals are still alive or at least went extinct just a few million years ago.[57]

The speculative expeditions of Anthropocenarian earth governance experts also today dream of animals that have not survived, but they believe

---

55. Theodor W. Adorno, *Lectures on Negative Dialectics: Fragments of a Lecture Course 1965/1966*, ed. Rolf Tiedemann (Cambridge: Polity, 2008), p. 96.

56. Adorno, "Boy from the Heath," in *Minima Moralia*, pt. 3, no. 103.

57. Adorno, "Mammoth."

humanity might resurrect entire species in vast "de-extinction" experiments to revive dying ecosystems with once long-dead species. Therefore, one finds:

> Zoological gardens originated from the same hope. They are laid out on the model of Noah's ark, for ever since they have existed, the bourgeois class has been waiting for the Biblical flood. The use of zoos for entertainment and instruction seems to be a thin pretext. They are allegories of the possibility that a specimen or a pair can defy the doom which befalls the species as a species. That is why the all too richly outfitted zoological gardens of major European cities seem like signs of decline: anything more than two elephants, two giraffes, and a hippopotamus is a bad sign.[58]

The Anthropocene's qualities are captured here in vividly fascinating ways: despite the ecocatastrophes billowing up around us, how can any human beings, as executioners of the "specimen in question," still believe that they can outlive all other species on a damaged planet?

This realization continues to be ignored. It is the mammoth, so to speak, sitting in the room of every environmental conference, ecology lab, or energy lab, because the allusion makes clear what the Anthropocene actually is: "humanity mired in powerlessness," as men and women now accept such "collective projections of the monstrous total state"[59] within which they survive, even though survival itself is being degraded with each passing year. Politics is being grounded within deep time itself, and historical time itself also is politicized.

Like *Telos*, however, Adorno does not end his accompaniment on a sour note. He sustains the spirit of hope that all of the living beings thriving in "creation might survive the injustice done to them by human beings, if not humanity itself, and bring forth a better species, which finally succeeds."[60] At best, if there is some good to be found, the environmental speculations in Anthropocene discourses are perhaps only the latest mystified "allegories of the possibility"[61] that allow some to believe we now are defying doom. Maybe we are, but many voices in *Telos* since

58. Ibid.
59. Ibid.
60. Ibid.
61. Ibid.

1968 have stressed in their environmental critiques and ecological ethics how this ethical and political project is crucial for the critical theory of the contemporary, striving to determine truths worthy of anchoring genuine hope rather than churning out worn-out leftist diamat hopes that are mistaken for truth.

Also from Telos Press Publishing

A Journal of No Illusions:
Telos, *Paul Piccone, and the Americanization of Critical Theory*
Edited by Timothy W. Luke and Ben Agger

For a New Naturalism
Edited by Arran Gare and Wayne Hudson

Mastering the Past: Contemporary Central and Eastern Europe
and the Rise of Illiberalism
Ellen Hinsey

Free Radicals: Agitators, Hippies, Urban Guerrillas,
and Germany's Youth Revolt of the 1960s and 1970s
Elliot Neaman

Europe and the World:
World War I as Crisis of Universalism
Edited by Kai Evers and David Pan

Eumeswil
Ernst Jünger

The Forest Passage
Ernst Jünger

On Pain
Ernst Jünger

The Tyranny of Values and Other Texts
by Carl Schmitt

Land and Sea: A World-Historical Meditation
Carl Schmitt

Theory of the Partisan
Carl Schmitt

The Nomos *of the Earth*
in the International Law of the Jus Publicum Europaeum
Carl Schmitt